# International Humanitarian Law Series

*Editors-in-Chief*



VOLUME 73

The International Humanitarian Law Series is a series of monograhs and edited volumes which aims to promote scholarly analysis and discussion of both the theory and practice of the international legal regulation of armed conflict.

The series explores substantive issues of International Humanitarian Law, including:

- Protection for victims of armed conflict and regulation of the means and method of warfare
- Questions of application of the various legal regimes for the conduct of armed conflict
- Issues relating to the implementation of International Humanitarian Law obligations
- National and international approaches to the enforcement of the law and
- The interactions between International Humanitarian Law and other related areas of international law such as Human Rights, Refugee Law, Arms Control and Disarmament Law, and International Criminal Law.

The titles published in this series are listed at *brill.com/ihul*

The Evolution of Humanitarian Intervention in International Law

# The Evolution of Humanitarian Intervention in International Law

*From the Ottoman Empire to the Russia-Ukraine War*

*By*

Cian Moran

BRILL | NIJHOFF

LEIDEN | BOSTON

Cover illustration: An OH-58 Kiowa helicopter overflies a US soldier (L) from the 3rd Battalion, 187th Infantry Regiment as he speaks to Iraqi boys atop a hill during a seven-hour joint air assault mission with Iraqi forces in search for weapons caches across agricultural belts in Shakiriyah, just south of Baghdad, on May 12, 2008. A ceasefire was agreed between anti-American Shiite cleric Moqtada al-Sadr and the Iraqi government to end weeks of fighting which killed hundreds of people in Baghdad's impoverished Shiite Muslim Sadr City district of eastern Baghdad. AFP/Mauricio Lima.

Library of Congress Cataloging-in-Publication Data

Names: Moran, Cian, author.
Title: The evolution of humanitarian intervention in international law: from the Ottoman Empire to the Russia-Ukraine War / Cian Moran.
Description: Leiden; Boston: Brill/Nijhoff, 2025. | Series: International humanitarian law series, 1389-6776 ; volume 73 | Includes bibliographical references and index. | Summary: "This book examines a central and important question in the field of international law, namely whether a right of states to engage in humanitarian intervention exists based on customary international law and state practice"– Provided by publisher.
Identifiers: LCCN 2024039099 (print) | LCCN 2024039100 (ebook) | ISBN 9789004696389 (hardback) | ISBN 9789004696396 (ebook)
Subjects: LCSH: Humanitarian intervention–History. | Humanitarian law. | Intervention (International law) | Customary law, International. | Turkey–History–Ottoman Empire, 1288-1918. | Russian Invasion of Ukraine, 2022.
Classification: LCC KZ6369 .M65 2025 (print) | LCC KZ6369 (ebook) | DDC 341.5/84–dc23/eng/20240826
LC record available at https://lccn.loc.gov/2024039099
LC ebook record available at https://lccn.loc.gov/2024039100

Typeface for the Latin, Greek, and Cyrillic scripts: "Brill". See and download: brill.com/brill-typeface.

ISSN 1389-6776
ISBN 978-90-04-69638-9 (hardback)
ISBN 978-90-04-69639-6 (e-book)
DOI 10.1163/9789004696396

# Contents

# Foreword

This book examines a central and important question in the field of international law, namely whether a right of states to engage in humanitarian intervention exists based on customary international law and state practice. The growing public interest in the law of international armed conflict and the desire for accountability within applicable international legal frameworks underpins both the relevance and importance of this work which is timely and apposite. Particularly where the horrors of war can now be brought to our screens at the touch of a button or click on a link as it were.

The examination of this 'right of states' is rigorously undertaken in this book through a clever combination of historical and legal methods taking the reader through an important chronological narrative from the Ottoman Empire to the present war in Ukraine. A unique and indeed clever mix of legal and military history that is eminently accessible to the reader. In my view, this book signposts very clearly, in terms of understanding such a complex and indeed controversial doctrine, that we can't understand where we are without understanding where we've been. Dr Moran's work certainly manages to achieve this.

It is clear that Dr. Moran's own military career has provided him with a unique meaning perspective, appreciation and critical comprehension of the important and complex material contained in this book.

Certainly, anyone involved with international law – academics, lawyers, students of the *jus ad bellum* and teachers – will profit greatly from using this book. Moreover, military officers and military legal advisors of all ranks will find this an invaluable resource when grappling with the strategic, military, political and legal lines of operation that dominate the use of force between states and indeed military operations.

Through this excellent book, Dr. Moran makes a significant contribution to the intellectual understanding of what is a controversial doctrine in international law, the impact of which still resonates to-day in theatres of operations throughout the world.

*Richard Brennan* BA, LLB, BL, MA (LMDS)
*Colonel*
*Director of the Defence Forces Legal Service*

# Acknowledgements

First, it seems only appropriate to thank Professor Ray Murphy, who first instilled in me an interest in international law when I was a law student. Having a mentor with a background in both the military as well as academia was invaluable.

I must also thank all my colleagues and friends from the Irish Centre for Human Rights for their camaraderie and support, particularly Andrew Forde, Thamil Venthan Ananthavinayagan, Sarah Creedon, Tanja Florath, Mesenbet Assefa, Leonard Taylor and Sally Anne Corcoran.

Sincere thanks to my cadet class; Ryan English, Orla Donnellan, Andrew Kearney, Jason Daniels, Chris Malcolm, Cúan Kenneally, Cáit McKeown, Brian Holland, Conor Hayes, Cathal McMahon, David Stack, Damian Fox and Fergus Munday. I would also like to thank Richard Brennan, Shane Mulcahy, Stuart Donaldson, and Maria O'Callaghan for their support as well as Aonghus Ó Neachtain, Sean Linehan, Tom Mullaney, Paddy Kearns, Marcus Ryan, Cormac Gillick and Niall Kavanagh for being such great shipmates.

I must also thank my friends. Peter O'Toole, George Kaar, Kev Power, Allen King, Chris Bond, Heber Rowan, Andrew Carroll, Dominick Barrett, Conor Ryan, Mickey Finn, Niall McNelis, and Eoin Mangan. Thank you for everything.

My parents, Gerard and Clodagh instilled in me a lifelong love of learning and books which will never leave me. I'm also blessed for my siblings, Eoghan, Cillian and Caoimhe as well as my niece Alma. I must also thank my family of in laws, particularly David and Mary O'Keeffe.

Finally, none of this would have been possible without my incredible, beautiful, and talented wife Clare. I love you. And of course, I must also thank my sons, Senan, and Malachy.

# Acronyms

| | |
|---|---|
| AL | Awami League |
| AU | African Union |
| FUNSK | Kampuchean United Front for National Salvation. |
| GCC | Gulf Cooperation Council |
| ICC | International Criminal Court |
| ICISS | International Commission on Intervention and State Sovereignty |
| ICJ | International Court of Justice |
| KFOR | Kosovo Force |
| NATO | North Atlantic Treaty Organisation |
| NTC | National Transitional Council |
| OAU | Organisation of African Unity |
| OIC | Organisation of Islamic Cooperation |
| OUP | Operation Unified Protector |
| P5 | The five Permanent Members of the UN Security Council |
| PRK | People's Republic of Kampuchea |
| R2P | Responsibility to Protect |
| RGF | Rwandan Government Forces |
| RPF | Rwandan Patriotic Front |
| UN | United Nations |
| UNAMIR | United Nations Assistance Mission in Rwanda |
| UNGA | UN General Assembly |
| UNSC | United Nations Security Council |

# Cases

International Court of Justice. *Allegations of Genocide under the Convention on the Prevention and Punishment of the Crime of Genocide* (*Ukraine v Russian Federation*) (26 February 2022)

International Court of Justice. *Asylum Case* (*Colombia/Peru*) ICJ Reports 266 (Judgment of 20 November 1950)

International Court of Justice. *Case Concerning the Continental Shelf Judgement* (*Libyan Arab Jamahiriya/Malta*) ICJ Reports 13 (Judgement of 3 June 1985)

International Court of Justice *Certain Expenses of the United Nations* (*Article 17, Paragraph 2 of the Charter*). ICJ Reports 155 (Advisory Opinion of 20 July 1962)

International Court of Justice *Corfu Channel case* (*UK v Albania*). ICJ Reports 4. (Judgement of April 9th, 1949)

International Court of Justice *Legality of Use of Force* (*Serbia and Montenegro v Belgium*) (Provisional Measures, Oral Proceedings CR 1999/15) (10 May 1999)

International Court of Justice *Legality of Use of Force* (*Serbia and Montenegro v Belgium*) Summary 2004/3 (15 December 2004)

International Court of Justice *Legality of Use of Force* (*Serbia and Montenegro v Belgium*) (Request for the Indication of Provisional Measures) (Order of 2 June 1999)

International Court of Justice *Legality of Use of Force* (*Yugoslavia v Spain*) (*Provisional Measures*) (Order of 2 June 1999)

International Court of Justice *Legality of Use of Force* (*Yugoslavia v United States*) *ICJ* (Application instituting proceedings) (29 April 1999)

International Court of Justice *Legality of Use of Force* (*Yugoslavia v United States of America*) (Provisional Measures, Order of 2 June 1999)

International Court of Justice *Nicaragua v United States of America*. ICJ Reports 14. (Judgement of 27th June 1986)

International Court of Justice *North Sea Continental Shelf Cases* (*Federal Republic of Germany/Denmark; Federal Republic of Germany/Netherlands*) ICJ Reports 3. (Judgement of 20th February 1969)

International Criminal Court *Decision on the 'Prosecutor's Application Pursuant to Article 58 as to Muammar Mohammed Abu Minyar Gaddaffi, Said Al-Islam Gaddaffi and Abdullah Al-Senussi* ICC-01/11-01/11-1 (27th June 2011)

International Criminal Tribunal for the former Yugoslavia *Prosecutor v Dusko Tadic* Case No IT-94-1 (Decision on the Defence Motion for Interlocutory Appeal of Jurisdiction 2nd October 1995)

International Criminal Tribunal for the former Yugoslavia *Prosecutor v Milutinovic et al* Case No IT-05-87 (Judgement of 26 February 2009)

Nuremberg Trial Proceedings Volume 3 Twelfth Day (Tuesday, 4 December 1945). http://avalon.law.yale.edu/imt/12-04-45.asp Accessed 10th March 2024

CHAPTER 1

# Introduction

> Tho' all the world betrays thee,
> one sword, at least, thy rights shall guard.
> The Minstrel Boy (THOMAS MOORE, 1779–1852)

∵

In recent times, humanitarian intervention has been prominent in the minds not just of academics, but also policy makers and the public.[1] It is a truism that people should be protected from abuse but exactly how is mired in controversy.[2] This is particularly the case when the response involves the use of military force, commonly known as humanitarian intervention. Despite the ongoing debate on humanitarian intervention, its status under international

1 Jahn, Beate. 'Humanitarian intervention – What's in a name?' *International Politics* (Vol 49, Iss.1, 2012) p.36.

2 Heraclides, Alexis and Dialla, Ada. *Humanitarian Intervention in the long Nineteenth Century. Setting the precedent.* (Manchester, 2015) p.2. For academic critics of humanitarian intervention, see Dinstein, Yoram. *War Aggression and Self Defense* (Cambridge, 2017) pp.76, Ronzitti, Natalino. *Rescuing Nationals Abroad through Military Coercion and Intervention in Grounds of Humanity* (Dordrecht, 1985) pp.89–113. Franck, Thomas and Rodley, Nigel. 'After Bangladesh: The Law of Humanitarian Intervention by Military Force' *American Journal of International Law* (Vol. 67, 1973) p.305, Donnelly, Jack. 'Human Rights, Humanitarian Intervention and American Foreign Policy: Law, Morality and Politics' *Journal of International Affairs* (Vol.37, No.2, 1984) p.317 and Mentan, Tatah. *The United Nations Organization: (in) Securing Global Peace and Security* (Bamenda, 2020) p.196. For supporters see Teson, Fernando. *Humanitarian Intervention: An Inquiry into Law and Morality* (Ardsley, 2005) p.415, Wolf, Daniel. 'Humanitarian Intervention' *Michigan Yearbook of International Studies* (Vol.9, 1988) p.353, Lillich, Richard. 'Intervention to Protect Human Rights' *McGill Journal of International Law* (1969) p.207, Fonteyne, Jean-Pierre. 'The Customary International Law Doctrine of Humanitarian Intervention: its Current Validity under the UN Charter' *California Western International Law Journal* (Vol.4, 1973–1974) p.258. Chesterman sees justifications for humanitarian intervention as 'shaky indeed' (Chesterman, Simon. *Just War and Just Peace: Humanitarian Intervention and International Law* (Oxford, 2001) pp.87–88), while Walling sees it as 'increasingly legitimate' but 'elective and rare'. (Walling, Carrie Booth. *All Necessary Measures: The UN and Humanitarian Intervention* (Philadelphia, 2013) p.244).

 | DOI:10.1163/9789004696396_002

law is unclear at best.[3] Even the definition is contentious,[4] however, this book will limit the term 'humanitarian intervention' to the following definition:

> The threat or use of force across state borders by a state (or group of states) aimed at preventing or ending widespread and grave violations of the fundamental human rights of individuals other than its own citizens, without the permission of the state within whose territory force is applied.[5]

Despite humanitarian intervention's dubious legitimacy, the tension between preserving state sovereignty and ending atrocities remains pressing.[6]

## 1 Research Question

The basis of this book is to assess whether a right of states to engage in humanitarian intervention exists based on customary international law and state practice. The main question being whether there is a legal right to humanitarian intervention, and if so, according to what criteria?[7] Humanitarian intervention is weak as a justification for the use of force, given its lack of invocation by governments, while academics are far more likely to use humanitarian intervention as a justification than states.[8] As will be explored, contemporary humanitarian intervention faces a major obstacle given the controversy surrounding whether it goes against the UN Charter's

3 See Czapliński, Władysław. 'Customary International Law on the Use of Force' *Wroclaw Review of Law, Administration & Economics* (Vol.8, Iss.2, 2018) p.100.

4 Franck and Rodley. *Supra* note 2. p.305. Even the term 'intervention' is problematic, potentially encompassing anything from diplomatic or economic pressure right up to armed invasion (International Commission on Intervention and State Sovereignty. *The Responsibility to Protect* (Ottawa, 2001) Para.1.37). Notably, international law prohibits intervention that interferes with the state's ability to decide for itself as per its sovereignty under international law. (International Court of Justice *Nicaragua v. United States of America* (Judgement of 27 June 1986) Para.205.) Likewise, civilian aid staff often resent the association of military force with humanitarianism. See Weiss, Thomas. *Humanitarian Intervention* (Cambridge, 2018) p.16.

5 Holzgrefe, J.L 'The Humanitarian Intervention Debate' in Holzgrefe, J.L and Keohane, Robert. *Humanitarian Intervention: Ethical, Legal and Political Dilemmas* (Cambridge, 2003) p.18.

6 See Walling. *Supra* note 2. p.10.

7 See Heinze, Eric. A. *Waging Humanitarian War: The Ethics, Law, and Politics of Humanitarian Intervention* (New York, 2009) p.5.

8 Chesterman *Supra* note 2. p.47.

prohibition on the use of force.[9] The research question in this book is to determine whether humanitarian intervention exists under customary international law. It will do this by empirically analysing its evolution and the key interventions where there is scope for arguing a humanitarian justification. While humanitarian intervention has a long historical basis,[10] it was often accepted that it is a recent concept.[11] This is important, as without a historical context, one cannot comprehend the legal system within which humanitarian intervention operates.[12]

While first studying humanitarian intervention, the author was surprised by how segmented current scholarship towards the area is, without any full-length study of how the doctrine developed. While numerous scholars have researched humanitarian intervention,[13] there is a lacuna in charting its evolution under international law. Humanitarian intervention is ultimately a doctrine with origins in the nineteenth century[14] and while several academics have analysed humanitarian intervention in this period, none have followed humanitarian intervention's development consistently through to the present. Simms and Trim's *Humanitarian Intervention: A History*[15] is a wide-ranging collection of essays on humanitarian intervention throughout history, with a particular focus on the nineteenth century. However, it fails to provide a continuous account of humanitarian intervention's evolution over time. In addition, the focus is not on international law and most of its contributors are historians and international relations scholars. At the same time, it omits key

9 See Wheeler, Nicholas. *Saving Strangers: Humanitarian Intervention in International Society* (Oxford, 2010) pp.44–47. Chesterman *Supra* note 2. pp.47–53. This will be explored further in Chapter 2, Section 1.

10 Klose, Fabian. 'The Emergence of Humanitarian Intervention' in Klose, Fabian. (Ed.) *The Emergence of Humanitarian Intervention: Ideas and Practice from the Nineteenth Century to the Present* (Cambridge, 2018) p.2.

11 See Simms, Brendan and Trim, D.J.B 'Towards a history of humanitarian intervention' in Simms, Brendan and Trim, D.J.B (Eds.) *Humanitarian Intervention: A History* (Cambridge, 2011) p.8.

12 Thompson, Andrew. 'Humanitarian interventions, past and present' in Klose, Fabian. (Ed.) *The Emergence of Humanitarian Intervention: Ideas and Practice from the Nineteenth Century to the Present* (Cambridge, 2018) p.356.

13 See Wheeler. *Supra* note 9, Teson *Supra* note 2, Chesterman *Supra* note 2, Lepard, Brian. *Rethinking Humanitarian Intervention: A Fresh Legal Approach Based on Fundamental Ethical Principles in International Law and World Religions* (University Park, 2002), Walling. *Supra* note 2, DiPrizio, Robert. *Armed Humanitarians: US Interventions from Northern Iraq to Kosovo* (Baltimore, 2002) and Holzgrefe. *Supra* note 5.

14 Fonteyne. *Supra* note 2. p.206, Heraclides, and Dialla. *Supra* note 2 p.12. It has further origins that will be explored in Chapter 2.

15 Simms and Trim. *Supra* note 11

interventions such as India's intervention in East Pakistan and Tanzania's intervention in Uganda. Bass's *Freedom's Battle*[16] focusses on three interventions in the Ottoman Empire during the nineteenth century. Although well written and informative, it does not focus on the legal aspects of international law in the nineteenth century. Likewise, Rodogno's *Against Massacre*[17] is an excellent account of humanitarian intervention in the nineteenth century Ottoman Empire but remains focused on this area. Heraclides and Dialla have a similarly well-researched work[18] on humanitarian intervention in the nineteenth century with a focus on international law, but again, its scope rests within the nineteenth century.

As such, this research will analyse humanitarian intervention from the nineteenth century to the contemporary period and the rise of the Responsibility to Protect (R2P) doctrine,[19] before analysing whether humanitarian intervention exists under customary international law. This is especially important, as despite humanitarian intervention's establishment in the nineteenth century,[20] the UN has repeatedly failed to protect people, even since the end of the Cold War and its impact on international relations.[21] Considering protecting people from atrocities cannot be divorced from ethics or common humanity, the use of humanitarian intervention transcends law and enters public debate worldwide. Due to the implications that either normalising or proscribing humanitarian intervention involves, this is a key area to analyse.

## 2 Methodology and Structure

Humanitarian intervention can be considered from ethical, political or legal perspectives, but a historical analysis is required in each case study to determine whether it strengthens humanitarian intervention's status under customary international law. An interdisciplinary approach is vital, as humanitarian intervention's legality cannot be easily separated from its historical development. The research required extensive use of primary sources,

16 Bass, Gary. *Freedom's Battle: The Origins of Humanitarian Intervention* (New York, 2008).

17 Rodogno, Davide. *Against Massacre: Humanitarian Intervention in the Ottoman Empire, 1815–1914*. (Princeton, 2012).

18 Heraclides and Dialla. *Supra* note 2.

19 See Chapter 5, Section 5. The Responsibility to Protect (R2P).

20 See *Supra* note 14.

21 See Lebor, Adam. *Complicity with Evil: The United Nations in the Age of Modern Genocide* (Bury St Edmunds, 2006).

especially government documents, newspaper reports, and the correspondence of political leaders. As both international law and records developed, minutes from the UN Security Council (UNSC), UN documents and NGO reports provide important sources. As this is a book relying heavily on historical analysis, secondary sources of both history and law will be used throughout the research.

The book will be divided into several chapters to determine successive stages in the development of humanitarian intervention Chapter 2 will demonstrate why humanitarian intervention is incompatible with the UN Charter and the need for customary international law as a source for humanitarian intervention. It will then chart humanitarian intervention's origins through the Just War theory and embryonic international law. This area of the book touches upon theology, ethics, and the formation of international relations. Nonetheless, it is a vital foundation for international law's development.

Following the establishment of humanitarian intervention's roots, Chapter 3 will explore interventions conducted by Europe's Great Powers to protect Christians within the Ottoman Empire and how this created a norm of humanitarian intervention under international law. It will focus on three key interventions: the 1827 multilateral intervention by the UK, France and Russia during the Greek War of Independence, France's intervention to protect Maronite Christians during the 1860 Lebanon conflict and Russia's 1877 unilateral intervention against the Ottoman Empire over the suppression of the Bulgarian rebellion. Primary sources are especially important given the historical basis of the research, but they must be understood in the historical era they arise from, with Euro-centric and often racist mindsets influencing both state practice and public opinion. There are other arguable examples of humanitarian intervention during the nineteenth century and even before but the allied intervention in Greece is seen as the first armed intervention on humanitarian grounds in history,[22] so this will be the starting point. Two other interventions will also be analysed as these are best placed to chart the development of humanitarian intervention, given they also involve European intervention in the Ottoman Empire.

Chapter 4 will look at the growth of humanitarian intervention in the twentieth century, initially with the League of Nations but then in the aftermath of the United Nations' foundation and its impact on the status of humanitarian intervention. The case studies here will focus on three interventions: India's 1971 intervention in East Pakistan, the Vietnam-Cambodia war of 1978, and

22 Heraclides and Dialla. *Supra* note 2. p.105.

the Uganda-Tanzania war of 1979.[23] These interventions took place against the backdrop of the foundation of the United Nations and the ongoing Cold War. They also occurred in a radically different context than those analysed in Chapter 3, with international law dominated by Europe's Great Powers being replaced by a legal system based on (nominally at least), sovereign equality and greater restrictions on the use of force.[24] Public documents (such as UNSC records) are used extensively to demonstrate how states characterise their actions, while records such as diplomatic cables are also important to show private interests.

Chapter 5 will then approach the issue of humanitarian intervention following the end of the Cold War and the newfound possibilities for the UNSC to protect civilians. However, the UNSC manifestly failed in this duty, most notably in Iraq (1991), Rwanda (1994) and Kosovo (1999).[25] Chapter 5 will examine the NATO led interventions in Iraq and Kosovo, neither of which was

---

23 Chesterman identifies eleven potential cases of humanitarian intervention. He deems the interventions by Belgium in the Congo (1960), Belgium and the USA in the Congo (1964), the USA in the Dominican Republic (1965), Israel in Uganda (1976) and Belgium and France in Zaire (1978) as being interventions for the protection of nationals. He deems French intervention in the Central African Republic (1979) as punishing the leader of a former French colony rather than preventing massacre. Furthermore, he rejects American intervention in Grenada (1983) as humanitarian given the US explicitly rejected it as a humanitarian intervention operation. (Chesterman *Supra* note 2. pp.64–84) while the US intervention in Panama (1989) was claimed to be in support of its democratically elected government. (Ibid. pp.103–104). Consequently, Chesterman highlights that only the interventions in East Pakistan, Uganda and Cambodia are seen favourably by the international community, although he highlights that humanitarian intervention was not invoked in these three cases. (Ibid. p.84).

24 UN Charter. (1 UNTS XVI, 1945) Article 2(1). See Wood, Michael. 'Use of force, prohibition of threat' in Wolfrum, Rudiger (Ed.), The Max Planck Encyclopaedia of Public International Law (online Ed) http://opil.ouplaw.com/view/10.1093/law:epil/9780199231690/law-9780199231690-e428?rskey=sfhUPW&result=2&prd=EPIL Accessed 10th March 2024.

25 These were chosen for their importance to the concept of humanitarian intervention: the intervention in Iraq as it was the first potential case of humanitarian intervention after the Cold War, and notably, a 'groundbreaking case' (See Walling. *Supra* note 6. p.18). Other examples of UN authorised peacekeeping and peace enforcement missions include Somalia (which took place in the absence if a functioning government), Bosnia-Herzegovina (where peacekeeping took place with the consent of the recognised Bosnian government) or Sierra Leone (where intervention took place in support of the deposed elected government) (See Walling. *Supra* note 2. p.259). NATO's intervention in Kosovo is a vital area to analyse as although unauthorised by the UNSC, the intervention in Kosovo is 'widely seen as an almost perfect example of humanitarian intervention' and humanitarian concerns were given as justification. (Heinze. *Supra* note 7. p.76). Likewise, Rwanda is taken as a case study given it took place amidst UN inaction to ongoing genocide, in

authorised by the UNSC. These will be compared with the UNSC authorised French intervention in response to the Rwandan genocide. Chapter 5 continues with the rise of the R2P doctrine in the aftermath of the UN's failure to protect civilians in the 1990s. This analyses the difference between R2P and traditional humanitarian intervention. R2P will then be considered in the context of the 2011 UNSC authorised intervention in Libya, an 'unprecedented' example of humanitarian intervention, which arguably disproves the concept that humanitarian intervention during the 1990s was a temporary deviation from UNSC practice.[26] It then analyses the ongoing Russia-Ukraine War and Russia's claims on the need to prevent Ukraine's government committing atrocities.

The conclusion is then drawn. Namely, that humanitarian intervention's existence under customary international law was extinguished over the course of the twentieth century. While humanitarian intervention arguably existed under international law in the nineteenth century, state practice over the course of the twentieth century demonstrates theat any right of humanitarian intervention has long since been eroded.

---

one of the greatest crises of the post-war era. (Schlesinger, Stephen. *Act of Creation: The Founding of the United Nations* (Boulder, 2003) p.286).

26 Walling. *Supra* note 2. p.18.

CHAPTER 2

# The Role of Humanitarian Intervention in Customary International Law

## 1 Humanitarian Intervention, the UN Charter and Customary International Law

Although of limited importance in domestic legal systems, custom is a prominent, if not a preeminent factor in international law.[1] The legal framework of international relations relies on the existence of a 'backdrop' of customary law.[2] Condorelli notes that they are rules 'whose existence is considered proven once their actual social effect is established'.[3] Given the lack of a universal authority, international law is fundamentally customary[4] and one of the more common arguments made to justify humanitarian intervention's legality is customary international law.[5] Customary international law offers humanitarian intervention a legal exception to the prohibition on the use of force[6] for operations that would otherwise be seen as aggression.[7]

Customary international law initially came about by necessity, given international relations required some rules, and it eventually became apparent that customary rules were insufficient, leading to the rise of law by treaty alongside customary law.[8] Writing at the start of the twentieth century, Oppenheim

1 Murphy, John F. *The Evolving Dimensions of International Law: Hard Choices for the World Community.* (Cambridge, 2010). p. 16.

2 Condorelli, Luigi. 'Customary International Law: The Yesterday, Today and Tomorrow of General International Law' in Cassese, Antonio (Ed.) *Realizing Utopia: The Future of International Law.* (Oxford, 2012) p.147.

3 Ibid. p.148.

4 Focarelli, Carlo. *International Law* (Cheltenham, 2019) p.114.

5 Heinze, Eric. A. *Waging Humanitarian War: The Ethics, Law, and Politics of Humanitarian Intervention* (New York, 2009) p.73.

6 International Law Association, Committee on the Use of Force (2010–2018), *Final Report on Aggression and the Use of Force, Sydney Conference* (2018) p.21.

7 In 1974, the UNGA passed a resolution defining aggression as 'the use of armed force by a State against the sovereignty, territorial integrity, or political independence of another State, or in any other manner inconsistent with the Charter of the United Nations'. Although advisory and not binding on the UNSC, the Resolution is nonetheless worth noting. See UN General Assembly *Definition of Aggression* UN Doc A/RES/3314(XXIX) (14 December 1974) Annex 1.

8 Oppenheim, Lassa *International Law: A Treatise, Vol. 1-Peace* (London, 1905) pp.16–17.

 DOI:10.1163/9789004696396_003

noted that custom occurs when continuous actions take place under the conviction that these are legally necessary or right.[9] When a rule reflecting the 'frequently adopted international conduct of states' is considered legally necessary or right, the rule becomes part of customary international law.[10]

The importance of customary international law remained after the League of Nations was founded, and the statute of the Permanent Court of International Justice highlighted 'international custom' as one of the four sources of international law.[11] This continued after the foundation of the United Nations, when the Statute for the ICJ's Article 38(1) (widely seen as authoritative on the sources of international law)[12] repeated custom as one of international law's four key sources.[13]

In 1950, one of the ICJ's judges noted the four key criteria for customary international law:

1) Concordant practice by a number of states with reference to a type of situation falling within the domain of international relations.
2) Continuation or repetition of the practice over a considerable period of time.
3) Conception that the practice is required by, or consistent with prevailing international law.
4) General acquiescence in the practice by other states.[14]

Essentially, customary international law must be looked for both in the actions and *opinio juris* of states.[15] The state practice must be 'in accordance with a constant and uniform usage'[16] and generally consistent.[17] Such practices need not be universal[18] but require no persistent opposition to their existence.[19] In

9 Ibid. pp.22–23.
10 Ibid.
11 Statute of the Permanent Court of International Justice. (L.N.T.S 6: 170, 1920) Article 38.
12 Shaw, Malcolm. *International Law* (Cambridge, 2017) p.51.
13 Statute of the International Court of Justice. (U.K.T.S 67, 1946) Article 38.
14 Hudson, Manley O. 'Article 24 of the Statute of the International Law Commission' *Yearbook of the International Law Commission* (Vol. II, 1950) p.26.
15 International Court of Justice. *Case Concerning the Continental Shelf Judgement (Libyan Arab Jamahiriya/Malta)* ICJ Reports 13 (Judgement of 3 June 1985). Para.27.
16 International Court of Justice *Asylum Case (Colombia/Peru)* ICJ Reports 266 (Judgment of 20 November 1950) p.14.
17 International Court of Justice *Nicaragua v. United States of America* (Judgement of 27 June 1986) ICJ Reports 14. Para 186.
18 Shaw. *Supra* note 12. p.57.
19 Heffes, Ezequiel. 'Some Reflections on the Theory of Sources of International Law: Re-Examining Customary International Law' *Israel Law Review* (Vol.51, No.3, 2018) p.485.

international law, custom can be created by a few powerful states to reflect geopolitical reality: Space law for example, was heavily developed by the USSR and US given these were the two key states with space programs, while maritime law would be gravely undermined without the input of major seafaring states[20] Although it is unclear how many states can create a norm under customary international law, a single state cannot do so unilaterally.[21]

For *opinio juris,* the state must not only perform certain actions but also see them as a legal obligation,[22] rather than carried out for convenience or political expediency.[23] For a rule to become binding under customary international law, it must be 'accepted and recognized by the international community of states as a whole as a norm from which no derogation is permitted.'[24] Just how extensive this recognition must be remains debatable.[25] Overall, the rules governing customary international law's creation are 'fraught with uncertainty' and can occur only when a significant number of states repeat actions over a considerable period of time, which can be extinguished at any time.[26]

To summarize, for something to exist under customary international law, it would require both the objective element of (general) state practice, be it actions or omissions, along with the subjective element of *opinio juris.*[27] For the principle of humanitarian intervention to exist under customary international law both of these elements are therefore required. However, it must also be acknowledged that critical to the status of humanitarian intervention under international law is the UN Charter's prohibition on the use of force against

20 See Shaw. *Supra* note 12. pp.58–59 and Dinstein, Yoram.*The Conduct of Hostilities under the Law of International Armed Conflict.* (Cambridge, 2010). p.11.

21 Focarelli. *Supra* note 4. p.120.

22 Charlesworth, Hilary and Chinkin, Christine. *The Boundaries of International Law. A Feminist Analysis* (Manchester, 2000). p.63 See International Court of Justice. *Nicaragua Case.* Supra note 17. Para 207 and International Court of Justice *North Sea Continental Shelf Cases (Federal Republic of Germany/Denmark; Federal Republic of Germany/Netherlands)* ICJ Reports 3. (Judgement of 20 February 1969). Para.77.

23 International Court of Justice. *Asylum case. Supra* note 16. p.15.

24 Vienna Convention on the Law of Treaties. (155 U.N.T.S. 331, 1969) Article.53.

25 Some ICJ judgements state that to invoke a rule under customary international law, its use must be 'constant and uniform' (International Court of Justice. *Asylum Case. Supra* note 16. p.14) or 'extensive and virtually uniform' (International Court of Justice. *Continental Shelf case. Supra* note 22. Para.74). However, a later judgement by the ICJ held that customary international law does not require 'absolute rigorous conformity' (International Court of Justice. *Nicaragua Case. Supra* note 17. Para 186).

26 Buchanan, Allen. 'Reforming the international law of humanitarian intervention' in Holzgrefe, J.L and Keohane, Robert. *Humanitarian Intervention: Ethical, Legal and Political Dilemmas* (Cambridge, 2003) p.135.

27 Dinstein. *Supra* note 20. pp.10–11.

the territorial integrity or political independence of any UN member state or in a manner inconsistent with UN principles.[28] The reason for this being that throughout history, one of the main drivers of conflict has been the threat and the use of force.[29] The key exception to this is when a state uses force in self-defence, with a government's obligation to protect its people being so vital[30] that the right of a state to use force in self-defence is 'inherent' and while recognised in the UN Charter, exists independently from it.[31] Unsurprisingly, such a right of self-defence is the most frequently cited justification in contemporary international law.[32]

The UNSC may authorise the use of force to maintain international peace and security in certain circumstances.[33] While the UN is a cornerstone for the protection of international human rights and the rule of law, one might expect the UNSC to authorise the use of force to end atrocities and blatant aggression. This is especially the case as the UN is the principal global actor in conflict resolution.[34] In practice, the UNSC is frequently unable to act due to a lack of unanimity among the UNSC's permanent members, which was especially notable during the Cold War with the polarisation between capitalist

28 UN Charter. (1 UNTS XVI, 1945) Article 2(4). For a more detailed analysis of Article 2(4), see Reisman, W. Michael. 'Article 2(4): The Use of Force in Contemporary International Law' Article 2(4): The Use of Force in Contemporary International Law' *Proceedings of the Annual Meeting (American Society of International Law)* (Vol.78, April 12–14, 1984) pp.74–87 and Gray, Christine. *International Law and the Use of Force* (Oxford, 2004) pp.29–58.

29 Frohlich, Manuel. 'The Responsibility to Protect. Foundation, transformation, and application of an emerging norm' in Klose, Fabian. (Ed.) *The Emergence of Humanitarian Intervention: Ideas and Practice from the Nineteenth Century to the Present* (Cambridge, 2018) p.300.

30 De Vattel notes that self-defence against aggression is not just a nation's right, but also 'one of her most sacred duties' (De Vattel, Emer. *The Law of Nations* (1758) p.487. http://files.libertyfund.org/files/2246/Vattel_1519_LFeBk.pdf Accessed 10th March 2024).

31 UN Charter. (1 UNTS XVI, 1945) Article 51. For a concise analysis of the issues surrounding the right of self-defence under the UN Charter, see Greig, D.W. 'Self-Defence and the Security Council: What Does Article 51 require?' *The International and Comparative Law Quarterly* (Vol.40, No.2, April 1991) pp.366–402.

32 Hoffman, Tamás. 'War or peace? – International legal issues concerning the use of force in the Russia–Ukraine conflict' *Hungarian Journal of Legal Studies* (Vol.63, No.3, 2022) p.209.

33 UN Charter. (1 UNTS XVI, 1945) Chapter VII. See Corten, Oliver and Simma, Bruno. *The Law Against War: The Prohibition on the Use of Force in Contemporary International Law* (Oxford, 2010) pp.311–400.

34 Fox, Gregory, Book Kristen and Jenkins, Isaac. 'The Contributions of United Nations Security Council Resolutions to the Law of Non-International Armed Conflict: New Evidence of Customary International Law' in *The American University Law Review* (Vol. 67, Iss. 3, 2018). p.651.

and communist members ensuring the UNSC was frequently deadlocked.[35] Likewise, even when the UNSC does authorise action, unless states are willing to provide the necessary military and logistical capacity, the UN can do little. In situations where egregious human rights abuses are taking place but the UN is unable to act, the question arises as to whether the use of force to end atrocities will be accepted by the international community. In this way, the issue of humanitarian intervention raises a key problem given it involves using force outside of the UN framework that appears incompatible with the UN Charter.[36] Indeed, the UN Charter's provisions were not intended to authorise humanitarian intervention, as the term is currently understood.[37] Nonetheless, the UN Charter's drafting history and UNSC practice strongly support the claim that humanitarian intervention which has been authorised by the UNSC is a lawful exception to the prohibition on the use of force.[38]

As the Charter prohibits the use of force 'against the territorial integrity and political independence of any state', the question arises as to whether humanitarian intervention is permissible, provided it does not involve annexation or subjugation.[39] This should be considered in the context of the UN Charter's lack of an explicit rejection of humanitarian intervention to permit the use of force to end human rights abuses.[40] This is problematic[41] and it can certainly be argued that Article 2(4) maintains its absolute prohibition on the

35 See Eichelberger, Clark. 'The Role of the United Nations in the East-West Dispute' *The Annals of the American Academy of Political and Social Science* (Vol.336, July 1961) pp.106–113.

36 Tams, Christian. 'Prospects for Humanitarian Uses of Force.' in Cassese, Antonio (Ed.) *Realizing Utopia: The Future of International Law.* (Oxford, 2012) p.361.

37 MacQueen, Norrie. *Humanitarian Intervention and the United Nations* (Edinburgh, 2011) p.13.

38 Holzgrefe, J.L 'The Humanitarian Intervention Debate' in Holzgrefe, J.L and Keohane, Robert. *Humanitarian Intervention: Ethical, Legal and Political Dilemmas* (Cambridge, 2003) p.43.

39 See Wolf, Daniel. 'Humanitarian Intervention' *Michigan Yearbook of International Studies* (Vol.9, 1988) p.339.

40 This is argued by Teson who claims a genuine humanitarian intervention 'does not result in territorial conquest or political subjugation' See Teson, Fernando. *Humanitarian Intervention: An Inquiry into Law and Morality* (Ardsley, 2005) p.193.

41 The wording of Article 2(4) of the UN Charter was not intended to be restrictive but to give additional safeguards to small states (See Brownlie, Ian. *International Law and the Use of Force* (Oxford, 2002) pp.266–267). Indeed, for such an argument to be made, each case of claimed humanitarian intervention would need to be examined on a case-by-case basis, which would fail to simplify or expand the norm (Fonteyne, Jean-Pierre. 'The Customary International Law Doctrine of Humanitarian Intervention: its Current Validity under the UN Charter' *California Western International Law Journal* (Vol.4, 1973–1974) p.254).

use of force, save for the exceptions explicitly listed in the Charter.[42] Explicit state support for humanitarian intervention is negligible and its strongest opponents tend to be from the Global South and former communist states.[43] This is largely due to self-interest. While member state sovereignty was an indispensable aspect of the UN's foundation,[44] it does not correlate to political equality.

Despite the seeming clarity on the prohibition on the use of force under international law, it remains open to interpretation and was written when the main threat to international security was from inter-state conflict.[45] Nowadays, intra-state conflicts constitute the majority of conflicts, rendering a focus on sovereignty as a potential threat to international order, rather than a protector of it.[46] Article 2(4) establishes an absolute prohibition on the use of force (outside of express exceptions in the UN Charter), and is widely accepted among academics.[47] Nonetheless, the decisions of the ICJ mean the UN Charter's prohibition on the use of force remains strong, even in situations where force is not used against a state's territorial integrity or political

42 This position is widely supported in state practice. In 1965, the UN General Assembly passed the *Declaration on the Inadmissibility of Intervention* which prohibited armed intervention 'for any reason whatsoever' (General Assembly Resolution XX. (21 December 1965) Para.20). Likewise, the 1970 Declaration on Principles of International Law states that the practice 'of any sort of intervention' violates the UN Charter and endangers international peace and security (UN Doc. A/Res/25/ (24 October 1970) Annex Preamble). In addition, the General Assembly's *Resolution on the Definition of Aggression* states that aggression includes the use of force against the sovereignty of a state, not just its territorial integrity or political independence (UN General Assembly *Definition of Aggression* UN Doc A/RES/3314(XXIX) (14 December 1974) Article 1).

43 Afro-Asian states relationship with intervention is complicated: while they support intervention to enable self-determination of peoples under colonial or racist control, they generally oppose intervention against governments, no matter how undemocratic or brutal these are (Ronzitti, Natalino. *Rescuing Nationals Abroad through Military Coercion and Intervention in Grounds of Humanity* (Dordrecht, 1985) pp.XVI–XVII). This is given Global South states tend to see humanitarian intervention as serving Western interests. (Thompson, Andrew. 'Humanitarian interventions, past and present' in Klose, Fabian. (Ed.) *The Emergence of Humanitarian Intervention: Ideas and Practice from the Nineteenth Century to the Present* (Cambridge, 2018) p.331).

44 Schulte, Jan Erik. 'From the Protection of sovereignty to humanitarian intervention? Traditions and developments of United Nations Peacekeeping in the twentieth century' in Klose, Fabian. (Ed.) *The Emergence of Humanitarian Intervention: Ideas and Practice from the Nineteenth Century to the Present* (Cambridge, 2018) p.262.

45 Frohlich. *Supra* note 29. p.301.

46 Ibid.

47 Ronzitti. *Supra* note 43. p.18.

independence.[48] Consequently, there is strong evidence to the effect that humanitarian intervention is not an exception to the prohibition on the use force under Article 2(4) of the UN Charter.[49]

The Article 2(4) prohibition on the threat or use of force is indisputably part of customary international law[50] and seems to permit no derogation for humanitarian intervention. At the same time, international law does not exist in a vacuum and evolves over time.[51] This is relevant given the increasing acceptance that human rights are no longer exclusively internal issues for states[52] with the post-World War II era seeing the rapid growth of international human rights law.[53] Likewise, the UN Charter states that one of the

48 These terms were not intended to restrict the prohibition on the use of force, but to protect weaker states (See International Law Association, Committee on the Use of Force (2010–2018), *Final Report on Aggression and the Use of Force, Sydney Conference* (2018) p.5). In the *Corfu Channel* case, The United Kingdom argued its minesweeping in Albanian waters was not a breach of the UN Charter, as it did not threaten Albania's territorial integrity or political independence. This was rejected by the ICJ, which held that 'the respect for territorial sovereignty is an essential foundation of international relations'. Furthermore, regardless of Albania's actions, the UK had violated Albania's sovereignty, with a right of intervention having no place in international law, 'whatever be the present defects in international organisation' (International Court of Justice *Corfu Channel case (UK v Albania)*. ICJ Reports 4, (Judgement of April 9, 1949) p.35). Although the ICJ made no explicit reference to humanitarian intervention, opponents of humanitarian intervention claim its judgement reaffirmed the general prohibition on intervention, humanitarian or otherwise (Bazyler. Michael. 'Re-examining the Doctrine of Humanitarian Intervention in Light of the Atrocities in Kampuchea and Ethiopia' *Stanford Journal of International Law* (Vol.23, 1987) pp.575–576). Likewise, in the *Nicaragua case*, the ICJ noted that the widely accepted principle of non-intervention forbids states from interfering in the internal or external affairs of others (International Court of Justice. *Nicaragua Case. Supra* note 17. Para 205). Although the US did not rely on humanitarian intervention in its support for rebel groups against Nicaragua's Sandinista government, the ICJ nonetheless concluded that the use of force is not an appropriate method to enforce human rights. (International Court of Justice. *Nicaragua Case. Supra* note 17. Para 268).

49 This is disputed by Teson, who argues it is a 'distortion' to claim humanitarian intervention is prohibited by Article 2(4), whose language does not prohibit the use of force to end serious human rights abuses (Teson. *Supra* note 40. pp.193–194). This is countered by Chesterman who claims this involves an 'Orwellian' interpretation of the Charter (Chesterman, Simon. *Just War and Just Peace: Humanitarian Intervention and International Law* (Oxford, 2001) p.53).

50 International Law Association, Committee on the Use of Force (2010–2018), *Final Report on Aggression and the Use of Force, Sydney Conference* (2018) pp.2–3.

51 International Court of Justice. *Nicaragua Case. Supra* note 17. Para 207.

52 Abiew. *Supra* note 42. p.98. See also, Teson. *Supra* note 40. p.178.

53 This was evident in the UN Charter, with the UN Commission on Human Rights seeking to give effect to the UN Charter's human rights provisions to lead what is known as the International Bill of Human Rights. This consists of the UN's Universal Declaration

UN's basic purposes is to protect human rights[54] with all member states agreeing to promote universal respect for these rights.[55] To this end, it is arguable that humanitarian intervention is compatible with the UN Charter as it seeks to execute the UN's duty to protect such rights.[56] The increased emphasis on human rights arguably necessitates a change in the UN's approach to their protection[57] and it is evident that human rights are mainstreamed within international law.[58] Although the UN was successful in creating human rights standards, there are significant shortcomings in ensuring the implementation and observance of such rights.[59] Despite the growth of human rights instruments, human rights remain subject to weak enforcement mechanisms, largely relying on supervisory committees and self-reporting by states.[60] Furthermore, human rights were not initially intended to be included in the UN Charter[61] and are not central to it, making it unlikely they were intended to be unilaterally enforceable by military means.[62] Although human rights are no longer strictly domestic concerns,[63] it is doubtful the UN Charter's focus on human

of Human Rights that was passed by the UN General Assembly in 1948 and the 1996 International Covenant on Civil and Political Rights and International Covenant on Economic, Social and Cultural Rights. (See Ramcharan, B.G. 'The Legal Status of the International Bill of Human Rights' *Nordic Journal of International Law* (Vol.55, 1986) p.366).

54 UN Charter. (1 UNTS XVI, 1945) Article 1(3).

55 Ibid. Article 55.

56 Holzgrefe, J.L 'The Humanitarian Intervention Debate' in Holzgrefe, J.L and Keohane, Robert. *Humanitarian Intervention: Ethical, Legal and Political Dilemmas* (Cambridge, 2003) p.39.

57 Stanulova, Maya. 'Has Humanitarian Intervention Become an Exception to the Prohibition on the Use of Force in Article 2(4) of the UN Charter?' *Atlantic Community* (2010) p.11 https://economia.uniroma2.it/ba/globalgovernance/corso/asset/YToo0ntzOjI6ImlkIjtzOjM6IjMyMyI7czozOiJpZGEiO3M6NToiNDEoODEiO3M6MjoiZWoiO047czox OiJjIjtzOjU6ImQ2YjgyIjt9 Accessed 10th March 2024.

58 International Commission on Intervention and State Sovereignty. *The Responsibility to Protect* (Ottawa, 2001) Para.1.25.

59 Korey, William. 'A Global Ombudsman' *The Saturday Review* (12 August 1967).

60 Donnelly, Jack. 'Human Rights, Humanitarian Crisis and humanitarian intervention' *International Journal* (Vol.48, Autumn 1993) p.624.

61 Schlesinger, Stephen. *Act of Creation: The Founding of the United Nations* (Boulder, 2003) pp.123–124. Although they were included, they are largely exhortative in nature (Chesterman. *Supra* note 49. p.45).

62 Franck, Thomas and Rodley, Nigel. 'After Bangladesh: The Law of Humanitarian Intervention by Military Force' *American Journal of International Law* (Vol. 67, 1973) p.300.

63 Teson. *Supra* note 40. p.178.

rights can be used as a justification for intervention,[64] even against especially heinous crimes such as genocide.[65] This is not to say human rights have no enforcement mechanism under international law, but to argue that this creates a right of intervention is weak at best.

Despite the above, international legal scholars have continued to recognise an inherent right of humanitarian intervention, regardless of UN authorisation.[66] This arises primarily from customary international law, which is a vital source of public international law, comprising international law which is unwritten but which is accepted from practice.[67] However, 'customary law can exist *infra* the UN Charter, *praetor* the Charter and perhaps also *contra* the Charter.'[68] Such customary international law is vital as article 51 of the UN Charter refers to the 'inherent' right of self-defence, which exists independently of the Charter and so humanitarian intervention could still exist

64 Karoubi noting that despite the Charter's emphasis on human rights, they do not create any binding obligations on member states (Karoubi, Mohammed Taghi. *Just or Unjust War?* (Aldershot, 2004) p.223). This was also concluded by the Independent International Commission on Kosovo who noted that while it is 'reasonable and necessary' to give stronger protection to human rights under the UN Charter, the Security Council does not have authority under the Charter to take action against or to prevent human rights abuses (Independent International Commission on Kosovo. *Kosovo Report* (Oxford, 2000) p.196).

65 Article 1 of the 1948 Convention on the Prevention and Punishment of the Crime of Genocide requires contracting parties to 'prevent and punish' genocide. However, it does not appear to authorise states to use force against others and instead Article 8 allows them to call upon the 'competent organs' of the UN to act. In practice, this would be the Security Council but in cases such as Darfur, where many states and UN organs accused the Sudanese government of committing genocide, the Security Council took no effective action (Hehir, Aidan. *Humanitarian Intervention: An Introduction* (Basingstoke, 2010) p.95). As such, humanitarian intervention without UN authorisation to avert genocide is still an ostensible breach of the UN Charter. Furthermore, the Genocide Convention has significant shortcomings in that it is reactive rather than preventive, ensuring that action can only be taken when it may be too late to help the victims of genocide (Organisation of African Unity *Rwanda: The Preventable Genocide* (2000) Para.1.11). For further analysis humanitarian intervention and genocide, see Donnelly, Jack. 'Genocide and Humanitarian Intervention' *Journal of Human Rights* (Vol.1, No.1, 2002).

66 Bazyler. *Supra* note 48. p.576. It must be noted that such academics are heavily concentrated in the Global North (Hassan, Farooq. 'Realpolitik in International Law: After Tanzanian-Ugandan Conflict Humanitarian Intervention Re-examined' *Willamette Law Review* (Vol.17, Issue.4, Fall 1981) pp.883–884).

67 International Law Commission. 'Draft conclusions on identification of customary international law, with commentaries.' *Yearbook of the International Law Commission* (Vol. II, Part 2, 2018) p.122.

68 Czapliński, Władysław. 'Customary International Law on the Use of Force' *Wroclaw Review of Law, Administration & Economics* (Vol.8, Iss.2, 2018) p.100.

outside of the UN Charter, having survived as a right of customary international law.[69] Indeed, a customary law of humanitarian intervention would not be against the Charter as it would be, by definition, an exception to it.[70] However, even if such a situation did occur, it would be difficult to prove, given the requirements for a norm to be deemed part of customary international law.[71] Analysing the status of humanitarian intervention in history provides cogent evidence to help determine whether it constitutes a norm of customary international law, which would maintain its existence independently from the UN Charter.

## 2 The Origins of Humanitarian Intervention

Humanitarian intervention has its philosophical origins in the Just War tradition,[72] as does R2P.[73] Although force was used by European states in the sixteenth and seventeenth centuries to aid others, this was primarily for reasons of religious solidarity.[74] St Augustine of Hippo is frequently regarded as a key founder of the Just War doctrine[75] and unlike modern approaches to the

69 The use of force continuing to exist under customary international law and outside of the UN Charter is a contentious one. Dinstein argues that the prohibition on the use of force under Article 2(4) is now part of customary international law (See Dinstein, Yoram. *War Aggression and Self Defense* (Cambridge, 2017) p.99). This was highlighted by the ICJ (International Court of Justice. *Nicaragua Case. Supra* note 17 Para.188) who also noted the UN Charter does not cover all forms of the use of force under international law, with treaty law and customary international law continuing to exist and 'do not overlap exactly' (International Court of Justice. *Nicaragua Case. Supra* note 17. Para 176). Hassan argues that if humanitarian intervention survives under customary international law, it is only in the following circumstances: First, the intervening state must be disinterested and have no primarily self-interested motive from the action. Second, it must be in response to atrocities of 'genocidal magnitude'. Third, the sovereign must have actively or passively complied with the atrocities and finally, major powers must act collectively against the atrocity (Hassan. *Supra* note 66. p.885).

70 Heinze. *Supra* note 5. p.81.

71 See Oppenheim. *Supra* note 8 pp.22–25, Kunz, J. 'The Nature of Customary International Law' *American Journal of International Law* (Vol.47, 1963) p.662 and Voyiaka, Emmanuel. 'A Disaggregative View of Customary International Law Making' *Leiden Journal of International Law* (Vol.29, No.2, June 2016) pp.365–366.

72 Heinze. *Supra* note 5. p.2.

73 Frohlich. *Supra* note 29. p.305.

74 Fonteyne. *Supra* note 41. pp.205–206.

75 It must be noted that Just War has deeper roots in the work of Cicero and early Church Fathers (Syse, Henrik. 'Augustine and Just War' in Syse, Henrik and Reichberg, Gregory. *Ethics, Nationalism and Just War: Medieval and Contemporary Perspectives* (Washington

prohibition on the use of force, St Augustine's doctrine does not prohibit offensive wars, provided they are carried out in the name of justice.[76] Christian theory on Just War was expanded by St Thomas Aquinas who argued that a war's legality required the authority of a lawful sovereign, a just cause and rightful intent.[77] Aquinas supports some foundations for humanitarian intervention in arguing 'wars are lawful and just in so far as they protect the poor and the entire common weal from suffering at the hands of the foe'.[78] Such theological and ethical arguments on Just War influenced humanitarian intervention, offering a lens whereby the motives behind the use of force could be evaluated.

Aiding strangers was considered by the Spanish theologian, Francisco de Vitoria who rejected divine law as a basis for Spanish colonialism and instead argued in favour of natural law.[79] De Vitoria expanded on the Just War doctrine, arguing that only a lawful sovereign (those without a superior lord) could declare war, and that war required a just cause, namely that of a wrong received which must be of sufficient gravity to necessitate war.[80] In addition to developing international law and the use of force, De Vitoria touched on the use of force to defend others.[81]

---

D.C, 2007) p.36). See also Nussbaum, Arthur. 'Just War: A Legal Concept?' *Michigan Law Review* (Vol.42, No.3, Dec 1943) pp.453–455.

76 Syse. *Supra* note 75. p.37. To St Augustine, war was reconcilable with Christ's teachings as just military actions prevented evil and were therefore an act of love. (Russell, Frederick. *The Just War in the Middle-Ages* (Cambridge, 1977) p.17).

77 Aquinas, Thomas. *Summa Theologicae* (1485) Second Part of the Second Part: L.39, C.2, Article 1. https://www.documentacatholicaomnia.eu/03d/1225-1274,_Thomas_Aquinas,_Summa_Theologiae_%5B1%5D,_EN.pdf Accessed 10th March 2024.

78 Ibid. L.39, C.2, Article 2.

79 Anghie, Antony. 'Francisco de Vitoria and the Colonial Origins of International Law' *Social and Legal Studies* (Vol.5, No.3, 1996) p.323. Taking a (for the time) progressive approach to Spain's Native American subjects, De Vitoria rejected claims that they were subhuman, arguing that they were rational humans, capable of exercising reason (De Vitoria, Francisco. *De Indis De Jure Belli. Relectiones Theologicae XII. (1583)* Part 2 http://legalhistorysources.com/Law508/VitoriaDeIndis.htm Accessed 10th March 2024). The Native American's capacity for reason ensured they were governed by international law (Jus Gentium) which applies to all nations and their rejection of Papal authority was not cause to make war upon them (Ibid).

80 De Vitoria, Francisco. *De Indis De Jure Belli. Relectiones Theologicae XII. (1583)* Part 3 http://legalhistorysources.com/Law508/VitoriaDeIndis.htm Accessed 10th March 2024.

81 De Vitoria argues that some acts such as cannibalism are so tyrannical and against natural law that anyone can use force to protect its victims and that 'it is especially the business of princes to do so' (De Vitoria. *Supra* note 79.) However, De Vitoria also justified Spanish colonialism, seeing it as beneficial to the Indians and an intervention in the name of humanity. See Heraclides, Alexis and Dialla, Ada. *Humanitarian Intervention in the long Nineteenth Century. Setting the precedent.* (Manchester, 2015) p.20.

While De Vitoria laid secular foundations for protecting strangers, it was developed by Hugo Grotius, whose work formed a key basis for international law's development.[82] This is evident in *De Jure Belli ac Pacis* where Grotius asserts that the 'common tie of one common nature' is enough to impose obligations on men to aid one another.[83] Sovereigns have authority within their own borders but can lose natural law's protection by committing atrocities, justifying others to act against them.[84] As such, sovereigns have the right (although not the duty) to inflict punishments 'for gross violations of the law of nature and of nations, done to other states and subjects'.[85]

Grotius laid the fundamental principles for modern international law and he was the sole international law jurist whose work was widely recognised in the seventeenth century.[86] Likewise, his work is notable for forming a secular basis to his natural law approach.[87] Opposition to humanitarian intervention was also evident, particularly in the work of the de Vattel, who believed states are obliged to help one another promote 'the perfection of others', but that using force violated their liberty.[88]

Although European nations were fragmented by legal systems, languages and denominations, certain accepted norms of law between nations took root. This became especially important in the seventeenth century, which saw the embryonic formation of statehood.[89] This had a major impact on

82 Oppenheim. *Supra* note 8. p.4. For an analysis on Grotius and his work, see Oppenheim. *Supra* note 8. pp.76–81.

83 Grotius, Hugo. *On the Law of War and Peace* (1625) Book II, Ch.25, Art.VI. https://socialsciences.mcmaster.ca/econ/ugcm/3ll3/grotius/Law2.pdf Accessed 10th March 2024. p.247.

84 Ibid. Art. VIII. p.247.

85 Ibid. Book II Ch.20, Art. XL. p.207. While Grotius was aware of the risk that humanitarian claims risked being used to cloak selfish goals, he concluded that 'right does not necessarily lose its nature from being in the hands of wicked men.', comparing them to swords which can be used for lawful defence, but will sometimes be used by robbers (Ibid. Book II Ch.25, Art.VIII). This has contemporary echoes: few would deny that states have the right to use force in self-defence and though the right of self-defence is frequently used to justify selfish aims, self-defence remains accepted within international law.

86 Hershey, Amos. 'History of International Law since the Peace of Westphalia' *American Journal of International Law* (Vol.6, No.1, Jan 1912) pp.31–32.

87 Chesterman. *Supra* note 49. pp.12–13.

88 Furthermore, De Vattel rejects Grotius' assertions that sovereigns have the right to take up arms against nations committing crimes against nature. (De Vattel. *Supra* note 30. p.265).

89 The modern concept of statehood was still absent and prior to 1789, there were few fully independent and autonomous states in Europe, with Catholic powers technically subordinate to Papal authority and most major powers formed from recognisable smaller political units with varying degrees of independence (Doyle, William. *The Old European Order. 1660–1800* (Oxford, 1992) p.221). The rise of statehood was heavily underpinned by military developments and the rise of professional, standing militaries.

international law, strengthening governmental power and the modern state, permitting governments to maintain their territorial sovereignty and engage in international relations.[90] Likewise, governments' growing domestic and military power was matched by sophisticated approaches to external affairs, with diplomacy becoming formalised and conducted by foreign ministries rather than sovereigns.[91] This allowed a new approach to be taken to international law. Especially important was the 1648 Peace of Westphalia, which established modern foundations of international law in relation to sovereignty.[92]

The Peace of Westphalia laid out many important aspects of contemporary international law such as territorial sovereignty and a prohibition on interference,[93] and highlights that sovereigns have full jurisdiction within their own territory.[94] Above all, retrospective analysis of Westphalia ensured non-intervention became an important legal principle associated with sovereignty.[95] This led to a new approach in international law towards regulating conduct between states. International law evolved and gradually, the governance of international relations by natural law was superseded by positivism based on shared European legal practices.[96] Though the Peace of Westphalia is often seen as maintaining state sovereignty, this was subordinate to the balance of power,[97] which dominated European diplomacy.[98] It was the balance of power rather than the sovereignty or rights of independent states, which governed international relations. While every nation had rights, the Great

90 Dandeker, Christopher. 'War and the Military Establishment' in Freedman, Lawrence (Ed.) *War* (Oxford, 1994) p.110.

91 Doyle. *Supra* note 89. pp.267–268.

92 Weiss, Thomas. *Humanitarian Intervention* (Cambridge, 2018) p.23.

93 Treaty of Westphalia (1648). Article LXIV https://avalon.law.yale.edu/17th_century/westphal.asp Accessed 10th March 2024.

94 Ibid. Article LXVII. It must be noted that this did not mean a state had absolute sovereignty within its borders. See Trim, D.J.B 'Conclusions: Humanitarian intervention in historical perspective' in Simms, Brendan and Trim, D.J.B (Eds.) *Humanitarian Intervention: A History* (Cambridge, 2011) pp.381–382.

95 Heraclides and Dialla. *Supra* note 81. p.23.

96 Palabiyik, Mustafa Serdar. 'The Emergence of the Idea of 'International Law' in the Ottoman Empire before the Treaty of Paris (1856)' *Middle Eastern Studies* (Vol 50, No.2, 2014) pp.233–234.

97 Trachtenberg, Marc. 'Intervention in Historical Perspective' in Reed, Lauren and Kaysen, Carl (Eds.) *Emerging Norms of Justified Intervention* (Cambridge, MA, 1993) p.19.

98 Brownlie. *Supra* note 41. p.16. While small nations were frequently absorbed into stronger nations to suit the interests of the Great Powers, it is important to note that this was not merely the case of strong states using international law to oppress weaker ones. Even strong nations would be collectively opposed if they threatened stability. The 1713 Treaties of Utrecht which ended the War of Spanish Succession being a notable example.

Powers noted 'Europe also has her rights'.[99] This became especially important due to growing international trade and the rise of colonialism.[100]

It would be a mistake to adopt an entirely Euro-centric approach to modern international law but international law's progress at the time was reliant on the (European) Great Powers.[101] While the seventeenth century had seen the world's most sophisticated legal systems being found in Asia,[102] the nineteenth century saw European states becoming hegemonic on the world stage, rapidly gaining military and economic power while previously formidable non-European empires like the Ottoman, Chinese and Mughal Empires were forced into subordinate relationships by European states.[103] The nineteenth century also witnessed the concept of 'Christian society' being replaced by an international society that saw Europe as the standard for civilisation, and international law as involving European states and those states of European extraction.[104] While international law was seen to exist, European states only saw it as applying to relations between European states and not to their colonial domains.[105] This ensured a heavily Euro-centric approach to the development of international law, which evolved to include non-European states, initially Christian and subsequently non-Christian.[106] This became especially pressing as the nineteenth century saw the rise of solidarity across ethnic and religious boundaries, inducing intervention.[107]

---

99 Cited by Lingelbach, William. 'The doctrine and practice of intervention in Europe' *Annals of the American Academy of Political and Social Science* (July 1900) p.7.

100 Karns, Margaret and Mingst, Karen. *International Organisations: The Politics and Processes of Global Governance* (Boulder, 2004) p.65.

101 Oppenheim. *Supra* note 8. p.163.

102 Pirie, Fernanda. *The Rule of Laws: A 4,000-Year Quest to Order the World* (London, 2021) p.315.

103 France, John. *Perilous Glory: The Rise of Western Military Power* (New Haven 2011) pp.216–217.

104 Heraclides, Alexis and Dialla, Ada. *Humanitarian Intervention in the long Nineteenth Century. Setting the precedent.* (Manchester, 2015) pp.31–32.

105 Snyder, Timothy. *The Road to Unfreedom: Russia, Europe, and America* (London, 2019) p.75.

106 Wheaton, Henry. *Elements of International Law* (London, 1916) pp.18–19.

Oppenheim. *Supra* note 8. p.32, pp.48–50. See also, Schwarzenberger, Georg. The Rule of Law and the Disintegration of the International Society' *American Journal of International Law.* (Vol.33, Iss.1, January 1939) p.63. Likewise, Anghie notes that by the end of the nineteenth century, European expansion meant that European international law had become universal (Anghie, Antony. 'The evolution of international law: Colonial and postcolonial realities' *Third World Quarterly.* (Vol.27 (5), 2006). p.746). The foundations of international law arising from Western nations is also highlighted by Shaw (Shaw. *Supra* note 12. p.10).

107 Bazyler. *Supra* note 48. p.582.

CHAPTER 3

# Humanitarian Intervention in the Ottoman Empire

Following Napoleon' s defeat by the Sixth Coalition, a conference was convened at Vienna in 1814 to ensure European stability.[1] The resulting Concert of Europe is notable from an international law perspective where after years of conflict, the European Powers sought to solve disputes through collective negotiations.[2] The Concert had many issues to address that would have a key impact on international law, particularly maintaining the balance of power, which the Great Powers saw as vital to ensure stability and prevent future unilateral aggression.[3] This ensured the Concert treated France leniently and avoided destabilising it through ruinous indemnities,[4] before France eventually became a member of the Concert. The sovereignty of small nations was a minor legal concern compared to the overarching balance of power and the Concert forcibly unified smaller states with larger ones to ensure buffer zones.[5]

The coercion of smaller states was a major problem in the nineteenth century when states' rights to use force to coerce others were extremely broad.[6] The use of force was not unlimited due to the balance of power and a European state that threatened stability would likely find itself facing a coalition of opposition. Likewise, although the right of pre-emptive use of force existed under international law, it was subject to restrictions as evidenced in the 1837 *Caroline* affair.[7]

---

1 For a detailed analysis of the Congress of Vienna, see Chapman, Tim. *The Congress of Vienna: Origins, Processes and Results* (London, 1998) and Langehorne, Richard. 'Reflections on the Significance of the Congress of Vienna' *Review of International Studies* (Vol.12, No.4, October 1986) pp.313–324.

2 Rie, Robert. 'The Origins of Public Law and the Congress of Vienna' *Transactions of the Grotius Society* (Vol.36, 1950) p.209. Negotiations were hindered due to sharp divisions between the Great Powers, particularly Britain's constitutional monarchy against authoritarian Russia, Austria and Prussia. Austria's Foreign Minister, Prince Metternich sought to maintain stability at any cost while his British counterpart, Viscount Castlereagh preferred constitutional reform. Collins, Bruce. *War and Empire: The Expansion of Britain 1790–1830* (Harlow, 2010) p.441.

3 France, John. *Perilous Glory: The Rise of Western Military Power* (New Haven 2011) p.214.

4 Castlereagh; Richelieu; Wellington. *Cobbett's Political Register*, (2 December 1815).

5 Adair, Robert. *The Declaration of England against the acts and projects of the Holy Alliance* (London, 1821) p.8.

6 Brownlie, Ian. *International Law and the Use of Force* (Oxford, 2002) p.19.

7 'Correspondence between Great Britain and the United States, respecting the Arrest and Imprisonment of Mr. McLeod, for the Destruction of the Steamboat Caroline' (March,

 | DOI:10.1163/9789004696396_004

Following Napoleon's return and defeat at Waterloo, two new agreements were concluded in 1815, namely the Quadruple Alliance[8] and the Holy Alliance.[9] The authoritarian states of Austria, Prussia and Russia feared the rise of nationalism and liberalism and were adamant that the Quadruple and Holy Alliances should be used to suppress revolutions and maintain Europe's status quo.[10] Britain, mindful of its own Glorious Revolution was less interventionist[11] and Britain's Foreign Minister, Viscount Castlereagh noted the Quadruple Alliance was intended to free the continent from French military domination rather than supervise 'the internal affairs of other States'.[12] To Castlereagh, intervention was only permissible when there was a threat to the balance of power and thus international peace and security.[13] This shows one

---

April 1841) *British Foreign and State Papers* (Vol.29. 1840–1841) pp.1126–1139. Here, British forces penetrated into US territory and destroyed a ship which had been used to conduct raids in British-Canada. See Rogoff, Martin and Collins, Edward. 'The Caroline Incident and the Development of International Law' *Brooklyn Journal of International Law* (Vol.16, No.3, 1990) p.495. Although Britain defended the attack as necessary, the US Secretary of State, Daniel Webster noted that self-defence could only exist when it was 'instant, overwhelming, leaving no choice of means and no moment for deliberation' and that self-defence 'justified by the necessity of self-defence, must be limited by that necessity and clearly kept within it' (see Jennings, R.Y. 'The Caroline and McLeod Cases' *American Journal of International Law* (Vol.32, No.1, Jan 1938) p.89). These principles were accepted by the British government and are now acknowledged as part of customary international law (Shaw, Malcom. *International Law* (Eight Ed. Cambridge, 2017) p.861).

8 This was aimed at maintaining geopolitical stability and declared its opposition to revolution and support for collective action to maintain European peace. See Sharp, Alan. 'Reflections on the Remaking of Europe: 1815, 1919, 1945, Post-1989' *Irish Studies in International Affairs* (Vol.8, 1997) p.14.

9 The Holy Alliance was set up by Russia's Tsar Alexander I which sought to replace international law with 'the sublime truths which the Holy Religion of our Saviour teaches'. The Holy Alliance Treaty. (1815) Preamble. https://www.napoleon-series.org/research/government/diplomatic/c_alliance.html (Accessed 10th March 2024) See Anonymous 'Europe's Poisonous Remedies' *Advocate of Peace through Justice* Vol.84.11, (November 1922). Although Russia, Prussia and Austria acceded to the Holy Alliance, it was a vague 'entente' rather than an enforceable contract. Mowat, R.B. *A History of European Diplomacy 1815–1914* (London, 1922) p.26. Castlereagh dismissed it as a 'piece of sublime mysticism and nonsense' and even Metternich saw it as 'loud-sounding nothing' Shepardson, Whitney. 'Nationalism and Free Trade' *Foreign Affairs* (April 1934).

10 Gildea, Paul. *Barricades and Borders: Europe 1800–1914* (Oxford, 1996) p.64.

11 Langehorne. *Supra* note 1. p.321.

12 Castlereagh, Robert Stewart. 'Lord Castlereagh's Confidential State Paper of May 5th, 1820' in Ward, Adolphus, William and Gooch, George Peabody (Eds.) *The Cambridge History of British Foreign Policy, 1783–1919* (Cambridge, 2012) p.627.

13 Trachtenberg, Marc. 'Intervention in Historical Perspective' in Reed, Lauren and Kaysen, Carl (Eds.) *Emerging Norms of Justified Intervention* (Cambridge, MA, 1993) p.22.

of the key problems of nineteenth century international law, in that the Great Powers worked well on facing common threats (such as French hegemony) but divisions arose between them on other issues.[14]

During the 1820s, the Great Powers deployed troops to crush liberal and nationalist revolts[15] demonstrating interventions in what had previously been internal matters.[16] Interventionism worried Castlereagh who feared intervention in domestic issues becoming normalised, which he viewed as 'utterly impractical and objectionable'.[17] International law was also facing radical change but its Euro-centric and Christian approach raised questions as to the status of non-Christians,[18] especially as European states engaged in increased colonisation and relations with independent non-European states. Although European states had conducted external relations for centuries, this had primarily been based on negotiation rather than conquest.[19] This changed during the nineteenth century when European imperialism and technological superiority ensured international law became dominated by Western state practice,[20] marking a key development in international relations.[21] Europe's

14 A Russian proposal for the 1818 Congress of Aix La Chapelle would have created an alliance where the Great Powers would collectively guarantee each other's territories and governments. Castlereagh was alarmed and opposed force being 'prostituted to the support of established power, without any consideration of the extent to which it was abused' (Castlereagh *Robert Stewart. Memorandum on the Treaties of 1814 and 1815* (October 1818)). A further conference was convened at Troppau which sought to create an allied military league to intervene in domestic unrest, but this was rejected by Britain and France. (Anonymous. *Supra* note 9. p.369).

15 See Miller, Marion. 'A 'Liberal International'? Perspectives on Comparative Approaches to the Revolutions in Spain, Italy, and Greece in the 1820s' *Mediterranean Studies* (Vol.2, Greece, and the Mediterranean, 1990).

16 Bew, John. 'From an Umpire to a competitor' Castlereagh, Canning, and the issue of international intervention in the wake of the Napoleonic Wars' in Simms, Brendan and Trim, D.J.B (Eds.) *Humanitarian Intervention: A History* (Cambridge, 2011) p.120.

17 Castlereagh. *Supra* note 12. p.631.

18 Oppenheim, Lassa *International Law: A Treatise, Vol. 1-Peace* (London, 1905) p.148.

19 Alexandrowicz, C.H. 'Freitas vs Grotius' *British Yearbook of International Law* (Vol.35, 1959) p.164.

20 Brownlie. *Supra* note 6. p.49.

21 While Europeanised Christian states like the United States of America were accepted into the international legal regime, nations which were neither Christian nor European had no such protection. Intervention was common during the nineteenth century and used for everything from the protection of nationals to the enforcement of debts (see Trachtenberg. *Supra* note 13. p.23). A prime example is China which had a developed empire, but was coerced by European nations into accepting the 'Unequal Treaties' which imposed major infringements of Chinese sovereignty in a manner which would have been unacceptable between Western powers (see Chiu, Hungdah. 'China's Struggle

disdain for foreign sovereignty was especially evident in the Ottoman Empire, whose multi-ethnic and Islamic empire had long been involved in European affairs.[22] Ottoman weakness gave rise to the Eastern Question: problems relating to Ottoman decline and its impact on the European balance of power. This was especially dangerous to European stability as the Porte[23] provided a key buffer zone and its collapse risked European war and instability.

## 1 Humanitarian Intervention in Greece 1827

Ottoman instability was evident in the Balkans, where unrest grew due to Ottoman taxes and repression. Rebellion broke out in 1821 in Greece with the rebels invoking 'the aid of all civilised nations of Europe'.[24] Although the Greeks committed atrocities,[25] the Ottoman response caused horror across Europe.[26] While the Ottoman Empire was not part of the Congress of Vienna, Ottoman instability was a grave threat to the balance of power, ensuring the Great Powers denounced the uprising but watched events closely,[27] particularly as it soon became apparent that the Ottomans were unable to suppress the rebellion.

This situation caused friction in the Holy Alliance,[28] whose commitment to Christianity required aiding the Greeks while its counter-revolutionary sentiment meant supporting the Porte. The consequences of Ottoman collapse

---

against the Unequal Treaties, 1927–*1946' Chinese (Taiwan) Yearbook of International Law and Affairs* (Vol.5, 1985) p.2).

22 In the Early-Modern period, the Ottoman Empire conquered the Byzantine Empire and threatened to sweep across Europe but by the nineteenth century, it was an empire in decline, with an outdated military, economic stagnation, and ineffective government. See Palmer, Alan. *The Decline and Fall of the Ottoman Empire* (London, 1992).

23 The Sublime Porte being the metonym for the Ottoman Empire's central government.

24 Manifesto Addressed to Europe by Petros Mavromikhalis (28 March 1821) in Gordon, Thomas. *History of the Greek Revolution, Volume 1* (Edinburgh, 1844) p.183.

25 Gordon. *Supra* note 24. pp.168–169.

26 Reports of Ottoman brutality resulted in European outrage particularly in more liberal states like Britain and France whose relatively uncensored press regimes reported on the atrocities. Even authoritarian Austria was disturbed by the massacres of innocent Greek civilians and clergymen ('Massacres at Constantinople' *Observer* (18 June 1821)). This led to accusations of the Holy Alliance being responsible for allowing such atrocities to happen and of upholding an 'antichristian and barbarous' power in Europe ('State and Prospects of the Greeks' *Scotsman* (13th July 1822)).

27 Heraclides, Alexis and Dialla, Ada. *Humanitarian Intervention in the long Nineteenth Century. Setting the precedent.* (Manchester, 2015) p.107.

28 See *Supra* note 9.

in the Balkans were severe, threatening the balance of power and drawing the Great Powers into war with one another.[29] Tsar Alexander I saw a chance to expand Russian influence in the region whilst Russian trade was suffering from an Ottoman blockade of the Greeks.[30] Russia also sought control of Constantinople for reasons both mystical and pragmatic.[31]

Russian public opposition to the Ottomans continued to grow.[32] Russia avoided intervention but its representative in Constantinople urged the Great Powers to send ships to defend Greek Christians.[33] The other Powers did not support this and Russia withdrew its ambassador to the Porte, with Alexander I warning that Russia could not surrender fellow Christians to the 'mercy of blind fanaticism'.[34] As an autocracy, Russia's foreign policy largely amounted to the Tsar's personal interests and despite his unpredictability, Alexander I was aware of both Russia's isolation and the risks it faced from nationalism.[35] Greek leaders sought support from the Tsar, arguing that Russia had the right and obligation to intervene on their behalf under the 1774 Treaty of Kutchuk Kainardji.[36] Russia's claimed right of intervention risked further destabilising the region but Alexander I believed in a multilateral approach to maintaining peace, particularly in combating revolutionaries.[37] Overall, Alexander I's sympathy for the Greeks did not override his opposition to nationalism[38] and the Porte felt Russian intervention was unlikely.[39]

Austria's position was more problematic. Like Russia, Austria was a multiethnic empire and its Foreign Minister, Prince Metternich, sought to maintain the Ottoman Empire as a counterweight to Russian expansionism in the Balkans, fearing that a challenge to the Sultan's authority threatened

29 This was a reasonable fear, with the First World War being triggered by conflict in the Balkans. See Chapman. *Supra* note 1. p.71.
30 Bartlett, C.J *Castlereagh* (London, 1966) p.225.
31 Goodwin, Jason. *Lords of the Horizon. A History of the Ottoman Empire* (London, 1998) p.293.
32 This was particularly the case after the hanging of Patriarch Gregory V. See Gordon. *Supra* note 24. p.187.
33 Ibid.
34 Brewer, David. *The Greek War of Independence* (Woodstock, 2003) p.107.
35 Bartlett. *Supra* note 30. p.229.
36 Article XIV of the Treaty provided for the building of a Greek Orthodox Church in Constantinople under Russian care, but Russia interpreted this as placing all Ottoman Orthodox Christians under Russian protection. See Quatert, Donald. *The Ottoman Empire 1700–1922* (Cambridge, 2000) p.40.
37 Seton-Watson, Hugh. *The Russian Empire 1801–1917* (Oxford, 1967) p.176.
38 Westwood, J.N. *Endurance and Endeavour: Russian History 1812–1992* (Oxford, 1973) p.24.
39 Palmer. *Supra* note 22. p.87.

the legitimacy of monarchs everywhere.[40] Metternich was suspicious of the Russians, arguing that Russia's Foreign Minister sought for 'the waters to remain troubled [...] until they had no hope of being cleared'.[41]

Britain's politicians were generally pro-Ottoman given Britain needed a buffer zone to prevent other Great Powers expanding into the Middle East[42] and supported the Ottoman Empire as a regional counterweight to Russia.[43] Britain was also a democracy (albeit a limited one) and Castlereagh knew British public opinion was mostly anti-Russian rather than pro Greek.[44] Although Britain's Whigs criticised Castlereagh for his complicity in intervention to support authoritarian powers, neither did they support humanitarian intervention.[45] Britain was also motivated by its distrust of Russia, with a contemporary periodical noting, 'the Muscovite is already a formidable rival and would be a worse neighbour'.[46] This was a credible threat and the relevance of the Ottoman Empire to British naval supremacy was a cornerstone of Britain's foreign policy.[47] Ottoman collapse in the Balkans would create a dangerous power vacuum, allowing Russia to expand which threatened both British imperial interests and the very existence of Austria.[48]

Although sympathetic to the Greeks,[49] Castlereagh genuinely believed in non-intervention.[50] While he opposed using force to buttress authoritarian

40 Seton-Watson. *Supra* note 37. p.180.

41 Prince Metternich to the Marquess of Londonderry' (26 October 1821) in Vane, Charles (Ed.) *Memoirs and Correspondences of Viscount Castlereagh Volume XII* (London, 1853) pp.429–432.

42 Spagnolo, John. *France and Ottoman Lebanon 1861–1914* (London, 1977) p.12.

43 Temperely, Harold. *The Foreign Policy of Canning 1822–1827* (London, 1925) pp.320–321.

44 Western, Jon. 'Prudence or outrage? Public opinion and humanitarian intervention in historical and comparative perspective' in Klose, Fabian. (Ed.) *The Emergence of Humanitarian Intervention: Ideas and Practice from the Nineteenth Century to the Present* (Cambridge, 2018) p.174.

45 Bew. *Supra* note 16. p.121.

46 Anonymous 'Report on the Present State of the Greek Confederation' *The Eclectic Review Vol.20* (December 1823) p.528.

47 Bartlett. *Supra* note 30. p.225.

48 Derry, John. *Castlereagh* (London, 1976) p.214.

49 Once the Greeks had surrendered, Castlereagh wanted the Great Powers to make diplomatic representations to protect the Greeks from Ottoman reprisal in the interests of humanity. (Ibid).

50 Castlereagh had opposed the Troppau Protocol and the use of force against national revolts that did not threaten European stability (Castlereagh. *Supra* note 12.) His non-interventionism was supported by Britain's Prime Minister, Lord Liverpool (Rodogno, Davide. *Against Massacre: Humanitarian Intervention in the Ottoman Empire, 1815–1914.* (Princeton, 2012), p.71). Castlereagh acknowledged non-interventionist sentiment in a letter to his brother, noting that British involvement with authoritarian intervention

governments, Castlereagh warned Alexander I that the Greek rebellion was part of the revolutionary fervour sweeping Europe that threatened Alexander I's own regime.[51] Rather than appealing to international law or morality, Castlereagh appealed to Russian self-interest, highlighting the threat the Greek rebellion posed to Russia's authoritarian empire, with Russia's rivalry with the Porte being secondary to the need to maintain European stability.[52]

### 1.1 *Inaction and Intervention in Greece*

The Greek Revolt attracted particular interest in Europe,[53] enabling the Greeks to solicit aid from sympathetic Europeans known as Philhellenes,[54] with pressure among elite Europeans and Americans to aid the Greeks.[55] Europeans even took up arms to fight for the Greek cause[56] notably the famed English poet Lord George Byron who arrived in Missolonghi in 1823.[57] Meanwhile, Castlereagh was worn down, which was compounded by his failure to appreciate the importance of parliamentary support and public opinion.[58] His mental health continued to deteriorate before he committed suicide in 1822.[59]

Castlereagh's successor was George Canning who appreciated the dangers of a Russo-Turkish war and initially invoked British neutrality in the Greek War of

---

would be criticised by Parliament and render Britain liable for the actions of authoritarian allied forces. (Castlereagh. 'Lord Castlereagh to Lord Stewart' (16 September 1820) in Vane. *Supra* note 41. p.311).

51 Castlereagh. 'The Marquess of Londonderry to his Imperial Majesty, the Emperor of all the Russians' (16 July 1821) in Vane. *Supra* note 41. pp.403–408.

52 Castlereagh. 'Lord Castlereagh to Sir Charles Bagot (14 December 1821) in Vane. *Supra* note 41. pp.443–446.

53 Craig, Gordon. *Europe Since 1815* (New York, 1967) p.25.

54 Droz, Jacques. *Europe between Revolutions 1815–1848* (London, 1967) p.224.

55 Heraclides and Dialla. *Supra* note 27. p.110.

56 See St Clair, William. *That Greece Might Still Be Free: The Philhellenes in the War of Independence* (Oxford, 1972). p.356.

57 Byron swiftly found stories of Greek victories either exaggerated or false and became disillusioned but stayed on to fight nonetheless. (See Byron, George. *Letter to Charles Barry* (8bre (sic) 25 1823) from Marchand, Leslie (Ed.) *Lord Byron: Selected Letters and Journals* (London, 1982) p.306). The Philhellenes' disillusionment was compounded at the Battle of Petta when a Philhellene battalion was abandoned by their Greek allies and slaughtered by Ottoman forces. (Gordon. *Supra* note 24. p.390).

58 Nicholson, Harold. *The Congress of Vienna* (London, 1946) p.260. As leader of the House of Commons, he was forced to defend unpopular government policies with *The Times* noting he was blamed for the errors of his colleagues See *The Times* (14 August 1822).

59 Castlereagh was hissed in the street, and he suffered from depression, paranoia, and overwork, telling the king 'I am mad. I know I am mad' (Derry. *Supra* note 31. p.227). Even in death, he faced criticism, with his funeral procession jeered by a mob. See 'Funeral of the Late Marquis of Londonderry' *The Times* (21 August 1822).

Independence.[60] This became problematic as Ottoman atrocities continued. Canning was more aware than Castlereagh of the importance of popular opinion and support for the Greeks, necessitating government action.[61] This came to a head in 1824 when it was clear the Porte's campaign against the Greeks had made little progress. Although the Greeks had some advantages,[62] they lacked the organisation or strategy to defeat the Ottomans.[63] Sultan Mahmud II's priority was to reform his empire and he became increasingly desperate to resolve the rebellion and thus engaged his viceroy, the Pasha of Egypt whose son, Ibrahim Pasha, deployed a modernised Egyptian military to Greece.[64]

Tsar Alexander I died suddenly in 1825 and was succeeded by his brother, Tsar Nicholas I. Initially, Nicholas opposed intervention[65] but Russian public support for intervention was significant,[66] while Canning feared Russia would intervene to aid the Greeks.[67] Canning managed to avoid unilateral Russian intervention by dispatching the Napoleonic war hero, Arthur Wellesley, Duke of Wellington to the Tsar.[68] At the same time, Ibrahim's ruthless tactics alienated Europeans, particularly after the Russians had 'positive information' that the Porte entered an agreement with Egypt that any territory conquered by Egypt would see its Greek population carried off to slavery and the land repopulated by Muslims[69] although this was denied by the Porte.[70] Such action

60 Rodogno. *Supra* note 50. p.72.

61 Craig. *Supra* note 53. p.27.

62 Notably, high morale, excellent sailors, and control of easily defensible terrain ('State and Prospects of the Greeks' *Scotsman* (13th July 1822)). Consequently, they were capable of 'maintaining a more than equal conflict with the Turks' (*The Times* (13th August 1822)).

63 Hupchick, Dennis. *The Balkans from Constantinople to Communism* (New York, 2001) p.222.

64 Gordon, Thomas. *History of the Greek Revolution, Volume 2* (Edinburgh, 1844) p.151.

65 Nicholas feared intervention would induce his own subjects to rebel (see Lord Strangford to Bagot (7 March 1826) in Bagot, Josceline (Ed.) *George Canning and His Friends, containing hitherto unpublished letters, Jeux d'esprit, etc Volume II* (London, 1909) p.335) and crushed the reformist Decembrist revolt which included many Russian Philhellenic officers.

66 Heraclides and Dialla. *Supra* note 27. p.110.

67 Western. *Supra* note 44. p.174.

68 Mowat. *Supra* note 9. p.48.

69 Canning, George. *Some Official Correspondences of George Canning Volume 1* (London, 1887) p.315. The exact veracity of the report is debatable. There was no evidence of such a strategy (see Schwartzberg, Steven. 'The Lion and the Phoenix: British Policy towards the Greek Question' *Middle Eastern Studies* (Vol.24 (2), April 1988) p.161).

70 Canning, George. 'Mr Canning to Viscount Granville (26 April 1826)' in Stapleton, Edward (Ed.). *Some Official Correspondences of George Canning Volume 2* (London, 1887) p.34. Ibrahim denied the allegation to Britain's ambassador to the Porte, Stratford Canning, but Stratford claimed Ibrahim was engaged in extermination, enslavement and forced conversion. See Heraclides and Dialla. *Supra* note 27. p.114).

ensured Britain's interests were endangered: it had strong trade links with the Porte[71] but was not opposed to Greek independence (though it was 'diffident on the issue').[72] Outright removal of Christians could not be ignored, and Russia would be outraged at such a flagrant breach of the Treaty of Kutchuk-Kainardji . Canning feared the possible outcomes of Greece being occupied by the Egyptians or turned into a Russian satellite state.[73]

Unlike Castlereagh, who acted in the collective interest of Europe, Canning was more concerned with British interests.[74] Canning was also pragmatic and knew it was sometimes in British interests to intervene.[75] He also appreciated that multilateral intervention was necessary to maintain peace while collective intervention could force the Sultan to grant Greek autonomy, which would prevent unilateral Russian expansion.[76] Wellington worked with the Tsar and signed a protocol that offered allied mediation of the Greek conflict to create an autonomous Greece within the Ottoman Empire. The resulting St Petersburg Protocol was of monumental importance, expressly mentioning the Greeks and effectively giving them international recognition.[77]

Canning became Britain's Prime Minister in 1827, which saw the St Petersburg Protocol gain greater prominence and become the Treaty of London,[78] concluded between Britain, France and Russia, and providing for an autonomous Greek state under Ottoman sovereignty.[79] Furthermore, it provided for the Great Powers to act as mediators, which if rejected by the Porte, 'impose upon the High Contracting Parties the necessity of taking immediate measures for

71 *House of Commons Debate 15 June 1819 Volume.40 Column.1178.*

72 Anonymous. *Supra* note 46. p.527.

73 Rodogno. *Supra* note 50. p.79. Both options were detrimental to British interests and Canning was painfully aware of the need to prevent Ibrahim's plan without strengthening Russia's influence in the region. Furthermore, by this point, Canning saw the Greek conflict not as a civil war but as a war between the Ottoman and Greek nations with an autonomous Greece within the Ottoman Empire as a possible solution. (Schwartzberg. *Supra* note 69. p.159).

74 Bew. *Supra* note 16. p.126.

75 Canning was helped in that British public opinion was staunchly anti-Russian, seeing it as an imperial, expansionist power predestined to 'always to conquer and add territory to territory (Anonymous 'The Political State of England and Europe' *The Monthly Magazine of Politics, Literature and the Belles Lettres* Vol.8 (47), (November 1829) p.482). Canning was also conscious that British public opinion risked forcing him to act against Ibrahim's alleged plans for depopulating Greece (Temperely. *Supra* note 43. p.353).

76 Derry. *Supra* note 31. p.215.

77 Hinde, Wendy. *George Canning* (London, 1973) p.408.

78 *'Treaty for the Settlement of Greece' The Times (12th July 1827).*

79 Treaty of London (1827) Article II. https://sourcebooks.fordham.edu/mod/1827gktreaty.asp Accessed 10th March 2024.

forming a connection with the Greeks', involving establishing commercial and diplomatic links with the Greeks and a secret additional article provided for the threat of armed force.[80]

While the Treaty of London noted the need for intervention to prevent piracy, trade disruption and chaos, it also highlighted the need for intervention to prevent further bloodshed. The Treaty explicitly stated it was 'an arrangement called for, no less by sentiments of humanity, than by interests for the tranquillity of Europe'[81] and sought to '[put] a stop to the effusion of blood and of preventing the evils of every kind'.[82] Canning's sudden death in 1827 meant he never saw the Treaty of London come to fruition. A joint British, French and Russian fleet was dispatched to the Mediterranean[83] under the de-facto command of British Vice-Admiral Codrington who had been given the vague task of blockading the Egyptians without engaging in hostilities.[84] Initially, the fleet contacted Ibrahim Pasha, warning him that they were there to 'terminate this cruel war' and prevent further Egyptian action in Greece,[85] while Codrington claimed he gave strict orders for the fleet to use force solely in self-defence.[86] Ibrahim relented and promised a ceasefire until he heard from the Porte.[87] He then landed his troops in Morea and committed atrocities, causing the allies to head to Navarino to prevent further Egyptian action.[88] The Egyptians opened fire and in the ensuing battle, were decisively vanquished. With the defeat of the Egyptian fleet, the Ottoman Empire had 'broken down to its foundations'.[89]

Ottoman-Russian relations continued to deteriorate. Russia declared war on the Porte in 1828 based on enforcing Turkish compliance with Russian treaty rights and sought to march on Constantinople.[90] This threatened the balance of power and though Britain and France readied their navies, they

80 Ibid. Additional Article.
81 Ibid. Preamble.
82 Ibid. Preamble.
83 *The Times.* (14 November 1827).
84 'The Earl of Aberdeen to Vice Admiral Sir Edward Codrington (May 1828) in Wellington, Arthur. *Despatches, Correspondence, and Memoranda of Field Marshal Arthur, Duke of Wellington Volume V* (London, 1873) p.5.
85 *The Times.* (12th November 1827).
86 'Total destruction of the Turkish and Egyptian fleets' *The Times.* (12th November 1827).
87 Temperely. *Supra* note 43. p.406.
88 Laughton, J.K. 'Codrington, Sir Edward'. *Oxford Dictionary of National Biography* (Oxford, 2004) http://www.oxforddnb.com/view/article/5796 Accessed 10th March 2024.
89 Anonymous. *Supra* note 75. p.481.
90 Bitis, Alexander. 'The 1828–1829 Russo-Turkish War and the Resettlement of Balkan Peoples into Novorossiia' Jahrbücher für Geschichte Osteuropas (Vol.53, No.4, 2005) pp.510–511.

were unwilling to assert themselves[91] before the Sultan conceded in 1829.[92] The resulting Treaty of Adrianople provided for Greek autonomy within the Ottoman Empire and in 1830, the London Protocol was signed by Great Britain, France and Russia, established a sovereign Greek state.

Not only had aid been given to nationalist Greek rebels but also a shift in the balance of powers had taken place. Outraged that it did not receive its promised reward for supporting the Porte, Egypt rebelled in 1831 and threatened to march on Constantinople. With Britain and France too preoccupied with internal matters to help, Russia forced a peace agreement between Cairo and Constantinople, fearing the emergence of a powerful Egyptian empire.[93] Pragmatism caused Russia to aid the Porte, showing the continued importance of the balance of power over legal norms.

The Greek intervention was also notable for its impact on contemporary international relations. Metternich's fear of a collapse of the conservative powers was fulfilled, with liberals and nationalists taking heart from the rebellions and their support by Great Powers.[94] Indeed, France dispatched a peacekeeping force to supervise the withdrawal of Egyptian troops from Greece, showing France's return as a Great Power, further altering the balance of power.[95]

The Great Powers were neither consistently liberal nor conservative in the modern sense. Rather, stances shifted when interests were threatened. Overall, there was a generally accepted balance of power and no country could unilaterally expand its own power.[96] This should not be misinterpreted as general European support for non-interventionism, particularly given the intervention against liberal regimes, but Castlereagh showed a non-interventionist inclination, whether against authoritarian empires or revolutionary liberals. This proved impossible to maintain, and the question arises whether intervention in Navarino can be seen as setting a precedent for humanitarian intervention.

Public opinion was a factor in the use of force during the Greek War of Independence. Due to a mixture of religious, liberal and antiquarian sympathies, European public opinion was pro-Greek.[97] This was helped by the comparatively free press of Britain that reported Ottoman atrocities and helped

91 Rendall, Matthew. 'Defensive Realism and the Concert of Europe' *Review of International Studies* Vol.36 No.3 (July 2006) p.531.

92 Despite initial successes, Russia was ill equipped, and its troops were forced in sieges while suffering heavy casualties from disease. See Bitis. *Supra* note 90. p.511.

93 Anderson, M.S. *The Eastern Question* (London, 1966) p.80.

94 Droz. *Supra* note 54. p.228.

95 Seton-Watson. *Supra* note 37. p.301.

96 Craig. *Supra* note 53. p.36.

97 Anderson. *Supra* note 93. p.57.

stoke support for allied intervention. Despite rebel atrocities against Ottoman civilians, there was never any question of intervention to protect Muslim civilians from Greek rebels.[98] While the Greeks sought foreign aid, the Porte did not and while the Holy Alliance might have helped crush the revolutionaries (as they had done in Naples and Piedmont), this would have been a counter-revolutionary intervention rather than a humanitarian one.[99]

Growing public outrage against Ottoman atrocities coincided with Britain's realisation that non-intervention was not always in British interests. Canning was acutely aware of this and Derry argues that Canning acted as much out of British interest as he did in sympathy with the Greeks.[100] Although a limited democracy, by the 1820s, Britain was seeing a growing prospect for parliamentary reform,[101] forcing greater attention to public opinion. Multilateral intervention allowed the British authorities to prevent Russian expansion and accommodate domestic sympathy for the Greeks, while Bew highlights that Britain was 'sucked' into intervention not out of humanitarian sympathy but due to the need to prevent Russia from growing too powerful in the Balkans.[102] Mowat argues that even if Russia had not intervened, public opinion in Britain and France would have still forced government action.[103]

Bass underlines how continued Ottoman atrocities forced Britain to abandon neutrality and towards intervention.[104] The impact of the Philhellenes cannot be discounted, and neither can public opinion. The radical *Scotsman* warned the Holy Alliance that the British press would inform on the atrocities

---

98 To the credit of many Philhellenes, they were not blind to Greek atrocities and sought to avoid brutality. The Greeks were aware of this and during the siege of Tripolis, idealistic Philhellenes were sent away before the city fell to Greek forces, lest they witness the 'hell of fire and blood' that took place. (See Brewer. *Supra* note 34. p.120) Likewise, Byron released Ottoman prisoners, hoping that such a gesture would set a precedent for the treatment of prisoners. See Byron, George. 'Letter to Yusuff Pasha' (23 January 1824) http://www.lordbyron.org/monograph.php?doc=ThMoore.1830&select=AD1824 Accessed 10th March 2024. Such actions were isolated and mutual atrocities stoked a vicious circle of violence and reprisal.

99 Rodogno. *Supra* note 50. p.66.

100 Derry. *Supra* note 31. p.215.

101 Machin, Ian. *The Rise of Democracy in Britain* (Hampshire, 2001) p.10. This formed the nucleus for the democratic push that would soon lead to the Great Reform Act of 1832: the government was aware of the increasing tension underlying Britain, with Canning in particular recognising the importance of public opinion.

102 Bew. *Supra* note 16. p.136.

103 Mowat. *Supra* note 9. p.47.

104 Bass, Gary. *Freedom's Battle: The Origins of Humanitarian Intervention* (New York, 2008) p.49.

they shared by their inaction.[105] This was echoed by segments of British society who supported intervention, which was often anti-Russian but also motivated by genuine sympathy for the Greeks with even the anti-populist Castlereagh fearing British public opinion would force him to intervene.[106] Canning was even more aware of public opinion's impact and Britain did not act entirely in its own geopolitical interests, especially given that purely maintaining the balance of power would have led Britain to oppose the creation of a Greek state.[107]

Britain could have supported the Ottoman Empire against Russian expansionism but it did not do so. This would have been unpopular with the British public that was playing an increasingly important role: Hupchick highlights that British public sympathy for the Greeks prevented Britain from opposing the Greek revolution.[108] Humanitarianism as well as self-interest played a key role in Britain's foreign policy. France's approach is less clear, though there was considerable French public support for intervention in Greece. Constant argued that France had a particular interest in intervening: the Ottoman Empire was no longer a French ally against Russia and Austria and an independent Greece could operate as an effective barrier.[109] The French government's attitude was quite neutral and while it theoretically supported Metternich in his opposition to revolution, France did not attempt to limit aid going to the Greek cause.[110]

Although Russia's authoritarianism made it less susceptible to public opinion, Alexander I was susceptible to the feelings of his subjects.[111] Public opinion in Russia demanded action and Alexander I noted that his 'people demand war',[112] which Britain was aware of.[113] Though public opinion was more important in relatively liberal states like Britain and France, it nonetheless did have an impact in Russia, leading Britain to fear the Tsar would attempt to strengthen his authority by placating Russian Philhellenes.[114] Bew highlights the paradox

105 'State and Prospects of the Greeks' *Scotsman*. (13th July 1822).
106 Bartlett. *Supra* note 30. pp.229–230.
107 Schwartzberg. *Supra* note 69. p.145.
108 Hupchick. *Supra* note 63. p.249.
109 Constant, Benjamin. *Appel aux nations Chrétiennes en faveur des Grecs* (Paris, 1825) pp.8–9.
110 St Clair. *Supra* note 56. p.57.
111 Temperely. *Supra* note 43. p.322.
112 Temperely, Harold. 'Princess Lieven and the Protocol of 4 April 1826' *The English Historical Review* Vol.39, No.153 (January 1924) p.60.
113 As early as 1821, Britain's ambassador to Russia warned Westminster that Russia needed little provocation to go to war and was mobilising troops along the Turkish border. See Vane. *Supra* note 41. pp.429–432.
114 Hinde. *Supra* note 77. p.405.

of interventionist authoritarian states like Austria opposing intervention while non-interventionist Britain and France were willing to intervene.[115] Britain and France had generally subscribed to legal positivism while the Holy Alliance adhered to 'traditionalist' jurisprudence, whereby intervention was lawful when done to bolster traditional (and therefore legitimate) authorities.[116]

### 1.2 *Humanitarian Intervention and Greece*

In his seminal text on international law in the nineteenth century, Wheaton[117] wrote that intervention in Greece showed 'the principles of international law authorising such an interference [...] where the general interests of humanity are infringed by the excesses of a barbarous and despotic government'.[118] It is arguable that realpolitik rather than humanitarian interests dictated the Greek intervention. Bew highlights Canning's acceptance of intervention and that this could have arisen from a realisation that Great Power intervention was imminent and Britain needed to cooperate to protect its own interests.[119] This is reinforced by Temperely who argues Britain knew conflict was inevitable and needed to act with and restrain Russia.[120]

It can certainly be argued that the Navarino intervention was motivated by strategic rather than humanitarian concerns. The allied fleet at Navarino was dispatched to deter any breaches of the Treaty of London: it could only use force in self-defence and returned fire only when attacked by the Egyptian fleet while Britain's subsequent response suggests Codrington acted outside of his mandate.[121] Rodogno rejects the view that Navarino can be seen as a

115 Bew. *Supra* note 16. p.128.

116 Schwartzberg. *Supra* note 69. p.141.

117 Initially published in 1836, Wheaton's work was very influential for a long time. See Segesser, Daniel Marc. 'Humanitarian Intervention and the issue of state sovereignty in the discourse of legal experts between the 1830s and the First World War' in in Klose, Fabian. (Ed.) *The Emergence of Humanitarian Intervention: Ideas and Practice from the Nineteenth Century to the Present* (Cambridge, 2018) p.59.

118 Wheaton, Henry. *Elements of International Law* (London, 1916) pp.102–103.

119 Bew. *Supra* note 16. p.130.

120 Temperely. *Supra* note 43. p.398.

121 The cabinet of Canning's successor, Lord Goderich collapsed and was replaced by the Tory government of Wellington who opposed the use of force outside of war and felt Codrington's intervention had advanced Russian interests. See Brewer. *Supra* note 34. p.334. Codrington was relieved of command. 'The Earl of Aberdeen to Vice Admiral Sir Edward Codrington (May 1828) in Wellington. *Supra* note 84. p.7. British public support for Greece made the government reluctant to rebuke him. See Laughton, J.K. 'Codrington, Sir Edward'. *Oxford Dictionary of National Biography* (Oxford, 2004) http://www.oxforddnb.com/view/article/5796 Accessed 10th March 2024.

humanitarian intervention given it did not save civilians or provide humanitarian aid to Greek civilians and was predicated on a rumour of ethnic cleansing.[122]

Nonetheless, the alleged depopulation strategy could not be ignored, given the severity and the insistence of the Russian ambassador.[123] Canning doubted Britain could avoid intervening if the British public knew of such atrocities.[124] Although the depopulation strategy was possibly fabricated, Ottoman atrocities did occur and these caused genuine outrage among Europeans. Brownlie reinforces that the intervention's 'substantial motive' was the prevention of 'racial extermination' but this was a legal concept that likely did not exist at the time.[125] The fact that preventing the repopulation of Greece was used as a justification for intervention shows how humanitarian concerns had entered international law.

The Holy Alliance supported intervention to uphold established autocracies while Britain had been generally non-interventionist. Canning opposed ethnic cleansing, and as both a liberal and a Christian, felt unable to turn his back on the Greeks[126] while Schwartzberg claims Canning's primary motive was his sympathy for the Greek cause.[127] Although this ignores British geopolitical concerns, it highlights how Britain was guided by more than self-interest. Canning openly justified collective intervention on both British political interests as well as Ottoman 'outrage on Christendom and humanity'.[128] This can be further seen in the Treaty of London, which highlighted that such a treaty was needed for humanitarian, as well as strategic reasons.[129] This is notable given a monarch's jurisdiction over his subjects was a cornerstone of sovereignty and international law.[130]

The enforcement of the Treaty also shows a humanitarian impulse, given the allied fleet's broad operational parameters. The allied commanders agreed on the need to stop the atrocities and signed a joint protocol, highlighting that

---

122 Rodogno. *Supra* note 50. p.83.

123 Heraclides and Dialla. *Supra* note 27. p.113.

124 Bass. *Supra* note 104. p.126.

125 Brownlie. *Supra* note 6. p.339.

126 Stapleton. *Supra* note 70. p.46.

127 Schwartzberg. *Supra* note 69. p.162.

128 Stapleton. *Supra* note 70. p.393.

129 Treaty of London (1827) Preamble https://sourcebooks.fordham.edu/mod/1827gktreaty.asp Accessed 10th March 2024.

130 Fonteyne, Jean-Pierre. 'The Customary International Law Doctrine of Humanitarian Intervention: its Current Validity under the UN Charter' *California Western International Law Journal* (Vol.4, 1973–1974) p.207.

they were enforcing the Treaty of London and preventing Ibrahim continuing 'warfare more devastating and destructive than before'.[131] Codrington himself highlighted that he sought to 'induce Ibrahim Pacha [sic] to discontinue the brutal war of extermination which he has been carrying on'.[132] In effect, the allies sought to operate as a proto-peacekeeping force to prevent further atrocities, with the 'imposing presence of the squadrons' acting as a deterrent.[133]

Few other than Canning would have known if Codrington acted within his mandate, although Canning's biographer feels he would have celebrated Greek independence.[134] The British public generally approved of Codrington's actions while he received chivalric orders from France, Greece and Russia.[135] It cannot be denied that such an intervention was at least partially justified on humanitarian grounds. The Great Powers had occasionally aided rebels but this had always been done for strategic reasons while the intervention in Greece was conducted 'in no small measure out of sheer humanitarian instinct'.[136] This is echoed by Stowell who writes that the allied intervention in Greece had a primarily humanitarian basis.[137] Had the elites in Britain, France and Russia not identified and sympathised with the Greeks, no intervention would have taken place.[138]

The Ottoman Empire saw the intervention as a flagrant violation of international law[139] but found little support among the Great Powers. Geopolitics cannot be discounted and collective humanitarian intervention allowed the Great Powers to intervene without setting a precedent for unilateral intervention.[140] This does not detract from the fact that military intervention took place to enforce the Treaty of London that was grounded 'no less by sentiments of humanity, than by interests for the tranquillity of Europe'.[141] This is critical

131 'Total destruction of the Turkish and Egyptian fleets' *The Times* (12th November 1827).
132 Ibid.
133 Palmer. *Supra* note 22. p.98.
134 Hinde. *Supra* note 77. p.458.
135 Black, Jeremy. *Slavery: A New Global History* (London, 2011) p.153.
136 Boot, Max. *Invisible Armies: An Epic History of Guerrilla Warfare from Ancient Times to the Present* (New York, 2013) p.107.
137 Stowell, Ellery. *Intervention in International Law* (Washington DC, 1921) p.489.
138 Heraclides and Dialla. *Supra* note 27. p.121.
139 Palabiyik, Mustafa Serdar. 'The Emergence of the Idea of 'International Law' in the Ottoman Empire before the Treaty of Paris (1856)' *Middle Eastern Studies* (Vol 50, No.2, 2014) p.241.
140 Rodogno. *Supra* note 50. p.88.
141 Treaty of London (1827) Preamble https://sourcebooks.fordham.edu/mod/1827gktreaty.asp Accessed 10th March 2024.

given that it was the first time that a humanitarian concern was invoked as a justification for intervention.[142]

There can be little doubt that the intervention was guided by realpolitik, with Russia anxious to expand in the Balkans and Britain seeking to prevent Russian expansion. They were also influenced to varying degrees by public opinion and humanitarianism, evidenced by the Treaty of London and the opposition to the reported repopulation strategy. The Battle of Navarino was not a clear-cut case of humanitarian intervention but neither was the allied intervention detached from any sympathy for the Greeks, being at least partially caused by the European public's horror at Ottoman atrocities[143] and the impact on public international law should not be ignored. Such intervention was only possible due to European sympathy for the Greeks (for historical or religious reasons) and should not be seen as a universal approach to human rights and intervention, especially given antipathy for the Ottomans. Rather than intervention being used to suppress liberal-nationalist revolution, it was used to support Greek nationalism, with humanitarian concerns entering the realm of international law. The sincerity of such claims is debatable, but an intervention had taken place at Navarino that had at least a partial humanitarian basis.

## 2 Humanitarian Intervention in Ottoman Syria 1860

In the decades after Navarino, the Ottoman Empire continued to decay further.[144] The Great Powers remained as divided as ever on the Eastern Question, particularly after the Crimean War of 1853–1856[145] saw a defeated Russia forced to curb its ambitions in the Balkans with the 1856 Treaty of Paris. The Treaty did admit the Ottoman Empire to the Concert of Europe, giving it the rights and obligations of international law ('Public Law') and a collective European guarantee of Ottoman territorial integrity.[146] Although the Ottoman Empire had previously been subject to international law by its adoption of European

142 Fonteyne. *Supra* note 130. p.208.
143 Oppenheim. *Supra* note 18. p.186–187.
144 See Palmer. *Supra* note 22. Especially pp.105–128.
145 The causes of the Crimean War are complex but included heightened tension between Catholic and Orthodox Ottoman subjects over the supervision of Christian holy sites in Jerusalem. See Badem, Candan. *The Ottoman Crimean War* (1853–1856) (Leiden, 2010), especially pp.64–65.
146 Treaty of Paris (1856) Article VII. https://content.ecf.org.il/files/M00934_TreatyOfParis1856English.pdf Accessed 10th March 2024.

customary law and treaties,[147] it was a landmark event in the extension of international law, given a state that was neither Christian nor European was accepted into the Family of Nations.[148]

The Great Powers' acceptance of the Ottoman Empire was largely a result of British and French insistence rather than any real perception of Ottoman equality and European interference in Ottoman affairs continued.[149] The Treaty established the Sultan's role in protecting Ottoman Christians and the signatories committed not to interfere in relations between the Sultan and his subjects.[150] Ultimately, the Ottomans entered the European balance of power as provisional members of the Westphalian system but they were more seen as a factor to consider in the balance of power rather than an independent decision maker.[151]

Syria[152] had long been home to numerous religious minorities, including Mount Lebanon whose Maronite Christian majority grew in influence at the expense of the Druze[153] minority.[154] Although the different groups had traditionally lived peacefully, tensions were rising in the mid-nineteenth century: growing European influence in the region stoked competition for political and economic power between Maronites and Druze.[155] The Ottoman Empire was reforming under the *Tanzimat* reforms,[156] which had the potential for the Ottoman Empire to adopt a European model of governance.[157] Among these was the 1856 Firman (Royal Decree) which removed many restrictions on

147 Palabiyik. *Supra* note 139. p.247.

148 Oppenheim. *Supra* note 18. pp.32–33.

149 Spagnolo. *Supra* note 42. p.19.

150 Treaty of Paris (1856) Article IX. https://content.ecf.org.il/files/M00934_TreatyOfParis1856English.pdf Accessed 10th March 2024.

151 Kissinger, Henry. *World Order: Reflections on the Character of Nations and the Course of History* (London, 2014) p.110. See also Heraclides and Dialla. *Supra* note 27. p.46.

152 In this section, 'Syria' will be used in its pre-World War I definition: the territory encompassing the modern states of Lebanon, Syria, Israel, Palestine, and Jordan.

153 The Maronites are an Eastern Catholic church who maintain strong links with the Roman Catholic Church while the Druze are a splinter group from Shiite Islam. For a brief history of their involvement in Lebanon, see Churchill, Charles Henry. *The Druzes and the Maronites under the Turkish Rule from 1840 to 1860* (London, 1862) pp.10–20.

154 Spagnolo. *Supra* note 42. p.2.

155 Kloepper, Stephen. 'The Syrian Crisis: 1860–61. A Case Study in Classic Humanitarian Intervention' *Canadian Yearbook of International Law* (Vol.23, 1985) p.249.

156 For an in-depth analysis of the Tanzimat reforms, see Shaw, Stanford and Shaw, Ezel Kural. *History of the Ottoman Empire and Modern Turkey Volume 2* (Cambridge, 1977) pp.55–171.

157 Heraclides and Dialla. *Supra* note 27. p.45.

non-Muslims within the Ottoman Empire, disquieting Ottoman Muslims who saw their dominance being weakened.[158]

France was then ruled by Napoleon III[159] who felt he could not ignore events in Syria, given France's historical role as the protector of the Ottoman Maronites,[160] Paris saw the Maronites as their 'pet[s] and protégé [and] anything against [them] offends French dignity'.[161] France also had strategic interests, having long been jealous of Britain's influence with the Ottoman Empire.[162] With French influence over the Maronites, Britain supported the Druze who were known as the 'English of the East',[163] and saw them as useful counterweights to French influence.[164]

With both confessional groups backed by Great Powers, tensions rose even further and on 15 July 1858, Christians in Jeddah were killed.[165] This led to the stockpiling of arms by Maronites and Druze and tensions came to a head in 1860 when Britain's consul in Beirut reported increased agitation among Druze and attacks on Christians.[166] Soon afterwards, violence broke out between the two groups.

---

158 Firman of the Sultan, relative to Privileges and Reform in Turkey. (18 February 1856) in Herslet, Edward. *The Map of Europe by Treaty, Vol. II* (London, 1875) pp.1243–1249.

159 The nephew of the famed Napoleon Bonaparte I, Louis-Napoleon Bonaparte was elected in 1848 as President of France's Second Republic in 1848 but installed himself as Emperor Napoleon III in 1851. See Hearder, Harry. *Europe in the Nineteenth Century 1830–1880* (Harlow, 1966) p.197.

160 The Maronites had been declared under French protection by Louis XIII in the seventeenth century. See Perry, Harold. 'England and France in the East' *The National Review* (No.6, August 1883) p.797), which were further extended by the Ottoman Capitulations, concessions granting legal and commercial privileges to the subjects of designated European Christian monarchs. See Brown, Phillip. 'The Capitulations' *Foreign Affairs* (Vol.1, No.4, 15 June 1923). Successive Ottoman Capitulations to France gave French protection of Catholics within the Ottoman Empire. See de Vogüé, Melchior. Les Événements de Syrie (Paris, 1861) pp.9–13.). This was partially pragmatic (extending French influence in the region) but also ideological, with France claiming guardianship of sacred sites in Jerusalem due to concessions granted to Charlemagne by the Abbasid Caliphate. See Spagnolo. *Supra* note 42. p.5.

161 'Sir Bulwer to Lord Russell' (24 April 1860) in British Parliamentary Papers *LXVII.499 'Papers relating to administrative and financial reforms in Turkey. 1858–61' (London, 1861)*) p.33.

162 Spagnolo, John. 'Franco-British rivalry in the Middle East' in Shehadi, Nadim and Mills, Dana Haffer (Eds.) *Lebanon: A history of conflict and consensus* (London, 1988) p.110.

163 Churchill. *Supra* note 153. p.204.

164 Gorce, Pierre. *Histoire du Second Empire, tome troisieme* (Paris, 1906) p.300.

165 'Massacre of Christians at Jeddah' *The Examiner* (17 July 1858).

166 'Consul-General Moore to Sir Bulwer' (18 May 1860) *in British Parliamentary Papers LXVII.599 'Reports received from Her Majesty's consuls relating to the condition of Christians in Turkey. 1860' (London, 1861)* pp.1–2.

### 2.1 *The Maronite-Druze Civil War of 1860*

By July 1860, Graham estimated that up to four thousand Christians had been killed while tens of thousands were internally displaced.[167] Responsibility for the conflict is difficult to deduce[168] but the violence soon amounted to a civil war. The Druze were better organised,[169] and Christians were killed while their villages were razed.[170] Ottoman impotence was compounded by the weakness of their garrisons,[171] though Graham argued that had the Ottomans 'used the slightest exertions', the entire conflict could have been averted.[172] Initially, the Christians sought Ottoman protection[173] but Ottoman help was generally not forthcoming[174] and many Ottoman soldiers failed to protect Christians.[175]

---

167 'Mr Graham to Lord Dufferin (18 July 1860) in British Parliamentary Papers *LXIX.675 Supra* note 168. p.45.

168 Cyril Graham, a British traveller was in the region at the time and claims that the conflict started with the murder of a Christian monk, outraging Maronites and inducing a vicious circle of retaliation (see 'Mr Graham to Lord Dufferin (18 July 1860) in British Parliamentary Papers *LXIX.675 'Further Papers Relating to the Disturbances in Syria'* (*London, 1860*) pp.40–41) while the British diplomat Col. Charles Churchill bluntly blamed the Druze for the conflict, claiming the Maronites only responded to Druze attacks and with far less ferocity (Churchill. *Supra* note 153. pp.139–141). Meanwhile Britain's ambassador to the Ottoman Empire noted that while the Ottoman Empire was lax in its response, the Maronites' actions bore responsibility for the outbreak of violence ('Sir Bulwer to Lord Russell' (27 June 1860) in British *Parliamentary Papers LXIX.553 'Papers relating to the disturbances in Syria'* (London, 1860) p.18). This was also the view of Lord Dufferin, Britain's representative to the International Commission for Syria. 'Lord Dufferin to Lord Russell' (10 March 1861) in British Parliamentary Papers *LXVIII.17 'Correspondence Relating to the Affairs of Syria 1860–61'* (London, 1861) p.486.

169 Fawaz, Leila Tarazi. *An Occasion for War: Civil Conflict in Lebanon and Damascus in 1860* (Berkeley, 1994) p.54.

170 It must be noted that the atrocities were not just directed against Maronites: all Christians were targeted, regardless of confessional group. See 'Intervention of France and England' *New York Times.* (24 July 1860).

171 Spagnolo. *Supra* note 42. pp.30–31.

172 'Mr Graham to Lord Dufferin' in British Parliamentary Papers *LXIX.675. Supra* note 168. p.41.

173 'Memorials of the Maronite Patriarch and Bishops to Khorsheed Pasha' (10 June 1860) in *British Parliamentary Papers LXIX.553 Supra* note 168. pp.19–20.

174 Not all Ottoman authorities were inactive: Christians from Zibdaneh safely reached Damascus under Ottoman escort, despite Druze demands for them to be handed over (Consult Brant to Sir Bulwer' (13th June 1860) in in *British Parliamentary Papers LXIX.553 Supra* note 168. p.25).

175 See 'Captain Paynter to Vice Admiral Martin' (28 June 1860) in Ibid. p.48, 'Massacre of the Christians at Mount Lebanon' *Observer.* (15 July 1860), De Vogüé. *Supra* note 160. p.5, and Churchill. *Supra* note 153. pp.150–151). It must be noted that responsibility rested on local Ottoman authorities rather than the Porte and although France was incensed by Ottoman inaction to the massacres, Thouvenel acknowledged the Porte's severe financial

Although a peace treaty was eventually signed, violence subsequently erupted in Damascus that was governed by Ahmad Pasha who took few steps to prevent violence in a city swollen by refugees and sectarian tension. Damascus' Christian Quarter was overrun by Muslim rioters (rather than Druze)[176] in July 1860. The governor's response was impotent: Ottoman soldiers took little action before withdrawing from the Christian Quarter and many joined Muslim rioters,[177] slaughtering men and abducting women.[178] Overall, thousands of Christians were killed (though exact estimates vary) and their district was destroyed.[179] It must be noted that sympathetic Muslims saved many Christians,[180] although the exact number is unknown.[181] Soon afterwards, a peace treaty was signed that gave an amnesty to the atrocities' perpetrators, which was reported in the *Times* as being 'too much for the patience of Europe'.[182]

### 2.2 *French Intervention*

The French Foreign Minister, Édouard Thouvenel felt the massacres needed a collective European response and forwarded French intelligence on Syria to Britain's Foreign Minister, Lord Russell.[183] Likewise, the French ambassador to the Porte was informed that the French government was moved by the massacres, with 'humanity demanding prompt action and urgent measures'.[184] Napoleon III ordered ships to be sent to Beirut on a 'mission of humanity'[185] but France did not act unilaterally. Napoleon III favoured multilateral action and highlighted the Great Powers' collective responsibility for Ottoman

problems 'paralysed its means of action' See 'Minister for Foreign Affairs to the Marquis of Chateaurenard' (5 July 1860) in *French Documents Diplomatiques 1860.* (1861) p.19).

176 'Lord Dufferin to Lord Russell' (10 March 1861) in British Parliamentary Papers LXVIII.17. *Supra* note 168. p.485.

177 Fawaz. *Supra* note 169. p.88.

178 Churchill. *Supra* note 153. pp.214–215.

179 Fawaz. *Supra* note 169. pp.132–133.

180 Most notably by the Algerian Muslim, Abd el-Kader who saved 15,000 Christians by sending his men on search-and-rescue missions throughout Damascus and giving Christians sanctuary at his house. See Churchill, Charles Henry. *Life of Abd el-Kader: Ex-Sultan of the Arabs of Algeria: written and compiled from his own dictation from other Authentic Sources* (London, 1867) pp.311–318.

181 Fawaz. *Supra* note 169. p.98.

182 *The Times* (25 July 1860).

183 'Minister for Foreign Affairs to the Marquis of Chateaurenard' (5 July 1860) in *French Documents Diplomatiques 1860.* (Paris, 1861) p.193.

184 'The Minister for Foreign Affairs to the Marquis of Lavalette' (6 July 1860) Ibid. p.196.

185 'The Naval Minister to the Minister for Foreign Affairs' (7 July 1860) Ibid. p.196.

Christians under the 1856 Treaty of Paris.[186] Opposition was not limited to France and Russell noted the 'feelings of horror, resentment and indignation' that the atrocities caused in Britain.[187] Britain initially pressured the Porte to protect its Christians and dispatched ships to Syria to do so.[188] This changed following the Damascus massacres and an even stronger deployment was seen as necessary.[189]

Britain could no longer ignore the Syrian unrest while France expanded its plans for intervention, suggesting a force of 6800 soldiers under the command of General Charles-Marie-Napoléon de Beaufort d'Hautpoul a former advisor to Ibrahim Pasha.[190] As the violence continued, Britain's cabinet had no objection to a multilateral (but mostly French) force being dispatched to Syria, although Westminster sought to limit its own involvement to naval support,[191] while other European powers raised little objection.[192]

News of the initial violence reached Constantinople causing the Sultan's ministers to convene on 'the most prompt and effective measures enacted by his Majesty to end the flow of blood and rescue all the miserable.'[193] The Porte's outrage at the inaction of local authorities was genuine and it saw their negligence as disgraceful to the Ottoman military.[194] Mindful of this and the need to prevent European intervention, Sultan Abdulmecid I telegrammed Britain's Queen Victoria[195] and Napoleon III,[196] promising prompt action.[197] Abdulmecid released an edict affirming the equality of all Ottoman subjects and dispatched his Foreign Minister, Fuad Pasha with 'all the civil and military powers' to end the conflict, restore order and punish the guilty according to

186 House of Commons Debate 23 July 1860 Vol.160 Cols. 15–16.

187 'Lord Russell to Sir Bulwer' (25 August 1860) in British Parliamentary Papers *LXVII.499 Supra* note 161 p.48.

188 'Lord Russell to Sir Bulwer' (10 July 1860) in British Parliamentary Papers LXVIII.17. *Supra* note 168. p.3.

189 Bass. *Supra* note 104. p.175.

190 'Earl Cowley to Lord Russell' (25 July 1860) in British Parliamentary Papers LXVIII.17. *Supra* note 168. p.21.

191 UK House of Commons Debate 23 July 1860 Vol 160 Col.16.

192 Austria supported intervention if it avoided contributing its own troops ('Earl Cowley to Lord Russell' (22 July 1860) in British Parliamentary Papers LXVIII.17. *Supra* note 168. p.14.) while Russia was also favourable to intervention. ('Mr Erskine to Lord Russell' (11th July 1860) Ibid. p.6).

193 Edwards, Richard. *La Syria 1840–1862* (Paris, 1862). p.164.

194 Heraclides and Dialla. *Supra* note 27. p.139.

195 'The Sultan [Abdumecid I] to Her Majesty, the Queen [Victoria I]' (16 July 1860) in British Parliamentary Papers LXVIII.17. *Supra* note 168. p.22.

196 'The Sultan [Abdulazid I] to the Emperor of the French' (16 July 1860) Ibid. p.10.

197 'The Sultan [Abdulazid I] to Her Majesty, the Queen [Victoria I]' (16 July 1860) Ibid. p.22.

the Sultan's Imperial Code.[198] Fuad sought to avoid giving the Great Powers an excuse to intervene and informed France that he would 'avenge the honour of humanity and stop the flow of blood'.[199]

Had the Damascus riots not occurred before Fuad was ready to depart, he might have averted European intervention.[200] Fuad arrived in Beirut on 17 July 1860, distributing aid and instructing the Ottoman commander at Aleppo to fight to the 'last man' to maintain order.[201] As the peace agreement between the Maronites and Druze in Beirut largely held, he turned his attention to Damascus where he arrived at the end of July, rapidly pacifying the city.[202]

Britain was especially pleased with Fuad's actions that restored order without requiring European action, but the Damascus massacres obliged Britain to support French demands for a military expedition.[203] Russell also knew Britain needed to prevent Syria's destabilisation, avert unilateral French expansion and supported an agreement between the Great Powers and the Ottoman Empire with a convention to regulate the intervention's mandate.[204] Consent from the Porte was forthcoming: although the Sultan claimed intervention risked destabilising the region, he nonetheless accepted an expeditionary force, provided it had unanimous support from the Great Powers.[205]

Napoleon III appreciated the legal necessity in securing European agreement before entering a region as unstable as Syria[206] and in August 1860, a protocol was signed between Britain, Austria, France, Prussia, Russia and the Ottoman Empire for the pacification of Syria.[207] The Protocol was not framed as external intervention but as aiding the Porte in protecting its subjects.[208] Although France was to supply half of the necessary troops, if necessary, the Protocol authorised a multinational European force to 're-establish

198 'Firman' (Undated) Ibid. pp.32–33.

199 Edwards, Richard. *La Syria 1840–1862* (Paris, 1862). p.165.

200 Rodogno. *Supra* note 50. p.103.

201 'Colonel O'Reilly to Sir Bulwer' (18 July 1860) in British Parliamentary Papers LXVIII.17. *Supra* note 168. pp.55–56.

202 'Fuad Pasha's Measures at Damascus' *Manchester Guardian.* (24 August 1860).

203 'Lord Russell to Earl Cowley' (23 July 1860) in in British Parliamentary Papers LXVIII.17. *Supra* note 168. p.15.

204 UK House of Commons Debate 23 July 1860 Vol 160 Col.16.

205 'Mr Musurus to Lord Russell' (30 July 1860) in British Parliamentary Papers LXVIII.17. *Supra* note 168. p.28.

206 Kloepper. *Supra* note 155. p.251.

207 'Protocol of a Conference held the 3rd August.' (1860) Preamble. In British Parliamentary Papers LXVIII.17. *Supra* note 168. p.36.

208 Ibid.

tranquillity' in Syria.[209] It also established a timeframe for the force, mollifying Great Powers' fear of unilateral French occupation. Although the Protocol did not become a formal convention for another month,[210] it was effective immediately, with Napoleon III addressing his troops that they were being dispatched to Syria to ensure the victory of 'rights of justice and humanity.[211]

By this point, over 11,000 Christians had been killed[212] and the French expeditionary force arrived in Syria on 16 August 1860 where Maronites welcomed them.[213] The French commander, General Beaufort used explicitly humanitarian language to justify his mission, telling his troops that they were 'defenders of all the great and noble causes', there to avenge 'humanity disgracefully vilified'.[214] Fuad was aware of the need to avoid antagonising the Great Powers and proclaimed the French were there with the Sultan's consent, lest Muslims see them as 'a crusade of the Cross against the Crescent'.[215] Likewise, Napoleon told his troops they were there to assist the Porte restore order.[216] Nonetheless, clashes were inevitable, given that the Ottomans and French had the same mandate, while Fuad's shrewdness ensured he had the upper hand when dealing with Beaufort.[217]

The French troops achieved little as a fighting force when they sought to pacify Mount Lebanon. The region had been utterly devastated but Fuad dispatched thousands of soldiers to pacify the region[218] while as predicted by the *Times*,[219] the Druze melted away before the French. Subsequently the French took on nation-building roles,[220] providing security to the Christians[221] and

209 Ibid.

210 See British Parliamentary Papers LXVIII.1 *'Convention between Great Britain, Austria, France, Prussia, Russia, and Turkey, respecting measures to be taken for the pacification of Syria'. (London, 1861).*

211 Edwards, Richard. *La Syria 1840–1862* (Paris, 1862). p.197.

212 Churchill. *Supra* note 153. p.219.

213 'Consul-General Moore to Lord Russell' (22 August 1860) in British Parliamentary Papers LXVIII.17. *Supra* note 168. p.82.

214 Fawaz. *Supra* note 169. p.119.

215 'Fuad Pasha's Measures at Damascus' *Manchester Guardian.* (24 August 1860).

216 Heraclides and Dialla. *Supra* note 27. p.140.

217 Fawaz. *Supra* note 169. pp.119–121.

218 'Major Fraser to Lord Russell' (21 September 1860) in British Parliamentary Papers LXVIII.17. *Supra* note 168. pp.152–154.

219 The *Times.* (10 August 1860).

220 Bass. *Supra* note 104. p.213.

221 It must be noted that while the French protected Christians, they indirectly induced further atrocities as emboldened by the French presence, Maronites began attacking Druze across the region. Overall, some one hundred Muslims were killed although Beaufort punished any guilty Christians who were caught (Churchill. *Supra* note 153. p.247).

helping them rebuild their destroyed villages.[222] Beaufort disdained such humanitarian tasks but they were vital components of what would now be acknowledged as peace building.[223]

While the massacres in Damascus involved Muslims attacking Christians, the violence in Mount Lebanon was more nuanced, with two guilty parties requiring a delicate balance to satisfy the Maronites without alienating the Druze.[224] Christians were used to help arrest those who committed atrocities and Druze leaders were imprisoned, (most were subsequently released).[225] Churchill notes that while Syrian Muslims initially fled from the French, they soon learned to trust them.[226]

Britain soon suspected French interests in the region: Russell argued that Beaufort and Fuad had achieved their 'work of humanity and justice' and to maintain French troops in Syria would change their original purpose.[227] The Eastern Question remained the dominant factor in how the Great Powers approached the Ottoman Empire with Britain seeking to prevent French expansion. Likewise, the Porte was keen to reassert its independence but ran into opposition from the Great Powers with divergence on whether to extend the duration of France's expedition.[228]

France convened a conference in Paris to seek an extension of their mandate but maintained they would withdraw their troops if this were the consensus.[229] The Paris Conference quickly showed the division between the Great Powers.[230] Eventually, in March 1861, a compromise was reached whereby France proposed the mandate be extended by three months to 5 June: as it had a defined date for French withdrawal, the Great Powers accepted the

222 Ibid. pp. 248–249.

223 Rodogno. *Supra* note 50. p.107.

224 Fawaz. *Supra* note 169. p.180.

225 Churchill. *Supra* note 153. pp.232–240.

226 Ibid. p.250.

227 'Lord Russell to Earl Cowley' (7 November 1860) in British Parliamentary Papers LXVIII.17. *Supra* note 168. p.186.

228 Bass. *Supra* note 104. p.219.

229 'M. Thouvenel to Count de Flauhaut (18 January 1861) in British Parliamentary Papers LXVIII.17. *Supra* note 168. p.330.

230 Napoleon III hoped to extend the duration of the French expedition indefinitely (see 'Summary of News: Foreign' *Guardian.* (23 February 1861)) and was supported by Russia although neither opposed the deployment of non-French troops. See 'Russia and the Syrian Conference' *Observer.* (25 February 1861). However, they were opposed by the Ottoman Empire and Britain while Austria and Prussia were mostly passive. See Bass. *Supra* note 104. p.223.

proposal.[231] On 7 June 1861, the French troops withdrew from Syria despite Maronite protests[232] and in 1861, the Great Powers and the Ottoman Empire sought to prevent further violence by restructuring Mount Lebanon into an autonomous mutasarrifate with a Maronite majority and Christian governor.[233]

### 2.3 *Humanitarian Intervention and Ottoman Syria*

By the time of the intervention in Syria, most humanitarian intervention theorists at the time (and many jurists) supported humanitarian intervention.[234] This makes the Syrian intervention fascinating from an international law perspective, particularly as the expedition was not purely military and the French soldiers primarily engaged in nation building.[235] It is important to note that the mission of the French expedition was to rescue Christians while the mandate prohibited territorial acquisition.[236] While no states acted against their geopolitical interests, they nonetheless responded to the massacre of civilians and without the Damascus riots, the intervention might have been unnecessary.[237] The resolution to the Syrian crisis was largely due to Fuad's measures and the French force did little,[238] with Fuad's actions rendering the expedition mostly irrelevant.[239] This deprived France of a justification to occupy Damascus[240]

231 'Lord Russell to Earl Cowley' (7 March 1861) in British Parliamentary Papers LXVIII.17. *Supra* note 168. p.424.

232 Fawaz. *Supra* note 169. p.131. European intervention had support among Syrian Christians who treated the French as heroes. When it was announced that the French expedition would withdraw, hundreds of Syrian Christians petitioned the Great Powers for the expedition to continue and begged the French troops to remain (see Bass. *Supra* note 104. pp.226–228).

233 Abu-Manneh, Butrus. 'The Province of Syria and the Mutasarrifiyya of Mount Lebanon (1866–1880)' Turkish Historical Review (Vol.4, 2013) pp.119–120.

234 Heraclides and Dialla. *Supra* note 27. p.134.

235 The International Commission for Syria convened in Beirut to investigate the roots of the conflict, ensure justice, prevent further violence, and administer European relief funds to the destitute (see Churchill. *Supra* note 153. pp.259–260). Overall, the Commission was dominated by Fuad Pasha and Lord Dufferin who represented the Ottoman Empire and Britain respectively and had similar goals in maintaining Ottoman sovereignty which strongly contributed towards the conflict's successful resolution (See Fawaz. *Supra* note 169. pp.196–197).

236 'Protocol of a Conference held the 3rd August'. (1860) Preamble. In British Parliamentary Papers LXVIII.17. *Supra* note 168. p.38.

237 Rodogno. *Supra* note 50. p.103.

238 Churchill argues that this was due to a lack of support, particularly from Westminster and the Porte. See Churchill. *Supra* note 153. p.251.

239 Shaw and Shaw. *Supra* note 156. p.143.

240 Spagnolo. *Supra* note 42. p.35.

and forced the French soldiers to focus on providing humanitarian aid.[241] The French engaged in a manner that would now be seen as peacekeeping rather than peace enforcement.[242] The Porte did not try to disguise the atrocities committed by Druze and Muslims, although it also highlighted atrocities committed by Christians[243] but disclaimed any initial knowledge of the conflict.[244]

While the intervention was accepted by the Great Powers, as was common under nineteenth century international law, morality was subordinate to the balance of power. There is certainly an argument to be made for the intervention's humanitarian nature given France did not gain territory or unilateral commercial privileges[245] and while it asserted French power in protecting Paris' Maronite protégés, it was an intervention to protect civilians. Although Fuad had mostly restored order before the French arrived, it is unclear how the Porte would have responded without the threat of Great Power involvement. Overall, there were three key players in the Syrian intervention: Britain, France and the Ottoman Empire, all of whom were guided by their own interests.

A key factor in French support for intervention was the importance of foreign policy. French geopolitical interests cannot be discounted but neither can the importance of the intervention to Napoleon III's regime. The intervention demonstrated French military prowess, bolstered Napoleon III's domestic support while French commercial interest in Syrian silk was also a likely a factor in their intervention.[246] The French intervention had a humanitarian goal in saving civilians and France framed its involvement in humanitarian terms, both to French soldiers[247] and to the Great Powers.[248] Bass also highlights that

241 Pogany, Istvan. 'Humanitarian Intervention in International Law: the French Intervention in Syria re-examined' *The International and Comparative Law Quarterly* (Vol.34, No.1. January 1986) p.186.

242 Heraclides and Dialla. *Supra* note 27. p.140.

243 'Sir Bulwer to Lord Russell' (27 June 1860) in *British Parliamentary Papers LXIX.553 Supra* note 168. p.18.

244 Spagnolo. *Supra* note 42. p.30.

245 Rodogno. *Supra* note 50. p.114.

246 Firro, Kais. 'Silk and Agrarian Changes in Lebanon, 1860–1914' *International Journal of Middle East Studies* (Vol. 22, No. 2. May 1990) p.154.

247 The French expeditionary force had the humanitarianism of their mission stressed to them by both Napoleon III (see 'Earl Cowley to Lord Russell (8 August 1860) in British Parliamentary Papers LXVIII.17. *Supra* note 168. pp.40–41) and General Beaufort (Fawaz. *Supra* note 169. p.119) while Thouvenel informed the Minister for War that Beaufort's instructions were to stop the flow of blood, end the attacks on Christians and punish the guilty (see Edwards, Richard. *La Syria 1840–1862* (Paris, 1862). p.199).

248 Thouvenel wrote to the other Great Powers referring to France's 'work of humanity ('M. Thouvenel to Count de Flauhaut (18 January 1861) in British Parliamentary Papers LXVIII.17. *Supra* note 168. p.330).

there was genuine French support for humanitarian intervention, although the government influenced such views and France had strategic interests in the Levant.[249] The French diplomat Melchior Vogüé feared Russia was usurping France's role as the protector of Christians in the Middle East but hoped French intervention could protect Syrian Christians while preventing Russian expansion into the region.[250] Overall, French geopolitical interests in Syria cannot be ignored but as the *Times* acknowledged France was also acting for humanitarian reasons.[251]

Although British press coverage was less detailed than that of France, it was more independent and could report more objectively.[252] While British public opinion opposed non-intervention, foreign policy concerns rather than public pressure induced Britain to support French intervention.[253] Russell's primary motives were not humanitarian but guided by fears of French motives as well as the risk of a joint Franco-Russian intervention.[254] As in Navarino, British intervention was influenced by a need to prevent unilateral action threatening the balance of power, but neither was Britain dismissive of the atrocities. While Britain supported the intervention (and to provide troops if needed),[255] it opposed extending the expedition's mandate, to avoid a precedent for European occupation in the region.[256] Russell accepted Thouvenel's claim that France's key motive was humanitarian though he was quick to highlight the Porte's sovereignty meant Britain would oppose occupation.[257]

Although the Porte wanted to solve the Syrian crisis itself, it knew it had to consent to Great Power intervention.[258] While the intervention took place with the Porte's consent, it was given under duress.[259] Neither the Porte nor the

249 Bass. *Supra* note 104. pp.156–157.

250 De Vogüé. *Supra* note 160. p.23.

251 *The Times.* (10 August 1860).

252 Bass. *Supra* note 104. p.184.

253 Rodogno, Davide. 'The 'principles of humanity' and the European Powers' intervention in Ottoman Lebanon and Syria in 1860–1861' in Simms, Brendan and Trim, D.J.B (Eds.) *Humanitarian Intervention: A History* (Cambridge, 2011) p.180.

254 Ibid. p.173.

255 'Earl Cowley to Lord Russell' (21 September 1860) in British Parliamentary Papers LXVIII.17. *Supra* note 168. pp.129–130.

256 'Lord Russell to Earl Cowley' (7 November 1860) in British Parliamentary Papers LXVIII.17. *Supra* note 168. p.186.

257 'Lord Russell to Earl Cowley' (24 January 1861) in British Parliamentary Papers LXVIII.17. *Supra* note 168. p.331.

258 Churchill. *Supra* note 153. p.256.

259 Fonteyne. *Supra* note 130. pp.208–209. Stowell likewise notes the Sultan only gave his consent 'through constraint' and thus is an example of intervention. (Stowell. *Supra* note 137. p.66).

Great Powers challenged the legality of the intervention and the expeditionary force involved European nations supporting the Porte in resolving the crisis rather than usurping Ottoman authority.[260] In this, it showed shadows of the Responsibility to Protect, with the Porte being helped to protect its citizens by the wider international community. The Ottoman Empire maintained that external interference had instigated the massacres while further intervention prevented them from checking the unrest.[261]

Some Europeans remained suspicious of an Ottoman commitment to justice.[262] In the end, Britain supported intervention only as a last resort, but after the massacres at Damascus, Ottoman control of Syria was demonstrably fragile enough that Britain felt obliged to support the French expedition.[263] France argued that French troops empowered Fuad to take action against the guilty.[264] The Ottoman Grand Vizier, Ali Pasha, rejected this, claiming the Porte was capable of enforcing control, but it accepted a European expeditionary force to 'act in concert with the Porte's Commissioner' and highlighted the importance of Constantinople satisfying both domestic and European public opinion.[265] This view of the French force as complementary to the Porte was reinforced by Napoleon III himself who informed his troops that as well as fighting for justice, they were working with, not against the Sultan.[266] Fuad's actions in Syria achieved what the Porte hoped. As predicted by the *Times*, effective action by Fuad ensured there was little for France to do and the expeditionary force operated mainly as support for Fuad's troops.[267] This prevented France from being able to expand its role in the region and highlighted to the Great Powers the Porte's ability to reform. It also allowed the violence to be addressed without overly antagonising the Ottoman Empire that could claim

260 Spagnolo. *Supra* note 42. p.46.

261 Fawaz. *Supra* note 169. p.214.

262 De Vogue suspected the Ottomans allowed the Druze to massacre the Maronites before reasserting control, ridding them of troublesome Christians while maintaining favour with the Great Powers (De Vogüé. *Supra* note 160. p.9). Likewise, Dufferin felt the Porte was using the Druze as a proxy to quash nascent Maronite independence (Lord Dufferin to Lord Russell (10 August 1861) in British Parliamentary Papers LXVIII.17. *Supra* note 168. p.485).

263 'Lord Russell to Sir Bulwer' (1 August 1860) Ibid. p.31.

264 'Earl Cowley to Lord Russell' (1 September 1860) Ibid. pp.82–83.

265 'Ali Pasha to Ahmed Vefyk Efendi' (27 July 1860) in British Parliamentary Papers LXVIII.17. *Supra* note 168. p.57.

266 Edwards, Richard. *La Syria 1840–1862* (Paris, 1862). p.197.

267 *The Times.* (10 August 1860).

the International Commission had an advisory role, with the Porte maintaining sovereignty over Mount Lebanon.[268]

The Syrian intervention has generated a considerable amount of academic interest. Bass highlights its importance in so far that the Sultan himself sanctioned it and it did not amount to outright French coercion, given French troops worked with the consent of the Great Powers and the Ottoman Empire.[269] This has parallels with today and the issue of 'coerced consent'.[270] Heraclides and Dialla note that while France did have some genuine humanitarian intentions, it was also guided by self-interest to expand French influence in the region and demonstrate Napoleon III's prowess.[271] Furthermore, they note that all of the international lawyers that cite the case highlight its substantial humanitarian component.[272] Nonetheless, they also draw attention to the particular issues, with the case being seen as an example of humanitarian intervention. Namely, that it took place with Ottoman consent (albeit under duress), that Fuad had pacified the region before French troops arrived and the role of the Maronites in contributing to the conflict's origins.[273]

Anderson maintains Napoleon III sought to force the Sultan to cease his opposition to the construction of the Suez Canal and establish an independent, pro-French Syria.[274] Fawaz concluded that Napoleon III probably used the Syrian crisis as an opportunistic way to assert French foreign policy.[275] Rodogno asserts that while the intervention was 'disinterested', Napoleon's actions were not entirely humanitarian as the expedition simultaneously protected French interests and expanded French prestige.[276] Rodogno concludes that the intervention was broadly humanitarian, given the primary motivation was to end the massacres.[277] Kloepper supports the substantial humanitarian aspect of the intervention, noting the extensive array of support this view has among international law scholars who have examined the case.[278] Kloepper concludes that French intervention in Syria was humanitarian intervention, justifiable under international law of its time.[279] Brownlie is even blunter,

268 Spagnolo. *Supra* note 42. p.46.
269 Bass. *Supra* note 104. p.231.
270 See Weiss, Thomas. *Humanitarian Intervention* (Cambridge, 2018) p.29.
271 Heraclides and Dialla. *Supra* note 27. p.141–142.
272 Ibid.
273 Ibid. pp.142–143.
274 Anderson. *Supra* note 93. p.156.
275 Fawaz. *Supra* note 169. p.110.
276 Rodogno. *Supra* note 253. p.179.
277 Ibid. p.181.
278 Kloepper. *Supra* note 155. p.255.
279 Ibid. p.258.

noting that the intervention in Syria is the world's only possible case of genuine humanitarian intervention.[280] Although Brownlie highlights the suspicion of the Great Powers of French ambition in Syria, he concludes that the 'motive of humanity' was real.[281]

On balance, it appears that there is a consensus that the French expedition was broadly humanitarian, even though France did not act entirely selflessly. The humanitarian aspect of the French intervention was evident: while France had mixed motives, they engaged in genuine humanitarian work, spurring the Porte to address the crisis and helping build an enduring peace that would last for decades. Although France had its own motives for intervening, it acted with the consent of the Great Powers, ensuring French intervention ended atrocities without disrupting the balance of power. Critically, the intervention took place with the (grudging) consent of the Porte.[282] As with other nineteenth century interventions, it was selective rather than entirely humanitarian. Although the Druze were engaging in a 'resolution to exterminate all the mountaineers who believe in Christ',[283] the Maronites in Mount Lebanon were merely less effective in their violence and there was never a European push to intervene on behalf of Mount Lebanon's Muslims. With an integrated approach to peace building, the expedition to Mount Lebanon and its background demonstrates a surprisingly advanced approach to not only end massacres but also prevent their reoccurrence and restore justice.

## 3 Humanitarian Intervention in Bulgaria 1877

The Porte hoped the *Tanzimat* reforms[284] would lead the Great Powers to accept the Ottoman Empire as their equal[285] but the reforms stalled by the mid-1870s and it was noted that 'the condition of the mass of people had greatly deteriorated'[286] while the Porte was bankrupt[287] and 'honeycombed

280 Brownlie. *Supra* note 6. p.340.
281 Ibid.
282 See *Supra* note 259.
283 'Vice Consul Abela to Consul-General Moore' (3 June 1860) in *British Parliamentary Papers* LXIX.553. *Supra* note 168. p.27.
284 See *Supra* note 156
285 Pavlowitch, Stevan. *A History of the Balkans 1805–1945* (Harlow, 1999) pp.101–102.
286 Letter to Mr. Tait from Richard Cobden, Esq., (The 'Manchester Manufacturer') on the Eastern Question *Tait's Edinburgh Magazine.* (February 1841) p.78.
287 'The Sick Man Again' *New York Times.* (27 August 1827).

with corruption'.[288] The political landscape of Europe had undergone substantial changes[289] and to maintain stability, German Chancellor Bismarck created the League of Three Emperors, uniting Austria-Hungary, Germany and Russia in a conservative, counter-revolutionary alliance.[290] The League was undermined by conflicting Austro-Hungarian and Russian interests in the Balkans, which by the 1870s faced unrest under Ottoman mismanagement, bad harvests and rising nationalism.

Insurrection in the Ottoman provinces of Bosnia and Herzegovina was of particular interest to Austria-Hungary, as it feared instability on its borders. Attempts by the League of Three Emperors to induce further Ottoman reform failed,[291] while unrest spread to the Ottoman vassal state of Serbia that declared war on the Ottoman Empire in June 1876.[292] Although Tsar Alexander II tried to avoid conflict, Russian patriotism and sympathy for their fellow Slavs resulted in a stream of Russian volunteers '[risking] making the Serbian war a Russian war'.[293] Another Russo-Turkish war was of concern to the Eastern Question and something staunchly opposed by Britain. Further instability was to arise, in the Ottoman province of Bulgaria.

### 3.1 *The Bulgarian Rebellion of 1876*

Due to its strategic location, the Ottoman Empire had extensively settled Muslims in Bulgaria leading to dissatisfaction among its native Christians[294] and a rebellion erupted in April 1876.[295] Troop shortages forced the Porte to rely on *bashibazouk* irregulars who massacred Bulgarian civilians while Ottoman authorities ordered Muslim villagers to turn on their Christian neighbours.[296]

288 Pears, Edwin. *Forty Years in Constantinople: The Recollections of Sir Edwin Pears 1873–1915* (New York, 1916) p.5.

289 France was no longer a counterweight to British interests in the Middle East given its weakened state from its decisive defeat in the 1870 Franco-Prussian War and was preoccupied with recovery rather than expanding its interests. Likewise, the newly unified state of Italy was accepted as one of the Great Powers but lacked the strength to exert international influence. A major development was the newly formed German Empire that was focussed on preventing a French resurgence and maintaining the balance of power.

290 Gildea. *Supra* note 10. p.230.

291 Seton-Watson. *Supra* note 37. p.450.

292 'Servia [sic] and Turkey: Reported Declaration of War' *Manchester Guardian.* (30 June 1876).

293 'Prospects of Russian Intervention'. *Manchester Guardian.* (5 October 1876).

294 Hupchick. *Supra* note 63. pp.208–209.

295 MacGahan, J.A. *Turkish Atrocities in Bulgaria* (London, 1876) pp.39–40.

296 Pears. *Supra* note 288. p.15.

*The Times* reported on the massacre of Bulgarian civilians by *bashi bazouks* but there was otherwise little information on the ongoing massacres.[297]

In many ways, the Balkan crisis of the 1870s echoed that of the Greek revolt, with each of the Great Powers seeking to protect its own interests in the Balkans. Austria-Hungary supported the Porte[298] while Germany was mostly indifferent to the Eastern Question.[299] France was too weakened from its 1870 defeat by Prussia to be overly concerned with the Eastern Question[300] while Italy was keen to assert itself but lacked strength.[301] As such, it was Austria-Hungary, Russia and Britain that would determine the Great Power's response to the Bulgarian crisis.

## 3.2 *Britain and the Bulgarian Rebellion*

Ideological and strategic support for the Ottoman Empire in maintaining the balance of power was a key factor in Britain's foreign policy, but the government's actions were constrained by Britain's increased democratisation and the rise of mass media. Key was the *Daily News* that built up a strong following while Edwin Pears, its foreign correspondent, reported on the Ottoman response to the Bulgarian insurrection.[302] Pears therefore urged Britain to either withdraw all support to the Ottomans or to intervene out of 'duty to an oppressed people and to humanity' to prevent unilateral Russian action.[303] Pears' reporting attracted attention, and was referenced in the House of

297 *The Times.* (1 June 1876).

298 Vienna was acutely aware that without the Ottoman Empire, it would be forced to maintain the Balkans itself (Stoyanovich, Mihailo. *The Great Powers and the Balkans 1875–1878* (London, 1939) pp.30–31). While Austria-Hungary could have expanded at Ottoman expense, its ethnic diversity meant this was not in their interests (Gladstone, William. *Bulgarian Horrors and the Question of the East* (London, 1876) p.32).

299 Any interest Germany had on the region was due to Berlin's strategic need to maintain good relations between Russia and Austria-Hungary which both had vital interests in the Balkans. See Shannon, R.T. *Gladstone, and the Bulgarian Agitation 1876* (Hassocs, 1963) p.20. Likewise, there was negligible public support in Germany for action on the Bulgaria crisis. *The Times.* (20 September 1876).

300 This was compounded by the French public's silence on the issue, save for some prominent intellectuals like Victor Hugo. See *The Times.* (20 September 1876).

301 Harris, David. *Britain and the Bulgarian Horrors of 1876* (Chicago, 1939) p.25.

302 Pears described *bashi bazouks* massacring thousands of civilians and razing hundreds of villages while highlighting the Porte's confidence that Britain would protect them from Russian intervention (Pears, Edwin. 'The Assassinations of Constantinople' *Daily News.* (23 June 1876)).

303 Ibid.

Commons, although Britain's Prime Miniser, Benjamin Disraeli was dismissive.[304] In response to this, Pears began sending the *Daily News* lists of destroyed villages, urged Westminster to form a commission and enlisted the help of an American journalist, Januarius MacGahan.[305]

Accompanied by Eugene Schuyler (the American Consul-General), MacGahan arrived at the village of Batak where thousands of Bulgarians had been massacred by *bashi bazouks*. MacGahan's lurid account of Batak described a village filled with rotting corpses and 'everywhere horrors upon horrors.'[306] MacGahan was particularly critical about Disraeli joking about Ottoman treatment of prisoners and for European diplomacy, 'discussing the matter over their coffee and cigars' while Bulgarians starved and died.[307] MacGahan's report was also objective, and while he received support from Schuyler,[308] his investigation was done independently of the British embassy or Ottoman authorities.[309] The article drew a strong response from the British public,[310] while Disraeli was blindsided by his own poor intelligence.[311] Disraeli

304 Disraeli assured the Commons that the Porte was deploying regular troops and had taken steps to prevent further atrocities (UK House of Commons Debate 26 June 1876 Vol. 230 Cols. 424–6). Furthermore, he denied Russian claims that he was indifferent to Bulgarian suffering, while rebels were labelled as foreign *agent provocateurs* rather than Bulgarians (Disraeli to Queen Victoria' (29 June 1876) in Moneypenny, William and Buckle, George (Eds.) *The Life of Benjamin Disraeli, Earl of Beaconsfield, Vol.6* (New York, 1920) p.35). While Disraeli did not deny that atrocities took place, he questioned their extent and severity, joking that Ottomans tend to 'terminate their connection with culprits in a more expeditious manner' rather than engage in torture or mass-imprisonment (*House of Commons Debate 10 July 1876 Vol. 230 Col.1182*).

305 Pears. *Supra* note 288. pp.17–18.

306 MacGahan, J.A 'The Turkish Atrocities in Bulgaria' *Daily News.* (22 August 1876).

307 Ibid.

308 Schuyler's own report corroborated MacGahan's findings, detailing rape, murder, and slaughter and estimating that at least 15,000 civilians were killed. See MacGahan. *Supra* note 295. p.91.

309 MacGahan. *Supra* note 295.p.vi.

310 British newspapers (especially ones based outside of England's Home Counties) began drawing far more attention to the atrocities ('The Turkish Atrocities in Bulgaria' *Daily News.* (24 August 1876) and received numerous letters demanding action against the atrocities, particularly the *Daily News*. See 'The Turkish Atrocities in Bulgaria' *Daily News.* (24 August 1876). In addition, town hall meetings were held across Britain to urge British intervention and the Christian League in Aid of the Christians of Turkey was founded to 'aid the Christians in obtaining their freedom from Mussulman (sic) oppression'. 'The Christian League in Aid of the Christians of Turkey' *Manchester Guardian.* (5 April 1876).

311 Harris. *Supra* note 301. p.24. Disraeli received a detailed report from the British consul in Rustchuk that referred to the atrocities as 'rumours which are probable'. ('Disraeli to Queen Victoria' (29 June 1876) in Moneypenny and Buckle *Supra* note 304. p.35.) 'Disraeli to Lord Derby' (14 July 1876) Ibid. pp.44–45. Publicly, Disraeli dismissed the report as

knew he needed to be better informed and dispatched a commissioner, Walter Baring, to the Balkans to investigate. Despite doubts over Baring's partiality,[312] he proved himself an honest investigator.[313] Baring's report concluded that some atrocities were exaggerated,[314] but nonetheless found evidence of massacres particularly by *bashi bazouks*.

The Porte's response was ineffectual[315] and their own report claimed that the Bulgarians were induced to rebel by Russian-funded agents with instructions to massacre civilians.[316] It was especially emphasised that the insurgents committed gruesome atrocities on Muslims, which was stressed by the Porte[317] and was useful for Westminster to repeat in order to avoid intervening: it is one thing to rescue innocent civilians and another to get involved in a civil war. Likewise, Derby argued that the conflict 'was not a case of lambs and wolves but of some savage races fighting in a peculiarly savage manner'.[318] MacGahan dismissed this, highlighting how Britain had no one on the ground to verify such claims and relied on biased Ottoman reports[319] and overall, atrocities committed by Ottoman troops dwarfed rebel ones.[320]

---

'coffee house babble' and argued that any atrocities were committed by irregulars over whom the Ottomans had little control. *House of Commons Debate 31 July 1876 Vol.231 Col.203*. This was also the line taken by the Ottoman Empire who claimed brutality arose from Muslims who the Porte had no control over ('Sir Elliot to the Early of Derby' (9 August 1876) in British Parliamentary Papers XC.1 *Correspondence respecting the affairs of Turkey (London, 1877) p.28*). However, this was disputed by MacGahan (MacGahan. *Supra* note 295.pp.28–29).

312 Baring was seen as a Turcophile and as he had Elliot's confidence, his integrity was questioned, particularly by Russia's ambassador to Constantinople, Count Ignatiev ('Sir Elliot to the Earl of Derby' (9 August 1876) in British Parliamentary Papers *XC.1 Supra* note 311. p.28).

313 Harris. *Supra* note 301. p.165.

314 Baring, Walter. 'Report by Mr Baring on the Atrocities Committed upon the Christians in Bulgaria'. *The London Gazette* (19 September 1876). p.5119.

315 It must be noted that Ottoman authorities did arrest the most egregious committers of atrocities. See Harris. *Supra* note 301. p.257).

316 'Report to the Sublime Porte by the Extraordinary Tribunal instituted at Philippopolis to judge persons implicated in the late events in Bulgaria' in British Parliamentary Papers *XC.1 Supra* note 311. pp.186–187.

317 'Sir Elliot to the Early of Derby' (9 August 1876) in British Parliamentary Papers *XC.1 Supra* note 311. pp.28–29.

318 *The Times*. (15 July 1876).

319 MacGahan. *Supra* note 295.p.13.

320 Baring's report noted that it was easier to document the numbers of Bulgarian Muslims killed and concluded that around 300 were killed by Christians in the Philippopolis region, as were numerous Romani (Baring. *Supra* note 314. p.5123). Baring estimated that Ottoman military casualties were small (Ibid. pp.5123–5124.) and overall concluded that a Bulgarian Christian rebellion took place which needed to be halted but that 'the manner

The Bulgarian crisis continued to be raised in the House of Commons and Disraeli was criticised by MPs, many of whom referenced the *Daily News* and Baring's report. Disraeli tried to play down the extent of the atrocities[321] and British strategic interests were the cornerstone of its policy in the Balkans.[322] The damage was done. Disraeli came under sustained fire for his perceived indifference on Ottoman atrocities, making him fear the British public had been brainwashed by Russia.[323] This led to Elliot being directed to warn the Porte that the continuation of the conflict would lead to outside intervention,[324] most likely from Russia.

### 3.3 *Russia and the Bulgarian Rebellion*

Although worried by domestic nationalism, Russia saw Balkan nationalism as an ideal tool to escape the Treaty of Paris' constraints while Panslavism[325] gained momentum, aided by Russia's ambassador to Constantinople, Count Ignatiev. Panslavism was opposed by Russia's Foreign Minister, Prince Gorchakov, who only supported intervention as part of multilateral action with British leadership.[326] Alexander II concurred, seeing Panslavism as dangerous populism that hindered Russian foreign policy.[327]

---

in which the rising was suppressed was inhuman', with 'fifty innocent persons suffering for every guilty one'. (Ibid. p.5139). Likewise, MacGahan found evidence of Romanis being killed by Bulgarians, the rebels did not engage in the brutality that the Ottomans did (MacGahan. *Supra* note 295.pp.81–82).

321 Disraeli highlighted how many allegations were refuted by the Baring report and that out of 3,700,000 Bulgarians, only 12,000 were killed (UK House of Commons debate 11 August 1876 Vol.231 Cols.1078–147).

322 UK House of Commons debate 11 August 1876 Vol.231 Cols.1078–147. Britain's Mediterranean fleet had been anchored in Besika Bay to protect the small English colony in Pera. This was seen as Britain shielding the Ottoman Empire from foreign intervention, enabling the commission of atrocities, although Elliot claimed Balkan Christians felt the fleet limited Ottoman atrocities in the region. See 'Sir H Elliot to the Earl of Derby' (27 August 1876) in British Parliamentary Papers *XC.1 Supra* note 311. pp.113–114.

323 'Disraeli to Lady Chesterfield' (31 August 1876) in Disraeli, Benjamin. *The Letters of Disraeli to Lady Chesterfield and Lady Bradford Volume Two* (New York, 1929) p.83.

324 'Lord Derby to Sir Elliot' (18 August 1876) British Parliamentary Papers *XC.1 Supra* note 311. p.33.
MacGahan. *Supra* note 295.p.33.

325 Panslavism involved Orthodox Slavic unity under Russian leadership. Russian state-funded Panslavist societies who promoted Slav culture within the Ottoman Empire were gaining increasing momentum and attracted many officers and civil servants (see Seton-Watson. *Supra* note 37. pp.446–447).

326 'Lord Loftus to Lord Derby' (15 August 1876) in British Parliamentary Papers *XC.1 Supra* note 311. p.43. See also Anderson. *Supra* note 93. p.181.

327 Rodogno. *Supra* note 50. p.142.

The Bulgarian atrocities drew the attention of Disraeli's political nemesis, William Gladstone, whose obsession with the Bulgarian question drew him out of retirement. Initially, Gladstone had shown little interest in Bulgaria, but his faith led him to write the *Bulgarian Horrors* where he criticised the government for supporting the Porte in crimes 'so vast in scale as to exceed all modern example'.[328] Gladstone was critical of the Ottomans[329] and demanded their total administrative withdrawal 'one and all, bag and baggage' from Bulgaria.[330] He demanded action, arguing that there were areas where humanity could not be bound by international law, and urged multilateral action to end Ottoman control of Bulgaria.[331] Disraeli was outraged by the pamphlet,[332] and his fear over public pressure over the Bulgarian question proved well founded.[333] Especially critical was Gladstone addressing a rally in Blackheath, where thousands attended and to wild cheers, Gladstone highlighted how support for the Bulgarians was based on 'common humanity'.[334]

The atrocities in Bulgaria continued to draw outrage in Russia, with extensive public sympathy for the Bulgarians.[335] Although Gorchakov assured Britain that Russian foreign policy would not change, the British ambassador warned London that further atrocities in Bulgaria could result in public pressure to force Russia to intervene.[336] Such mass appeal worried

328 Gladstone. *Supra* note 298. p.10.

329 Notably, Gladstone referred to the Ottomans as 'the one great anti-human specimen of humanity' (Ibid. p.10.).

330 Ibid. pp.34–39.

331 Ibid. pp.30–38.

332 Gladstone sent a copy of *Bulgarian Horrors* to Disraeli who found it as 'unprincipled as usual but less 'ill-written as is [Gladstone's] custom' ('Disraeli to Lady Bradford' (9 September 1876) in Disraeli. *Supra* note 323. p.88). Disraeli was particularly outraged by what he perceived to be Gladstone's racist proposal to remove Ottomans from Europe 'for ethnological reasons no less' (Disraeli to Lady Bradford (11th September 1876) Disraeli. *Supra* note 323. p.90). However, it must be noted that Gladstone was not advocating what would now be deemed ethnic cleansing but was referring to ending Ottoman rule of Bulgaria (Shannon, Richard. *Gladstone: Heroic Minister 1865–1898* (London, 1999) p.174).

333 *Bulgarian Horrors* sold forty thousand copies within four days and two hundred thousand copies within a month (Shannon. *Supra* note 299. p.109). Meanwhile, numerous public meetings were held to demand that the government take action (*The Times.* (19 September 1876)). Overall, some four hundred and fifty-five petitions were sent to the Foreign Office, with Christian groups and trade unions criticising the government's pro-Ottoman stance (Shannon. *Supra* note 299. p.148). Unlike elite Philhellenism, British outrage over the Bulgarian atrocities was a mass phenomenon (Bass. *Supra* note 104. p.274).

334 'Mr Gladstone on the Eastern Question'. *Manchester Guardian.* (11th September 1876).

335 MacGahan. *Supra* note 295.p.20.

336 'Lord Loftus to the Earl of Derby' (16 August 1876) in British Parliamentary Papers *XC.1* *Supra* note 311. pp.44–45. Alexander II's authority had been undermined making it hard

Disraeli[337] who felt without the agitation, peace would have been far easier to achieve.[338] The Ottoman Sultan, Murad V had been following the Eastern Question in British politics, with British unrest hindering its ability to negotiate a settlement.[339]

The British public response meant Westminster was forced to change its approach. Elliot warned the Porte that their atrocities were such that they offended the 'entire civilised world'.[340] An Ottoman report rejected claims of Ottoman brutality, claiming that the Bulgarians had exaggerated their situation in order to induce the involvement of the Great Powers.[341] By this point, Russia claimed Britain had aided Ottoman atrocities by supporting the Porte[342] and began mobilising. With war seemingly imminent, Disraeli mused that Gladstone's attempts to avenge the Bulgarians would lead to the 'butchery of the world'.[343] Fearing an Austro-Hungarian war, Germany sought British support to partition the Ottoman Empire between Austria-Hungary, Russia and Britain.[344]

It must be noted that there were notable opponents of intervention in Britain both within the press[345] and among British religious minorities.[346]

to resist pan-Slavist fervour (Anderson. *Supra* note 93. p.187). Likewise, Russian public support for Ottoman Slavs grew to the extent that not even the Tsar could ignore it (Westwood. *Supra* note 38. p.108). Such public pressure was turning Russian foreign policy even further against the Ottoman Empire (Bass. *Supra* note 104. p.284). This was helped by Britain's atrocitarian movement: the Porte relied on British protection and British domestic opposition to the Ottoman Empire was a huge boon to Russian foreign policy, particularly when *Bulgarian Horrors* was translated into Russian, where it sold ten thousand copies in one month (Palmer. *Supra* note 22. p.146).

337 Disraeli felt that the public was being brainwashed by Russia ('Disraeli to Lady Chesterfield (31 August 1876) in Disraeli. *Supra* note 323. p.83).

338 'Disraeli to Lady Bradford' (24 September 1876) in Ibid. p.92.

339 Bass. *Supra* note 104. p.278.

340 UK House of Commons Debate 09 July 1877 Vol. 235 Col.1023.

341 'Saadoulah Bey to the Grand Vizier' (21 Ramazan 1876) in British Parliamentary Papers *XC.1 Supra* note 311. pp.749–750.

342 'Prince Gorchakov to Count Schouvaloff' (3 November 1876) in Ibid. pp.736–737.

343 'Disraeli to Lady Bradford' (29 September 1876) in Disraeli. *Supra* note 323. p.95.

344 Anderson. *Supra* note 93. p.188.

345 *The Saturday Review* highlighted that Russia had no interest in defending Balkan Christians except to extend Russian despotism and that British 'incendiary philanthropy' risked turning Britain into an accessory to a brutal war ('Incendiary Philanthropy' *The Saturday Review of Politics, Literature, Science and Art.* (2 October 1876)). Meanwhile *The Economist* argued British intervention risked making the war worse ('The Turkish Atrocities' *The Economist.* (12th August 1876)) although it also opposed Britain supporting the Porte against the Bulgarians (Harris. *Supra* note 301. p.211).

346 Britain's Jewish community generally supported the Porte, given Ottoman tolerance of Jews and their belief in the anti-Semitism of many atrocitarians (Shannon. *Supra* note

Broadly, British public support for the Bulgarians made it impossible for Britain to support the Porte in any conflict with Russia.[347] Although the newly installed Sultan Abdulhamid II declared a range of reforms,[348] they were insufficient, leading Britain to put pressure on the Porte,[349] most notably warning that rejecting a suggested armistice would see Britain stop protecting the Ottoman Empire.[350] This was of great concern to the Porte, given their military was struggling to maintain internal security, let alone fighting another country.

The Great Powers began pressuring the Ottoman Empire into accepting their mediation at an international conference where 'the independence and integrity of Turkey must be subordinated to the guarantees demanded by humanity, the sentiments of Christian Europe and the general peace'.[351] While Abdulhamid felt humiliated by such intrusion into Ottoman internal affairs, he knew the alternative was the Great Powers convening without Ottoman input, while Russia threatened war,[352] forcing Ottoman acquiescence.[353]

## 3.4 *The Conference of Constantinople and the Russo-Turkish War of 1877–1878*

The Conference of Constantinople began, with representatives from Russia, Germany, France, Austria-Hungary, Britain, Italy and the Ottoman Empire. Although the Powers accepted the need to protect the Balkans, they were unable to agree on how this was to be done, with a particular fear of Russia entering Bulgaria.[354] The Great Powers were divided in their geopolitical interests,[355] preventing a cohesive approach and causing friction, particularly

332. p.183) Likewise, British Catholics were also unsupportive. (Harris. *Supra* note 301. pp.344–345).

347 Anderson. *Supra* note 93. p.184.

348 'Safvet Pasha to Musurus Pasha' (12th October 1876) in British Parliamentary Papers *XC.1* *Supra* note 311. pp.459.

349 Elliot had met with the Sultan and demanded action, although British intervention would be opposed by other powers, particularly Austria-Hungary (Moneypenny and Buckle *Supra* note 304. p.69).

350 'Disraeli to Lady Chesterfield' (12th October 1876) in Disraeli. *Supra* note 323. p.98.

351 'Prince Gorchakov to Count Schouvaloff' (7 November 1876) in British Parliamentary Papers *XC.1* *Supra* note 311. pp.720–722.

352 Shannon. *Supra* note 332. p.193.

353 Palmer. *Supra* note 22. p.146.

354 'The Eastern Question' *The Times*. (23 December 1876).

355 Britain and Austria shared the key goal of maintaining the Ottoman Empire while Russia remained the biggest obstacle to peace. Alexander II had made it clear that Russia would act unilaterally if the Conference failed to achieve the reforms Russia deemed necessary (Anderson. *Supra* note 93. p.191).

over Bulgaria. Eventually, a programme was decided on, whereby Bosnia, Herzegovina and Bulgaria would become autonomous within the Ottoman Empire, and the Porte would offer amnesty to all Christians and disarm the Muslim irregulars.[356]

The Porte was already opposed to the conference, arguing that no state had the right to invade Ottoman territory or meddle in internal Ottoman affairs.[357] As such, while the conference was ongoing, the Sultan proclaimed a new constitution that was insufficient from a Russian perspective.[358] The Porte hoped to retain British support and knew Russia would have little support from the other powers.[359] Accordingly, the Porte then rejected the conference's proposals, arguing that the new constitution was sufficient.[360]

The assembled powers were outraged but too divided to organise an effective response.[361] Disraeli's key concern was Russian intervention that risked destroying the Ottoman Empire, particularly Russian control of the Turkish straits and threatening British interests in the region, potentially as far as British India.[362] There were still many Britons opposed to Ottoman atrocities[363] but Russia had

356 Rodogno. *Supra* note 50. pp.162–163.

357 'The Eastern Question' *The Times.* (23 December 1876).

358 Although the constitution enshrined equality among all Ottoman subjects and provided for an elected parliament, it provided no autonomy for Ottoman Christians and mainly served as a proclamation of Ottoman patriotism. See Cleveland, William. *A History of the Modern Middle East* (Oxford, 2004) pp.85–86.

359 Pears. *Supra* note 288. pp.23–24.

360 'The Eastern Question' *The Times.* (19 January 1877).

361 Although Russia was keen to go to war with the Ottoman Empire, it wanted to do so as a European representative rather than unilaterally. However, Britain was particularly suspicious of Russian aims and contingency plans were formed whereby if the Conference failed and Russia occupied Bulgaria, a fleet would be sent to safeguard British interests in the region (Gathorne-Hardy, Gathorne. *Gathorne Hardy, First Earl of Cranbrooke: A Memoir with Extracts from His Diary and Correspondence* (London, 1910) p.377).

362 Heraclides and Dialla. *Supra* note 27. p.152.

363 Notably, just before the Constantinople Conference, The National Conference of the Eastern Question was held in St James' Hall, London where one thousand delegates listened to Gladstone demanding intervention 'as an absolute necessity' while the Duke of Westminster urged British cooperation with Russia and for Britain to dispatch its forces to coerce Ottoman compliance ('The Conference on the Eastern Question' *Irish Times.* (9 December 1876)). Gladstone wrote another pamphlet pushing for British action given Bulgarian massacres were 'key to the Eastern Question' (Gladstone, William. *Lessons in Massacre* (London, 1877) p.29). However, this had far less of an impact than *Bulgarian Horrors* as the atrocitarian movement was losing momentum. Britain's failure to resolve the Eastern Question raised domestic British criticism, with the Conference of Constantinople being criticised for failing to ameliorate Ottoman internal governance or provide for the security of Europe (UK House of Lords Debate 20 February 1877 Vol. 232 Col.660).

little support from the other powers. Ignatiev toured the Great Powers, seeking their support in coercing the Ottoman Empire into enacting the reforms proposed at the Constantinople Conference,[364] but Russian isolation caused the Porte to reject the proposals. On the 24 April 1877, Russia declared war on the Ottoman Empire, arguing that Russian intervention was necessary to protect Ottoman Christians.[365] Although the Great Powers refused to support Russia, the Porte's refusal to enact meaningful reform ensured the Ottoman Empire stood alone.[366]

The Russo-Turkish war was exactly what Britain had feared. The Suez canal remained a key British concern, while Disraeli feared Russia would capture Constantinople before taking the Suez Canal[367] and despite her prior sympathy for Balkan Christians, Queen Victoria was adamant that Britain's responsibilities as a Great Power necessitated its willingness to fight to prevent Russian occupation of Constantinople.[368] British public outrage at Ottoman actions in Bulgaria meant that Britain could only remain neutral while keeping a close eye on its interests in the East.[369] Gladstone was increasingly politically isolated[370] while Queen Victoria was alarmed by reports of Russian soldiers committing atrocities against Ottomans[371] although the prevention of further atrocities offered Britain a humanitarian justification for intervening. The Russo-Turkish war ended with the Treaty of San Stefano that was severe on the Porte[372] and threatened Austro-Hungarian interests.[373]

---

364 'The New Russian Ultimatum' *Manchester Guardian.* (*14 March 1877*).

365 'Russian Declaration of War against Turkey' *Manchester Guardian.* (25 April 1877).

366 Schulz, Matthias. 'The guarantees of humanity: the Concert of Europe and the origins of the Russo-Ottoman War of 1877' in Simms, Brendan and Trim, D. J.B (Eds.) *Humanitarian Intervention: A History* (Cambridge, 2011) p.202.

367 Moneypenny and Buckle *Supra* note 304. pp.84–85.

368 'Queen Victoria to Disraeli' (25 April 1877) in Ibid. p.133.

369 Ibid. p.134.

370 Gladstone sought to introduce resolutions in the House of Commons that condemned Ottoman brutality and sought to invoke Canning's intervention in Greece as a basis for securing Ottoman reform 'for the purposes of humanity and justice, for effectual defence against intrigue, and for the peace of the world.' (UK House of Commons Debate 30 April 1877 Vol. 234 Col.101). However, the resolution was defeated. (Mr Gladstone's Resolutions' *Irish Times.* (16 May 1877)).

371 'Disraeli to Queen Victoria' (16 July 1877) in Moneypenny and Buckle *Supra* note 304. p.151.

372 Notably, the Treaty of San Stefano gave independence to Romania, Serbia and Montenegro, free passage of the Straits for Russian bound ships and for a large, autonomous Bulgaria with access to the Aegean Sea. See the Treaty of San Stefano. (1878) https://pages.uoregon.edu/kimball/1878mr17.SanStef.trt.htm Accessed 10th March 2024.

373 As soon as Russia began pushing towards San Stefano, Austria-Hungary had begun marshalling its forces until it learned of Britain's fleet being deployed (Pears. *Supra* note 288. p.31). Likewise, After the Treaty of San Stefano, Austro-Hungarian fears of a Russian

The deteriorating relations between Austria-Hungary and Russia led Bismarck to mediate, ever mindful of the need to maintain French isolation.[374] The Congress of Berlin was then convened to redraw the Treaty of San Stefano and was attended by the Great Powers. Although Russia's gains from San Stefano were reduced, the Treaty of Berlin still represented an overall Russian victory.[375]

## 3.5 *Humanitarian Intervention and Bulgaria*

It was only with the Treaty of Paris that the Ottoman Empire was formally admitted to the rights and duties of European Public Law[376] although in practice it was still seen as inferior by the other powers. This offered a key justification for intervention: the Ottoman Empire could be interfered with in a manner that would be seen as unacceptable to a 'civilised' nation, thus permitting a right of intervention.[377] While nineteenth century European jurists accepted that individuals possessed certain rights, they generally rejected the idea that the abuse of such rights justified intervention but the atrocitarians saw the Ottoman Empire as a special case, with Ottoman moral inferiority giving Europeans a right to intervene in protecting Christians.[378] This was especially promoted by Russia with Gorchakov arguing that Ottoman integrity and independence was subordinate to the 'guarantees demanded by humanity, Christian Europe and interests of peace'.[379] While many British politicians highlighted the atrocities committed by Bulgarian Christians against Muslims, these were probably intended to justify British non-intervention rather than any genuine sympathy for the Ottomans.[380] Nonetheless, when Britain sought to use force in aid of the Ottoman Empire it was mainly for strategic, rather than humanitarian reasons.

It would be a mistake to overemphasise the humanitarian aspect of European involvement given that it was primarily driven by sympathy for Christians

satellite state on its borders intensified, leading Emperor Francis Joseph II to warn Alexander II that Russia could not unilaterally decide the Eastern Question (Anderson. *Supra* note 93. p.200).

374 Shannon. *Supra* note 332. p.217.

375 Anderson. *Supra* note 93. p.216.

376 Treaty of Paris. (1856) Article VII. https://content.ecf.org.il/files/M00934_TreatyOfParis1856English.pdf Accessed 10th March 2024.

377 Heraclides and Dialla. *Supra* note 27. pp.46–47.

378 Rodogno. *Supra* note 50. pp.158–159.

379 'Prince Gortchakow to Count Schouvaloff' (7 November 1876) in British Parliamentary Papers *XC.1* *Supra* note 311. p.722.

380 'Disraeli to Benjamin Austin' (1830) in Ibid. pp.158–159.

rather than a universal humanitarian impulse: the Great Powers left Bulgarian Muslims at the mercy of their Christian neighbours after the Russo-Turkish war.[381] Such indifference to the plight of Bulgarian Muslims casts doubts upon the humanitarian commitment of the European Powers. In addition, European policy makers at the time did not see the intervention as humanitarian.[382] The Great Powers were acting to maintain stability, convening the Conference of Constantinople but humiliating the Porte. The Conference certainly involved a large amount of interference in domestic Ottoman affairs, but the Great Powers' aims were aimed at maintaining peace but appreciated the role of humanitarianism, if only for pragmatic ends. Salisbury was instructed to demand justice from the Porte for the Bulgarian atrocities[383] and Britain highlighted that the Porte needed to ensure justice for Bulgarian Christians for practical reasons, if nothing else.[384] This makes sense, given Russia's unilateral invasion of the Ottoman Empire stoked British Russophobia and enabled Disraeli to avert intervention, although he failed to protect his political career.[385]

The issue of British humanitarian intervention in relation to the Bulgarian atrocities is difficult given that there was so much division on the subject. *The Times* generally supported non-intervention while highlighting the balance of power could necessitate British intervention[386] while the liberal *Daily News* highlighted that without British intervention (or at least ending aid to the Porte), Russia would unilaterally intervene to protect the Bulgarians.[387] The public was similarly divided and support for intervention showed marked differences depending on background. Support was weak among Jews,[388] Catholics,[389] Disraeli's Tories and the Church of England[390] but stronger among Liberals, the labour movement and outside the Home Counties.[391] Although some Liberals merely wanted Britain to end its support of the Ottoman Empire,[392] others supported more proactive measures. MacGahan

381 'The Tranquilisation of Roumelia' *Manchester Guardian.* (11th September 1878).
382 Heraclides and Dialla. *Supra* note 27. p.162.
383 'The Earl of Derby to the Marquis of Salisbury' (24 November 1876) in British Parliamentary Papers XC.1 *Supra* note 311. p.14.
384 'The Earl of Derby to the Marquis of Salisbury' (24 November 1876) Ibid. p.15.
385 Bass. *Supra* note 104. p.237.
386 *The Times* (23 May 1876).
387 *Daily News.* (23 June 1876).
388 Shannon. *Supra* note 332. p.183.
389 Harris. *Supra* note 301. pp.344–345.
390 Bass. *Supra* note 104. p.276.
391 Bass. *Supra* note 104. pp.276–277.
392 Harris. *Supra* note 301. p.128.

saw no solution for the atrocities without European intervention,[393] while the *Manchester Guardian* highlighted that it was a European duty to end the struggle should it 'degenerate into savage warfare'.[394]

The atrocitarians' success is debatable: Britain pressured the Porte to reform its administration of Bulgaria but it is unclear if Westminster was forced by British public outrage.[395] By 1878, even Derby admitted that deploying the British fleet to Constantinople might be in 'the interests of humanity',[396] while Disraeli was politically hindered by his indifference to the Bulgarians and was subsequently removed from office in 1880 due to an expanded electorate, a powerful press and humanitarian campaigners.[397] Schulz notes how the strength of the atrocitarian movement 'overwhelmed British jingoists' and forced the government to consider the British public's views.[398] Britain's reaction to the Russo-Turkish war demonstrates how nuanced the humanitarian impulse was, with Ottoman atrocities and rejection of British advice after the Conference of Constantinople meaning it could no longer rely on British protection while public opposition prevented the Tories from adopting their usual pro-Ottoman policies.[399] The prospect of Russian expansion threatened Britain's strategic interests enough that British public sympathy for the Bulgarians altered matters. According to Bass, Disraeli only managed to prevent British humanitarian intervention due to Russia's belligerence and fears of Russian expansionism allowed the government to reassert control and prevent British intervention.[400] Likewise, Harris argues that strong governmental condemnation of the atrocities in the summer of 1876 would at least have prevented English unrest.[401] There is certainly merit in this, with Disraeli's indifference to the atrocities being a key catalyst in the atrocitarian movement. It must be noted that Britain's interests were to support the Ottoman Empire against Russia that Disraeli was prevented from doing due to public horror over the atrocities in Bulgaria.[402]

---

393 MacGahan, J.A. Turkish Atrocities in Bulgaria (London, 1876), p.75.

394 'Latest News: The Impending War' *Manchester Guardian* (11th July 1876).

395 Rodogno claims that public opinion alone did not change Britain's foreign policy (Rodogno. *Supra* note 50. p.141) while Harris agrees the agitation did not unilaterally force Britain to push for peace negotiations, but it was 'probably a strong influence (Harris. *Supra* note 301. pp.332–333).

396 UK House of Lords Debate 31 January 1878 Vol. 237 Col.690.

397 Bass. *Supra* note 104. p.236.

398 Schulz. *Supra* note 366. p.194.

399 Trachtenberg. *Supra* note 13. p.25.

400 Bass. *Supra* note 104. p.237.

401 Harris. *Supra* note 301. p.329.

402 Hupchick. *Supra* note 63. p.264.

Nowhere was the clash over interventionism more evident than between Gladstone and Disraeli. It was common knowledge that Disraeli and Gladstone were reliving the humanitarian debate during the Greek War of Independence.[403] Both Disraeli and Castlereagh focussed on Britain's security interests (although Disraeli was mainly concerned with Britain's imperial interests while Castlereagh saw Britain's fate as bound to Europe), Disraeli was aware of the parallels and wrote that Russian occupation of Constantinople would lead to another Navarino.[404]

By contrast, Gladstone channelled the Philhellene movement and admired Canning's foreign policy, viewing him as an exemplary Foreign Secretary,[405] 'one of the most brilliant names of our political history'.[406] When arguing on the need for morality in foreign policy, Gladstone extolled the 'great example of Mr. Canning'[407] while praising Byron and the Philhellenes for bringing 'the dawn of emancipation' to the Greeks.[408] Gladstone was not opposed to intervention, provided it was like Canning's in that it was 'rare, deliberate, decisive in character and effectual'.[409] Gladstone also claimed that there were situations where abuses were so egregious that 'sympathy refuses to be confined by the rules [...] of international law'.[410] Overall, he favoured a Canning-like agreement with Russia to solve the Eastern Question.[411] Gladstone's humanitarian impulse cannot be denied and he frequently used humanitarian arguments to criticise the Ottomans for their actions in Bulgaria.[412] Both Gladstone and Disraeli failed in their desired resolution to the Eastern Question. Gladstone was unsuccessful in invoking British intervention in Bulgaria while Disraeli

403 Bass. *Supra* note 104. p.310. This was also remarked in an editorial in *The Times* drawing strong parallels between the Greek and Bulgarian rebellions, remarking that there would be far less surprise at Ottoman atrocities in Bulgaria if the public remembered the Greek atrocities that led to Navarino (*The Times*. (14 August 1876)).

404 'Disraeli to Lord Salisbury' (1 December 1876) in Moneypenny and Buckle *Supra* note 304. p.106.

405 Speech by Gladstone (27 June 1850) in Bassett, Arthur. *Gladstone Speeches: Descriptive Index and Bibliography* (London, 1916) p.147.

406 Gladstone, William. *The Hellenic Factor in the Eastern Problem with Other Tracts* (Leipzig, 1877) p.24.

407 Gladstone. *Supra* note 363. p.29.

408 Gladstone. *Supra* note 406. p.52.

409 Speech by Gladstone (27 June 1850) in Bassett. *Supra* note 405. p.148.

410 Gladstone. *Supra* note 298. p.30.

411 Shannon. *Supra* note 332. p.238.

412 However, he differed from the Philhellenes in one critical area: Gladstone drew on public support, turning the Bulgarian Horrors into a mass phenomenon, unlike the privileged Philhellenes (Rodogno. *Supra* note 50. p.15). This was vital given Britain's expanded electorate and mass media, where public outrage could be channelled into votes.

failed in his efforts to prevent a Russo-Turkish war or to support the Ottoman Empire.[413] Britain risked being forced to intervene and it was only that Russian expansion posed such a threat to British interests that humanitarian concerns were overridden. Had Russia not gone to war, mounting public pressure could well have pushed Britain into a second Navarino.[414]

Russia used explicitly humanitarian language in declaring war on the Ottoman Empire and the outrage in Russia was genuine.[415] It is arguable that the Panslavists had little impact on Russian foreign policy as claimed by Rodogno[416] and Pavlowitch.[417] Westwood highlights that Alexander was influenced more by his Minister for War than the Panslavists, but even the Tsar had to pay attention to his subjects' outrage at the Porte's treatment of Balkan Christians.[418] It can even be argued the British atrocitarian movement helped induce Russian intervention, with Britain's traditional role as the Porte's guardian being compromised by its own domestic agitation.

British public opinion prevented Britain from supporting the Porte against Russia,[419] forcing Britain to push for Ottoman reforms and jeopardising British protection of the Ottoman Empire altogether.[420] Many Britons were unconvinced by Russia's humanitarian claims with Queen Victoria nothing that Russia was as barbarous as the Ottomans and was engaging in war for selfish rather than altruistic reasons.[421] Initially Russia sought to avoid war, with Gorchakov fearing continued atrocities risking Panslavist fervour dragging Russia into war with the Porte that would force a strong reaction from the other Great Powers.[422] On this basis, Gorchakov consistently sought multilateral European action to induce Ottoman reform rather than unilateral Russian intervention.[423] Ottoman intransigence meant the Porte stood alone when

413 Harris. *Supra* note 301. p.335.

414 Bass. *Supra* note 104. p.312.

415 As evidenced by the mass relief efforts in aid of the Bulgarians while Britain's ambassador warned London that further Ottoman atrocities risked forcing Russian intervention 'Lord Loftus to the Earl of Derby' (16 August 1876) in British Parliamentary Papers XC.1 *Supra* note 311. pp.44–45.

416 Rodogno. *Supra* note 50. p.141.

417 Pavlowitch. *Supra* note 285 p.151.

418 Westwood. *Supra* note 38. p.108.

419 Anderson. *Supra* note 93. p.188.

420 Letter to Lady Chesterfield (12th October 1876) in Disraeli. *Supra* note 323. (p.98).

421 'Queen Victoria to Disraeli' (27 June 1877) in Moneypenny and Buckle *Supra* note 304. p.148.

422 Schulz. *Supra* note 366. p.191.

423 See *Supra* note 326.

St Petersburg declared war and although Russia unilaterally declared war, no Great Power opposed it.[424]

Overall, save for Britain, Russia's intervention was treated with 'benign neutrality'.[425] There was established evidence of Ottoman atrocities and Russia used force as a last resort, ensuring Russia's intervention was effectively mandated by the key international authority of the time, the Concert of Europe.[426] Once the war began, the military took control and ensured Russian humanitarian claims were eclipsed by imperialism until reined in at the Congress of Berlin.

Rodogno argues that by the 1870s, the Great Powers agreed that while intervention could take place to prevent massacres within the Ottoman Empire, this was subordinate to collective security interests.[427] This explains why no collective intervention took place to protect the Bulgarians as this threatened British interests, while Austria-Hungary had its own concerns in the region.[428] Russia used humanitarian justifications for its intervention,[429] which was believed by many Russians who supported protecting Christians from Ottoman brutality and they were genuinely surprised that Disraeli could stand behind the Ottomans.[430] This ignores Russia's strategic benefits from the conflict and Russia remained an absolute monarchy, mitigating the pressures of public opinion. Despite its claims to be acting in the name of religion and humanity, Russia was seeking to achieve its longstanding aim of expanding its geopolitical interests.[431] Heraclides and Dialla note that the Russian intervention was different from the interventions in Greece and Syria as it involved full scale war, it was carried out unilaterally (albeit with the benevolent neutrality of the other powers, save Britain), and also involved the greater role of the press and a final high level peace conference.[432]

Although British suffrage was limited, it was a democracy nonetheless and there was genuine outrage at the Bulgarian atrocities, as evidenced by support for Gladstone, public meetings and the petitions received by the Foreign Office.[433] Such mass opposition to Britain's foreign policy worried Disraeli

424 See *Supra* note 366.
425 Heraclides and Dialla. *Supra* note 27. p.225.
426 Schulz. *Supra* note 366. p.203.
427 Rodogno. *Supra* note 50. p.168.
428 See *Supra* note 298.
429 'Russian Declaration of War against Turkey' *Manchester Guardian.* (25 April 1877).
430 Pears. *Supra* note 288. pp.33–35.
431 Woolsey, Theodore. *America's Foreign Policy* (New York, 1898) p.74.
432 Heraclides and Dialla. *Supra* note 27. p.163.
433 See Bass. *Supra* note 104. pp.273–276.

and induced Britain to demand Ottoman action. No British humanitarian intervention took place, likely due to Russia's intervention that discredited the atrocitarian movement: British public support for Balkan Christians did not mean compromising Britain's interests and the extent of Britain's humanitarianism is doubtful.

Overall, the Great Powers response to the Eastern Question was far from purely humanitarian. Britain and Austria-Hungary operated primarily to curb Russia's desire to expand while Germany sought to maintain Austro-Russian relations. However, the humanitarian dimension cannot be overlooked. The mass public outrage in Britain and Russia did not drastically alter foreign policy but neither could either government discount public opinion, particularly in Britain. Ultimately, as with Navarino, humanitarianism shaped foreign policy, but both responses were subordinate to national strategic interests.

## 4 Humanitarian Intervention in the Nineteenth Century

Humanitarian intervention has evolved but it would be a mistake to see humanitarianism as being the main factor in interventionism. This was apparent throughout the nineteenth century, with the Great Powers having strategic goals that guided their attitude to the Eastern Question. The impact of humanitarianism cannot be discounted, with all three interventions ending atrocities while enjoying support from the local inhabitants.[434] However, at no point did any state act against its own geopolitical interests and the cases analysed in this chapter were always conducted when useful to the intervening power.

Over the course of the nineteenth century, the Great Powers were vigilant in their primary motivation of maintaining the balance of power. The start of the nineteenth century saw 'un-humanitarian' intervention as the norm.[435] Such a system favoured by Metternich collapsed with the intervention in Navarino, where military force was used in support of rebels rather than an established empire. This was a striking development[436] and continued during the nineteenth century, with humanitarian language being used by European powers to justify helping rebels in Greece,[437]

434 Heraclides and Dialla. *Supra* note 27. p.226.

435 See Stapleton, Augustus. *Intervention and Non-Intervention or the Foreign Policy of Great Britain 1790–1865* (London, 1866) pp.28–31.

436 Heraclides and Dialla. *Supra* note 27. p.106.

437 Treaty of London (1827) Preamble https://sourcebooks.fordham.edu/mod/1827gktreaty.asp Accessed 10th March 2024.

Syria[438] and Bulgaria.[439] In this way, humanitarian intervention became widely (although not unanimously) accepted as a principle of pre-UN Charter customary international law.[440]

Public opinion also had a role in nineteenth century humanitarian intervention.[441] Media impact was considerable, informing the public outside of government channels and increasing demands for intervention. This was especially the case in Britain that saw a rise in press freedom and mass media, which combined with democratisation to reduce Westminster's ability to decide unilaterally foreign policy.[442] While the Philhellenes were an elite (rather than mass phenomenon),[443] British public opinion nonetheless prevented Britain aiding the Porte, with Greek autonomy satisfying both British strategic interests and public sentiment. The British public was also not reflexively anti-Ottoman as British support of the Ottoman Empire against Russia in the Crimean War was initially popular and the British public was often more belligerent than Westminster.[444]

Initially, Castlereagh who was ideologically opposed to intervention, held British and Russian outrage over Greece in check,[445] while Alexander I's opposition to revolution often overrode his sympathy for fellow Orthodox Christians.[446] This changed after their respective deaths. Canning became Britain's Foreign Secretary and eventually Prime Minister, while Nicholas I succeeded as Tsar. Canning knew Britain could not continue supporting the Ottoman Empire as a bulwark against Russia while an autonomous Greece would satisfy British strategic interests and mitigate against Russian expansion.[447] Meanwhile, though a counter-revolutionary, Nicholas I was hostile to the Ottoman Empire as well as supportive of Orthodox Christianity inducing Russian involvement in the Greek question. Overall, as evidenced by the Treaty of London, allied involvement in the Greek conflict resulted from both political and humanitarian concerns. This was even more evident during the Bulgarian crisis where Britain's increasingly enfranchised male working class

---

438 'Protocol of a Conference held the 3 August. (1860) Preamble. In British Parliamentary Papers LXVIII.17. *Supra* note 168. p.36.

439 'Russian Declaration of War against Turkey' *Manchester Guardian.* (25 April 1877).

440 Fonteyne. *Supra* note 130. pp.234–235.

441 Heraclides and Dialla. *Supra* note 27. p.228.

442 See *Supra* note 97 to *Supra* note 103.

443 Bass. *Supra* note 104. p.274.

444 Badem. *Supra* note 145. p.323.

445 See *Supra* note 13.

446 See *Supra* note 38.

447 See *Supra* note 76.

combined with mass media to render the government even more susceptible to public pressure.[448]

It must also be noted that the concept of nineteenth century sovereignty was not seen as absolute and even at its zenith, the Westphalian model did not provide for either total sovereignty or an 'unconditional principle of non-intervention'.[449] Intervention at the time was seen as an extension of the legal principle of international community and an expression of sovereignty rather than an interference in the sovereignty of others or a breach of the norm of non-intervention.[450] This can also be seen in the work of contemporary jurists.

Wheaton wrote in 1880 that sovereignty ensured states had the right to pursue their interests by lawful means, but that the rights of other states limited this.[451] However, Wheaton also highlighted that a fundamental legal principle was non-interference in the affairs of other sovereigns, but there were numerous examples of intervention 'in the interests of humanity' or to maintain the balance of power.[452] Nonetheless, Wheaton specified that international law permitted the 1827 intervention in Greece due to the 'general interests of humanity'.[453] Hall noted in the late nineteenth century, that international law focused on the relations between states and that a state's treatment of its people did not factor into this.[454] Nonetheless, Hall deemed interventions carried out against cruelty needed authorisation by the 'whole body of civilised states'.[455] Oppenheim noted that 'many jurists' supported intervention in the name of humanity, but this is debatable.[456] Nonetheless, he concluded that both public opinion and the great powers support such interventions and

448 While Russophobia precluded British intervention, British outrage over the Bulgarian atrocities was enough to prevent Britain supporting the Porte against Russia (Shaw and Shaw. *Supra* note 156. p.183). Despite its authoritarianism, Russia could not ignore public opinion, with Alexander I noting the views of his subjects risked forcing his hand (Temperely. *Supra* note 112. p.60).

449 Trim, D.J.B 'Conclusions: Humanitarian intervention in historical perspective' in Simms, Brendan and Trim, D.J.B (Eds.) *Humanitarian Intervention: A History* (Cambridge, 2011) p.384.

450 Kroll, Stefan. 'The legal justification of international intervention' in Klose, Fabian. (Ed.) *The Emergence of Humanitarian Intervention: Ideas and Practice from the Nineteenth Century to the Present* (Cambridge, 2018) pp.73–74.

451 Wheaton *Supra* note 118. p.90.

452 Ibid. pp.91–92.

453 Ibid. p.103.

454 Hall, William Edward. *International Law* (Oxford, 1880) p.245.

455 Ibid. p.247.

456 Oppenheim, Lassa *International Law: A Treatise, Vol. I-Peace* (London, 1905) pp.186–187.

that international law may yet recognise a right of collective intervention for humanitarian reasons.[457]

Intervention in the nineteenth century was notable from a legal perspective, as it was so heavily selective. International law at the time prioritised European states, with the sovereignty of non-European states like the Ottoman Empire or China being limited.[458] Despite the utility of the Ottoman Empire to the Great Powers, they did not see it as their sovereign equal despite its long history of involvement and alliances with European powers.[459] The Porte was certainly seen as a power to be brought within 'civilised nations', but was regarded as less civilised than its European counterparts were.[460] It was not until 1856 that the Ottoman Empire was accepted into the Family of Nations in the Treaty of Paris and even then, this was mostly nominal.[461] This outsider status permitted intervention in the Ottoman Empire in a way different to those of a European state.[462] European influence within the Ottoman Empire had its roots centuries ago in the Ottoman Capitulations.[463] The Capitulations ensured diplomatic equality was nominal and these continued until the twentieth century, demonstrating the Ottoman Empire's inferior status under international law.

This meant the legitimacy of the Ottoman Empire was problematic, given European legal scholars did not see the Ottoman Empire as part of the Family of Nations but as backward and thus unprotected by the Law of Nations.[464] Consequently, they broadly saw intervention in 'civilised' (European) nations as illegal but accepted it in respect of intervention in 'uncivilised' nations

457 Ibid.

458 Heraclides and Dialla. *Supra* note 27. p.32. For international law and its applicability to China, Japan and the Ottoman Empire, see Ibid. pp.39–49.

459 Traditionally, the Porte had taken its own approach to international relations and in many ways, was ahead of European states in areas like diplomatic immunity while the Quran's rules ensured the Porte placed a premium on adhering to treaties. Initially the Ottoman perceptions of their superiority meant diplomacy was not seen as negotiations between equals (Quatert. *Supra* note 36. p.77) but Ottoman decline forced it to adopt European standards of international law and diplomacy (Horowitz, Richard. 'International Law and State Transformation in China, Siam, and the Ottoman Empire during the Nineteenth Century' *Journal of World History* (Vol.15, No.4, Dec.2004) p.451).

460 Segesser. *Supra* note 117. p.71.

461 Palabiyik. *Supra* note 139. pp.233–234.

462 See Heraclides and Dialla. *Supra* note 27. pp.46–47.

463 As Ottoman power declined, the Capitulations were used for flagrant European interference in Ottoman internal affairs including the adoption of Ottoman minorities as protégés by European nations (Brown. *Supra* note 160. p.73).

464 Rodogno. *Supra* note 50. p.48.

such as the Ottoman Empire.[465] The Ottoman Empire witnessed numerous atrocities during the nineteenth century with European humanitarians and interventionist governments seeing such brutality as a result of the Porte's backwardness and seeing their own civilisation as inherently superior.[466] Nonetheless, it must be noted that it was not just a case of intervention being used to help those deemed white and Christian, given force was also used to help Jewish minorities and free black Africans from the slave trade.[467]

Although the Ottoman Empire was weaker than the Great Powers, it was still a powerful empire but lacked legal protection despite being scarcely more repressive or backward than, Russia for example, which was seen as a full member of the Concert of Europe,[468] even it was seen as alien by the rest of Europe and swung between periods of rapprochement and alienation.[469] Nonetheless, even after its admittance into the Family of Nations in 1856, the *de facto* inferiority of the Porte was evident in the continued Western interference in Ottoman internal affairs[470] while there was little uproar over European atrocities in their colonies or within Russia. This led to some strange results, with authoritarian Russia benefitting from Gladstone's humanitarianism while the Duke of Westminster sought for 'cordial cooperation' with Russia and using force to 'coerce the Turk'.[471] The selectiveness and mixed motives of nineteenth

465 France's Benjamin Constant argued that the Ottoman's brutality and lack of regular succession meant they had no legitimacy: 'Do we not offend [the name of] legitimacy when we speak in its name of violence and crime?' (Constant. *Supra* note 109. p.15). Britain's Richard Cobden argued that it was in Britain's interests to refrain from intervention in the Ottoman Empire and opposed the idea of Britain being responsible for preserving world peace (Cobden, Richard. *The Political Writings of Richard Cobden,* Vol.I, Part II (London, 1835)). Cobden also argued that international law's prohibition on intervention did not apply to the barbaric Ottoman Empire which he saw as suffering from 'a chronic disease of the heart' (Letter to Mr. Tait from Richard Cobden, Esq. (The 'Manchester Manufacturer') on the Eastern Question *Tait's Edinburgh Magazine* (February 1841) p.79). Likewise, Churchill claimed that the principle of non-intervention did not apply to the Ottoman Empire (Churchill. *Supra* note 153. pp.8–9).

466 Rodogno. *Supra* note 50. p.12.

467 Kroll. *Supra* note 450.

468 This was a point made by the Porte who argued that the Christian powers did not attempt to prevent Russia from deporting its subjects to Siberia (Rodogno. *Supra* note 50. p.69) No humanitarian missions took place to save oppressed minorities within Russia, aside from diplomatic representations made on Russia's oppression of Poles (Stowell. *Supra* note 137. p.89). Nor was intervention undertaken against Britain, France or Belgium for atrocities committed in their colonies. (See Heraclides and Dialla. *Supra* note 27. p.22).

469 Sixsmith, Martin, with Sixsmith, Daniel. *Putin and the Return of History: How the Kremlin Rekindled the Cold War* (Dublin, 2024) pp.84–85.

470 Palabiyik. *Supra* note 139. pp.233–234.

471 'The Conference on the Eastern Question' *Irish Times.* (9 December 1876).

century humanitarian interventions is undeniable but the interventions in the Ottoman Empire were still 'humanitarian' as they had the result of protecting civilians from Ottoman atrocities or inaction.[472]

Although there was a broad acceptance of intervention among the nineteenth century's Great Powers, the underlying balance of power remained critical in order for humanitarian intervention's continued existence. Key in this was multilateralism. The Great Powers could tolerate intervention, provided the intervener did so with their consent and without altering the balance of power. This can be clearly seen in the intervention in Syria, where Ottoman authorities carried out most of the work, while French forces were able to operate with a high degree of independence. As the French were operating with European consent and oversight (particularly by Britain which feared a prolonged expedition turning into an occupation), their actions were unopposed by European nations.[473]

By contrast, where a state acted unilaterally and threatened stability, the other Great Powers, regardless of professed humanitarianism, would oppose it. This is especially evident with Russia's claims to be the protector of Ottoman Christians being seen as such a threat to the balance of power that it led to the Crimean War where Britain and France supported the Porte.[474] Likewise, despite Ottoman atrocities against Bulgarians, the resulting Russo-Turkish war risked such destabilisation that Russian gains in the Treaty of San Stefano were reduced at the Treaty of Berlin.[475] It is especially critical to highlight that this does not establish a norm of unilateral humanitarian intervention.[476] Any evolution of humanitarian intervention in the nineteenth century cannot be disassociated from multilateralism.

There were some marked similarities with the contemporary era, with a centralised body of the world's most powerful states making collective decisions to maintain geopolitical equilibrium. Likewise, similar arguments relating to sovereignty, ulterior motives and moral responsibility were also evident in respect to nineteenth century humanitarian intervention.[477] It operated at a time when the use of force was more permissible under international law

472 Bazyler. Michael. 'Re-examining the Doctrine of Humanitarian Intervention in Light of the Atrocities in Kampuchea and Ethiopia' *Stanford Journal of International Law* (Vol.23, 1987) p.583.

473 Bass. *Supra* note 104. p.231.

474 See *Supra* note 145.

475 See *Supra* note 373 and 374.

476 Franck, Thomas and Rodley, Nigel. 'After Bangladesh: The Law of Humanitarian Intervention by Military Force' *American Journal of International Law* (Vol. 67, 1973) p.282.

477 Bass. *Supra* note 104. p.5.

than today, and at a time when 'civilised' states exercise[d] de facto tutorial rights over uncivilised ones'.[478] Although members of the Concert of Europe would act against other Great Powers to prevent them becoming too powerful (as in the Crimean War or the 1878 Treaty of Berlin), smaller states were created and abolished in the interests of the Great Powers.[479] As nominal as sovereign equality can be today, it was even weaker in the nineteenth century.[480] Humanitarian intervention was invoked by the Great Powers as a justification for the use of force, as evidenced by the Treaty of London, 3 August 1860 Protocol and the statements of Canning[481] and Napoleon III.[482] These were multilateral with a joint allied fleet at Navarino while the French intervention in Syria operated according to strict parameters under the auspices of the other Great Powers. By contrast, Russia's intervention in Bulgaria was unilateral and therefore endangered the balance of power. Overall, humanitarian intervention in the nineteenth century saw similarities to contemporary interventions, being opaque, selective, and riddled with mixed motives. The problems of humanitarian intervention in the nineteenth century and the balance between humanitarianism, sovereignty and geopolitics continue to resonate. Nineteenth century international law accepted humanitarian intervention under certain circumstances; but neither did it lead to numerous cases of humanitarian intervention.[483] The balance of power was the main motivator in European acceptance of intervention and where intervention threatened stability, the other Great Powers would resist it. Intervention to save others would be accepted where it did not disturb the balance of power, with the consent of the Great Powers being critical. Although selective and with mixed motives, humanitarian intervention in the Ottoman Empire had humanitarian

---

478 Franck and Rodley. *Supra* note 476. p.281.

479 See *Supra* note 5 and Bartlett. *Supra* note 30. p.145.

480 Even an empire as large and advanced as China was forced to sign a series of treaties that saw it forced to conduct relations with Western powers on subordinate terms (Wang, Dong. 'The Discourse of Unequal Treaties in Modern China' Pacific Affairs (Vol.76, No.3 Fall 2003) p.402). Likewise, although the Ottoman Empire was admitted as an apparently full member of the Concert of Europe (and thus giving it the rights and responsibilities of contemporary international law), it was still subject to domestic interference and coercion in a manner which would be unacceptable to other European nations. While states such as the Ottoman Empire and China had their sovereignty recognised by European states, they were not seen as equal (Donnelly, Jack. 'Genocide and Humanitarian Intervention' *Journal of Human Rights* (Vol.1, No.1, 2002) p.98).

481 Stapleton. *Supra* note 70. p.393.

482 Edwards, Richard. *La Syria 1840–1862* (Paris, 1862) p.197.

483 Heraclides and Dialla. *Supra* note 27. p.225.

aims.[484] The fact humanitarian motives were used as a justification was a major development in international law and crucial in analysing humanitarian intervention's evolution.

484 This is highlighted by Franck and Rodley who note that although European nations intervened in the Ottoman Empire had self-interested reasons for intervening in the Ottoman Empire, their humanitarian motives should 'probably not be dismissed as bogus' (Franck and Rodley. *Supra* note 476. p.281). Likewise, Heraclides and Dialla highlight that while humanitarian intervention in the nineteenth century operated on a double standard, the overriding motive of European publics (and some policy makers) was humanitarian. (Heraclides and Dialla. *Supra* note 27. p.227).

CHAPTER 4

# Humanitarian Intervention in the Twentieth Century

As the nineteenth century became the twentieth century, humanitarian intervention remained broadly recognised as a norm of international law.[1] This was a time when the use of force was a widely accepted means of resolving disputes[2] and the prohibition on the use of force was so lax that laws governing its use had debatable legitimacy.[3] This contributed to World War I[4] and the Concert of Europe's collapse. Although economic and technological development and peace between the Great Powers ensured that early twentieth century Europe was optimistic regarding an end to conflict, World War I changed everything.[5] So devastating was the Great War that afterwards, it was recognised that international law's broad parameters on the use of force were problematic, requiring the institutional prevention of conflict.[6]

Also important was the reduction in the importance of race and religion in being deemed 'civilised'. Rather, once a state like Japan was deemed to meet

1 Fonteyne, Jean-Pierre. 'The Customary International Law Doctrine of Humanitarian Intervention: its Current Validity under the UN Charter' *California Western International Law Journal* (Vol.4, 1973–1974) p.223. See also, Teson, Fernando. *Humanitarian Intervention: An Inquiry into Law and Morality* (Ardsley, 2005). p.219. Abiew, Francis Kofi. *The Evolution of the Doctrine and Practice of Humanitarian Intervention* (The Hague, 1999) p.40. Brownlie, Ian. *International Law and the Use of Force* (Oxford, 2002) p.338. Lillich, Richard. 'Intervention to Protect Human Rights' *McGill Journal of International Law* (1969) p.210. Heraclides and Dialla note that of publicists between 1830 and 1930 who address humanitarian intervention, the vast majority were supportive. (Heraclides, Alexis and Dialla, Ada. *Humanitarian Intervention in the long Nineteenth Century. Setting the precedent.* (Manchester, 2015), p.59.) There were certainly critics of the norm: see Segesser, Daniel Marc. 'Humanitarian Intervention and the issue of state sovereignty in the discourse of legal experts between the 1830s and the First World War' in in Klose, Fabian. (Ed.) *The Emergence of Humanitarian Intervention: Ideas and Practice from the Nineteenth Century to the Present* (Cambridge, 2018) pp.71–72.

2 Wolf, Daniel. 'Humanitarian Intervention' *Michigan Yearbook of International Studies* (Vol.9, 1988) p.337.

3 Hehir, Aidan. *Humanitarian Intervention: An Introduction* (Basingstoke, 2010) p.32.

4 Karoubi, Mohammed Taghi. *Just or Unjust War?* (Aldershot, 2004) p.93.

5 Carnegie Commission on Preventing Deadly Conflict. *Preventing Deadly Conflict: Final Report* (Washington DC, 1997) p.11.

6 Drake, Durant. 'Will the League of Nations Work' *International Journal of Ethics* (Vol.29 (3) 1919) p.340.

 | DOI:10.1163/9789004696396_005

'minimum standards of civilisation', it would be capable of engaging with international law[7] and the law of nations was expanded to all sovereign states in their mutual dealings.[8] Notably, referring to states as 'civilised' (or not) was increasingly dropped during the interwar period.[9]

In the aftermath of World War I, the League of Nations was created in 1919 and sought to ensure peace through collective security and disarmament. This was a major development in international law, given it sought to impose a legal regime on the conduct of nations.[10] Unlike the ad-hoc Concert of Europe meetings, the League was the first legal regime charged with collective security,[11] with Article 10 of the League's Charter requiring its members to 'respect and preserve as against external aggression the territorial integrity and existing political independence of all Members of the League'. Furthermore, it was not limited to European nations and included states from Brazil to Abyssinia to China. While the League required its members to seek peaceful settlements before going to war, it also recognised states could resort to war under customary international law,[12] with the League's Covenant maintaining that the use or threat of war against a League member state was a matter for the whole League.[13]

The League had some successes[14] but its powerlessness soon became apparent, particularly as action by the League Council or Assembly required unanimity, giving each country a veto.[15] Although the League successfully resolved conflicts between small nations,[16] it failed when confronted by stronger

---

7 Heraclides and Dialla. *Supra* note 1. p.33. Indeed, Japan was effectively treated as a Western state by the League of Nations. (See Anghie, Antony. 'The evolution of international law: Colonial and postcolonial realities' *Third World Quarterly.* (Vol.27 (5), 2006). p.747).

8 Schwarzenberger, Georg. The Rule of Law and the Disintegration of the International Society' *American Journal of International Law.* (Vol.33, Iss.1, January 1939) p.63.

9 Heraclides and Dialla. *Supra* note 1. p.38.

10 France, John. *Perilous Glory: The Rise of Western Military Power* (New Haven 2011) p.307.

11 Henderson, Christine. 'The Centrality of the United Nations Security Council in the legal regime governing the Use of Force' in White, Nigel and Henderson, Christine (Eds.) *Research Handbook on International Conflict and Security Law* (Cheltenham, 2013) p.121.

12 Brownlie. *Supra* note 1. p.56.

13 Covenant of the League of Nations (1919) Article.11 (1924).

14 Notably in social and economic advancement and initially there was a high level of trust among League members, with smaller nations seeing it as a guarantor of their independence and strong nations supporting it as an effective way of maintaining stability (Pearce, Malcom and Stewart, Geoffrey. *British Political History: 1867–2001* (London, 2002) p.304).

15 'Statement by Big 5 on Yalta Voting Plan' *New York Times.* (9 June 1945).

16 Notably between Greece and Bulgaria ('At Geneva' *Time.* 28 December 1925) and averted war between Sweden and Finland ('An Argument for League' *New York Times.* 21 September 1921).

nations, particularly as powerful states like the US, Japan and Nazi Germany were not members of the League and not bound by League decisions.[17] Against such nations, the League could do little. It sought to use persuasion, diplomacy and economic sanctions to prevent war, but when these failed, the League had no military of its own.[18] The League's Covenant was also ineffective as it only sought to curtail war and made no provision for other forms of armed attack or coercion.[19] In effect, the League was at best, a mediator, and could do little to ensure peace,[20] ensuring the League's powerlessness condemned it to irrelevance before it was formally abolished in 1946.[21]

Mirroring the League's optimistic approach to restraining the use of force were the Locarno Treaties of 1925.[22] These were a notable development given

17 This was highlighted by Mussolini who noted 'The League is all right when sparrows quarrel. It fails when eagles fall out' (Murphy, Derrick and Morriss, Terry. *International Relations: 1879–2004* (London, 2008) p.55). There is merit to Mussolini's argument given the League was impotent to counter aggressive expansionism by strong state. Nonetheless, it is important to note that preventing warfare between small nations was crucial in maintaining international stability: the entangling nature of alliances could combine with the balance of power to drag powerful nations into the disputes of weaker ones. It was conflict between tiny Serbia and the militarily weak Austro-Hungarian Empire that dragged in stronger allies and instigated World War I. As such, the League's ability to defuse conflicts between minor powers was significant, given such conflicts could embroil larger ones.

18 When Fascist Italy invaded Abyssinia in 1935, the League's two strongest states, France and Britain favoured appeasement, fearing a strong response would drive Fascist Italy closer to Nazi Germany ('Oil on Troubled Waters' *Irish Times.* (2 September 1935)). In the end, while the League imposed sanctions on Fascist Italy, these did not include war resources (especially oil), allowing Italy to continue its invasion ('The League of Nations Stands Firmly on Covenant in Italo-Ethopian Conflict' *New York Times.* (1 January 1936)). Likewise, a military coup against Spain's elected government, the USSR's invasion of Finland and Nazi Germany's aggressive expansionism all met with minimal League action showing its ineffectiveness against aggression by strong states.

19 See International Law Association, Committee on the Use of Force (2010–2018), *Final Report on Aggression and the Use of Force, Sydney Conference* (2018) p.3 and Buell, Raymond Leslie. 'The World's Peace Machinery Undergoes Its Severest Test' *New York Times.* (25 October 1931). This became apparent in the case of Japan's invasion of Chinese Manchuria, where Tokyo made no formal declaration of war to provoke China into doing so first. ('China and Japan' *Irish Times.* (10 October 1931)). Had China declared war, it would have been in breach of the Covenant despite operating in self-defence against Japanese aggression (Brownlie. *Supra* note 1. p.60).

20 Schlesinger, Stephen. *Act of Creation: The Founding of the United Nations* (Boulder, 2003) p.259.

21 '1919–1946: End of the League. Experience That Can Help U.N.O' *Manchester Guardian.* (20 April 1946).

22 The Locarno Treaties involved reciprocal agreements between Germany, Britain, Italy, France, and Belgium, where they pledged not to use force outside of self-defence or in pursuance of the League's Covenant (Treaty of Mutual Guarantee between Germany,

they were reciprocal agreements that normalised Germany's international status after World War I.[23] This was important, as until their renunciation by Berlin in 1936, the Locarno Treaties demonstrated international law's attempts to limit the use of war in the inter-war era.[24] This is also evident in the widely signed Kellogg-Briand pact of 1928 that required parties to settle disputes peacefully and renounce war as an instrument of international relations,[25] although it did not prejudice the right of states to self-defence.[26] Above all, the pact formed the nucleus for prosecuting German and Japanese war criminals for crimes against the peace after World War II[27]and its key provisions were incorporated into the United Nation's Charter.[28]

Although humanitarian intervention was neither supported nor opposed by the League of Nations,[29] its existence was weakened in the inter-war period, with few states relying on it to justify the use of force.[30] Due to World War

Belgium, France, Great Britain, and Italy (LNTS, 54, 1925) Article 2). Such a pledge was guaranteed by Britain and Italy who agreed to aid any party subject to aggression (Anonymous. 'The Locarno Treaties' *Bulletin of International News* (Vol.1, No.21, 2 November 1925) p.2).

23 Grigg, Edward. 'The Merits and Defects of the Locarno Treaty as a Guarantee of World Peace' *International Affairs* (Vol. 14, No. 2. Mar- Apr 1935) pp.181–182.

24 Franck, Thomas. *Recourse to Force: State Action against Threats and Armed Attacks* (Cambridge, 2002). pp.10–11.

25 Kellogg-Briand Pact. (1928) Articles I–II. See Lesaffer, Randall. 'Kellogg-Briand Pact (1928) in Wolfrum, Rudiger (Ed.), The Max Planck Encyclopaedia of Public International Law (online ed) http://opil.ouplaw.com/view/10.1093/law:epil/9780199231690/law-9780199231690-e320?rskey=sXnVjt&result=1&prd=EPIL Accessed 10th March 2024.

26 The Kellog-Briand pact was concluded outside of the League, and was widely signed (including by the US). It remains in force today but proved ineffective at preventing war. Although it has seldom been referred to in state practice since 1946, its spirit was maintained, and most states took collective action against those states that engaged in aggression (Brownlie. *Supra* note 1. pp.113–114). However, it is important to note that despite still being in force, the drafters' consensus on the Kellog-Briand Pact is long gone. (Reisman, W. Michael. 'Article 2(4): The Use of Force in Contemporary International Law' Article 2(4): The Use of Force in Contemporary International Law' *Proceedings of the Annual Meeting (American Society of International Law)* (Vol.78, April 12–14, 1984) p.75).

27 White, Nigel. *International Conflict and Security Law* (Cheltenham, 2014) p.28.

28 Hehir. *Supra* note 3. p.85.

29 Karoubi. *Supra* note 4. p.218.

30 Ronzitti, Natalino. *Rescuing Nationals Abroad through Military Coercion and Intervention in Grounds of Humanity* (Dordrecht, 1985) p.91. The key exception to this was Nazi Germany which vowed to use force to protect ethnic Germans from their 'oppressors' ('Hitler's Speech' *Manchester Guardian.* (13th September 1938)). This led Berlin to invade and occupy Czechoslovakia, emboldening Nazi aggression and leading to World War II. Likewise, one of Hitler's justifications for the invasion of Poland was the claimed need to protect ethnic Germans from oppression in Poland (Bazyler. Michael. 'Re-examining

I, states were reluctant to use force on behalf of others, in an era known as the 'eclipse of humanitarian intervention'.[31] Although Europe's democracies eventually went to war with Nazi Germany, this only occurred when Berlin's aggression threatened the European balance of power[32] and despite systematic Nazi atrocities such as the Holocaust, they did little to protect persecuted groups within the Third Reich. This did not mark the end of humanitarian intervention under international law and at the Nuremburg War Crimes Tribunal, the UK's Attorney General and Chief Prosecutor highlighted that the right of humanitarian intervention had long been recognised as 'part of the law of nations'.[33] Likewise, Lauterpacht, the prominent international lawyer and ICJ judge, noted in 1946 that while humanitarian intervention was not a 'fully acknowledged' part of international law, it provided a warning that was occasionally acted upon and paved the way for the UN Charter's focus on human rights.[34]

Following World War II, there was a push for a new system to maintain peace but improve on the League's mistakes. This led to the creation of the UN, which remains the principle institution for collective security, given membership is universal while its competence in peace and security matters is expansive.[35] The UN's formation was a landmark development in international law, particularly the sovereign equality of all its members.[36] In practice, this is far from the case, with only the UNSC being capable of authorising the use of force, subject

---

the Doctrine of Humanitarian Intervention in Light of the Atrocities in Kampuchea and Ethiopia' *Stanford Journal of International Law* (Vol.23, 1987) p.584). Such interventions by the Nazis discredited humanitarian intervention in the aftermath of the Second World War. (See Klose, Fabian. 'The Emergence of Humanitarian Intervention' in Klose, Fabian. (Ed.) *The Emergence of Humanitarian Intervention: Ideas and Practice from the Nineteenth Century to the Present* (Cambridge, 2018) p.25).

31 Marrus, Michael. 'Holocaust Bystanders and Humanitarian Intervention' *Holocaust Studies* (Vol.13, No.1, 2007) p.9 See also Klose. *Supra* note 30. p.21.

32 This is disputed by Teson who argues the Allies fought the Axis for humanitarian as well as security reasons. Teson. *Supra* note 1. p.227.

33 Nuremberg Trial Proceedings Volume 3 Twelfth Day (Tuesday, 4 December 1945) http://avalon.law.yale.edu/imt/12-04-45.asp Accessed 10th March 2024.

34 Lauterpacht H. 'The Grotian Tradition in International Law' *British Yearbook of International Law* (Vol.23, 1946) p.46.

35 Tsagourias, Nicholas and White, Nigel. *Collective Security: Theory, Law, and Practice* (Cambridge, 2013) p.91.

36 UN Charter. (1 UNTS XVI, 1945) Article 2(1). See Wood, Michael. 'Use of force, prohibition of threat' in Wolfrum, Rudiger (Ed.), The Max Planck Encyclopaedia of Public International Law (online Ed) http://opil.ouplaw.com/view/10.1093/law:epil/9780199231690/law-9780199231690-e428?rskey=sfhUPW&result=2&prd=EPIL Accessed 10th March 2024.

to the wishes of its permanent five members (the P5). While the maintenance of international peace and security was premised on the UNSC's ability to enforce collective security through military forces under UN command and control, this proved unachievable, resulting in a partially decentralised system of collective security emerging, whereby a state or states could be authorised to take military action on behalf of the UNSC.[37]

At the drafting of the UN Charter, it was inconceivable that the two superpowers of the USSR and USA would have joined the UN without a veto power, which would have rendered the UN powerless.[38] Above all, the UNSC sought to avoid the League of Nations' mistakes and create an organisation that worked with, rather than against the 'realities of power'.[39] The veto system ensures that the UNSC does not adopt resolutions against the P5 that would be unenforceable or indeed, risk war.[40] As such, collective security is unenforceable against the P5, despite their being the states that pose the greatest threat to international peace and security.[41] Although inconsistent with the equality of states principle,[42] the veto system is inherently practical.[43]

Notably, the UNSC is not entirely dominated by the P5 as although weaker than the P5, the non-permanent members have a collective veto of their own.[44] Even if united, the P5 still need to secure the consent of non-permanent members to achieve a majority for any resolution.[45] It nonetheless ensures that humanitarian intervention has never been used against a powerful or Western nation. Generally, Western states emphasise human rights while other states focus on non-intervention to protect their sovereignty.[46] It is also notable

37 White, Nigel. 'Towards Integrated Peace Operations: The Evolution of Peacekeeping and Coalitions of the Willing' in Odello, Marco and Piotrowicz, Ryszard (Eds.) *International Military Missions and International Law* (Leiden, 2011) p.2. This will be explored further in Chapter 5.

38 Schlesinger. *Supra* note 20. p.284.

39 Briggs, Herbert. 'Power Politics and International Organization' *American Journal of International Law* (Vol.39, No.4, October 1945) p.670.

40 Franck, Thomas and Rodley, Nigel. 'After Bangladesh: The Law of Humanitarian Intervention by Military Force' *American Journal of International Law* (Vol. 67, 1973) p.300.

41 Murphy, Ray. *UN Peacekeeping in Lebanon, Somalia, and Kosovo* (Cambridge, 2007) p.11.

42 This was a point made by several smaller states prior to the San Francisco Conference's where the UN Charter was drafted. See Schlesinger. *Supra* note 20. pp.100–101.

43 The P5 are among the most militarily and economically powerful states in the world, ensuring their agreement is vital to ensure an action can be enforced.

44 'Statement by Big 5 on Yalta Voting Plan' *New York Times*. (9 June 1945).

45 Walling, Carrie Booth. *All Necessary Measures: The UN and Humanitarian Intervention* (Philadelphia, 2013) p.6.

46 Abiew. *Supra* note 1. p.66.

that legal scholars opposing humanitarian intervention are frequently from the Global South.[47] Furthermore, with veto power available to each of the P5, genuinely collective enforcement action by the UN was rendered far more difficult.[48]

The seeming ban on the use of force or intervention invoked in the UN Charter saw the debate over humanitarian intervention wane after World War II.[49] However, several potential humanitarian interventions still took place during the Cold War, none of which were conducted by P5 nations.[50] There is a consensus that just three examples of military intervention can be seen as humanitarian, which will be explored below.[51]

## 1 Humanitarian Intervention in East Pakistan, 1971

In 1947, the British Raj was partitioned into the states of Pakistan and India, with accompanying ethnic violence killing hundreds of thousands while displacing millions more.[52] Adding to the difficulties was the separation of Pakistan into two provinces a thousand miles apart and further divided by ethnic, linguistic and cultural differences, with ensuing unrest in East Pakistan.[53] Pakistan's President Yahya Khan introduced democratic elections for Pakistan's National Assembly that took place in December 1970 amidst high turnout and universal

---

47 Bazyler. *Supra* note 30. p.574. It can be argued that for Global South countries, solidarity against former colonial powers is often more important than acting against atrocities. (See Lebor. *Supra* note 189. p.183 and 204–209).

48 MacQueen, Norrie. 'Cold War peacekeeping versus humanitarian intervention' in Klose, Fabian. (Ed.) *The Emergence of Humanitarian Intervention: Ideas and Practice from the Nineteenth Century to the Present* (Cambridge, 2018) p.237.

49 Klose. *Supra* note 30. p.6.

50 There are several other potential examples of humanitarian intervention during the Cold War, but these are mired in controversy. (See Chesterman, Simon. *Just War and Just Peace: Humanitarian Intervention and International Law* (Oxford, 2001) pp.63–84). The three interventions examined in this chapter are those that are most relevant to humanitarian intervention's status under customary international law.

51 Heraclides and Dialla. *Supra* note 1. pp.2–3.

52 Bose, Sugata and Jalal, Ayesha. *Modern South Asia: History, Culture, Political Economy* (Delhi, 1998) pp.87–89.

53 East Pakistan had a larger population than its western counterpart and was linguistically and ethnically homogenous, with most of the population being Bengali Muslims while West Pakistan was overwhelmingly Muslim but ethnically diverse (Sanaullah, M. 'Second and Third Release from the Second Population Census of Pakistan, 1961' *The Pakistan Development Review* (Vol. 2, No. 1, Spring, 1962) pp.110–111).

adult suffrage.[54] East Pakistan's large population ensured most of the seats went to the Bengali nationalist Awami League (AL) party[55] whose demands for sweeping provincial autonomy[56] caused uproar in West Pakistan.[57] Yahya announced the postponement of the National Assembly's opening on 1 March 1971.[58] The AL responded by declaring a general strike and on the 25th March 1971, the Pakistani military conducted Operation Searchlight in East Pakistan,[59] claiming the need to prevent an Awami League coup and protect West Pakistanis and Biharis[60] from extermination by Bengalis.[61] In practice, the military went far beyond this and conducted widespread atrocities,[62] although the exact numbers of victims vary.[63]

---

54 Blood, Archer. *The Cruel Birth of Bangladesh: Memoirs of an American Diplomat* (Dhaka, 2002) p.128.

55 Ghauri, S.R 'Fear of deadlock in Pakistan' *Guardian.* (19 December 1970).

56 Memorandum from Harold Saunders and Samuel Hoskinson of the National Security Council Staff to the President's Assistant for National Security Affairs (Kissinger) (1 March 1971) http://2001-2009.state.gov/r/pa/ho/frus/nixon/xi/45604.htm Accessed 10th March 2024.

57 The election was of critical importance given the National Assembly would draft Pakistan's new constitution by simple majority. Drafting a new constitution proved problematic given that the AL supported maximum devolution and reconciliation with India. By contrast, the second largest party, the Pakistan People's Party favoured centralisation and ongoing hostility to India. See Memorandum from the Staff Secretary of the National Security Council (Davis) to the Deputy Secretary of Defence (Packard) (3 March 1971) https://history.state.gov/historicaldocuments/frus1969-76ve07/d123 Accessed 10th March 2024).

58 Quoted by Blood. *Supra* note 54. pp.153–155.

59 Schanberg, Sydney. 'Kennedy in India, Terms Pakistani Drive Genocide' *New York Times.* (17 August 1971).

60 East Pakistani Muslims who were generally loyal to Islamabad.

61 'What Made Them Flee' *Economist.* (12th June 1971).

62 The US Consul in Dhaka described a city under military control while thousands of refugees fled (Blood. *Supra* note 54. p.198). Likewise, a British journalist in Dhaka described a 'crushed and frightened city' with the wilful killing of civilians and the targeting of Bengali intellectuals, policemen, soldiers, Hindus and Awami League supporters (Dring, Simon. 'Dacca Eyewitness: Bloodbath, Inferno' *Washington Post.* (30 March 1971)). Sexual violence was also used by the military, with mass-rape used to destroy Bengali women and society (Jones, Owen Bennett. *Pakistan: Eye of the Storm* (New Haven, 2002) p.343). As the Indian representative to the UN noted, this was done as a deliberate campaign of humiliation (UN Security Council. *Official Records, 26th Year, 1606th Meeting.* UN Doc S/PV.1606. (4 December 1971) Para.174).

63 The brutality of the Operation Searchlight was affirmed by the International Commission of Jurists which noted that the main features of the Pakistani army's campaign was the indiscriminate killing of civilians, the ethnic cleansing of East Pakistani Hindus, raping and looting on 'a scale difficult to comprehend' (International Commission of Jurists. *The events in East Pakistan, 1971* (Geneva, 1972) pp.26–27). A Pakistani Commission estimated

Although the show of force coerced East Pakistan's cities into submission, it posed a problem in the countryside where the territory favoured guerrilla warfare[64] by the Mukti Bahini.[65] This led to an on-going insurgency, resulting in refugees fleeing to neighbouring India where they posed a major problem.[66] India was outraged, but Pakistan's military intelligence chief dismissed Indian criticism[67] at a time when Indo-Pakistani relations remained strained since India's military victory over Pakistan in 1965.[68] The refugees further poisoned Indo-Pakistani relations, alongside the fact that among those refugees were many Awami League supporters and deserting soldiers who set up a government in exile on Indian soil.[69]

In this, they were supported by local Indian authorities who recognised the rebels and gave them support.[70] While Pakistan's repression continued, New

---

that around 26,000 people were killed by the Pakistani military (Hamoodar Rahman Commission Report (1974) pp.20–22 http://img.dunyanews.tv/images/docss/hamoodur_rahman_commission_report.pdf Accessed 10th March 2024). This seems low but is nonetheless a Pakistani admission that huge numbers were killed. Likewise, even Yahya's key ally, US President Nixon acknowledged that 'countless thousands' had been killed (Nixon, Richard. 'Third Annual Report to the Congress on United States Foreign Policy.' (9 February 1972)). Upon Bangladesh's independence, its Police Chief estimated that 'millions' had been killed while the New York Times suggested that between 500,000 and 1.5 million had been killed (Who Knows How Many Millions Have Been Killed' in the East?' *New York Times.* (22 December 1971)). By contrast, R.J Rummel estimates the deaths at around 1.5 million (Rummel, R.J. 'Statistics of Democide' http://www.hawaii.edu/powerkills/SOD.CHAP8.HTM Accessed 10th March 2024).

64 'Unity at Gunpoint' *Economist.* (3 April 1971).

65 East Pakistani insurgents who waged a guerrilla campaign against the Pakistani military (International Commission of Jurists. *Supra* note 63. p.41). Islamabad's brutality also radicalised Bengalis, catalysing support for the rebels and shifting East Pakistani demands from autonomy to independence (Schanberg, Sydney. 'Pakistan Divided' *Foreign Affairs* (Vol.50, October 1971)). In this, the insurgents were greatly supported by the East Pakistani peasantry who supplied and sheltered the rebels (Telegram 10043 From the Embassy in Pakistan to the Department of State (October 4, 1971) http://2001-2009.state.gov/r/pa/ho/frus/nixon/e7txt/49190.htm Accessed 10th March 2024).

66 International Commission of Jurists. *Supra* note 63. p.87.

67 Pakistan's military intelligence chief claimed that the Bengalis who fled to India were common criminals, and that India was overstating the numbers of refugees to solicit international aid. See Brownes, Malcolm. 'War with India possible, Pakistan general asserts.' *New York Times.* (6 May 1971).

68 Kulke, Hermann and Rothermund, Dietmar. *A History of India* (Chatham, 1997) pp.339–340.

69 Jones. *Supra* note 62. p.168.

70 'Bangla Desh is Over the Border' *Economist.* (24 April 1971). Although India's central government denied helping the Mukti Bahini, there can be little doubt that the Mukti Bahini operated with India's help. See UN Security Council. *Official Records, 26th Year, 1607 Meeting* UN Doc S/PV.1607 (5 December 1971) Para.172. See also International Commission

Delhi accused Islamabad of 'planned carnage and systematic genocide'[71] and publicly expressed support for East Pakistani independence, risking another Indo-Pakistan war.[72]

The threat to stability was notable given the Cold War was in full swing and both superpowers had interests in the region.[73] The importance of Pakistan to Sino-American relations was vital,[74] so much so that while Pakistani troops were committing atrocities, US President Nixon wrote to Yahya to thank him for helping establish contact between the US and China.[75] Hitchens argues

---

of Jurists. *Supra* note 63. p.88. This was critical for the rebels who had safe havens from the Pakistani military, which greatly aided their guerrilla campaign.

71 'Bangla Desh (Sic) is Over the Border' *Economist.* (24 April 1971).

72 Dallek, Robert. *Partners in Power: Nixon and Kissinger* (New York, 2007) pp.335–336.

73 Despite India being the world's largest democracy and a key player in the Non-Aligned-Movement, the USSR supported New Delhi as a bulwark against China while India appreciated the backing of a superpower. Given India was a democracy, India might be expected to have the support of the US. Washington was irritated by India's non-alignment and was more supportive of Pakistan, ensuring the Pakistani military relied on the US for military hardware to use in East Pakistan (Bass, Gary. *The Blood Telegram: Nixon, Kissinger, and the Forgotten Genocide* (New York, 2013) p.67). Likewise, Nixon's National Security Advisor, Henry Kissinger was an archetypal realist, concerned with how South-Asian instability would threaten US interests. Kissinger understood that while US interests supported Pakistani unity, there was 'very little material left in the fabric of the unity of Pakistan' and the US needed a contingency plan for East Pakistani secession (Memorandum From the President's Assistant for National Security Affairs (Kissinger) to President Nixon, Washington (22 February 1971)) https://history.state.gov/historicaldocuments/frus1969-76ve07/d118 Accessed 10th March 2024).

74 Nixon sought to establish diplomatic relations with China and saw Pakistan as an ideal diplomatic route to do so, resulting in Kissinger flying to Peking via Islamabad in July 1971 (Herbers, John. 'Nixon is expected to visit China around end of year' *New York Times.* (17 July 1971)). Likewise, the US saw East Pakistan as a mollifying influence to West Pakistan's hostility to India (Memorandum from the Staff Secretary of the National Security Council (Davis) to the Deputy Secretary of Defence (Packard) (3 March 1971) https://history.state.gov/historicaldocuments/frus1969-76ve07/d123 Accessed 10th March 2024).

Kissinger viewed East Pakistan as being so poor and overpopulated that independence would lead to it becoming a 'cesspool [and a] ripe field for Communist infiltration' (Conversation between President Nixon and his Assistant for National Security Affairs (Kissinger), Washington (4 June 1971) https://history.state.gov/historicaldocuments/frus1969-76ve07/d136 Accessed 10th March 2024). Kissinger was aware that strengthening US links to China and Pakistan gravely weakened its standing with India but felt that once US relations with China had been established, Washington could win the Indians back in the near future (Conversation between President Nixon and his Assistant for National Security Affairs (Kissinger) Washington (6 December 1971) https://history.state.gov/historicaldocuments/frus1969-76ve07/d162 Accessed 10th March 2024).

75 Handwritten Letter from President Nixon to President Yahya (7 August 1971) http://www2.gwu.edu/~nsarchiv/NSAEBB/NSAEBB79/BEBB20.pdf Accessed 10th March 2024.

that Kissinger was not only motivated by his interest in China, but also with appeasing Nixon's hatred of India's Prime Minister Indira Gandhi while preventing East Pakistani secession.[76] Likewise, the US had realpolitik interests. Kissinger was a disciple of Prince Metternich's focus on the balance of power and opposed East Pakistani independence, lest it undermine a US ally in the region.[77] Washington was unwilling to get involved in the East Pakistan crisis although it was keenly aware of the ongoing atrocities, and could have used its influence over Pakistan to protect Bengalis,[78] or utilised the US Consul-General in Dhaka.[79]

To a realist like Kissinger, the priority was preventing war in South-Asia and maintaining US interests.[80] Nixon claimed the US had not supported Pakistan's military operations in East Pakistan[81] but he took no public action. Although Nixon admitted Islamabad was the 'heart of the problem', he made representations only using private channels,[82] and made no public statements against West Pakistani oppression.[83] Pakistan relied heavily on the US for military

76 Hitchens, Christopher. *The Trial of Kissinger* (London, 2001) pp.48–49.

77 Anderson, Jack. *The Anderson Papers* (London, 1973) pp.217–218.

78 Ibid. p.223.

79 The US consul, Archer Blood, warned the State Department how the Pakistani military was targeting Awami League members while supporting mobs attacking Bengalis and Hindus (Telegram 959 from the Consulate General in Dacca to the Department of State (28 March 1971). 2001–2009.state.gov/r/pa/ho/frus/nixon/e7txt/47241.htm Accessed 10th March 2024). In conjunction with other US diplomats in East Pakistan, Blood telegrammed the State Department, expressing horror at US 'moral bankruptcy' in failing to condemn atrocities and intervene against genocide (National Security Archive Project 'U.S. Consulate (Dacca) Cable, Dissent from U.S. Policy Toward East Pakistan, April 6, 1971' http://www2.gwu.edu/~nsarchiv/NSAEBB/NSAEBB79/BEBB8.pdf Accessed 10th March 2024). The so-called 'Blood Telegram' was a landmark development, marking the most public and vehement denunciation of US foreign policy by State Department officials ever recorded (Hitchens. *Supra* note 76. p.45). Washington simply recalled Blood from Dhaka, despite his being scheduled to remain for another 18 months (Holley, John. 'Archer K. Blood; Dissenting Diplomat' *Washington Post.* (23 September 2003)).

80 It must be noted that while the White House supported Pakistan, this was not shared across the American public and there was heavy press criticism for US inaction during the crisis (Transcript of Telephone Conversation Between Secretary of State Rogers and the President's Assistant for National Security Affairs (Kissinger) (3 December 1971). https://history.state.gov/historicaldocuments/frus1969-76ve07/d158 Accessed 10th March 2024.

81 Nixon, Richard. 'Third Annual Report to the Congress on United States Foreign Policy.' (9 February 1972).

82 Ibid.

83 Anderson. *Supra* note 77. p.215.

and economic aid but Nixon refused to rule out using these for leverage.[84] The atrocities continued, particularly against Bengali Hindus.

### 1.1 *The Indo-Pakistan War of 1971*

With Indo-Pakistani tensions already strained, Indian public outrage at Operation Searchlight and a constant flood of refugees fleeing to India, conflict between India and Pakistan was becoming increasingly likely. It is unclear when New Delhi realised war was inevitable but as Pakistan's campaign continued and refugees kept arriving, India accepted that an independent East Pakistan was in its own interests.[85] Border disputes erupted into armed conflict and India advanced into East Pakistan.

While Kissinger felt China was unlikely to attack India unprovoked, Beijing claimed they would support Pakistan in a war, although this was probably a bluff.[86] Kissinger warned India that war would be a disaster for both countries but assured them the US would take 'the gravest view of any unprovoked Chinese aggression against India'.[87] India was outraged with Washington and the US was vilified in the Indian parliament and media.[88] It also pushed New Delhi closer to Moscow despite India's traditional non-alignment. The USSR had seen a chance to assert itself as a mediator in South Asia during the 1965 Indo-Pakistan war, and a rapprochement between India and the USSR led to a bilateral Friendship Treaty in 1971.[89] With such involvement of the superpowers, there was a serious risk of escalation but Pakistan could not rely on much US help.[90] While the White House claimed it sought to end the conflict,

---

84 Bass. *Supra* note 73. p.149.

85 Jones. *Supra* note 62. p.172.

86 'Memorandum of Conversation, New Delhi, (7 July 1971) https://history.state.gov/historicaldocuments/frus1969-76ve07/d139 Accessed 10th March 2024.

87 Memorandum for the Record (Undated, 1971) https://history.state.gov/historicaldocuments/frus1969-76ve07/d156 Accessed 10th March 2024.

88 Schanberg, Sydney. 'U.S-India Relations: A New Low: New Delhi Regards Aid to Pakistan as a Betrayal' *New York Times* (27 July 1971).

89 Although not a military pact, the Friendship Treaty stated that should one party be attacked by a third party, the other was required to 'start mutual consultation with a view to eliminating the threat and taking appropriate effective measures to ensure peace and security for the countries' (Jones. *Supra* note 62). Therefore, it offered Soviet support to India in the event of war with China.

90 Despite Nixon's support for Pakistan, Congressional opposition prevented the US from supplying arms to Islamabad (Smith, Terence. 'US urges India and Pakistan to avoid an all-out-war' *New York Times*. (12th November 1971)). US arms continued to flow to Pakistan, with the State Department claiming that these had been contracted before the embargo began, precluding them from the embargo (Schanberg. *Supra* 65. Although Congress

it focussed chiefly on India, seeing New Delhi (with Moscow's backing) as the aggressor despite opposition from the State Department, Congress, the press and the US public.[91]

Conflict between two regional powers already posed a grave threat to international peace and security and superpower involvement risked even further escalation. The UN Secretary-General brought the crisis to the attention of the UNSC, arguing that the UN had an important role to play, given its experience in peacekeeping and conflict resolution.[92] Nine members of the UNSC then called for a UNSC meeting on the conflict, with India and Pakistan invited to participate. Pakistan's accusations against India were numerous, including stoking unrest in Pakistan, exploiting the refugee problem and blatant military aggression.[93] By contrast, India highlighted Pakistan's oppression of the democratically elected AL and that Pakistan was dismembering itself by suppressing the will of its people.[94] India accused Pakistan of 'refugee aggression' through the exodus of millions into India where they placed a heavy strain on Indian resources, which scarcely differed from 'the more classical type' of aggression.[95]

China claimed the crisis was an internal matter for Pakistan and stated its full support for Pakistan against Indian aggression and 'social imperialism'.[96] The USSR defended India, highlighting Pakistan's repression of the AL,[97] and the refugee crisis affecting India.[98] Furthermore, the USSR criticised China's claims of 'social imperialism', calling it a mere shield for states to engage in terrorism, dictatorship and the suppression of national liberation movements.[99] The US position was more nuanced, reflecting US public opposition

sought to end these, the White House ensured that such efforts failed, and the US continued to supply Pakistan with vital military spare parts (Bass. *Supra* note 73. p.234).

91 Dallek. *Supra* note 72. p.341.

92 UN Security Council. *Report of the Secretary-General.* UN Doc S/10410 (3 December 1971) p.4.

93 See UN Security Council. *Official Records, 26th Year, 1606th Meeting.* UN Doc S/PV.1606. (4 December 1971) Paras 70–75 and Paras 111–116. Furthermore, Pakistan's ambassador contrasted Pakistan's support for mutual military withdrawal and acceptance of the Secretary-General's involvement with India's rejection of both (Ibid. Paras 136–137). Likewise, Pakistan referred to the importance of sovereignty and India's traditional advocacy for non-intervention (Ibid. Paras 107–109).

94 Ibid. Para. 155.

95 Ibid. Para.161.

96 Ibid. Para.237–242.

97 Ibid. Para 253.

98 Ibid. Para 258.

99 Ibid. Para 249.

to Pakistan's brutality but also Washington's relationship with Islamabad and Beijing. Although the US did not condemn India, it highlighted that Pakistan had accepted the US' proposal of mutual military withdrawal and the Secretary-General's offer of his good offices while India had not.[100] Among the UNSC's other member states, there was widespread support for a ceasefire, reciprocal disengagement and the repatriation of refugees. However, few supported India's justification for the use of force. Somalia called for 'a scrupulous regard by both states for each other's territorial integrity'[101] and Syria for the territorial integrity of Pakistan to be accepted.[102] Only communist Poland joined the USSR in condemning Pakistan for its violation of Indian borders[103] and repression in East Pakistan.[104]

Given the division among the Great Powers, it is unsurprising that the UNSC was unable to adopt a resolution to address the crisis. A US draft resolution called for mutual military withdrawal and a strong role for the UN in brokering a ceasefire.[105] Although the resolution did not condemn India for aggression, New Delhi had little to gain from such a proposal, given it would maintain Islamabad's control of East Pakistan. As the UK pointed out to the US, any proposal to withdraw Indian troops from East Pakistan was unrealistic and unacceptable to the USSR.[106] Predictably, the USSR vetoed the US resolution while only Poland joined the USSR in voting against it. The US highlighted that it was time for the UN to step in and preserve peace,[107] but Washington's professed faith in the UN was disingenuous. While the US Ambassador to the UN claimed the UNSC needed to act immediately to avoid showing UNSC impotence,[108] Nixon and Kissinger only sought UN involvement as a cynical measure. They knew the USSR would veto any UNSC action against India, rendering

---

100 Ibid. Para.192–196.

101 Ibid. Para.217.

102 Ibid. Para.245.

103 Ibid. Para.303.

104 Ibid. Para.306.

105 UN Security Council. *Draft Resolution (Concerning the India-Pakistan Question)*. UN Doc S/2022/155 (25 February 2022).

106 Telegram 11295 from the Embassy in the United Kingdom to the Department of State (December 13, 1971) http://2001-2009.state.gov/r/pa/ho/frus/nixon/e7txt/49207.htm Accessed 10th March 2024.

107 UN Security Council. *Official Records, 26th Year, 1606th Meeting.* UN Doc S/PV.1606. (4 December 1971) Para.187.

108 Ibid. Para.342.

it a 'paper exercise' that Kissinger saw as useful political cover.[109] As Kissinger expected, although only Poland and the USSR voted against the resolution (with French and British abstentions), the USSR vote ensured the resolution was vetoed.[110] A further UNSC debate saw China propose a resolution condemning Indian aggression and demanding an Indian withdrawal but this was equally fruitless.[111]

By contrast, the USSR submitted a draft resolution calling for a political solution to the crisis (which would involve a cessation of hostilities) and require Pakistan to cease all hostile acts in East Pakistan.[112] The resolution failed to pass as only Poland and the USSR supported the motion, with China voting against and every other country abstaining.[113] Eight of the UNSC's non-permanent members sought an alternative by calling for an immediate ceasefire and mutual withdrawal without condemning either side.[114] Although less controversial, it would allow Pakistan to continue its campaign and require the withdrawal of Indian troops. This was opposed by Poland and the USSR, although China and the US supported it.[115] A third UNSC meeting met the same deadlock.[116]

While the UNSC has primary responsibility for maintaining peace and security, it is not exclusive and the UN General Assembly (UNGA) has an interest in the area.[117] UNSC deadlock had been notable in the past resulting in the Uniting for Peace Resolution,[118] whereby when the UNSC fails in its primary

109 Transcript of Telephone Conversation between President Nixon and His Assistant for National Security Affairs (Kissinger) (4 December 1971) https://history.state.gov/historicaldocuments/frus1969-76v11/d225 Accessed 10th March 2024.

110 UN Security Council. *Official Records, 26th Year, 1606th Meeting.* UN Doc S/PV.1606. (4 December 1971) Para.371.

111 UN Security Council. *Draft Resolution (Concerning the India-Pakistan Question).* UN Doc S/10421 (5 December 1971).

112 UN Security Council. *Draft Resolution (Concerning the India-Pakistan Question).* UN Doc S/10418 (4 December 1971).

113 UN Security Council. *Official Records, 26th Year, 1607th Meeting.* UN Doc S/PV.1607 (5 December 1971) Para.217.

114 UN Security Council. *Draft Resolution (Concerning the India-Pakistan Question).* UN Doc S/10423 (5 December 1971).

115 UN Security Council. *Official Records, 26th Year, 1607th Meeting.* UN Doc S/PV.1607 (5 December 1971) Para.240.

116 UN Security Council. *Official Records, 26th Year, 1608th Meeting.* UN Doc S/PV.1608 (6 December 1971).

117 International Court of Justice *Certain Expenses of the United Nations (Article 17, Paragraph 2 of the Charter).* ICJ Reports 155 (Advisory Opinion of 20 July 1962). p.163.

118 The Uniting for Peace resolution arose in 1950 at a time when the USSR was boycotting the Security Council in opposition to the anti-communist Chiang Kai-shek regime taking China's UN Security Council seat. The USSR boycott enabled the US to push through

responsibility to maintain international peace and security due to deadlock, the UNGA is empowered to recommend action.[119] However, such a power is recommendatory only and any coercive measures require UNSC authorisation.[120] With consensus impossible over the Indo-Pakistan War, the UNSC used the Uniting for Peace Resolution to refer the issue to the UNGA.[121] The UNGA result was a humiliation for India with 104 countries voting for an immediate ceasefire and troop withdrawal,[122] with only ten against and eleven abstentions.[123]

However, the UNGA was unable to enforce its decision[124] and India simply ignored the resolution and continued its military campaign that demonstrated UN impotence.[125] With India's failure to comply with the UNGA resolution, another UNSC meeting was convened on 12 December 1971. Citing India's 'defiance of world opinion', the US sought an end to the conflict, claiming it threatened international peace and security.[126] Both India and Pakistan's Foreign Ministers were present, and both gave eloquent defences of their respective

---

the Uniting for Peace Resolution (Walker, Martin. *The Cold War: A History* (New York, 1993) pp.74–78). The Uniting for Peace resolution arose due to a realisation that the UN's foundational consensus was at an end, necessitating an alternative form of collective security outside of the Security Council (White, Nigel. 'The Legality of Bombing in the Name of Humanity' *Journal of Conflict and Security Law* (Vol.5, No.1 2000)).

119 UN General Assembly. *Uniting for Peace*. UN Doc A/RES/377(V) (3 November 1950) Para.1. It must be noted that the General Assembly's capacity to make recommendations reinforces collective action as a Security Council prerogative (See Henderson. *Supra 11*. p.133).

120 Tsagourias and White. *Supra* note 35. p.104.

121 UN Security Council. *Security Council Resolution 303 (1971)*. UN Doc S/Res/303 (6 December 1971).

122 UN Security Council. *Questions Considered by the Security Council at its 1606th, 1607th and 1608th Meetings on 4, 5, 6 December 1971*. UN Doc. A/RES/2793(XXVI) (7 December 1971).

123 As with the debate, the voting was broadly along Cold War lines, with Western nations backing Pakistan and USSR-aligned countries supporting India. Despite India's prominence in the Non-Aligned movement, most Global South states supported Pakistan, given their fears of intervention as a cloak for imperialism. However, some Eastern Bloc nations like Romania voted for the Resolution while some Western nations like the UK and France abstained, as did some Global South countries like Senegal (UN General Assembly 26th Session, 2003rd Plenary Meeting, UN Doc A/PV.2003 (7 December 1971) Para.490).

124 Although the UN Charter allows the General Assembly to recommend peacekeeping operations to maintain international peace and security with the consent of the state (See 1 UNTS XVI, 1945) Article 11(2)), the authorisation of force under Chapter VII remains with the remit of the Security Council (International Court of Justice *Certain Expenses Case*. ICJ Report 155 (Advisory Opinion of 20 July 1962). pp.164–165).

125 Pace, Eric. 'Indians deride U.N move, Pakistanis express doubt' *New York Times*. (9 December 1971).

126 UN Security Council. *Official Records, 26th Year, 1611th Meeting*. UN Doc S/PV.1611 (12th December 1971) Para.16.

positions under international law. Again, India highlighted Pakistani repression caused refugees to flee to India, forcing India to take action to maintain its own security and stability.[127] The USSR warned India that the longer the war dragged on, it would be harder for the USSR to oppose a ceasefire in the UNSC.[128] It was therefore in India's interests for the conflict to be speedily resolved and while the UN debated, India sought to end its campaign in East Pakistan before the UNSC could act.

Pakistan was at a major military disadvantage against Indian forces[129] but Chinese involvement would be a key variable, given China had defeated India in 1962, with Nixon claiming India was 'petrified' of Chinese involvement.[130] Although China had reportedly assured Yahya of its support, Beijing had little to gain from going to war with India and while it supplied Pakistan, it was unlikely to use force.[131] On 6 December 1971, Gandhi announced India's recognition of East Pakistan as the independent state of Bangladesh.[132] Yahya had assured Pakistan's regional commander, Lt-Gen Niazi that China and the US would intervene but this support failed to materialise and he was forced to surrender.[133] Consequently, Pakistani forces withdrew and the state of Bangladesh was established.

Given the sheer scale of atrocities, one might expect India's use of force to be accepted under international law,[134] particularly given international inaction. However, India's primary justification for using force against Pakistan was self-defence.[135] Such a claim has merit as despite border skirmishes, Pakistan's air strikes went well beyond this, giving India a legitimate *casus belli*.[136] Although self-defence is an inherent right, it is not unlimited. While India's actions were

127 Ibid. Para.54.

128 Central Intelligence Agency Information Cable TDCS–315/07612–71 (December 15, 1971) http://2001-2009.state.gov/r/pa/ho/frus/nixon/e7txt/50165.htm Accessed 10th March 2024.

129 Pakistani forces in East Pakistan were surrounded by a hostile population (Jones. *Supra* note 62). India had air-superiority, a larger army and had local support.

130 Conversation between President Nixon and his Assistant for National Security Affairs (Kissinger), Washington (6 December 1971) https://history.state.gov/historicaldocuments/frus1969-76ve07/d162 Accessed 10th March 2024.

131 Anderson. *Supra* note 77. p.248.

132 'Mrs Gandhi says recognition is a tribute to freedom struggle' *Guardian.* (7 December 1971).

133 Young, Gavin. 'How Dacca fell: the inside story' *Observer.* (19 December 1971).

134 Wheeler, Nicholas. *Saving Strangers: Humanitarian Intervention in International Society* (Oxford, 2010) p.55.

135 See UN Security Council. *Official Records, 26th Year, 1606th Meeting.* UN Doc S/PV.1606. (4 December 1971) Para 163–164.

136 International Commission of Jurists. *Supra* note 63. p.90.

in reaction to a Pakistani armed attack, they swept through East Pakistan and enacted regime change that goes well beyond self-defence under international law.[137] India appeared to see Article 51 of the UN Charter as a weak defence for its actions and instead claimed its actions were in response to a different type of aggression, which India called refugee aggression.[138] India's response required more than merely defending its borders and Pakistan's internal actions were having grave consequences for India.[139] India could potentially claim self-defence that explains why India refused a ceasefire without any political settlement for East Pakistan as this would not resolve the crisis or stem the flow of refugees. The burden of the refugees on India was onerous[140] and the influx of so many displaced people into areas of India where there was already unrest placed even further strain on the country.[141]

India could simply have closed its borders but it did not do so and went to great efforts to sustain refugees, despite its own domestic problems.[142] An end to 'refugee aggression' would be nearly impossible without a political settlement in East Pakistan that was not forthcoming in the UNSC. Although India claimed it would help the East Pakistanis, it denied it was fighting on their behalf, noting that for 'so long as we have any light of civilized behaviour in us, we shall protect them. We shall not fight their battle [...] but whatever help we can give [...] we shall give it.'[143] It is likely that the refugee crisis was a key impetus that drove India to war as it simply could not cope with the numbers seeking shelter within its borders but neither could Indians turn their backs on Bengalis (especially Bengali Hindus) fleeing massacre. As the

137 This was noted by China that highlighted the problems with an expansive definition of self-defence being used to justify invasion. (See UN Security Council. *Official Records, 26th Year, 1606th Meeting.* UN Doc S/PV.1606. (4 December 1971) Para 238).

138 Wheeler. *Supra* note 134. pp.60–61. Supra note 137. Para.161.

139 This was a point made by the USSR when it highlighted that the East Pakistan crisis was now an international problem with international consequences (UN Security Council. *Official Records, 26th Year, 1607th Meeting* UN Doc S/PV.1607 (5 December 1971) Para.120). Likewise, Anderson noted that the refugees was arguably a form of aggression against India that had enough trouble feeding its own citizens, let alone millions of refugees (Anderson. *Supra* note 77. p.218).

140 By December 1971, India claimed it was sheltering over ten million refugees, an estimate accepted by impartial observers (International Commission of Jurists. *Supra* note 63. p.92). Although the exact number is debatable, the economic burden on India was severe at a time when it was already running a large budget deficit ('The cost of 5 million Refugees' *Economist.* (12th June 1971)).

141 Schanberg. *Supra* 65.

142 See *Supra* note 140.

143 UN Security Council. *Official Records, 26th Year, 1606th Meeting.* UN Doc S/PV.1606. (4 December 1971) Para.175.

International Commission of Jurists concluded, it is unlikely India acted solely in self-defence.[144]

India also claimed it was operating in East Pakistan at the invitation of the Bangladeshi government.[145] India could credibly claim that it was operating with the consent of Pakistan's legitimate authority, given the AL victory in the 1970 National Assembly election. This was particularly the case in East Pakistan where the Awami League had won a landslide victory.[146] Despite its authoritarianism, Yahya's regime was recognised internationally and the AL electoral mandate was for autonomy, not secession. It is therefore unlikely that East Pakistan had an inherent right of self-determination. However, given Yahya sought to impose a different sort of regime than that voted for by Pakistan's electorate,[147] the AL had an arguably greater authority than Yahya's unelected regime and the AL could claim the right to resist the Pakistani military by force.[148] India took months to recognise the Bangladeshi government in exile, likely reflecting its gradual understanding that East Pakistani secession was in their interests. Likewise, India argued that Islamabad's failure to retain East Pakistan's loyalty combined with its inability to maintain control gave legitimacy to Bangladeshi secession.[149]

### 1.2 *Humanitarian Intervention and East Pakistan*

There can be little doubt that there was a crisis in East Pakistan, with atrocities by the Pakistani army potentially amounting to genocide[150] while an official

144 International Commission of Jurists. *Supra* note 63. p.90.

145 UN Security Council. *Official Records, 26th Year, 1611th Meeting.* UN Doc S/PV.1611 (12th December 1971) Para.100.

146 Ghauri, S.R 'Fear of deadlock in Pakistan' *Guardian.* (19 December 1970).

147 International Commission of Jurists. *Supra* note 63. pp.97–98.

148 UN Security Council. *Official Records, 26th Year, 1611th Meeting.* UN Doc S/PV.1611 (12th December 1971) Para.100.

149 UN Security Council. *Official Records, 26th Year, 1608th Meeting.* UN Doc S/PV.1608 (6 December 1971). Para.124.

150 Hitchens summarises the problem as involving the suppression of an election, the use of 'genocidal policy' and the grave threat posed to international peace and security (Hitchens. *Supra* note 76. p.46). The International Commission of Jurists agreed the targeting of Bengali Hindus made a strong case for amounting to genocide but rejected the claim that Pakistani actions constituted genocide against the Bengalis as a whole (International Commission of Jurists. *Supra* note 63. p.57). This matched reports by the US consulate in Dhaka which noted that the term 'genocide' was inappropriate to use for the violence against Bengali Muslims, but the flagrant targeting of Bengali Hindus amounted to genocide (Blood. *Supra* note 54. p.216).

Pakistani inquiry commission found evidence of military atrocities.[151] India was left with few options to respond. Despite strong Indian political and public support for military action against Pakistan, Gandhi initially sought peaceful means to resolve the conflict.[152] She sought the help of numerous countries in changing Pakistan's course and used a 'fairly sophisticated diplomatic and public relations campaign' to change Pakistan's policy.[153] Although this was rendered futile by the general international consensus that East Pakistan was an internal matter for Islamabad, it does offer India a defence against accusations of a premature resort to force.[154] It was only after Gandhi despaired of a political solution that she resorted to military means.[155] Furthermore, India conducted itself well in East Pakistan.[156] India's behaviour, particularly when combined with its willingness to aid East Pakistani refugees, strengthens its humanitarian claims.

---

151 The Pakistani Commission was established under Hamoodur Rahman, a Bengali Chief-Justice. Although the Commission's report claimed many alleged atrocities were exaggerated or false, it concluded that there was 'substance in the allegations that during and after the military action excesses were indeed committed on the people of East Pakistan'. It also noted and that Awami League provocation could not justify atrocities being conducted by professional soldiers against their own people (Hamoodar Rahman Commission Report (1974) p.36 http://img.dunyanews.tv/images/docss/hamoodur_rahman_commission_report.pdf Accessed 10th March 2024). Likewise, a Pakistani officer admitted to the Hamoodur Rahman Commission that there was a general feeling of hatred towards Bengalis throughout the chain of command, with 'verbal instructions given to eliminate Hindus'. (Ibid. p.26) In addition, a Pakistani brigadier confirmed that soldiers were given written orders to kill Hindus (Ibid. p.27).

152 Schanberg. *Supra 65*.

153 Memorandum from Samuel Hoskinson of the National Security Council Staff to the President's Assistant for National Security Affairs (Kissinger) (26 May 1971) https://history.state.gov/historicaldocuments/frus1969-76ve07/d134 Accessed 10th March 2024.

154 Kulke and Rothermund. *Supra* note 68. p.342.

155 Bass. *Supra* note 73. p.258.

156 Despite outrage at Pakistani atrocities, Indian soldiers treated Pakistani POW humanely and unilaterally ended fighting once Pakistan surrendered (Anderson. *Supra* note 77. p.268). India also took steps to prevent further violence upon Bangladeshi independence, patrolling troubled areas of Dhaka to prevent reprisals against Biharis. ('Who Knows How Many Millions Have Been Killed' in the East?' *New York Times.* (22 December 1971)). It must be noted that many East Pakistanis committed atrocities with reprisals against Biharis and West Pakistanis taking place during and directly after the conflict. The International Commission of Jurists noted that while the scale of anti-Bihari violence probably meets the criteria to be considered crimes against humanity, it was spontaneous mob violence rather than an organised targeting of civilians and probably not genocide under international law (International Commission of Jurists. *Supra* note 63. pp.61–62). The new Bangladeshi government was mostly successful in ensuring that the courts, rather than mobs determined the fate of collaborators (Ibid. p.44).

Regional conflicts, particularly those involving the Great Powers, were of even graver importance during the Cold War and UN Secretary-General Thant warned both India and Pakistan that any hostilities risked jeopardising the 'wider peace'.[157] While the UNSC had the authority to determine the threat to international peace and security under Article 39 of the UN Charter before taking measures under Chapter VII, no action was forthcoming.[158] At any rate, such a move would almost certainly have been pointless, given the widely divergent views of the P5. The US and China would presumably veto any Resolution calling for East Pakistani independence, while the USSR demonstrated its willingness to veto any ceasefire that resulted in India withdrawing from East Pakistan. It was only when the Indo-Pakistan war broke out that the UNSC debated the issue and even then, limited its involvement to the conflict and not the alleged genocide, with the UNSC debates achieving nothing. As the US Assistant Secretary of Defence for International Security Affairs highlighted, India's actions showed UN impotence in maintaining international peace and security.[159]

This was apparent from the outset to Kissinger, who felt working with the UN was likely to be an 'exercise in futility', with the UN able to do little while the Soviet veto rendered the UNSC 'as a farce'.[160] This was also apparent to the UNGA, with Nicaragua warning that the UN's inability to resolve the crisis would damn it to irrelevance.[161] While India can be criticised for using force without seeking a UN resolution, the UN's failure to treat the causes of the conflict and UNSC deadlock shows that India's reluctance was well founded. Not only did the UN fail to prevent the crisis, but it also failed to stop the fighting or secure a political settlement.[162] With this in mind and India's prior attempts to resolve the crisis without direct intervention, India had a legitimate defence against accusations of a premature resort to force. Crucially, India's use of force was proportionate with ending the atrocities.[163]

---

157 UN Security Council. *Report of the Secretary-General.* UN Doc S/10410 (3 December 1971) p.5.

158 Wheeler. *Supra* note 134. p.75.

159 Memorandum from the Assistant Secretary of Defence for International Security Affairs (Nutter) to Secretary of Defence Laird (December 30, 1971) http://2001-2009.state.gov/r/pa/ho/frus/nixon/e7txt/50170.htm Accessed 10th March 2024.

160 Anderson, Jack. 'U.S., U.N. Damaged by Indian Blitz' *Washington Post.* (1 January 1972).

161 UN General Assembly. *Supra* note 123. Para.194.

162 Nanda, Ved. 'A Critique of the United Nations Inaction in the Bangladesh Crisis' *Denver Journal of International Law* (Vol.49, 1972–1973) p.55.

163 International Commission of Jurists. *Supra* note 63. p.96.

While India did not rush into war, its motives were debatable, with Pakistan being especially vocal that India was acting out of self-interest.[164] Despite India's claims to be acting in self-defence, it was evident that it would benefit from Pakistan's partition,[165] with the East Pakistan crisis offering India a chance to weaken its rival.[166] Nonetheless, India's claims of self-defence are weakened, given it went far beyond what was necessary to defend itself while Pakistan's military posed little threat to India.

A ceasefire as recommended by the international community would restore the status-quo after India had demonstrated its strength. As India noted at the UNSC, a cease-fire would merely free up Pakistani soldiers to continue their atrocities.[167] This view was endorsed by the USSR, which argued that a cease-fire without a political settlement permitted Pakistan to conduct further bloodshed.[168] Gandhi rejected calls for a cease-fire, saying that India would take all steps necessary to create an independent Bangladesh, referring to Pakistan as an occupier, whose oppression of the Bengalis forced India to go to their rescue.[169] The US State Department noted that India would likely accept a cease-fire once East Bengal was 'liberated' and would agree to a cease-fire should Pakistani forces surrender.[170] Likewise, Gandhi noted both that Pakistan's actions posed a threat to Indian security but also that India could not stand by while Bengalis were killed.[171] New Delhi could not permit Pakistan to maintain its campaign of terror, which would ensure a steady stream of refugees seeking shelter in India, but also due to widespread outrage within India at Pakistani atrocities.[172]

---

164 Pakistan was adamant that India was merely using the East Pakistan crisis as a cloak while dismembering Pakistan (UN Security Council. *Official Records, 26th Year, 1606th Meeting.* UN Doc S/PV.1606. (4 December 1971) Para.70) Likewise, Pakistan's Institute of International Affairs argued that India saw East Pakistan as a way to destroy Pakistan, having failed to do so in the 1965 Indo-Pakistan war (Hasan, K. Sarwar. 'Political Background of the East Pakistan Crisis' *Pakistan Horizon* (Vol.24, No.2, Second Quarter, 1971) p.4).

165 An independent Bangladesh would deprive Pakistan of over half its population, simultaneously weakening Pakistan and ensuring India had an ally on its eastern flank.

166 Bazyler. *Supra* note 30. p.589.

167 UN Security Council. *Official Records, 26th Year, 1606th Meeting.* UN Doc S/PV.1606. (4 December 1971) Para.172.

168 UN Security Council. *Official Records, 26th Year, 1608th Meeting.* UN Doc S/PV.1608 (6 December 1971). Para.57.

169 'India to fight until Bangla Desh free' *Irish Times.* (11th December 1971).

170 Anderson. *Supra* note 77. p.233.

171 Anonymous. 'E Bengal must be free says Gandhi' *Irish Times.* (1 December 1971).

172 Outrage at Pakistani atrocities was especially notable among Indian politicians (Bass, Gary. Bass. *Supra* note 73. p.89) while the Indian government soon described Pakistan's actions as genocide (Sterba, James. 'India Charges Genocide' *New York Times.* (17 April

Despite its numerous criticisms of Pakistan's brutality, India did not use explicitly humanitarian justifications for its intervention. India's representative at the UNSC warned against an overemphasis on sovereignty at the expense of human rights and justice,[173] but such claims were parenthetical. Although India initially claimed it was engaging in a rescue mission,[174] it received no support for this and quietly dropped this claim in favour of self-defence.[175] The likely reason for this was to ensure consistency between India's tradition as a champion of non-intervention and its use of force in East Pakistan.[176] Rather, India relied mainly on self-defence claims for its use of force, particularly in relation to 'refugee aggression',[177] which should not be disassociated from the genocide in East Pakistan.

In a letter to Nixon, Gandhi not only highlighted that India acted in self-defence but that Pakistan's cruel governance 'culminated in genocide' and sent millions fleeing into India's borders.[178] She also claimed that the war only came about when India's diplomacy failed and that while Pakistan's territorial integrity was 'sacrosanct, human rights, liberty were no less so', with a key link between states' inviolable territory and the consent of their citizens.[179] While India did not necessarily seek East Pakistani independence, it could not

1971)). Likewise, resolutions stating Pakistan's 'systematic decimation of people amounts to genocide' were unanimously passed in both chambers of India's parliament (Schanberg, Sydney. 'Parliament in India condemns Pakistani 'massacre' in East' *New York Times*. (1 April 1971)) Outrage was shared among the Indian public, with universal suffrage and a free press ensuring considerable public pressure on the East Pakistan crisis. To Indians, the Pakistani military's suppression of the elected will of the people was literally 'evil crushing good' (Schanberg. *Supra* 65). Likewise, India's Gen. Jacob responded to accusations of violating Pakistani sovereignty by asking how India could remain complacent when Pakistan was engaging in genocide, rape and forcing millions of refugees to stream into India (Cited by Bass. *Supra* note 73. pp.322–323).

173 UN Security Council. *Official Records, 26th Year, 1608th Meeting.* UN Doc S/PV.1608 (6 December 1971). Para.262.

174 UN Security Council. *Official Records, 26th Year, 1606th Meeting.* UN Doc S/PV.1606. (4 December 1971) Para.185.

175 Roy-Chaudhury, Rahul. 'The Security Council and the India-Pakistan Wars' in Lowe, Vaughan, Roberts, Adam, Welsh, Jennifer and Zaum, Dominik (Eds.) *The United Nations Security Council and War: The Evolution of Thought and Practice since 1945* (Oxford, 2008) p.339.

176 Fonteyne. *Supra* note 1. p.204.

177 See *Supra* note 95.

178 'Letter from Indian Prime Minister Gandhi to President Nixon' (5 December 1971) https://history.state.gov/historicaldocuments/frus1969-76v11/d226 Accessed 10th March 2024.

179 Letter from the Indian Ambassador (Jha) to President Nixon (15 December 1971) http://2001-2009.state.gov/r/pa/ho/frus/nixon/xi/45597.htm Accessed 10th March 2024.

permit Pakistan to continue its campaign. In a letter to the UN's Secretary-General, India highlighted the brutality that Pakistan was unleashing against its own citizens.[180] India also noted that while it had sympathy for oppressed East Pakistanis, it could have taken 'a detached view' had it not taken place in a neighbouring country, sending so many refugees to India's borders.[181]

India highlighted its longstanding policy of non-interference but noted that a state has few options when so many refugees are forced onto it by another.[182] India was not seeking to expand or destroy Pakistan as a rival but to end the flow of refugees, a point stressed by Gandhi who highlighted India wanted no territorial concessions.[183] This was confirmed by the UK who received Indian assurances to this effect.[184] Although some prominent Indians (including the Defence Minister and military officers) wanted to refuse a UN brokered cease-fire until Pakistan's military was destroyed and parts of Kashmir were under Indian control, this was rejected by Gandhi who was willing to accept a cease-fire once the AL took their elected place, a position supported by the USSR.[185]

To this end, it appears that India's motives were mixed. It stood to benefit from an independent Bangladesh but was unlikely to have gone to war had Pakistan not forced so many refugees upon it. Likewise, India only resorted to force once diplomacy failed, and it became apparent that the Mukthi Bahini would be unable to drive out Pakistani forces. Thus, India had few other options, and showed comparative restraint as it dealt with millions of refugees.

It is arguable that India's actions did not establish a right of humanitarian intervention under customary international law as it did not use humanitarian justifications. This is highlighted by Hassan, who notes that while many academics use East Pakistan as an example of humanitarian intervention, India did not take such a stance itself.[186] India's motives were not entirely selfish. New Delhi allowed refugees into its territory and went to great efforts to

180 UN Doc S/10445 (12th December 1971).

181 Ibid.

182 Ibid.

183 Gandhi, Indira. 'Text of Prime Minister Gandhi's Letter to President' *New York Times* (17 December 1971).

184 Telegram 11295 from the Embassy in the United Kingdom to the Department of State (December 13, 1971) http://2001-2009.state.gov/r/pa/ho/frus/nixon/e7txt/49207.htm Accessed 10th March 2024.

185 Central Intelligence Agency Intelligence Information Cable TDCS–314/13308–71 (December 13, 1971) http://2001-2009.state.gov/r/pa/ho/frus/nixon/e7txt/50163.htm Accessed 10th March 2024.

186 Hassan, Farooq. 'Realpolitik in International Law: After Tanzanian-Ugandan Conflict Humanitarian Intervention Reexamined' *Willamette Law Review* (Vol.17, Issue.4, Fall 1981) p.886.

sustain them.[187] Even if India did not act for purely humanitarian purposes, intervention simultaneously benefitted India's security problems, resolved the refugee crisis, and ensured Bangladeshi independence. Consequently, the humanitarian benefits cannot be ignored.[188]

Although India's actions had a humanitarian result, for its intervention to establish a norm under customary international law, it would need a high level of acceptance from the international community. Due to the Cold War, this was lacking and the UN was preoccupied with the humanitarian symptoms, rather than Pakistani atrocities.[189] The UNSC was predictably divided along Cold War lines, with geopolitics taking precedence over ideology.[190] Only China explicitly condemned India for aggression, with most states supporting a ceasefire and mutual military withdrawal. Although a Soviet resolution for a political solution was solely supported by Poland, the sole vote against was from China, with the rest of the UNSC abstaining[191] but even without the Chinese veto, the motion lacked enough votes to pass. The weak UNSC response highlights the problems with India's intervention. Although most of the states were unwilling to endorse India's actions, neither were they willing to condemn India for aggression. The reluctance to condemn India probably arose from an understanding of Pakistani brutality alongside its incursions into India. Another likely reason was that the USSR would veto any resolution condemning India, so efforts were made to avoid criticising India to create conditions where a ceasefire resolution could be adopted.

Further light on humanitarian intervention under international law can be gleaned from the UNGA debate. Here, India had few supporters with most states supporting an immediate ceasefire. The debate was broadly split along Cold War lines with most Western and Non-Aligned nations supporting the resolution, while those opposed were nearly all USSR-aligned nations.[192] Few (including

---

187 See *Supra* note 140.

188 Teson highlights, even if India's motives were not purely humanitarian, the result certainly was, with East Pakistan benefiting from India ending the genocide (Teson. *Supra* note 1. pp.250–251) Likewise, Bass concludes that although India had mixed motives, it was also motivated by genuine humanitarianism to aid East Pakistanis (Bass. *Supra* note 73. p.335).

189 Moses, Dirk. 'The United Nations, Humanitarianism and Human Rights: War Crimes/Genocide Trials for Pakistani Soldiers in Bangladesh, 1971–1974,' in Hoffman, Stefan-Ludwig (Ed.) *Human Rights in the Twentieth Century* (New York, 2011) p.268.

190 The US and Maoist China supported Pakistan's dictatorship while the communist USSR backed the non-aligned but democratic India.

191 UN Security Council. *Official Records, 26th Year, 1607th Meeting* UN Doc S/PV.1607 (5 December 1971) Para.217.

192 UN General Assembly. *Supra* note 123. Para.490.

China,[193] Portugal,[194] and Albania)[195] explicitly criticised India and these had their own ulterior motives.[196] Other states like Lebanon[197] and Sudan[198] highlighted territorial sovereignty and the principle of non-intervention but did not explicitly condemn India for aggression. Likewise, while Sweden criticised Pakistan's human rights record, it highlighted that the UN Charter forbids the use of force outside of self-defence.[199] Even those states like Czechoslovakia that opposed condemning India focussed on the need for a political settlement and did not justify India's actions as humanitarian intervention.[200]

Post-colonial countries mostly sided with Pakistan, viewing sovereignty as a bulwark against imperialism, particularly since such countries saw Pakistan as a small country standing up to a predatory larger neighbour.[201] Despite a lack of UN condemnation, the reality was more nuanced. Although China's resolution condemning Indian aggression was not adopted, neither was India's position endorsed by most UN states, either in the UNGA or in the UNSC. Rather, most states in both organs supported an immediate ceasefire and mutual military withdrawal. Consequently, it is difficult to argue that India's actions can be seen as strengthening humanitarian intervention under customary international law, given the lack of support from other states. Although few states explicitly criticised India, even fewer supported her with the majority refraining from commenting while supporting a ceasefire that was to Pakistan's benefit. Only the USSR's veto prevented a binding resolution from being adopted while the UNGA's inability to enforce its decisions ensured India simply ignored it.

Overall, it would appear that India's actions did not strengthen the status of humanitarian intervention under customary international law. Teson claims that India's actions were a legitimate form of humanitarian intervention, supporting the East Pakistanis in exercising self-determination while ending genocide.[202] Likewise, no organ of the UN condemned India, with a

193 Ibid.) Para.311.

194 Ibid. Para.264.

195 Ibid. Para.107.

196 China's rivalry with India has already been noted while India's annexation of Portuguese India in 1961 poisoned New Delhi's relations with Portugal's dictatorship and Albania was a key Chinese ally, having sided with China during the Sino-Soviet split.

197 UN General Assembly. *Supra* note 123. Para.53.

198 Ibid. Para.87.

199 Ibid. Para.302.

200 Ibid.) Para.149.

201 Moses, Dirk. 'The United Nations, Humanitarianism and Human Rights: War Crimes/Genocide Trials for Pakistani Soldiers in Bangladesh, 1971–1974,' in Hoffman, Stefan-Ludwig (Ed.) *Human Rights in the Twentieth Century* (New York, 2011) p.278.

202 Teson. *Supra* note 1. p.248.

non-condemnatory ceasefire having the most support in both the UNGA and UNSC. It could be argued that the UNSC's reluctance to condemn India arose from an understanding that the USSR would veto any such proposal. The UNGA has no such veto to worry about and still sought to broker a ceasefire rather than criticise India for breaching international law. Indeed, the UNGA seemed broadly reconciled to India's use of force and many nations swiftly recognised the new Bangladeshi state.[203] This somewhat strengthens the argument that India's intervention was broadly accepted by the international community. There was no overt support for India's actions as humanitarian, with neither India nor its allies using this as a justification. Likewise, India's actions were unsupported by most states who largely refrained from condemning India but supported an Indian withdrawal. This would maintain Pakistani control and give Islamabad little incentive to cease its brutal campaign.

Although Franck and Rodley concluded that at the time, humanitarian intervention lacked the criteria to be considered an exception to the prohibition on the use of force,[204] many other academics note India's actions would have been a leading example of humanitarian intervention and justifiable under international law, had India invoked humanitarian intervention.[205] Despite India's lack of reliance on humanitarian intervention as a justification, the International Commission of Jurists remarked that it would have been justified in doing so, given the refugee crisis, international inaction and the proportionate use of force that India used to end the atrocities in East Pakistan.[206] While the ongoing brutality in East Pakistan was a key mitigating factor in India's breach of the UN Charter, India's reliance on self-defence claims over humanitarian justifications is likely due to India's realisation that this was its best option for legitimising its intervention, particularly given the Cold War's polarisation.

---

203 Nanda. *Supra 162*. p.66.

204 Franck and Rodley. *Supra* note 40. pp.304–305.

205 Abiew. *Supra* note 1. p.117. Likewise, Fonteyne claims that despite India's reluctance to justify its actions under humanitarian intervention, its actions constituted the clearest contemporary example of humanitarian intervention (Fonteyne. *Supra* note 1. p.204). Wheeler highlights the intervention can be seen as humanitarian given India was guided by necessity and proportionality, but its methods and primary motivation were not incompatible with the humanitarian result (Wheeler. *Supra* note 134. p.75). Wheeler further notes that India's actions did not pose a major risk in normalising the use of force: states relying on the East Pakistan intervention as a precedent would need to demonstrate a similar security threat as faced by India (Ibid. p.76).

206 International Commission of Jurists. *Supra* note 63. p.96.

## 2 Humanitarian Intervention in Cambodia, 1978

Cambodia's history is one of invasions,[207] ensuring that during the Cold War, Cambodia's monarch, Prince Sihanouk, was primarily concerned with maintaining Cambodia's independence.[208] In 1970, Sihanouk was overthrown by General Lon Nol who was in turn overthrown by the Maoist Khmer Rouge who seized Phnom Penh in April 1975.[209] The Khmer Rouge, led by Pol Pot, was initially seen as severe rather than dangerous and its seizure of Phnom Penh was generally welcomed.[210] However, the Khmer Rouge quickly established itself as brutal towards its own population[211] and ethnic minorities.[212] The Khmer

207 In the postclassical era, Cambodia was the heartland of the Angkor Empire before being colonised by France in the nineteenth century and achieving independence in 1953 (CIA World Factbook 'Cambodia' https://www.cia.gov/the-world-factbook/countries/cambodia/ Accessed 10th March 2024). Unlike many other postcolonial countries, Cambodia was mostly ethnically and linguistically homogenous as well as heavily rural and isolated (Kiernan, Ben. *The Pol Pot Regime: Race, Power, and Genocide in Cambodia under the Khmer Rouge, 1975–1979* (New Haven, 2002) pp.4–5).

208 Sihanouk kept rigid control of power but was paternalist towards his subjects (Chandler, David. *A History of Cambodia* (Boulder, 2008) pp.242–244).

209 Lon Nol's anti-communism ensured he received support from a US anxious for a South-East Asian ally during the Vietnam War (Power, Samantha. *A Problem from Hell: America and the Age of Genocide* (New York, 2002) pp.92–93). US involvement stoked support for the Khmer Rouge, both domestically and internationally, particularly by China and Vietnam.

210 Although Phnom Penh's residents were not mostly Khmer Rouge supporters, they saw their arrival as heralding an end to the war (Lufty, James. 'Humanitarian Intervention: The Invasion of Cambodia' *New York Law School Journal of International and Comparative Law* (1980–1981) p.143), causing civilians to rejoice and weep with joy (Cazeaux, Jean-Jacques and Juvenal, Claude. 'Phnom Penh Fell First to Obscure Playboy' *Washington Post*. (8 May 1975)).

211 Families were split, children were brainwashed and encouraged to inform on their parents, radios were banned, schools were closed and currency abolished (Schanberg, Sydney. 'Cambodia' in Gutman, Roy, Dieff, David and Dworkin, Anthony. *Crimes of War* (New York, 2007) p.77). The nation was turned into a forced labour camp with refugees describing forced labour and severe food shortages (Greenway, H.D.S. 'The New Cambodia: A Harsh and Joyless Land' *Washington Post*. (2 February 1976)).

212 Despite communism's emphasis on class over race, the Khmer Rouge was explicitly racist, targeting ethnic minorities who had settled in Cambodia for centuries. Although hundreds of thousands of Vietnamese had left Cambodia during the 1970s, there were still some 30,000 Vietnamese citizens in Cambodia when the Khmer Rouge seized power (Amer, Ramses. 'The Ethnic Vietnamese in Cambodia: A Minority at Risk?' *Contemporary SouthEast Asia* (Vol. 16, No. 2, September 1994) pp.211-p.218). The Vietnamese were mercilessly targeted for extermination by the Khmer Rouge (Kiernan. *Supra* note 207. p.460). Likewise, the Muslim Cham were the largest indigenous minority in Cambodia and a remnant of the Kingdom of Champa, which had been defeated by Vietnam in 1471 (Ibid.

Rouge avoided aligning itself with other communist states and adopted a government radically different to other Marxist-Leninist regimes.[213] In this way, Cambodia was an isolated nation, ensuring minimal media coverage of ongoing human rights abuses.

Although US intelligence warned that Khmer Rouge victory would result in 'bloodletting' against members of the Lon Nol regime and the middle class would be subjected to indoctrination, the US still concluded that 'mass exemplary executions' were unlikely.[214] This proved hard to verify as the expulsion of foreign nationals exacerbated the lack of knowledge on the situation within Cambodia[215] that was compounded by the Khmer Rouge sealing the borders. This isolation made it difficult for human rights groups to confirm the sheer extent of atrocities within Cambodia. Amnesty International noted allegations made by refugees mandated 'deep concern' but that widespread reports of killing were 'unverifiable' due to the lack of reporters and restriction of information.[216] Refugee reports were so consistent and detailed that certainly some atrocities took place.[217] The US State Department highlighted it was impossible to estimate the precise number killed due to the lack of intelligence,[218] while the UN noted it was impossible to secure proof of atrocities without a thorough investigation.[219] Although Cambodia denied mass killings took place, insisting that only 'the worst criminals' were condemned,[220] the CIA reported that the Khmer Rouge was the most extreme of the world's

---

pp.252–253). Being an ethnic and religious minority, they were also targeted by the Khmer Rouge. Overall, ethnic minorities dropped from 10% of the Cambodian population to just 3% (Mysliwiec, Eva. *Punishing the Poor: The International Isolation of Kampuchea* (Oxford, 1988) pp.12–13).

213 'Research Study Prepared by the Central Intelligence Agency, Washington' (December 1976) https://history.state.gov/historicaldocuments/frus1969-76ve12/d95 Accessed 10th March 2024.

214 Intelligence Memorandum, Washington (31 January 1975) https://history.state.gov/historicaldocuments/frus1969-76ve12/d64 Accessed 10th March 2024.

215 'Minutes of the Secretary of State's Staff Meeting, Washington' (30 April 1975) https://history.state.gov/historicaldocuments/frus1969-76ve12/d65 Accessed 10th March 2024.

216 Amnesty International. *Amnesty International Report 1977* (London, 1977) p.167.

217 Greenway, H.D.S. 'the New Cambodia: A Harsh and Joyless Land' *Washington Post.* (2 February 1976).

218 US Senate. *Hearing before the Subcommittee on East Asian and Pacific Affairs of the Committee on Foreign Relations. 95 Congress, 2nd Session on the Current Situation in Indochina.* (August 1978) p.22.

219 UN Economic and Social Council. Subcommission on Prevention of Discrimination and Protection of Minorities. *Analysis of Information Materials on the Situation of Human Rights in Democratic Kampuchea.* UN Doc E/CN.4/1335 (30 January 1979) p.7.

220 Amnesty International. *Supra* note 216. p.190.

totalitarian governments[221] and so many Cambodians had been killed[222] that the case that genocide occurred is arguable.[223]

Nevertheless, the international community did little to end the violence given Cambodia posed little threat to international peace and security. Rather, Cambodia pursued a policy of isolationist non-alignment, refusing even to ally itself with China, despite its total reliance on Beijing.[224] In the tense environment of the Cold War, few states wished to risk destabilisation, particularly given Soviet backing of Vietnam and China's support to the Khmer Rouge. Although the Khmer Rouge horrified most countries, no decisive action was taken.[225] It must be noted that although Cambodia was heavily censored and cut off from the rest of the world, the US was soon aware of the Khmer Rouge's brutality and yet did nothing.[226] This was also the case for nations such as UK,

---

221 'Research Study Prepared by the Central Intelligence Agency, Washington' (December 1976) https://www.cia.gov/the-world-factbook/countries/cambodia/ Accessed 10th March 2024. UN Under-Secretary-General Jackson noted the Khmer Rouge's slaughter in Cambodia was the 'greatest human tragedy of the twentieth century' (Mysliwiec. *Supra* note 212. P.iii). Likewise, the Khmer Rouge was described 'one of the most savage and repressive regimes of this Century' (Ibid. p.2) and it was surpassed in brutality only by the Third Reich (Wolf. *Supra* note 2. p.350).

222 By the time the Khmer Rouge were overthrown, some 1.5 to 2 million Cambodians had been killed, comprising some 20% of the population (Schanberg. *Supra* note 211. p.76). Kiernan likewise estimates that some 1.6 million were killed, a figure corroborated by death tolls within individual communities (Kiernan. *Supra* note 207. pp.458–459). Although most were killed through exhaustion, starvation, or inadequate medical care, around 400,000 were executed, primarily in provincial prisons (Chandler. *Supra* note 208. p.259).

223 This is debatable: although such atrocities primarily involved the Khmer Rouge slaughtering their fellow Khmers, it was an attempt to eradicate the Cambodian way of life, particularly Buddhism (Schanberg. *Supra* note 211. p.76). Consequently, a UN Rapporteur viewed the Khmer Rouge's actions as 'auto-genocide' that highlighted the existence of genocide within an ethnic group (UN Social and Economic Council. *Record of Meeting Held on 7 March 1979*. UN Doc E/CN.4/SR.1510 (9 March 1979) Para.22). Even if not deemed genocide, the Khmer Rouge committed crimes against humanity and minority groups such as the Cham were deliberately targeted.

224 'Research Study Prepared by the Central Intelligence Agency, Washington' (December 1976) https://history.state.gov/historicaldocuments/frus1969-76ve12/d95 Accessed 10th March 2024.

225 Ronzitti. *Supra* note 30. p.98.

226 Power. *Supra* note 209. p.90. Indeed, just days after the fall of Phnom Penh, Kissinger claimed to have conclusive evidence of the 'blood bath' going in on Cambodia ('Minutes of the Secretary of State's Staff Meeting, Washington' (30 April 1975) https://history.state.gov/historicaldocuments/frus1969-76ve12/d65 Accessed 10th March 2024). Although President Carter made human rights a cornerstone of his presidency, the memory of the Vietnam War ensured Washington would not deploy troops to South-East Asia (Power. *Supra* note 209. p.123). Likewise, with no aid programmes or diplomatic relations, the US

Canada, Australia and Norway.[227] The UN was little better and three years in, none of its organs had spoken out against atrocities in Cambodia.[228] However, intervention arose from elsewhere.

### 2.1 *The Vietnam-Cambodia War*

Cambodia going to war with Vietnam was perhaps inevitable, with the Khmer Rouge declaring that Vietnam was occupying Cambodian territory.[229] The Vietnamese civil war had ended with victory for the communists in 1975 but Vietnamese unification was marked by conservative leadership policies and international isolation.[230] Likewise, the government was authoritarian, with widespread internment in 're-education' camps.[231] However, it was still far less brutal than its Khmer Rouge neighbour.

The Khmer Rouge was expansionist and in 1975 sought to take advantage of South Vietnam's defeat to annex Vietnamese islands, though it was repulsed.[232] Further border disputes erupted in 1977 and Cambodia sought to annex Vietnamese territory arguing it was stolen from Cambodia in the nineteenth century.[233] Vietnam offered to negotiate a solution that was refused, but had Cambodia accepted, it is likely that Pol Pot's regime would have survived.[234]

---

had little leverage to use on the Khmer Rouge (US Senate. *Supra* note 218. p.2). Even if such leverage existed, there seemed to be little political will to use it. The key exception to this was US senator George McGovern who urged American humanitarian intervention in Cambodia. Although McGovern had opposed the Vietnam War, he highlighted the differences, given the Khmer Rouge had seized power and lacked popular support (US Senate. *Supra* note 218. p.24) Douglas Pike, a State Department expert on Indochina highlighted that military action would be difficult to achieve (Ibid. p.30).

227 UN Economic and Social Council. Subcommission on Prevention of Discrimination and Protection of Minorities. *Analysis of Information Materials on the Situation of Human Rights in Democratic Kampuchea*. UN Doc E/CN.4/1335 (30 January 1979) p.4.

228 Power. *Supra* note 209. p.125.

229 Kiernan. *Supra* note 207. p.360. There is some truth in this, given that pre-colonial Vietnam had expanded at Cambodia's expense (Amer. *Supra* note *229*. p.211). Likewise, Cambodians were suspicious of Vietnam's goal of an Indochina federation, fearing Vietnamese domination (Becker, Elizabeth. 'Sihanouk and the Saga of the Khmer Rouge' *Washington Post*. (28 January 1979)). This was shared across South East Asia given Hanoi's military was roughly equal in strength to all its non-communist neighbours combined (US Senate. *Supra* note 218. p.1).

230 CIA World Factbook 'Vietnam' https://www.cia.gov/the-world-factbook/countries/vietnam Accessed 10th March 2024.

231 Amnesty International. *Supra* note 216. p.227.

232 Chandler. *Supra* note 208. p.269.

233 Butterfield, Fox. 'Situation in Cambodia 'Excellent', Its Leader Says at Peking Banquet' *New York Times* (30 September 1977).

234 Kiernan. *Supra* note 207. p.388.

Instead, its intransigence meant tensions escalated and Vietnam realised that its security required the Khmer Rouge's neutralisation.[235]

Vietnam declared war on Cambodia in December 1978 and 150,000 Vietnamese soldiers invaded Cambodia, backed by 15,000 Cambodian dissidents,[236] known as the Kampuchean United Front for National Salvation (FUNSK).[237] Against weak resistance, the Vietnamese took Phnom Penh after two weeks of fighting and announced the People's Republic of Kampuchea (PRK) under Heng Samrin, a former Khmer Rouge commander who had rebelled and defected to Vietnam.[238] Although many Cambodians fled the country those who remained were relieved by Vietnam's intervention[239] with the vast majority of Cambodians rejoicing.[240] Likewise, an Oxfam report noted that despite their inherent suspicion of Vietnam, nearly all Cambodians saw the Vietnamese as liberators.[241] Although the PRK was authoritarian,[242] it was far less repressive than the Khmer Rouge, restoring freedom of movement, religion and education.[243] Nonetheless, some 200,000 Vietnamese soldiers remained in Cambodia.[244]

Although Heng's regime was swiftly recognised by Vietnam, Laos, Czechoslovakia, the USSR and many USSR aligned countries,[245] its recognition was opposed by the Khmer Rouge's primary backer, China, as well as many Western states. Even after Phnom Penh had fallen and the extent of Cambodian atrocities became apparent, the UK continued to maintain its recognition of Pol Pot's regime.[246] Despite controlling 90% of Cambodia's

235 Wheeler. *Supra* note 134. p.81.
236 Kiernan. *Supra* note 207. p.450.
237 FUNSK soldiers were largely Cambodians who sought refuge in Vietnam or Cambodian POW who Hanoi trained (Chandler. *Supra* note 208. p.272). However, the FUNSK was created by Vietnam itself out of Cambodian refugees and its independence was suspect. (Ronzitti. *Supra* note 30. p.99).
238 Mysliwiec. *Supra* note 212. P. XI.
239 Chandler, David. *The Tragedy of Cambodian History: Politics, War and Revolution since 1945* (New Haven, 1991) p.313.
240 Kiernan. *Supra* note 207. p.455.
241 Mysliwiec. *Supra* note 212. p.9.
242 Shawcross, William. *Deliver Us from Evil: Warlords and Peacekeepers in a World of Endless Conflict* (London, 2001) p.35.
243 Becker, Elizabeth. 'Sihanouk and the Saga of the Khmer Rouge' *Washington Post.* (28 January 1979).
244 Mirsky, Jonathan, 'China's 1979 Invasion of Vietnam: A View from the Infantry' *RUSI* (1 June 1981) p.52.
245 Shannon, Don. 'U.S Backs Sihanouk on U.N debate' *Los Angeles Times.* (11th January 1979).
246 UK House of Commons. Written answers (Commons) 25 October 1979. Vol.972, Col.268.

territory and population,[247] the PRK was denied representation at the UN.[248] This was opposed by the USSR and Vietnam who questioned why a powerless and unelected Khmer Rouge represented Cambodia.[249] The UN Credentials Committee decided to recognise the Khmer Rouge as Cambodia's legitimate representative at the UN.[250]

The Khmer Rouge therefore remained internationally recognised as Cambodia's government, where it waged a guerrilla war against the PRK.[251] Despite having been imprisoned by the Khmer Rouge, Sihanouk feared Vietnamese domination and though he acknowledged the Khmer Rouge's brutality, he urged support for it against the 'Hitlerian Vietnamese aggressors'.[252] Although Sihanouk acknowledged that life under Heng was better than under the Khmer Rouge and most Cambodians were far happier under the new government,[253] his actions were in line with his preoccupation with maintaining Cambodian independence.[254]

When the UNSC met to discuss the issue, Sihanouk offered a useful way for member states to oppose Vietnam without explicitly endorsing the Khmer Rouge. Vietnam's intervention had little international support, with China accusing the USSR of supporting Vietnam in its 'naked, large scale armed

247 Rowley, Kelvin. 'Second Life, Second Death: The Khmer Rouge After 1978' in Cook, Susan (Ed.) *Genocide in Cambodia and Rwanda: New Perspectives* (New Brunswick, 2007) p.192.

248 Schanberg. *Supra* note 211. p.78.

249 Shannon, Don. 'U.S Backs Sihanouk on U.N debate' *Los Angeles Times.* (11th January 1979).

250 Here, the global divergence on Cambodia was evident. Some states such as Pakistan and the US highlighted Khmer Rouge atrocities but still accepted that their credentials were valid. Others such as Belgium, Ecuador and Senegal maintained that the Committee's role was not to make decisions on a government's actions and so accepted the Khmer Rouge credentials. China argued the PRK had no legitimacy and defended the Khmer Rouge's role as Cambodia's government. Only the Congo, USSR, and Panama opposed recognising the Khmer Rouge's representative but nonetheless proposed keeping the seat temporarily unoccupied (UN General Assembly 34 Session, Credentials Committee First Report. UN Doc A/34/500 (20 September 1979) Paras. 7–22).

251 The Khmer Rouge were not the only anti-Vietnam groups: both Sihanoukists and the Khmer People's National Liberation Front formed non-communist resistance and controlled their own territory, though they were far weaker than the Khmer Rouge (Rowley. *Supra* note 247. pp.193–196).

252 Matthews, Linda. 'Sihanouk Vows to Support Fallen Cambodian Regime' *Los Angeles Times.* (9 January 1979).

253 Anonymous 'Sihanouk says Cambodia Better Off with Heng Samrin than Khmer Rouge' *Washington Post.* (3 April 1980).

254 Becker, Elizabeth. 'Sihanouk and the Saga of the Khmer Rouge' *Washington Post.* (28 January 1979).

aggression'[255] and the PRK was no more than a Vietnamese puppet.[256] While few members of the UNSC were as openly critical, all except the USSR and Czechoslovakia opposed letting the PRK participate in the UNSC discussion on Cambodia.[257] Even Bangladesh (a nation created by Indian intervention), refused to support the PRK as Cambodia's representative[258] and highlighted its support for Article 2(4) of the UN Charter.[259] Prince Sihanouk addressed the UNSC, where he accused Vietnam of orchestrating the invasion to stave off economic collapse, and highlighted Vietnam's annexation of Cambodian territory in the past.[260] Likewise, he dismissed the FUNSK as a 'pitiful smoke screen' for Vietnamese aggression[261] and demanded Vietnam be condemned and compelled to withdraw.[262]

France, who claimed that regardless of a government's actions, to support its overthrow by outside actors set a dangerous precedent, echoed opposition to Vietnam.[263] By contrast, Vietnam argued that it had shown restraint against Cambodian aggression but justified its actions under self-defence rather than humanitarian intervention.[264] Although it highlighted Khmer Rouge atrocities, it argued this induced revolt among Cambodians and commended the FUNSK for its war of self-determination.[265] Likewise, it vehemently denied that its forces had overthrown the Khmer Rouge.[266]

Unsurprisingly, Vietnam's actions were supported by its Soviet allies who argued that the Khmer Rouge were not the legitimate representatives of Cambodia, had engaged in 'cruel repression' and whose foreign policy threatened the region's stability.[267] They echoed Vietnam's claims that a domestic

255 UN Security Council. *Official Records, 34 Year, 2108 Meeting.* UN Doc S/PV.2108 (11th January 1979) Para.18.
256 Ibid. Para.52.
257 Ibid. Para.39.
258 Ibid. Para.65.
259 Ibid. Para.49.
260 Ibid. Paras. 76–78.
261 Ibid. Para.84.
262 Ibid. Para.88.
263 UN Security Council. *Official Records, 34th Year, 2109th Meeting.* UN Doc S/PV.2109 (12th January 1979) Para.36.
264 UN Security Council. *Official Records, 34th Year, 2108th Meeting.* UN Doc S/PV.2108 (11th January 1979) Paras.126–127.
265 Ibid. Paras.131–137.
266 UN Security Council. *Official Records, 34th Year, 2109th Meeting.* UN Doc S/PV.2109 (12th January 1979) Para.89.
267 UN Security Council. *Official Records, 34th Year, 2108th Meeting.* UN Doc S/PV.2108 (11th January 1979) Para.10.

liberation movement had toppled the regime.[268] In this, they were supported by the Soviet allies of Czechoslovakia, Hungary, the German Democratic Republic and Cuba who highlighted Khmer Rouge atrocities but insisted that the Khmer Rouge have been overthrown by domestic forces.

With the USSR supporting Vietnam, the UNSC could do little. A Chinese draft resolution that condemned Vietnam for aggression and violating international law[269] was never tabled. The Non-Aligned Movement (including Bangladesh) proposed a more moderate resolution. This called for a ceasefire and Vietnamese military withdrawal without explicitly mentioning Vietnam[270] while reaffirming the principle that any intervention was a violation of the UN Charter.[271] The USSR vetoed the resolution but only Czechoslovakia supported the USSR,[272] showing the widespread reluctance to criticise Vietnam. Likewise, the UNGA made no mention of Cambodia's atrocious human rights record and urged a withdrawal of Vietnamese troops and respect for Cambodia's independence.[273]

### 2.2 *Humanitarian Intervention and Cambodia*

Given Cambodia attacked Vietnam first,[274] Vietnam cannot be easily accused of aggression. Although it was defending itself, Vietnam then invaded Cambodia and self-defence was a weak justification given Hanoi was the dominant regional power and faced little threat once Cambodian forces were expelled.[275] Vietnam could argue that its security required it to overthrow the expansionist Pol Pot regime[276] and that it had the right to respond militarily to aggression. Nonetheless, its overthrow of Cambodia's recognised government was an over-reaction and a violation of the principle of proportionality. Indeed, Hanoi initially sought to establish a pro-Vietnam state in eastern Cambodia but the Khmer Rouge's military weakness made Vietnam realise it could take Cambodia itself.[277]

268 Ibid.

269 UN Security Council. *Draft Resolution* (*China*) UN Doc S/13022 (11th January 1979) Para.2.

270 UN Security Council. *Draft Resolution* (*Bangladesh, Bolivia, Gabon, Jamaica, Kuwait, Nigeria, and Zambia*). UN Doc S/13027 (15 January 1979) Para.2.

271 Ibid. Para.1.

272 UN Doc S/PV.2112 (15 January 1979) Para.4.

273 UN General Assembly. *The Situation in Kampuchea*. UN A/Res/34/22 (14 November 1979) Paras.7–9.

274 Kiernan. *Supra* note 207. p.386.

275 See *Supra* note 229.

276 Abiew. *Supra* note 1. p.130.

277 Chandler. *Supra* note 239. p.312.

The Khmer Rouge was one of the most brutal regimes of the twentieth century,[278] and its overthrow had a significant humanitarian result. The vast majority of Cambodians were relieved rather than outraged at Vietnam's arrival[279] while the international community's failure to respond to Khmer Rouge atrocities gave further legitimacy to Vietnam's actions.[280] Overall, the world's choice was between the Khmer Rouge and the PRK, both of whom were supported by powers with poor human rights records, ensuring most states preferred to prioritise the principle of non-intervention and the UN Charter.[281] Bazyler highlights that despite the brutality of the Khmer Rouge, Vietnam's unilateral intervention combined with its lack of humanitarian motives undermines any potential argument for humanitarian intervention: had Phnom Penh maintained cordial relations with Hanoi, no war would have taken place.[282]

Vietnam did not rely on humanitarian claims for intervention and sought justification for its actions by claiming support from Cambodian dissidents.[283] Although Vietnam highlighted Khmer Rouge atrocities,[284] this was largely done to reinforce their claim that Cambodia's government was so oppressive it induced domestic rebellion.[285] Vietnam certainly ended one of the twentieth century's' most notorious regimes but its motives were also to expand into a region it had long desired.[286] Further undermining Vietnam's humanitarian credentials was the fact it only criticised Cambodia's human rights record after the Khmer Rouge had invaded Vietnam[287] while Samrin was a former Khmer Rouge commander who participated in Cambodia's takeover.[288] Furthermore, overthrowing a neighbouring regime backed by China was of clear strategic

278 See *Supra* note 221.

279 Ibid. p.313.

280 Pruitt-Ham, Bruce. 'Humanitarian Intervention in SouthEast Asia in the Post-Cold War World: Dilemmas in the Definition and Design of International *Law' Pacific Rim Law and Policy Journal* (Vol.3, Issue.2 1994) p.188.

281 Franck, Thomas. 'Interpretation and Change in the Law of Humanitarian Intervention' in Holzgrefe, J.L and Keohane, Robert (Eds.) *Humanitarian Intervention: Ethical, Legal and Political Dilemmas* (Cambridge, 2003) p.219.

282 Bazyler. *Supra* note 30. pp.608–611.

283 Wheeler. *Supra* note 134. p.84.

284 UN Security Council. *Official Records, 34th Year, 2108th Meeting.* UN Doc S/PV.2108 (11th January 1979) Para.130.

285 Franck. *Supra* note 24. p.147.

286 Bazyler. *Supra* note 30. p.608.

287 Wheeler. *Supra* note 134. p.89.

288 It must be noted that Samrin's soldiers committed significantly fewer atrocities than other Khmer Rouge forces (Kiernan. *Supra* note 207. p.32).

interest to Hanoi[289] and Vietnam already feared Laos and Cambodia were dangerous as potential bases for invading forces.[290]

Vietnam's actions were arguably self-interested as in addition to ending Khmer Rouge atrocities, they created a puppet state and occupied the country for years.[291] Indeed, China and Sihanouk claimed Vietnam's invasion was part of their plan to create a Hanoi-dominated Indochinese federation.[292] Vietnam's position is further undermined by its repeated attempts to come to a peaceful agreement with the Khmer Rouge.[293] While this weakens any claims that Vietnam was aggressive and its extended occupation is partially mitigated by the country's sheer devastation;[294] the fact that Vietnam initially sought peace with the Khmer Rouge shows that Hanoi cared little for the people of Cambodia and the intervention was not to save the Cambodians but to protect Vietnamese security interests.[295] Even if Vietnam's intervention was not conducted for humanitarian reasons, its result was overwhelmingly humanitarian and Vietnam's harsh rule was far preferable to that of the Khmer Rouge.[296] The fact that Vietnam established its own authoritarian regime in Cambodia means that even Teson (normally a supporter of humanitarian intervention) is reluctant to classify Vietnam's intervention as humanitarian.[297]

As in the Indo-Pakistan War, realpolitik was the primary factor determining Washington and Beijing's support of the Khmer Rouge.[298] This led Beijing to

289 Mysliwiec. *Supra* note 212. p.9.

290 US Senate. *Supra* note 218. p.15.

291 Bazyler. *Supra* note 30. pp.607–608. The exact degree of Vietnamese control is debatable: while they undoubtedly had major influence immediately after the overthrow of Pol Pot, they gradually withdrew their troops during the 1980s (Amer. *Supra* note 229. p.219).

292 Matthews. *Supra* note 252.

293 Wheeler. *Supra* note 134. p.82.

294 Cambodia was ruined with no currency, industry, or education system while nearly all professionals such as lawyers, doctors and teachers had been executed (Mysliwiec. *Supra* note 212. pp.10–11). Such devastation gravely weakened the emergence of a functional state, and Vietnamese troops were arguably necessary to prevent the country plunging into anarchy.

295 Karnow, Stanley. *Vietnam: A History* (London, 1991) p.58.

296 Wheeler. *Supra* note 134. p.103.

297 Teson. *Supra* note 1. pp.119–121.

298 Despite US criticism of Khmer Rouge atrocities, the Cold War ensured that the US sided with the Khmer Rouge against the PRK due to the memories of the Vietnam War and Soviet backing of Hanoi (Power. *Supra* note 209. p.141) Likewise, China was motivated by its own security interests and feared that Cambodia would come under Vietnamese influence as Laos had, which would weaken China in the region (Szulc. Tad. 'The War We Left Behind' *New York Magazine* (16 January 1978)). In addition, Beijing feared Vietnam was attempting to assert regional dominance while the USSR was using Vietnam as an agent

respond to Vietnam's intervention by invading Vietnam in 1979 to teach Hanoi 'a lesson'.[299] Likewise, the Association of South East Asian Nations (ASEAN)[300] condemned Vietnam's intervention.[301] Even so, many countries saw Vietnam's invasion as more worthy of criticism than the Khmer Rouge, who received aid from Thailand, the UK, US, China and Singapore.[302] The key problem that most states had with the intervention was that it was conducted by Vietnam and had Thailand intervened it would likely have been treated as a 'great victory for the Free World and its methods'.[303] As Vietnam's intervention was by a Soviet-backed state, it had repercussions on how the invasion was perceived, making it seem like a regional power struggle rather than the overthrow of a brutal government. Most states felt unable to support either Cambodia or Vietnam and instead upheld the prohibition on the use of force.[304]

Overall, while Vietnam's actions were not taken for a humanitarian purpose, the humanitarian result is evident, liberating Cambodia from one of the most brutal regimes in the post-World War II era. Wheeler argues that while Vietnam's motives were not pure, its action should be accepted given it ended the Khmer Rouge's atrocities.[305] By contrast, Abiew argues that given the extent of the human rights abuses and international inaction, the Vietnamese intervention was the only way the atrocities would cease.[306] The international reaction to Vietnam's actions was broadly negative and Vietnam's prolonged occupation of Cambodia raises grave doubts that its intervention can be seen as humanitarian.

---

in its own quest for 'global hegemonism' (UN Security Council. *Official Records, 34th Year, 2108th Meeting.* UN Doc S/PV.2108 (11th January 1979) Para.105).

299 Mirsky. *Supra* note 244. p.49. This proved a mistake: although China deployed 300,000 troops against Vietnam, Vietnam resisted and inflicted significant casualties on Chinese forces, forcing Chinese withdrawal (Zhang, Xiaoming. 'China's 1979 War with Vietnam: A Reassessment' *The China Quarterly* (Vol.184, December 2005) pp.865–867 and pp.865–867).

300 Consisting of Indonesia, Thailand, Singapore, the Philippines, Brunei, Malaysia, and Indonesia.

301 UN Security Council. *Letter Dated 79/01/12 from the Permanent Representative of Indonesia to the United Nations.* UN Doc S/13025 (12th January 1979).

302 Power. *Supra* note 209. pp.146–147. There is also a significant amount of hypocrisy here: few countries showed any outrage over France's re-conquest of Cambodia after World War II or the US bombings in the early 1970s (Vickery, Michael. *Cambodia: 1975–1982* (Boston, 1984) p.247).

303 Ibid.

304 Franck. *Supra* note 24. pp.150–151.

305 Wheeler. *Supra* note 134. p.110.

306 Abiew. *Supra* note 1. p.131.

## 3 Humanitarian Intervention in Uganda 1979

Decolonisation also posed major problems in Africa where borders were arbitrarily drawn between colonial powers, with little regard for indigenous peoples. This was especially evident in the former British colony of Uganda.[307] Milton Obote was elected prime minister in 1962, but subsequently declared himself President with expansive executive power.[308] Obote alienated the military despite his reliance on them, particularly its army commander, Idi Amin, whose suitability for the job was dubious.[309] Obote trusted Amin,[310] but a coup by Amin in January 1971 saw little public opposition.[311] Amin's government was speedily recognised by the UK, Israel and the US although there was opposition from Tanzania, Zambia and the Organisation of African Unity (OAU).[312] Nonetheless, the OAU was non-interventionist due to African states' experience with colonisation.[313] The OAU's Charter was non-interventionist for postcolonial states[314] and no action was taken against Amin's coup which

---

307 Formed out of centralised kingdoms in East Africa. Uganda became independent in October 1962 but was hindered from emerging as a liberal democracy, given its citizens distrusted those outside their ethnic groups, particularly nationalist politicians who often came from different or even hostile tribes (Ibingira, Grace. 'The Impact of Ethnic Demands on British Decolonisation in Africa: The Example of Uganda' in Gifford, Prosser and Louis, WM. Roger. *The Transfer of Power in Africa: Decolonisation 1940–1960* (New Haven, 1982) p.285).

308 Although Obote was authoritarian, he was not a tyrant who killed opponents or terrorised the general population (Jackson, Robert and Rosberg, Carl. *Personal Rule in Black Africa: Prince, Autocrat, Prophet, Tyrant.* (Berkeley, 1982) p.252) but his actions alarmed Ugandans, eroded his legitimacy, and forced his reliance on the army to maintain his power.

309 Amin was originally a non-commissioned-officer in the British Empire's King's African Rifles (Martin, David. *General Amin* (London, 1974) p.15). Mindful of independence, black non-commissioned-officers like Amin were rapidly promoted, resulting in a strikingly uneducated officer corps (Lofchie, Michael. 'The Uganda Coup-Class Action by the Military' *The Journal of Modern African Studies* (Vol.10, No.1, May 1972) p.21). Just before independence, Amin's brutality had him on the verge of cashierment, but Amin was one of only two black Ugandan officers, sorely needed for Ugandan independence (Melady, Thomas and Melady, Margaret. *Idi Amin Dada: Hitler in Africa* (Mission, 1977) p.12).

310 Meredith, Martin. *The State of Africa: A History of Fifty Years of Independence* (London, 2005) p.232.

311 BBC News 'Idi Amin ousts Uganda president' (25 January 1971). http://news.bbc.co.uk/onthisday/hi/dates/stories/january/25/newsid_2506000/2506423.stm Accessed 10th March 2024.

312 Federal Research Division of the Library of Congress. *Uganda: A Country Study* (Washington DC, 1990) p.26.

313 Thomas, Caroline. *New States, Sovereignty, and Intervention* (Aldershot, 1985) pp.63–64.

314 Organisation for African Unity Charter (UNTS, 479, 1963) Article III.

is unsurprising given how many OAU governments had taken power the same way.[315]

### 3.1 *Uganda under Idi Amin*

Amin proved even more dictatorial than Obote, abolishing parliament, suspending political activity and granting extensive powers to Ugandan security forces.[316] A leaked document by one of his ministers described him as a racist, amoral dictator, with prisoners being arbitrarily detained, castrated, mutilated and force-fed their own flesh, with corpses being dumped in the rivers so frequently that the crocodiles were unable to eat them all.[317] Those targeted were mainly seen as a threat to Amin's rule, particularly soldiers from the Langi and Acholi tribes (groups close to Obote),[318] and legal professionals resulting in the absence of Ugandan judicial independence.[319]

The human rights abuses within Uganda were severe[320] and tens of thousands were killed.[321] Such killings were largely carried out by soldiers and the military became an even more privileged caste of Ugandan society,[322] with promotions based on loyalty and ethnicity rather than ability, ensuring an officer corps of low experience and competence.[323] Amin's delusions were considerable and he was frequently seen as a buffoon in the West: his apparent brutality,

315 Martin, David. *General Amin* (London, 1974) p.64.

316 International Commission of Jurists. *Violations of Human Rights and the Rule of Law in Uganda* (May 1974) pp.12–14.

317 Martin. *Supra* note 315. pp.225–226.

318 Munnion, Christopher. 'If Idi Amin of Uganda is a madman, he's a cunning and ruthless one' *New York Times*. (12th November 1972).

319 Centre for the Independence of Judges and Lawyers. 'Uganda' *CIJL Bulletin* (Vol.1, No.2, September 1978) pp.4–45.

320 US Senate. *Uganda: The Human Rights Situation: Hearings before the Subcommittee on Foreign Relations* (*95th Congress, 2nd Session*) (June 1978) p.11). See also Melady and Melady. *Supra* note 309. p.47 and Jackson and Rosberg. *Supra* note 308. p.258.

321 The exact death toll is difficult to ascertain but one of Amin's former ministers estimated that around 80–90,000 were killed in the first 2 years of his rule (Martin, David. 'The Unfunny Truth about Idi Amin' *Observer*. (23 June 1974)). The International Commission of Jurists estimated that by 1974, the casualties lie anywhere between 25,000 and 250,000 (International Commission of Jurists. *Supra* note 316. p.61). Overall estimates amount to some 100,000 to 300,000 murdered under his rule (Darnton, John. 'Idi Amin: A Saviour Who Became the Creator of 8 Years of Horror' *New York Times*. (30 April 1979)).

322 Even under Obote, Ugandan soldiers were privileged with the lowliest private earning more than double his Kenyan or Malawian counterparts (Lofchie. *Supra* note 309. p.21) and many times the average Ugandan national income (Nugent, Paul. *Africa Since Independence: A Comparative History* (Hampshire, 2004) p.207).

323 Federal Research Division of the Library of Congress. *Supra* note 312. p.26.

illiteracy and incompetence fitted Western racist stereotypes of Africans,[324] as did his arrogance.[325] Amin was no mere dictatorial caricature and his cruelty was not comedic.[326] He was not stupid and geared himself towards maintaining power.[327]

Such was the violence that by the late 1970s, Amin's popular support was negligible.[328] As one of Amin's ministers leaked, Amin had been advised by Israel to keep his army perpetually busy, which led to Amin seeking scapegoats from imaginary or exaggerated threats.[329] While Amin was initially supported by Israel (who was keen for an African ally), his excessive demands for military aid were rejected first by Israel and then the UK.[330] In a striking turnabout, Amin turned to Israel's enemy, Libya that offered him the military assistance he craved.[331] This led to Amin finding a newfound interest in his Islamic faith and the expulsion of Israeli technicians amidst virulently anti-Semitic statements.[332]

The expulsion of Israeli experts compounded Uganda's economic problems that were straining under Amin's military excesses with some 20–60% of GNP being spent on the military.[333] Amin's response was to disdain advice from his ministers and order the printing of even more money, causing hyperinflation and widespread shortages.[334] Exacerbating this was Amin's scapegoating of Ugandan's south-Asian community, who were prominent as entrepreneurs and businesspeople but unpopular among Uganda's African majority.[335] In August 1972, Amin claimed God appeared to him in a dream and instructed him to

---

324 Martin, David. 'The Unfunny Truth about Idi Amin' *Observer.* (23 June 1974).

325 Amin professed his military would liberate South Africa, declared his support for the Holocaust and offered himself as a mediator to resolve the Northern Ireland and Middle East conflicts (Munnion. *Supra* note 318).

326 US Senate. *Supra* note 320. p.1.

327 Jackson and Rosberg. *Supra* note 308. pp.260–261. Many who knew him highlighted his cunning, with even his most offensive statements being carefully calculated decisions ('Centre of an African Storm' *New York Times.* (28 February 1977)). Melady highlighted that Amin was clever and cunning with a gift for making the world 'laugh rather than cry' over the thousands he killed (Melady and Melady. *Supra* note 309. pp.9–11).

328 Nugent. *Supra* note 322. p.231.

329 Martin. *Supra* note 315. pp.224–225.

330 Melady and Melady. *Supra* note 309. pp.57–58.

331 Mann, Roger. 'Libya's Military Largesse Feeds Idi Amin's Anti-Zionism' *Washington Post.* (27 February 1977).

332 'Centre of an African Storm' *New York Times.* (28 February 1977).

333 US Senate. *Supra* note 320. p.7.

334 Meredith. *Supra* note 310. p.235.

335 International Commission of Jurists. *Supra* note 316. p.3.

banish Uganda's Asians, with some 50,000 being exiled,[336] which was disastrous for the economy.[337] Amin's response was to impose heavy punishments for smuggling, hoarding and embezzlement.[338] Only economic and military assistance from Libya and Saudi Arabia saved Uganda from economic collapse, with Amin responding by increasing his public professions of Islam.[339]

Knowledge of Amin's brutality was widely known but no action was taken, particularly as Uganda refrained from using force against its neighbours.[340] Although opposed by Tanzania and Zambia, Amin's showmanship ensured he had appeal in postcolonial Africa.[341] Likewise, the OAU's strict non-interventionist stance was a useful shield for African leaders who feared criticising Amin would leave them open to attacks for their own human rights records.[342] African states were willing to criticise atrocities committed by white regimes[343] ensuring a UNGA draft resolution condemning Uganda was opposed by African states[344] while an investigation of Ugandan human rights abuses by the UN Commission on Human Rights was stonewalled.[345] Likewise, the Arab League claimed it supported Amin's anticolonial struggle and would not interfere in Uganda's internal affairs.[346]

Criticism of Uganda was scarcely more forthcoming in the West and there was never any serious suggestion that a state would intervene to protect Ugandans from Amin. While the UNSC was willing to condemn South Africa and impose an arms embargo, it did nothing of the sort in respect to Uganda.[347]

---

336 Munnion. *Supra* note 318. Most of these were British citizens but even Ugandan citizens were deprived of their citizenship and banished in a manner that reminded Melady of the Nazi expulsion of the Jews (Melady and Melady. *Supra* note 309. p.88).

337 The expulsion of Uganda's Asians lowered government revenue by nearly 40% (Meredith. *Supra* note 310. p.236).

338 Decker, Alice. 'Idi Amin's Dirty War: Subversion, Sabotage, and the Battle to Keep Uganda Clean, 1971–1979' *The International Journal of African Historical Studies* (Vol. 43, No. 3 2010) p.507.

339 Mann. *Supra* note 331. Even after one of Amin's ministers leaked a damning report, documenting a country riven by brutality, chaos and economic meltdown, no action was taken by the international community (Martin. *Supra* note 315. p.227).

340 A notable exception was in 1972, when Uganda bombed a Tanzanian village in response to a raid by Tanzanian based Obote supporters (Mann. *Supra* note 331).

341 To many Africans, his expulsion of Asians, nationalisation of foreign companies and goading of Western leaders made him a hero (Martin. *Supra* note 315. p.231).

342 Abiew. *Supra* note 1. p.124.

343 Thomas. *Supra* note 313. p.92.

344 Ullman, Richard. 'Human Rights and Economic Power: The United States versus Idi Amin' *Foreign Affairs* (April 1978).

345 US Senate. *Supra* note 320. p.32.

346 Mann. *Supra* note 331.

347 Ullman. *Supra* note 344.

Although the British Commonwealth heads of government condemned the brutality of Uganda's regime, they refrained from using Amin's name[348] and there was no US support for intervention. However, military force was forthcoming from within the Global South.

### 3.2 *The Ugandan-Tanzanian War of 1979*

On 30 October 1978, Ugandan troops crossed into Tanzania in pursuit of deserting Ugandan soldiers.[349] The incursion turned into an annexation as Amin sought to distract his military and to intimidate Tanzanian president Julius Nyerere for supporting Ugandan dissidents.[350] Nyerere was incensed by the OAU attempts to broker a ceasefire and demanded the OAU condemn the Amin regime, something unprecedented in the OAU's history.[351] The OAU refused to do so, despite Uganda's aggression.[352] Instead, Nyerere mobilised the Tanzanian People's Defence Force and counter attacked while Ugandan dissidents in Tanzania formed the Ugandan National Liberation Front, with the Ugandan National Liberation Army as a military wing.[353] Ugandan troops were repulsed from Tanzania and pursued into Uganda itself.[354] Amin sought OAU intervention but this was not forthcoming, while his attempts at securing Arab aid saw small troop contributions from Palestine and Libya.[355]

Despite Nyerere being one of Africa's least martial leaders and Uganda's nominal military superiority,[356] Amin's forces soon found that their experience oppressing civilians was of little practical use.[357] Compared to the well-equipped but undisciplined Ugandan military were Tanzania's soldiers who

---

348 Melady and Melady. *Supra* note 309. p.117.

349 Thomas. *Supra* note 313. p.92.

350 'Small Battle, How Many Dead?' *Economist.* (18 November 1978).

351 Avirgan, Tony. 'Nyerere angry with OAU' *Guardian.* (7 December 1978).

352 Aminzade, Ronald. *Race, Nation, and Citizenship in Post-Colonial Africa: The Case of Tanzania* (Cambridge, 2013) p.200.

353 Anonymous. 'Fall of Idi Amin' *Economic and Political Weekly* (Vol.14, No.21, 26 May 1979) p.909.

354 Federal Research Division of the Library of Congress. *Supra* note 312 pp.30–31.

355 Hassan. *Supra* note 186. p.875.

356 'The Tottering Idi Amin' *New York Times.* (3 March 1979).

357 Although Amin had heavily invested in modern military hardware, it was ineffective in the Ugandan bush while his soldiers lacked the training to use them effectively (Anonymous. *Supra* note 353. p.910). Compounding Ugandan military weakness was a distinct lack of organisation and discipline combined with the promotion of uneducated soldiers to positions of command (Jackson and Rosberg. *Supra* note 308. p.257). As such, Uganda's ineffective troops focussed on looting while their Libyan allies did most of the fighting (Federal Research Division of the Library of Congress. *Supra* note 312. pp.30–31).

lacked training but distinguished themselves in battle.[358] International support for Amin was also not forthcoming, with his human rights abuses, nationalisation of foreign property and anti-Semitism alienating the West. While the USSR had initially supported him, it ended its aid to Uganda.[359] Amin could only rely on reactionary Islamic powers like Libya and Saudi Arabia, who lacked the strength to protect him. Amin fled Uganda while Ugandan civilians welcomed Tanzanian and Ugandan National Liberation Army units as liberators.[360] Although post-Amin Uganda remained impoverished, Tanzanian forces helped maintain order[361] and remained in Uganda for two years and at the government's invitation, giving legitimacy to their presence.[362]

### 3.3 *Humanitarian Intervention and Uganda*

Amin's regime was certainly guilty of human rights abuses.[363] Accusations of genocide were levelled in the US Senate,[364] by Melady[365] and by Obote[366] although these were hyperbolic. Amin was undoubtedly a dictator, but his intent was not to destroy a specific group. Rather, he sought to stay in power and plunder the country to placate his military, whose support he relied on to stay in power. It is clear he committed extensive human rights abuses, but the question arises as to whether this rendered Tanzania's actions legal.

Initially, Tanzania had a legitimate recourse to force under international law. Amin was blatantly engaging in aggression, justifying Tanzania defending

---

358 Aminzade. *Supra* 352. p.200.

359 Martin. *Supra* note 315. p.164.

360 Hassan. *Supra* note 186. pp.880–881.

361 Jaynes, Gregory. 'For Uganda, Nyerere's Army Has Overstayed Its Welcome' *New York Times*. (16 March 1980). While Tanzania's maintenance of troops in Uganda is questionable, their absence would have contributed to further chaos (Thomas. *Supra* note 313. p.118) and Wheeler notes that their presence is excusable on humanitarian grounds (Wheeler. *Supra* note 134. p.132).

362 Franck. *Supra* note 281. p.219.

363 Jackson and Rosberg claimed that Amin's regime was one of the most tyrannical to emerge in the developing world since World War II (Jackson and Rosberg. *Supra* note 308. p.259). Likewise, the International Commission of Jurists highlighted the government's tyranny combined with a military that engaged in 'massive and continuing violations of human rights' and a 'reign of terror' (International Commission of Jurists. *Supra* note 316. pp.62–63). Ullman notes that only Stalin and Hitler can compare to Amin's toxic cocktail of capriciousness and savagery (Ullman. *Supra* note 344) and Amin was compared to Hitler by US Ambassador to the UN Andrew Young and President Kaunda of Zambia (Melady and Melady. *Supra* note 309. pp.116–117).

364 US Senate. *Supra* note 320. p.38.

365 Melady and Melady. *Supra* note 309. p.6.

366 International Commission of Jurists. *Supra* note 316. p.33.

itself. However, Tanzania went beyond repelling Ugandan forces and breached the proportionality that the use of force in self-defence requires under the UN Charter,[367] with regime change scarcely justifiable under self-defence. Contemporary reports indicate that Uganda had a strong military advantage[368] and Amin had showed his aggressiveness. Even after Ugandan troops had retreated, Amin refused to renounce his territorial claims,[369] ensuring he posed a continuing threat to Tanzania. Nonetheless, it is difficult to reconcile the proportionality of responding to an invasion with regime change. Amin offered to withdraw if Tanzania gave assurances it would not invade Uganda or support Ugandan dissidents,[370] which Tanzania rejected.

It could be argued Nyerere only ousted Amin as a last resort. Nyerere offered a ceasefire if the OAU condemned Ugandan aggression, Amin provided compensation, renounced his territorial claims and offered assurances he would not invade Tanzania again.[371] Nyerere's sincerity is debatable, as he knew the OAU did not condemn member states.[372] Even with the atrocities of Amin's regime, Tanzania's actions seem a disproportionate response to protect human rights as its forces remained in Uganda until well after the war's end.[373] While initially Nyerere merely sought to punish Ugandan invaders, his goals soon changed to toppling Amin's regime, which he felt had dishonoured Africa.[374] Claiming Amin was a 'cancer' that needed to be destroyed, Nyerere rejected offers to mediate and resisted intense pressure from other African leaders for a ceasefire following the repulsion of Ugandan forces from Tanzania.[375] Likewise, Nyerere declared that there could be no peace in East Africa until Amin was toppled.[376]

Evidently, there were other motives at work. Thomas argues that Nyerere had two key motivations in toppling Amin, both responding to Amin's atrocities and restraining a dangerous neighbour.[377] Regime change in Uganda

367 Abiew. *Supra* note 1. p.122. Likewise, Hassan claims Uganda's *causus belli* was extinguished as soon as Ugandan troops were driven from Tanzanian territory, with Uganda posing no military threat to Tanzania (Hassan. *Supra* note 186. pp.902–903).
368 'The Tottering Idi Amin' *New York Times.* (3 March 1979).
369 Thomas. *Supra* note 313. p.98.
370 'Amin offers to withdraw from Tanzanian territory' *New York Times.* (9 November 1978).
371 Hassan. *Supra* note 186. p.873.
372 Ibid.
373 See *Supra* note 362.
374 Jackson and Rosberg. *Supra* note 308. p.263.
375 'Tanzania Prepares for Long War' *Guardian.* (20 November 1978).
376 'Tanzania and Uganda: Behind the Lies' *Economist.* (2 December 1978).
377 Thomas. *Supra* note 313. p.91.

would secure Tanzania's border, ensure a friendly Ugandan government and enable Tanzania to concentrate on South Africa.[378] Nyerere was adamant that Tanzania sought no territorial expansion, their war was against Amin, and not Uganda's oppressed people.[379] Rather, it saw itself as operating in a supportive role to Ugandan dissidents,[380] which was given weight given Nyerere did not seek to reinstate Obote.

It is important to qualify Tanzania's actions with political realities. A violent dictator ruled Uganda, with the UN and OAU unwilling to take action.[381] Tanzania's options were limited and the humanitarian aspect of Tanzania's actions should not be discounted.[382] Restoring Ugandan human rights was a key stated goal of Tanzania and the UNLF highlighted its commitment to human rights, while Uganda's new President Lulu declared that a return to dictatorship would be opposed (although Obote eventually returned to power and instituted a repressive regime).[383] This was mirrored by Tanzanian public support for the war, with the public outraged by the atrocities committed by Ugandan forces.[384] Neither was the conflict straightforward for Tanzania, which was one of the world's poorest nations with the war costing an estimated $1million a day.[385] Given Uganda's initial invasion and apparent military strength, Tanzania has a defence against accusations of aggression, although the proportionality of its response is debatable.

Criticism of Tanzania was not forthcoming on the world stage although the international community had made no effort to use force against Uganda or exert diplomatic methods.[386] The position of African states was ambiguous given their reluctance to criticise fellow postcolonial regimes and while they were willing to criticise Rhodesia and South Africa for racism, they remained mostly silent in relation to Tanzania's actions.[387] Sudan and Nigeria criticised

378 Darnton, John. 'Motives are Tangled in the War in Uganda' *New York Times*. (12th March 1979).

379 Thomas. *Supra* note 313. p.9.

380 Hassan. *Supra* note 186. p.867.

381 Bazyler. *Supra* note 30. p.591.

382 Although Tanzania was far from a model of human rights, by the time of the 1978 war, it had emerged as one of the more progressive African nations (Hassan. *Supra* note 186. p.891).

383 Teson. *Supra* note 1. p.232.

384 Darnton, Charles. 'Uganda Charges a Tanzanian Invasion' *New York Times*. (28 November 1978).

385 Federal Research Division of the Library of Congress. *Supra* note 312. p.31.

386 Thomas. *Supra* note 313. p.91.

387 Ibid p.99.

Tanzania,[388] but Botswana, Mozambique, Angola and Zambia condemned Amin's 'fascist and imperialist aggression' and expressed solidarity with Tanzania.[389] Even these emphasised Amin's initial aggression rather than his domestic brutality[390] and African states' silence highlights the OAU's unwillingness to condemn Tanzania for overthrowing Amin.[391] It is more likely that it was the OAU adhering to its traditional non-intervention principle, as neither did it condemn Amin for invading Tanzania. Given his commitment to non-intervention, Nyerere's willingness to use force against Amin's regime is of great significance.[392]

It is also notable that the OAU advised Amin not to appeal to the UN.[393] Amin sought urgent UNSC involvement after Tanzania penetrated Ugandan territory but was rebuffed on a technicality.[394] Furthermore, Uganda's deputy representative at the UN sought the UNSC's convening to address the Tanzanian 'aggression'[395] but the request was withdrawn due to an appeal by the African Group in New York[396] and Tanzania's victory.[397] Due to the brutality of Amin's regime, the international community generally avoided condemning Tanzania.[398] Tanzania was a key member of the Non-Aligned-Movement ensuring that the overthrow of Amin's regime was far less controversial or dangerous than if it had been conducted by a superpower.[399] The USSR ended its supply of arms to Uganda and endorsed Tanzania's actions while China and the US recognised the new government,[400] as did numerous Western nations, effectively endorsing Tanzania's actions.[401] This can be compared to the number of governments that refused to recognise the PRK while Vietnamese troops

388 Abiew. *Supra* note 1. p.124.

389 UN Security Council. *Letter Dated 79/03/05 from the Permanent Representative of Angola to the United Nations.* UN Doc S/13141 (5 March 1979).

390 Ibid.

391 Thomas. *Supra* note 313. p.109. Abiew argues that while most African states remained mute on the issue, lest they set a precedent for intervention into their own human rights abuses, this can be seen as supportive of Tanzania (Abiew. *Supra* note 1. p.124).

392 Jackson and Rosberg. *Supra* note 308. p.264.

393 Teson. *Supra* note 1. p.233.

394 'Rebuff for Amin at the UN' *Guardian* (15 February 1979).

395 UN Security Council. *Letter Dated 79/03/28 from the Deputy Permanent Representative of Uganda to the United Nations.* UN Doc S/13204 (28 March 1979).

396 UN Security Council. Letter Dated 79/04/05 from the Deputy Permanent Representative of Uganda to the United Nations. UN Doc S/13228 (5 April 1979).

397 Franck. *Supra* note 24. p.144.

398 Teson. *Supra* note 1. p.237.

399 Franck. *Supra* note 24. p.145.

400 Wheeler. *Supra* note 134. pp.123–124.

401 Thomas. *Supra* note 313. p.113.

remained. Tanzania's intervention took place in a region of no strategic interest to the Superpowers and impoverished Tanzania was of little threat to regional peace and security.

Overall, the case can certainly be made that Tanzania's actions had a strong humanitarian impulse, with Kofi Annan arguing that the nature of Amin's rule meant history has supported Tanzania's actions.[402] Academic opinion on whether Tanzania's actions constituted humanitarian intervention are mixed[403] and aside from Uganda's new government, no state justified Tanzania's actions on humanitarian grounds.[404] Rather, the reaction to Tanzania's overthrow of Amin was generally silence. Although it can be argued that this demonstrates a lack of support, it is important to highlight the importance of realpolitik. Tanzania was responding to aggression by a repressive regime without threatening Superpower interests or regional security. Such was Amin's volatility, Tanzania's actions arguably increased stability in East Africa. While endorsement of Tanzania's actions are lacking, so too was condemnation. The lack of international outcry is of vital importance. While it does not create a strong norm of humanitarian intervention under customary international law, it does show that the international community can tolerate even unilateral intervention. Although Tanzania maintained its adherence to self-defence rather than humanitarian justifications, it still involved humanitarian intervention which the UN's member states silently but notably supported.[405] Nonetheless, the lack of explicit support for Tanzania's actions renders its utility debatable in relation to humanitarian intervention's status under customary international law.

## 4 Humanitarian Intervention during the Cold War

The twentieth century saw rapid changes in the development of international law as international relations moved away from a system centred on the collective will of Europe's Great Powers and towards a system with the concept of sovereign equality between all states, evident in the UN.[406] This had major

402 Annan, Kofi. *The Question of Intervention* (1999) p.10.

403 Supporters include Teson (Teson. *Supra* note 1. p.238). Abiew (Abiew. *Supra* note 1. p.126), Franck (Franck. *Supra* note 24. p.145), Bazyler (Bazyler. *Supra* note 30. p.591), Thomas. (Thomas. *Supra* note 313. p.111). Opponents include Hassan (Hassan. *Supra* note 186. p.912) and Wheeler (Wheeler. *Supra* note 134. p.135).

404 Wheeler. *Supra* note 134. p.134.

405 Franck. *Supra* note 281. p.219.

406 See *Supra* note 36.

ramifications for the existence of humanitarian intervention as international law was now formed developed by former colonies that had seen their sovereignty eroded by colonialism and now sought to protect their sovereignty from intervention.[407] During the Cold War, the UN regime prioritised sovereignty over human rights.[408] Consequently, subsequent state practice in support of humanitarian intervention during the Cold War is weak,[409] and humanitarian intervention was generally seen as taboo at the time.[410] Although the UN Charter permitted the deployment of military forces under Chapter vii, it was essentially inoperable in this period due to the Cold War, with the Korean War being the only major departure.[411]

Humanitarian intervention's continued existence as a customary norm in the twentieth century is certainly disputed by academics and it is even more problematic as to whether such a right continued after the foundation of the UN.[412] The contemporary Great Powers in the nineteenth century broadly accepted humanitarian intervention and humanitarian justifications were used to authorise interventions in the Ottoman Empire.[413] Humanitarian intervention's existence under customary international law is vital and its cessation would require consistent state practice in opposition to it, which is arguably not the case.[414] Customary international law exists independently of the

407 Anghie. *Supra* note 7. p.748.

408 Weiss, Thomas. *Humanitarian Intervention* (Cambridge, 2018) p.27.

409 Of eleven possible humanitarian interventions that occurred during the Cold War, Chesterman feels that just three were seen favourably by the international community, with these three being the ones analysed in this chapter. See Chesterman. *Supra* note 50. pp.64–84.

410 Heraclides and Dialla. *Supra* note 1. p.2. Ronzitti. *Supra* note 30. p.108. Belgium later cited all three interventions as a precedent for humanitarian intervention (International Court of Justice. *Legality of Use of Force* (*Serbia and Montenegro v Belgium*) Provisional Measures, Oral Proceedings CR 1999/15 (10 May 1999). p.12).

411 White, Nigel. 'Towards Integrated Peace Operations: The Evolution of Peacekeeping and Coalitions of the Willing' in Odello, Marco and Piotrowicz, Ryszard (Eds.) *International Military Missions and International Law* (Leiden, 2011) p.1.

412 Brownlie argues that humanitarian intervention's legality from the nineteenth century was extinguished by the condemnation of intervention and the prohibition on force within the UN Charter (Brownlie. *Supra* note 1. p.342). Likewise, Ronzitti argues that prior customary rights on the use of force are extinguished by the UN Charter (Ronzitti. *Supra* note 30. p.19). Franck and Rodley claim that humanitarian intervention before 1945 does not support a customary right of humanitarian intervention due to alleged humanitarian interventions having a 'musty aura of racial-religious superiority mixed with self-interest' (Franck and Rodley. *Supra* note 40. p.285).

413 See Supra note 1

414 Teson. *Supra* note 1. p.201.

UN Charter, for example, the right of self-defence, which the Charter notes, is 'inherent'.[415] Although humanitarian intervention was applied inconsistently and was bound up with realpolitik, this does not detract from its existence.

The evolving situation can be analysed further through the three noted humanitarian interventions of the Cold War and it is notable that they were not conducted by imperial powers but by former colonies.[416] They all involved a repressive regime using force against a neighbour only for their attacks to be repulsed and their regime toppled. States have the right to use force in self-defence, giving legitimacy to the actions of Vietnam, India and Tanzania who all used force in response to armed attacks and used the language of self-defence.[417] It is widely accepted that the use of force in self-defence must be subject to the principles of necessity and proportionality[418] but self-defence involving regime change is a clear breach of the proportionality rule. Although Karoubi claims India and Cambodia tried to justify their actions in humanitarian terms,[419] this is not the case and self-defence was the justification used.[420]

The failure of the aforementioned cases to rely on humanitarian intervention was primarily for tactical rather than legal reasons.[421] The Cold War was in full swing and humanitarianism was subordinate to geopolitics.[422] The paradox of humanitarian intervention during the Cold War is evident by the international community's differing reactions to the overthrow of repressive regimes.[423]

415 See Chapter 2. *Supra* note 31.

416 Simms, Brendan and Trim, D.J.B 'Towards a history of humanitarian intervention' in Simms, Brendan and Trim, D.J.B (Eds.) *Humanitarian Intervention: A History* (Cambridge, 2011) p.23.

417 Frohlich, Manuel. 'The Responsibility to Protect. Foundation, transformation, and application of an emerging norm' in Klose, Fabian. (Ed.) *The Emergence of Humanitarian Intervention: Ideas and Practice from the Nineteenth Century to the Present* (Cambridge, 2018) p.310.

418 Gray, Christine. *International Law and the Use of Force* (Oxford, 2004) p.120.

419 Karoubi. *Supra* note 4. p.231.

420 See Heraclides and Dialla. *Supra* note 1. p.3.

421 Abiew. *Supra* note 1. pp.134–135.

422 Ibid.

423 Many states that recognised Uganda's new government were opposed to Cambodia's PRK, with even Bangladesh opposing Vietnam's intervention in Cambodia and advocating a strict interpretation of Article 2(4), despite only achieving independence through Indian intervention (UN Security Council. *Official Records, 34th Year, 2109th Meeting.* UN Doc S/PV.2109 (12th January 1979) Para.49). Likewise, while India had intervened in East Pakistan, it refused to recognise the PRK but was willing to establish relations with the Tanzanian installed government of Uganda (Thomas. *Supra* note 313. p.114). Although repressive, Amin's regime was far less ruthless than the Khmer Rouge and yet Tanzania's actions received far more acceptance than Vietnam's. This highlights the inconsistences of international law and international relations, with Western governments refusing to

The difference between the responses to the three interventions was largely to do with realpolitik. Vietnam and India were strong regional actors, backed by Great Powers and operating in strategically important regions. In contrast, Tanzania was nonaligned, of little threat to the global order and acting independently. Unlike the other two interventions, Tanzania's actions produced a negligible international reaction.[424] As in the nineteenth century, the balance of power was the key factor and where a state overthrew a brutal regime without threatening stability, it would attract little criticism, even if it acted unilaterally. By contrast, even when an intervention ended egregious human rights abuses and atrocities, it would be criticised should it threaten the balance of power.[425]

It must be noted that in all three cases, the intervening state stood to benefit from their intervention. This reflects that there are few humanitarian interventions where a humanitarian outcome was not also subject to less idealistic motives.[426] India's security was improved by the partition of Pakistan, Vietnam removed a rival backed by China and Tanzania neutralised an aggressive neighbour. India and Vietnam used force in response to aggression and when ceasefires failed, India was forced into action by the flood of refugees.[427] It is now accepted that large-scale flows of forced migration is a threat to international peace and security.[428] Had Islamabad not committed such atrocities in East Pakistan or granted its inhabitants' autonomy it is doubtful India would have invaded. Likewise, Vietnam had co-existed peacefully with Cambodia for years before the Khmer Rouge sought to annex Vietnamese territory and Hanoi only used force when the Khmer Rouge rejected ceasefires.[429] By contrast,

---

recognise the PRK but recognised Uganda's Tanzanian installed government. Although this can be explained by comparing non-aligned Tanzania to USSR backed Vietnam, this ignores Cambodian aggression against Vietnam and Western criticism of Vietnam's actions rather than motives (Wheeler. *Supra* note 134. p.124).

424 Ronzitti. *Supra* note 30. p.105.

425 This can be highlighted alongside the speed of disengagement once the intervention was over. Indian troops quickly withdrew from Bangladesh and Tanzanian troops remained in Uganda for just two years at the transitional government's request, in contrast to Vietnam's extended military presence in Cambodia and human rights abuses (Franck. *Supra* note 281. pp.218–219). Furthermore, Vietnam had no humanitarian motives in Vietnam (Bazyler. *Supra* note 30. p.609). Rather, Vietnam responded to Cambodian incursions by occupying its neighbour and instituting a compliant puppet state. This was a major difference between the interventions in Bangladesh and Cambodia (Lufty. *Supra* note 210. p.154).

426 Franck and Rodley. *Supra* note 40. p.290.

427 See *Supra* note 138–143.

428 Weiss. *Supra* note 408 p.59.

429 Kiernan. *Supra* note 207. p.388.

while Tanzania was certainly responding to Ugandan aggression, it went far beyond merely repulsing Amin's forces and instituted regime change, rejecting any ceasefire without OAU condemnation of Uganda, which Nyerere would have known was unlikely.[430]

The UN's reaction in all three cases was hesitant in the face of state atrocities and the Cold War ensured the UNSC was even more paralysed than usual. At the time, human rights were seen as domestic concerns, outside of the UNSC's remit.[431] Little effective action could be taken in Cambodia and East Pakistan due to the strategic interests of the P5, whose veto prevented any collective action being taken to avert the ongoing human rights abuses. Likewise, the veto system ensured the UNSC could not act against P5 backed states that engaged in intervention and both Vietnam and India evaded UNSC censure for their intervention. However, neither did they receive overt UN support, likely an attempt to avoid a USSR veto. Overall, while states could refrain from condemning the overthrow of authoritarian regimes (as happened in Uganda), the Cold War precluded this when intervention threatened a P5's interests as in the case of Cambodia.[432]

Both India and Tanzania were at least partially motivated by humanitarian concerns, with domestic outrage helping drive the governments to intervene.[433] Their use of force against the dictatorships of Pakistan and Uganda gave them a measure of credibility and their motivations and methods allow their interventions to be deemed humanitarian.[434] On the other hand, while Vietnam's actions had a humanitarian result in overthrowing the Khmer Rouge, Hanoi's extended occupation of Cambodia and imposition of a puppet PRK regime prevented the actions strengthening the case of humanitarian intervention.

It is debatable thatthe above interventions can be deemed 'humanitarian', weakening such interventions' status under international law.[435] There

430 Hassan. *Supra* note 186. p.873.

431 Walling, Carrie Booth. *All Necessary Measures: The UN and Humanitarian Intervention* (Philadelphia, 2013) p.2.

432 Franck. *Supra* note 24. p.145.

433 Crucially, India was a democracy and though Tanzania was a one-party state, Nyerere was widely admired as an honest and principled politician, both domestically and internationally (See Meredith. *Supra* note 310. p.249).

434 This echoes Kant's claims that the principle of non-intervention only applied to democratic governments (Karoubi. *Supra* note 4. pp.214–215) although the extent of this is debatable (Wilson, James Lindley and Monten, Jonathan. 'Does Kant Justify Liberal Intervention?' *The Review of Politics* (Vol. 73, No. 4, Fall 2011) p.636).

435 Heinze argues that only the intervention in East Pakistan can be seen as humanitarian, given India used humanitarian justifications (in tandem with self-defense) while Vietnam

is a distinct lack of states willing to invoke humanitarian intervention: India, Vietnam and Tanzania all claimed their use of force was in response to aggression and avoided justifying their actions under humanitarian intervention.[436] As the International Commission of Jurists noted, India could have justified its use of force under humanitarian intervention.[437] Likewise, given the international community's acceptance of Tanzania's intervention, it is arguable that this was due to the atrocities in Uganda and its humanitarian credentials are burnished by its prior criticism of Amin's human rights record. However, Vietnam's actions cannot be seen as having a humanitarian basis given it co-existed with Cambodia before the Khmer Rouge invaded Vietnamese territory and its own regime was oppressive, albeit less so than the Khmer Rouge.[438] Such an intervention seemed to be more about removing a troublesome neighbour that ending atrocities. Nevertheless, the humanitarian outcome following the overthrow of the Khmer Rouge cannot be denied. Even if the states did not invoke humanitarian justifications, international law requires an examination of states' actions as well their words.[439] In international law, the legal justifications are vital. The Cold War ensured that geopolitics and strategic interests were the primary factors in international relations and while the consequences of such interventions results should not be ignored, they do not demonstrate a continued existence for humanitarian intervention under customary international law.

---

and Tanzania did not. (Heinze, Eric. A. *Waging Humanitarian War: The Ethics, Law, and Politics of Humanitarian Intervention* (New York, 2009) p.76).

436 See *Supra* note 410.

437 International Commission of Jurists. *Part 9* (1972).

438 Amnesty International *Amnesty International Report 1978* (London, 1978) pp.195–197.

439 Wheeler. *Supra* note 134. p.286. It could be argued that states' actions are far more important than their words. This has key problems as it leaves an analysis of the states' actions as reliant on interpretation, which can vary considerably between different commentators which poses grave difficulties in an area as controversial as humanitarian intervention and prevents the emergence of *opinio juris* (See Chesterman. *Supra* note 50. pp.84–85).

CHAPTER 5

# Humanitarian Intervention in the Post Cold War Era

Despite the UNSC's deadlock between the Superpowers, geopolitical changes were taking place, culminating in the collapse of the USSR in 1991 and the end of the Cold War, leading to an 'era of cautious optimism'.[1] This was a monumental occurrence in modern history,[2] with the UN Secretary-General declaring that the Cold War's 'immense ideological barrier' had given way to a new global phenomenon where democratic regimes replaced authoritarian ones and new states arose, giving new impetus to the importance of state sovereignty.[3] Although this saw the rapid rise of democracy,[4] the Cold War had restrained many states' political developments and the USSR's collapse unleashed instability.[5] This saw the rise of militant nationalism that threatened the stability of states along ethnic lines.[6] At the time the Cold War ended, the UN was primarily a service organisation, with 90% of its resources devoted to issues such as famine, health and economic development.[7] With newfound conflict and atrocities, there was a pressing need for the UN to address such events but the newly hegemonic US and its European allies prioritised multilateral action. At the same time, Russia was still recovering from the USSR's collapse, Japan

1 Lebor, Adam. *Complicity with Evil: The United Nations in the Age of Modern Genocide* (Bury St Edmunds, 2006) p.13.

2 See Fukuyama, Francis. *The End of History and the Last Man* (London, 1992). By contrast, President Putin of Russia referred to the USSR's collapse as the 'the greatest geopolitical catastrophe' of the 20th century'. (BBC News. 'Putin deplores collapse of USSR' (2nd April 2005) http://news.bbc.co.uk/2/hi/4480745.stm Accessed 10th March 2024).

3 UN General Assembly and Security Council. *An Agenda for Peace: Preventative Diplomacy, Peacemaking and Peacekeeping*. UN Doc A/47/277 – S/24111 (17 June 1992) Paras.8–10.

4 Freedom House notes that in 1950, 31% of the world's population lived in democracies, with a further 11.9% of the world's population living in partial democracies. By the end of the twentieth century, this had changed to 58.5% of the world living in democracies, and a further 5% living in restricted democracies. (Freedom House. *Freedom in the World: The Annual Survey of Political Rights and Civil Liberties 1999–2000*. (*New York, 2000*) pp.8–9).

5 This was especially the case in in Southern and Eastern Europe where nationalism had been suppressed by the USSR (Gellner, Ernest. 'Nationalism and the New World Order' in Reed, Laura and Kaysen, Carl (Eds.) *Emerging Norms of Justified Intervention* (Cambridge, 1993) pp.152–153).

6 UN General Assembly and Security Council. *Supra* note 3. Para.11.

7 Schlesinger, Stephen. *Act of Creation: The Founding of the United Nations* (Boulder, 2003) p.286.

 | DOI:10.1163/9789004696396_006

remained staunchly pacifist after its World-War II militarism and few other states possessed force projection capabilities.[8]

Unlike the League of Nations, the UN's collective security role relied on the UNSC's ability to use military force to maintain peace.[9] Although the UN lacked its own forces, it was capable of utilising military forces in a manner unlike the League.[10] The UN Charter provides for peacekeeping under Chapter VI, where lightly armed soldiers supervise a ceasefire between consenting belligerents while a political solution is sought.[11] As such, traditional Chapter VI peacekeeping relies on consent, neutrality and the use of force solely in self-defence.[12] The UN Charter also permits peace-enforcement under Chapter VII, which empowers the UNSC to take 'such action by air, sea, or land forces as may be necessary to maintain or restore international peace and security' if non-military efforts prove inadequate.[13] Such peace enforcement is critically different from traditional peacekeeping given it does not require the host state's consent and the UN forces involved have a more robust use of force mandate, although peace enforcement is also based on the principle of impartiality.[14] This thesis will use the term 'peace operations' to refer to both peacekeeping and peace enforcement operations. Although often politically controversial, such peace-operations are authorised under the UN Charter[15] and thus distinct from any potential right of humanitarian intervention under customary international law.

Peace-operations had been used during the Cold War, but the polarisation and the P5 veto ensured that such operations overwhelmingly involved Chapter VI missions under the UN Charter.[16] During the Cold War, humanitarian tasks were not high on the UN's agenda for peacekeeping, with

8 Donnelly, Jack. 'Human Rights, Humanitarian Intervention and American Foreign Policy: Law, Morality and Politics' *Journal of International Affairs* (Vol.37, No.2, 1984) p.627.

9 White, Nigel. *Keeping the Peace: The United Nations and the Maintenance of International Peace and Security* (Manchester, 1997) p.115.

10 Van Den Berg, Ruud. 'Promising or Failing? League of Nations and United Nations Organisation' *Tillburg Foreign law Review* (Vol.4, Issue.2, 1994–1995) p.104.

11 Karns, Margaret and Mingst, Karen. *International Organisations: The Politics and Processes of Global Governance* (Boulder, 2004) p.82.

12 Weiss, Thomas. *Humanitarian Intervention* (Cambridge, 2018) p.13.

13 Charter of the United Nations (1 UNTS XVI, 1945) Article 41.

14 Murphy, Ray. *UN Peacekeeping in Lebanon, Somalia, and Kosovo* (Cambridge, 2007) p.13.

15 Murphy highlights that the key issue is not with the legality of Chapter VII missions, but controversy over the states that authorize them, and the criteria involved. See *Ibid.* p.14.

16 White, Nigel. 'Towards Integrated Peace Operations: The Evolution of Peacekeeping and Coalitions of the Willing' in Odello, Marco and Piotrowicz, Ryszard (Eds.) *International Military Missions and International Law* (Leiden, 2011) p.1.

humanitarian considerations failing to play a significant role in the decision to dispatch peacekeepers.[17] Nonetheless, the ability to deploy peace-operations is one of the most significant developments in the UN's efforts to secure international peace and security.[18]

Between the UN's foundation and the end of the Cold War, over 100 conflicts had taken place, with some 20 million deaths.[19] The UN was largely impotent due to Superpower division, leading to some 279 vetoes taking place, but the end of the Cold War gave the UNSC a newfound potential to promote peace and conflict resolution.[20] This led to the UN Secretary-General declaring that the UN's effectiveness was no longer in doubt, with the UNSC freed from the Cold War's immobilisation,[21] and enabling the UN to approach collective security in the way that was intended when the UN was founded.[22] As such, the end of the Cold War saw a marked development in the UNSC's competence in peace and security as well as a significant rise in peacekeeping operations.[23]

Such progress was vital given the changing nature of warfare and a shift from international to non-international armed conflict during the 1990s.[24] This posed a huge challenge to the UN in that its peacekeeping experience was in maintaining ceasefires between states.[25] Instead, new peacekeeping missions required the deployment of peacekeepers in heavily polarised environments

17 Schulte, Jan Erik. 'From the Protection of sovereignty to humanitarian intervention? Traditions and developments of United Nations Peacekeeping in the twentieth century' in Klose, Fabian. (Ed.) *The Emergence of Humanitarian Intervention: Ideas and Practice from the Nineteenth Century to the Present* (Cambridge, 2018) pp.265–266.

18 White. *Supra* note 9. p.207.

19 UN General Assembly and Security Council. *Supra* note 3. Para.14.

20 Ibid. Para.15. Notably, the end of the Cold War saw a reduction in the use of vetoes and a sharp rise in the number of resolutions and peacekeeping operations adopted by the UNSC. (See Walling, Carrie Booth. *All Necessary Measures: The UN and Humanitarian Intervention* (Philadelphia, 2013) p.6).

21 UN Doc A/46/1 (13th September 1991) p.2.

22 White, Nigel. 'The Legality of Bombing in the Name of Humanity' *Journal of Conflict and Security Law* (Vol.5, No.1 2000) p.31.

23 Tsagourias and White. *Supra* note 35. p.101.

24 Walling, Carrie Booth. *All Necessary Measures: The UN and Humanitarian Intervention* (Philadelphia, 2013) p.6. Between 1991 and 2001 saw rapid expansion of ethnic conflict and two genocides (Chua, Amy. *Political Tribes: Group Instinct and the Fate of Nations* (London, 2019) p.96). Such conflicts were also notable for atrocities, involving the deliberate targeting and brutalising of non-combatants, with casualties being largely civilian rather than military (Carnegie Commission on Preventing Deadly Conflict. *Preventing Deadly Conflict: Final Report* (Washington DC, 1997) P.XVII).

25 International Commission on Intervention and State Sovereignty. *The Responsibility to Protect* (Ottawa, 2001) Para.1.23.

alongside fragmented non-state-actors.[26] A new approach to peacekeeping was sought and the Secretary-General published *An Agenda for Peace*. Although UN peace-operations evolved in the 1990s, the lines between peacekeeping and peace-enforcement became increasingly blurred, with peacekeepers being thrust into exponentially more dangerous scenarios.[27] Consequently, 'second generation' peace-operations arose since 1985, with more numerous missions taking place which had increasingly complex mandates that encompass characteristics of both peacekeeping and peace enforcement operations.[28] This posed new challenges for UN forces who frequently found themselves without the resources, mandate or support necessary to carry out the increasingly complex operations they were deployed to implement.[29]

State actions that invoke a UNSC response under Chapter VII are distinct from those that breach Article 2(4) of the Charter,[30] as the UNSC has the potential to authorise intervention to protect civilians when conflicts threaten international peace and security. Although the UNSC does not have the authority to take measures against human rights abuses,[31] atrocities can have such a grave impact on international security that the UNSC can authorise deployments to end such violations.[32] The UNSC's ability to authorise such interventions is widely accepted by governments and academics,[33] which is important given the threat internal conflicts pose to stability.[34] The end of the Cold War ensured the UNSC was increasingly active and saw an expanded number of peace-operations, particularly under Chapter VII,[35] offering a critical UNSC role in ensuring humanitarian intervention. Despite authorising more peacekeeping

26 Findlay, Trevor. *The Use of Force in UN Peace Operations* (Oxford, 2002) pp.148–149.

27 Berdal, Mats and Ucko, David. 'The United Nations and the Use of Force: Between Promise and Peril' *The Journal of Strategic Studies* (Vol.37, No 5, 2014) p.666.

28 Murphy, Ray. 'United Nations Military Operations and International Humanitarian law: What Rules Apply to Peacekeepers?' *Criminal Law Forum* (Vol.14, No.2, 2003) p.167.

29 Krishnan, S. 'UN Peacekeeping, Responsibility to Protect and Humanitarian Intervention' *India Quarterly* (Vol.76, No.1, 2020) p. 122.

30 Tsagourias and White. *Supra* note 35. p.95.

31 Independent International Commission on Kosovo. *Kosovo Report* (Oxford, 2000) p.196.

32 International Criminal Tribunal for the former Yugoslavia *Prosecutor v Dusko Tadic* Case No IT-94-1 (Decision on the Defence Motion for Interlocutory Appeal of Jurisdiction 2 October 1995) Para.30.

33 Teson, Fernando. *Humanitarian Intervention: An Inquiry into Law and Morality* (Ardsley, 2005) p.188.

34 International Criminal Tribunal for the former Yugoslavia. *Supra* note32. Para.30.

35 Wood, Pia Christina 'France' in Sorenson, David and Wood, Pia Christina (Eds.) *The Politics of Peacekeeping in the Post-Cold War Era* (Abingdon, 2005) p.68.

mission in the mid-1990s than all previous years combined, the UN was constantly short of troops and resources.[36]

Although the post-Cold War era's increase in internal armed conflicts saw a marked increase in the need for peacekeeping, this was not forthcoming and while there was no alternative to collective action, the UN simply lacked the resources to address such conflicts effectively.[37] This created additional pressures on a post-Cold War NATO to act as a guarantor of international peace and security, given its military prowess. This became especially evident over the course of the 1990, with conflicts that saw egregious human rights abuses.

## 1 Humanitarian Intervention in Iraq and Operation Provide Comfort 1991

Human rights abuses were evident in Iraq, a country that faced many domestic difficulties under President Saddam Hussein's rule.[38] Baghdad competed for regional influence with neighbouring Iran, which had a larger population and US support for its pro-Western Shah.[39] As such, Hussein signed the Algiers Agreement in 1975, which recognised a long-standing border dispute in Iran's favour.[40] The status quo changed in 1979 when Iran's pro-Western Shah was overthrown and replaced by a Shiite theocracy under Ayatollah Khomeini. Iran's comparative military advantage over Iraq was greatly reduced[41] while Iranian-Iraqi relations deteriorated.[42] Consequently, Baghdad became increasingly

36 Off, Carol. *The Lion, The Fox, and the Eagle: A Story of Generals and Eagles in Rwanda and Yugoslavia* (Toronto, 2000) pp.23–24.

37 'Trotting to the Rescue' *Economist.* (25 June 1994).

38 Iraq was a heterogeneous state but dominated by Sunni Arabs like Hussein who comprised some 20% of the population, with Shiite Arabs comprising 50–55% of the population (primarily in the south), while 15–20% of Iraqis were Sunni Kurds and concentrated in Iraq's mountainous north (Human Rights Watch. *Human Rights in Iraq* (New Haven, 1990) pp.17–18).

39 Takeyh, Ray. *Guardians of the Revolution: Iran and the World in the Age of the Ayatollahs* (Oxford, 2009) p.82.

40 'Iraqis Said to Renew Fighting' *Washington Post.* (9 March 1975).

41 Tehran alienated American support and purged its officer corps, greatly weakening its military. Meanwhile, although Hussein had neutralised many competent Iraqi generals, his nationalisation of oil fields funded the acquisition of modern military equipment (Keegan, John. *The Iraq War* (London, 2004) pp.47–61).

42 Baghdad was outraged by Iran's intent to foment revolution in Iraq and sought to extend Iraq's regional influence (Wenger, Marcha and Anderson, Dick. 'The Gulf War' *Middle East Report* (No.148, Sep-Oct 1987) p.24).

aggressive, repudiated the Algiers Agreement and declared its intent to regain its lost territory through force.[43] The Iran-Iraq war began in 1980 and Iran's initial advantages were gradually mitigated by Iraq,[44] until a war of attrition ensued.[45] Anxious to break the stalemate and repel Iran from their territory, Iraq deployed chemical weapons against Iran.[46] The UNSC subsequently passed Resolution 620, which condemned the use of chemical weapons in the Iran-Iraq war, but refrained from blaming either side.[47] However, such was Hussein's utility as a bulwark against Iranian expansion that he received significant international backing, particularly from the US, which was reluctant to take action, despite the use of chemical weapons.[48]

The continued conflict exhausted Iran[49] and a cease-fire was signed in 1988 but Iraq had achieved little beyond a devastated infrastructure, high casualties, and war debt.[50] To finance the war, Iraq borrowed heavily from Gulf States whose Sunni rulers feared Iran's Shiite theocracy. One of Iraq's main creditors was neighbouring Kuwait which Baghdad saw as a seceded part of Iraq that

---

43 Ottaway, David. 'Iraq Cancels Border Pact with Iran' *Washington Post.* (18 September 1980).

44 Despite its pariah status, strategic shortcomings and insecure access to arms, Iran's revolutionary fervour ensured high morale and popular mobilisation (Takeyh, Ray. 'The Iran-Iraq War: A Reassessment' *Middle East Journal* (Vol 64, No.3, Summer 2010) p.365). Iran utilised human wave tactics, accrued consecutive military victories and advanced into Iraq, risking Iraqi military collapse and Iran's emergence as the dominant regional power (Sterner, Michael. 'The Persian Gulf: The Iran-Iraq War' *Foreign Affairs* (Fall, 1984)). While Iran had much larger manpower and higher morale, Iraq had air and artillery superiority and gradually adopted defensive manoeuvres to counter Iran's assaults (Jenkins, Loren. 'Iraq Appears to Be Paying High Price in War with Iran' *Washington Post.* (4 March 1986)).

45 Keegan. *Supra* note 41. p.64.

46 Tehran claiming some 50,000 casualties from Iraqi chemical weapons between 1983 and 1988 (Carus, W. Seth. 'The Genie Unleashed: Iraq's Chemical and Biological Weapons Program' *Washington Institute for Near East Policy Paper* No.14 (1989) p.3). Initially Iraq sought to obfuscate its use of chemical weapons but eventually confirmed their use (Hirst, David. 'Iraq admits to using chemical weapons and accuses Iran' *Guardian.* (2 July 1988)). A 1987 UN investigation found continued Iraqi use of chemical agents against Iranians military and civilian personnel (UN Security Council. *Report of the Mission Dispatched by the Secretary-General to Investigate Allegations of the Use of Chemical Weapons in the Conflict between the Islamic Republic of Iran and Iraq.* UN Doc S/18852 (8 May 1987) Paras 65–66), while a further UN investigation in 1988 found numerous Iranians (primarily civilians) and Iraqi soldiers suffering from chemical weapon injuries (UN Doc S/19823 (25 April 1988) Para.54).

47 UN Security Council. *Security Council Resolution 612 (1988).* UN Doc S/Res/612 (9 May 1988) Para.2.

48 Takeyh. *Supra* note 44. pp.377–382.

49 Ibid. p.380.

50 Human Rights Watch. *Supra* note 38. p.24.

hindered Iraq's recovery by keeping international oil prices low.[51] This combined with Kuwait's refusal to renounce Iraq's war loans resulted in Iraq invading Kuwait in 1990, claiming it was deploying to support the 'Free Provisional Government of Kuwait'.[52] Iraq's aggression against a sovereign state was already a significant violation of international law and Baghdad went even further by annexing Kuwait.[53] This jeopardised Middle-Eastern stability, demonstrating Hussein's aggressiveness and threatening Saudi Arabia's border.[54] Despite Hussein's utility as a source of oil and counterweight to Iran, the invasion of Kuwait shattered his international support.[55]

The UNSC swiftly convened to discuss the issue. Kuwait beseeched the UNSC to maintain international peace and security while protecting the sovereignty of small nations.[56] Iraqi aggression was widely condemned among the UNSC's members and the resulting Resolution 660 was adopted unanimously (save for Yemen, which abstained in the vote),[57] which condemned Iraq's invasion and demanded immediate Iraqi withdrawal.[58]

Continued Iraqi non-compliance led to a series of increasingly strict embargos until the UNSC convened under Chapter VII of the UN Charter.[59] The result was Resolution 678, which was widely supported on the UNSC[60] and authorised

51 Keegan. *Supra* note 41. pp.72–73.

52 UN Doc S/PV.2932 (2 August 1990) p.11.

53 Murphy, Kim. 'Undaunted Iraq Says It Has Annexed Kuwait' *Los Angeles Times.* (9 August 1990).

54 Matthews, Ken. *The Gulf Conflict and International Relations* (London, 1993) p.44.

55 Weiss, Thomas and Collins, Cindy. *Humanitarian Challenges and Intervention* (Boulder, 2000) p.79.

56 UN Doc S/PV.2932 (2 August 1990) p.7.

57 Ibid. p.27.

58 UN Doc S/Res/660 (2 August 1990) Paras.1–2.

59 The President opened the debate by quoting Haile Selassie, drawing on the League of Nation's failure to protect Abyssinian sovereignty in 1935 as a need to defend Kuwait (poignantly, the quote also referenced Fascist Italy's use of chemical weapons (See UN Security Council. *Provisional Verbatim Record of the 2963rd Meeting.* UN Doc S/PV.2963 (29 November 1990) pp.5–6). This comparison was reiterated by Ethiopia on the Security Council (Ibid, pp.49–50).

60 Only Cuba and Yemen opposed it while China abstained (Ibid. pp.64–65). Yemen opposed the Resolution on the basis that its use of force risked escalation, that the forces would not be under UN control and that the sanctions were sufficient to coerce Iraqi compliance (Ibid. pp.31–35). Although Cuba condemned Iraq's invasion of Kuwait, it criticised the sanctions regime for the effects it was having on Iraqi civilians (Ibid. p.53). Likewise, it highlighted the selectivity of Security Council enforcement and criticised the resolution as risking further war (Ibid. pp.56–60). China abstained: it felt unable to support the use of force to settle a dispute but recognised that the Resolution was necessary due to Iraq's aggression and continued intransigence (Ibid. pp.62–63).

UN member states to use 'all necessary measures' to enforce Iraqi compliance with Resolution 660.[61] A US led multinational Coalition was assembled under Operation Desert Storm comprising some sixteen states, including Arab nations,[62] marking the first time that the superpowers had cooperated in major military action under the UN umbrella.[63] Iraq was defeated,[64] forcing Baghdad to accept the Coalition's ceasefire terms and ending the so-called Gulf War.[65] The UNSC subsequently adopted Resolution 687, which set out Iraq's post-war obligations, urging Iraq and Kuwait to respect each other's borders, requiring Iraq to neutralise its stocks of long-range ballistic missiles, chemical and biological weapons and compensation measures by Iraq.[66] Hussein was allowed remain in power given his utility.[67] This is critical to understanding the subsequent intervention when Hussein faced sustained opposition from large segments of Iraqi society, notably the Kurds.

### 1.1 *The Iraqi Kurds*

Due to their numbers,[68] independence and inhabitation of areas rich in natural resources, the Kurds are marginalised by governments across the Middle East.[69] Iraq was no exception and Iraqi Kurdish discontent was longstanding.

61 UN Doc S/Res/678 (29 November 1990) Paras.1–2.

62 Keegan. *Supra* note 41. p.77.

63 Carey, Henry. 'US Domestic Politics and the Emerging Humanitarian Intervention Policy: Haiti, Bosnia and Kosovo' *World Affairs* (Vol.164 (2), Fall, 2001) p.72.

64 Although Iraq's military was large, experienced, and well equipped, it relied on fortified positions that had been effective against Iranian assaults but were vulnerable to bombardment and ensuring they were easily outflanked by Coalition forces. (Keegan. *Supra* note 41. p.80). Within 100 hours, up to 100,000 Iraqi soldiers were killed and most of their heavy weaponry was destroyed, captured, or abandoned (US Senate. *Civil War in Iraq Staff Report to the Committee on Foreign Relations United States Senate.* (Washington, 1991) p.1).

65 Coll, Steve and Gugliotta, Guy. 'Iraq Accepts All Cease-Fire Terms' *Washington Post.* (4 March 1991).

66 UN Security Council. *Security Council Resolution 687 (1991)*. Un Doc S/Res/687 (3 April 1991).

67 Although authoritarian and belligerent, Hussein appealed to many Arabs as a powerful leader, necessitating Iraq's preservation (Fuller, Graham. 'The Fate of the Kurds' *Foreign Affairs* (Vol.72, No.2, Spring 1993) p.118) and Iraq's welfare state meant Hussein had genuine popularity among many Iraqis. (Human Rights Watch. *Supra* note 38. p.34). Likewise, Iraq's invasion of Kuwait had some support in the Arab world, particularly among impoverished northern Arabs who felt Hussein would ensure fairer distribution of Gulf Arabs' wealth (Matthews. *Supra* note 54. p.56).

68 Numbering some 22 million, the Kurds are the fourth largest ethnic group in the Middle East and comprise the largest stateless people in the world, scattered across Turkey, Iran, Iraq, the former USSR, and Syria (Fuller. *Supra* note 67. pp.109–112).

69 See McDowall, David. *A Modern History of the Kurds* (London, 2004) pp.3–7.

Although repression was widespread throughout Iraq, the Kurds suffered disproportionately[70] resulting in rebellion.

Baghdad struggled to defeat the Kurds who utilised guerrilla tactics and received support from the USSR and the Shah of Iran, leading Hussein to soften his campaign against them.[71] Part of the Algiers Agreement saw Tehran end its support of Iraqi Kurds[72] Without Iranian support, Iraq's Kurds were gravely weakened and the day after the Algiers Agreement, Baghdad immediately began an offensive against them.[73] The Kurds gained a new opportunity during the Iran-Iraq War which diverted Hussein's attention and resources and by 1987, the main Kurdish factions united into the Kurdistan Front with Iranian support, presenting a significant threat to Hussein's rule.[74] In response, Iraqi authorities initiated the Al-Anfal campaign, where large numbers of Kurdish villages were razed, their inhabitants displaced and unknown casualties caused.[75] Further Kurdish collusion with Tehran resulted in Iraq using mustard gas,[76] becoming the first country to use chemical weapons against its own citizens.[77] Kurdish accounts of the chemical weapons attack were remarkably consistent across Kurdistan, rendering it unlikely that such diverse communities could fabricate matching stories.[78]

70 Human Rights Watch. *Supra* note 38. p.84.

71 Keegan. *Supra* note 41. p.59.

72 See *Supra* note 40.

73 Ibid.

74 'Iraq's Weapons of Terror' *Guardian* (24 March 1988).

75 US Department of State 1988). p.1170.

76 Especially egregious was Iraq's use of poison gas in 1988 on Halabja, a Kurdish town that was seized by a joint Iranian-Kurdish operation. Baghdad responded with artillery strikes before deploying chemical bombs, with visiting reporters finding civilian corpses lying in the streets (Tyler, Patrick. 'Gas Attack Envelopes Iraqi Town in Cloud of Death' *Los Angeles Times.* (24 March 1988)). Overall, some 5,000 Kurds were reportedly killed in Halabja and 100,000 forcibly resettled (Adelman, Howard. 'Humanitarian Intervention: The Case of the Kurds' *International Journal of Refugee Law* (Vol.4, No.1, 1992) p.7). Such was the severity of the Al-Anfal campaign that a UN Special Rapporteur deemed the campaign as bearing 'the marks of a genocide-type design' (UN Social and Economic Council. *Record on the Human Rights Situation in Iraq.* UN Doc E/CN.4/1992/31 (18 February 1992) Para.103) while parliaments in UK, South Korea, Norway, and Sweden condemned it as genocide (Barbarani, Sofia. 'Iraq Kurds Press States to Recognise Genocide' *Al Jazeera* (14 April 2014) http://www.aljazeera.com/indepth/features/2014/04/iraq-kurds-press-states-recognise-genocide-anfal-201441371637191288.html Accessed 10th March 2024).

77 Power, Samantha. *A Problem from Hell: America and the Age of Genocide* (New York, 2002) pp.186–187.

78 Human Rights Watch. *Supra* note 38. pp.115–116.

Although the UNSC condemned the use of chemical weapons in the Iran-Iraq war, it made no such condemnation of Iraq using chemical weapons against its own citizens.[79] Iraq continued to increase its campaign against the Kurds in an attempt to end the Kurdish problem, deploying 20,000 troops to Kurdistan towards the end of the Iran-Iraq war.[80] The Iran-Iraq war's end posed significant dangers to the Kurds who now lacked Iranian support and faced Iraqi retaliation. This allowed Iraq to engage in the mass resettlement of Kurds, causing huge numbers to flee to Turkey.[81] As in the Iran-Iraq War, Hussein's utility as a counterweight to Iran ensured Western states were reluctant to antagonise him.[82]

### 1.2 *Operation Provide Comfort*

Although the Al-Anfal campaign had weakened the Kurds, they saw Iraq's weakness after the Gulf War as an opportunity.[83] Meanwhile, domestic unrest arose in Iraq and rebellions broke out among Iraqi Shiites in 1991.[84] Despite US President Bush exerting Iraqis to revolt against Hussein, little aid was given to the rebels[85] who were crushed by Hussein while large numbers of civilians fled.[86]

The Kurds had also rebelled and after neutralising the Shiite rebellion, Iraqi forces crushed the Kurdish rebellion, causing two million Kurds to flee to the Turkish and Iranian borders where they overwhelmed relief efforts.[87] Turkey

79 Walling. *Supra* note 24. p.34.

80 Cowell, Alan. 'A Gulf Truce Leaves Rebels in a Quandary' *New York Times*. (28 August 1988).

81 McDowall. *Supra* note 69. pp.360–361.

82 Akhavan, Payam. 'Lessons from Iraqi Kurdistan: Self Determination and Humanitarian Intervention against Genocide' *Netherlands Quarterly of Human Rights* (Vol.11, No.1, 1993) p.43.

83 Walling. *Supra* note 24. p.42.

84 Human Rights Watch 'Iraq and Occupied Kuwait' (1992) http://www.hrw.org/reports/1992/WR92/MEW1-02.htm Accessed 10th March 2024.

85 Bush claimed the best way for the 'bloodshed to stop [was for] the Iraqi military and the Iraqi people [...] to force Saddam Hussein, the dictator, to step aside' ('A Cruel Hoax ... We will continue' *Guardian*. (16 February 1991)). The US did not anticipate the rebellions. (US Senate. *Supra* note 64. P.VII). Rather, the US hoped for an Iraqi military coup against Hussein (DiPrizio, Robert. *Armed Humanitarians: US Interventions from Northern Iraq to Kosovo* (Baltimore, 2002) p.28).

86 Ibrahim, Youssef. 'Iraq Hitting Hard, Reports Big Gains against the Kurds' *New York Times*. (29 March 1991).

87 Arkin, William. Durrant, Damian and Cherni, Marianne. *Greenpeace Study: On Impact: Modern Warfare and the Environment: A Case Study of the Gulf War* (May, 1991) p.49 http://www.greenpeace.org/international/Global/international/planet-2/report/1991/6/on-impact-modern-warfare-and.pdf Accessed 10th March 2024 p.49.

refused them entry due to its own problems with Kurdish unrest and its prior difficulties with Kurdish refugees during the Al-Anfal Campaign.[88] It was apparent that these displaced Kurds were the direct result of Iraq's internal repression,[89] although Iraq claimed that they were not refugees due to their remaining within Iraqi borders (and thus rendering it a domestic problem).[90] The two million Kurds trapped at the borders were dying at a rate of up to 2,000 people a day.[91] Harrowing images of this were broadcast directly to Western audiences, drawing a contrast between the Coalition's willingness to use force to protect Kuwait's autocracy but not Kurdish civilians.[92] Furthermore, it was apparent that Baghdad's human rights abuses were not only threatening regional peace and security but also its neighbours' territorial sovereignty.[93] Although the Allied powers warned Iraq against using chemical weapons, it otherwise took no firm action against what it saw as an Iraqi civil war.[94]

The UNSC adopted Resolution 688, which condemned Iraq for the repression of its civilians, and the subsequent refugee crisis to the extent that it threatened international peace and security, and called for an immediate end to such repression and for Iraq to open access to aid agencies.[95] Resolution 688 was notable as it was the first UNSC resolution to mention the Kurds as populating areas of Iraq (giving them legitimacy) and for its insistence on the UN's right of interference into a member state's domestic policy.[96] However, the question arose as to the best course of action. Coalition forces were reluctant to support Iraq's Kurds actively, fearing it would encourage Kurdish secession and destabilise the region.[97] This was a key impetus behind Washington's approach, given it was under pressure from Saudi Arabia and Turkey to prevent Iraqi dismemberment.[98]

---

88 Frelick, Bill. 'Operation Provide Comfort: False Promises to the Kurds' in Chaliand, Gerard (Ed.) *A People without a Country: The Kurds and Kurdistan* (London, 1993) p.235.

89 UN Social and Economic Council. *Record on the Human Rights Situation in Iraq*. UN Doc E/CN.4/1992/31 (18 February 1992) Para.136.

90 Harrington, Michael E. 'Operation Provide Comfort: A Perspective in International Law' *Connecticut Journal of International Law* (Vol.8, No.2, Spring 1993) p.640.

91 US Senate. *Supra* note 64. p.VI.

92 McDowall. *Supra* note 69. p.373.

93 Walling. *Supra* note 24. p.36.

94 Akhavan. *Supra* note 82. p.43.

95 UN Security Council. *Security Council Resolution 688 (1991)*. UN Doc S/Res/688 (5 April 1991) Paras.1–3.

96 McDowall. *Supra* note 69. p.375.

97 Ibid. p.370.

98 Wheeler, Nicholas. *Saving Strangers: Humanitarian Intervention in International Society* (Oxford, 2010) p.147. For all its brutality, Hussein's authoritarianism maintained Iraqi stability and Western governments were broadly tolerant of his regime (Matthews. *Supra*

Faced with deteriorating security and the risk of escalation,[99] the US began providing humanitarian relief in southern Turkey to Kurdish refugees under Resolution 688 .[100] A more lasting solution was needed, as the Kurds could not enter Turkey but feared Baghdad's retribution if they returned home.[101] This was unsustainable and Turkey pushed for the creation of safe havens within Iraq, a suggestion endorsed by the UK and then the US.[102] Operation Provide Comfort was initiated, creating a 3,600 square mile safe-zone above the 36th parallel in northern Iraq with a no fly zone protecting the Kurds from Iraqi helicopters (a major tool in Baghdad's repression of the Kurds).[103] It also involved the deployment of 21,000 ground troops (from NATO states and France), marking a groundbreaking case of humanitarian intervention.[104] Such safe zones were opposed by Iraq, which had agreed to UN administered humanitarian relief operations but claimed the safe zones violated its sovereignty.[105] Baghdad was in no position to resist and the allied military presence continued to expand, with the area off limits to Iraqi forces having doubled in size by the end of April 1991.[106]

### 1.3 *Humanitarian Intervention and Operation Provide Comfort*

Iraq's systemic human rights abuses tied in with an important year for the UNSC as it began analysing states' internal policies and how they affected international security while a focus on human rights drastically altered the

---

note 54. pp.37–38). Although Bush had expressed his hope that Hussein would be ousted, Washington maintained it never saw his removal as a political or military goal given the instability this would unleash and the bulwark Hussein provided against Iran (Devroy, Ann. 'Bush, aides keep quiet on rebels' *Washington Post.* (3 April 1991)).

99 Most dangerously, Turkey threatened unilateral Turkish intervention (Akhavan. *Supra* note 82. p.43). This was due to Turkey's fear that Iraqi dismemberment would see Iran expand into Iraq's Shiite south and Iraqi Kurds encourage insurrection among Kurds in Turkey (Habermans, Clyde. 'Worried Turks Prefer Iraq to Remain Whole' *New York Times.* (6 March 1991)).

100 Harrington. *Supra* note 90. p.644.

101 DiPrizio. *Supra* note 85. p.25.

102 McDowall. *Supra* note 69. p.375. Such safe havens would serve a vital purpose, staunching the flow of refugees to Turkey (a NATO member and vital Western ally) while addressing the concerns of the Western public who were horrified by the plight of Kurdish refugees (Frelick. *Supra* note 88. p.235).

103 Human Rights Watch. *Supra* note 84.

104 Power. *Supra* note 77. p.241.

105 UN Security Council. *Letter Dated 91/04/21 from the Permanent Representative of Iraq to the United Nations.* UN Doc S/22513 (22 April 1991) pp.2–4.

106 Montalbano, William. 'Allies double size of Iraq safe zone' *Los Angeles Times.* (29 April 1991).

UNSC's approach to military force.[107] Given Operation Provide Comfort did not have a UN mandate, its legal basis is debatable. Resolution 687 provided ceasefire terms to end the Iraqi occupation of Kuwait but made no mention of Iraqi civilians as a basis for intervention.

Resolution 688 was not much better, though Bush claimed that the US troops were creating safe zones as a 'humanitarian measure, consistent with Resolution 688',[108] which was echoed by the UK's Foreign Office.[109] While Resolution 688 certainly used strong language in condemning Iraqi mistreatment of civilians and demanded an end to their repression,[110] it did not authorise the use of force.[111] Furthermore, out of all the relevant UNSC resolutions following Iraq's invasion of Kuwait, it was the first that did not rely on Chapter VII of the Charter or even the previous resolutions.[112] It required Iraq to allow humanitarian aid access, but Operation Provide Comfort went far beyond this. The US and its allies interpreted this to include military forces used for humanitarian purposes.[113] However, at no point during the debate on the draft resolution did a state claim that the resolution authorised armed intervention to protect Iraqi civilians (although the UK and France highlighted that human rights were an international interest) and it is unlikely that a resolution authorising armed intervention would have been adopted.[114]

The issue of international law seemed ambiguous. The US claimed allied forces did not need Baghdad's consent to create the safe zones.[115] This was a novel step: while the French foreign minister had proposed a 'right to interfere', this was in relation to humanitarian aid and not the deployment of troops.[116]

---

107 Walling. *Supra* note 24. pp.34–35.

108 Bush George. 'Letter to Congressional Leaders on Iraq's Compliance with United Nations Security Council Resolutions' in *Public Papers of the Presidents of the United States: George Bush 1991 Book 1-January 1 to June 30, 1991* (Washington DC, 1992) p.522.

109 Marston, Geoffrey (Ed.) 'United Kingdom Materials on International Law 1992' *British Yearbook of International Law* (Vol.63, 1992) p.822.

110 UN Security Council. *Supra* note95. Paras.1–3.

111 Gray, Christine. 'The Use of Force for Humanitarian Purposes' in White, Nigel and Henderson, Christine (Eds.) *Research Handbook on International Conflict and Security Law* (Cheltenham, 2013) p.232.

112 Chesterman, Simon. *Just War and Just Peace: Humanitarian Intervention and International Law* (Oxford, 2001) p.131.

113 Harrington. *Supra* note 90. p.643.

114 Wheeler. *Supra* note 98. p.146. This was a key reason why the US and its allies did not seek a new mandate for military operations in Iraq: any such Resolution would be vetoed by Russia or China (DiPrizio. *Supra* note 85. p.32).

115 Harden, Blaine. 'US, Iraq Differ on Zone for Kurds' *Washington Post.* (20 April 1991).

116 Webster, Paul. 'France will deliver 80 tons of food aid' *Guardian.* (5 April 1991).

The UN Secretary-General questioned whether intervention could take place without clear UNSC authorisation.[117] The use of Resolution 688 was weak, but it still provided the strongest legal justification available. A new resolution to authorise the creation of safe zones explicitly would have provided a stronger legal justification for the Coalition's intervention but risked being vetoed. Operation Provide Comfort received no condemnation from the UNSC or UNGA, presumably, as it was a temporary operation, with no state wanting to oppose such a humanitarian mission.[118] While China's long-standing opposition to intervention would have obligated it to veto any UNSC authorisation of military force in Iraq, it could remain silent on such interventions outside of the UN's authority.[119] This enabled countries like China to refrain from criticising the Coalition's intervention, with Harrington highlighting the negligible opposition to Operation Provide Comfort as proof of the intervention's legality.[120]

Although lack of opposition can be seen as tacit consent to the intervention, it remains a weak argument to rely on, particularly given the unique background[121] and the unlikelihood that intervention would have been authorised by the UNSC. Furthermore, there was no clear evidence that a right of humanitarian intervention overrode the prohibition on the use of force under the UN Charter.[122] Even in the absence of Resolution 688, it is possible that intervention would have taken place, which would have required an alternative legal argument, presumably relying on the right of humanitarian intervention under customary international law.[123]

The UNSC debate on Resolution 688 is illuminating as it showed an understanding that a state's internal actions could threaten regional peace and security. In 1971, India received little support for arguing that Pakistan's brutality in East Pakistan resulted in 'refugee aggression' that was scarcely any different to more common concept of aggression.[124] By contrast, Turkey noted that while Iraq maintained its right to sovereignty, its oppression was inducing a

117 Lewis, Neil. 'Legal Scholars Debate Refugee Plan' *New York Times.* (19 April 1991).

118 Wheeler. *Supra* note 98. p.154.

119 Franck, Thomas. *Recourse to Force: State Action against Threats and Armed Attacks* (Cambridge, 2009) p.154.

120 Harrington. *Supra* note 90. p.647.

121 Operation Provide Comfort followed Operation Desert Storm, which was then the UN's most successful peace-enforcement operation (Donnelly. *Supra* note 8. p.633).

122 Akhavan. *Supra* note 82. p.45.

123 Wheeler. *Supra* note 98. p.167.

124 UN Security Council. *Official Records, 26th Year, 1606th Meeting.* UN Doc S/PV.1606. (4 December 1971) Para.161.

refugee crisis that threatened regional peace and security and Turkey expected 'immediate and forceful' UNSC action to end Iraq's repression of its civilians.[125] Indeed, despite its opposition to Indian intervention in 1971, Pakistan expressed horror at ongoing human rights abuses in Iraq that were inducing a refugee crisis.[126]

Although Iraq claimed that Resolution 688 was an unwarranted intrusion into its internal affairs, the resolution was overwhelmingly adopted with every state that spoke in favour of the motion highlighting Iraqi brutality and the impact that refugees were having on neighbouring states.[127] The only states to oppose the resolution were Yemen, Zimbabwe (which saw the resolution as an unwarranted intrusion into Iraq's internal affairs) and Cuba (which also highlighted that the CIA was aiding rebel groups within Iraq), while China and India abstained.[128] Interestingly, despite its 1971 intervention in East Pakistan, India claimed the UNSC's role should be limited to helping the refugees and demanding Iraq cease its actions, with any UNSC prescription a breach of Iraq's sovereignty.[129] It is notable that Resolution 688 itself highlights the refugees may pose a threat to international peace and security[130] (although it is important to note that the resolution saw the consequence of Iraqi brutality as threatening peace rather than the repression itself).[131] For this reason, Adelman argues that there were legal grounds for intervention, provided it merely restrained Iraq's government and did not threaten Iraq's territorial integrity.[132]

Although Operation Provide Comfort saved thousands of lives, it took place in response to a rebellion partially induced by Bush's encouragement.[133] The US was initially reluctant on the creation of a safe zone, fearing mission creep,[134] but soon warned Iraq to pull its military back from the 36th parallel.[135] American motives were primarily self-interested: in 1991, the Bush

125 UN Security Council. *Provisional Verbatim Record of the 2982nd Meeting*. UN Doc S/PV.2982 (5 April 1991) pp.6–8.

126 Ibid. pp.8–10.

127 Ibid.

128 Ibid.

129 Ibid. p.62.

130 UN Doc S/Res/688 (5 April 1991) Para.1.

131 Akhavan. *Supra* note 82. p.44.

132 Adelman. *Supra* note 76. p.24.

133 Understandably, many Iraqi refugees were bewildered that Washington incited them to revolt but failed to aid them, with the US espousing non-interference, fearing involvement in an Iraqi civil war (Human Rights Watch. *Supra* note 84).

134 DiPrizio. *Supra* note 85. p.29.

135 Tyler, Patrick. 'Bush sees accord on 'safe havens' for Kurds in Iraq' *New York Times*. (12th April 1991).

administration repeatedly criticised Baghdad for Iraqi atrocities in Kuwait but barely mentioned the widespread abuses taking place inside Iraq.[136] Bush used unexpectedly humanitarian language in justifying its intervention, claiming that the introduction of allied armed forces was not to interfere with Iraq's internal affairs but to save Iraqi civilians as a humanitarian measure.[137] It was only when the refugees posed a threat to Turkish stability that the US took action while the numerous refugees on the Iranian border elicited a negligible US response.[138]

The utility of the safe zones was a critical aspect to their creation and the only viable option,[139] which would simultaneously address the refugee problem while maintaining Iraqi sovereignty. Although many Arabs saw military intervention as a Western ploy to destroy Iraq, it is likely that protecting the Kurds enabled them to remain in Iraq and prevented Hussein's repression.[140] Consequently, the safe zones were devised to protect the Kurds while preventing the facilitation of their independence.[141]

The US was keen to extricate itself from the region but withdrawal risked endangering the Kurds and reigniting a refugee crisis. The US and its allies began seeking the deployment of UN police as a buffer zone between Kurdish and Iraqi forces, which was rejected by Baghdad.[142] Although such a force required a UNSC mandate, the US and the UK avoided tabling a resolution, knowing it would likely be opposed by Moscow and Beijing, while the UN refused to commit UN personnel to Iraq without Baghdad's consent.[143] Eventually, a

136 Human Rights Watch. *Supra* note 84.

137 Bush George. 'Letter to Congressional Leaders on Iraq' Compliance with United Nations Security Council Resolutions' in *Public Papers of the Presidents of the United States: George Bush 1991 Book 2-July 1 to December 31 1991* (Washington DC, 1992). p.896.

138 Ibid.

139 The Kurds were too numerous to be easily assimilated by their neighbours, especially given the problems Middle Eastern states faced with their own Kurdish population (Adelman. *Supra* note 76. pp.9–10). Neither could so many refugees be left to die on national borders, lest their desperation cause further regional destabilisation. Likewise, the provision of large-scale humanitarian aid might have kept the Kurds alive but would not have addressed the root of the problem and meant they would continue to cluster on Iraq's border, jeopardising regional security.

140 Fuller. *Supra* note 67. p.114.

141 The US refused to set up Kurdish 'enclaves', lest it catalyse demands for statehood (Tyler, Patrick. 'Bush sees accord on 'safe havens' for Kurds in Iraq' *New York Times.* (12th April 1991)). Likewise, the no-fly zone was only enforced above the 36th parallel that protected many Kurds but pointedly excluded Kirkuk, whose oil wealth would have greatly bolstered Kurdish secession (Chesterman. *Supra* note 112. p.198).

142 Tisdall, Simon. 'Iraq rejects UN police for Kurdish havens' *Guardian.* (10 May 1991).

143 Ibid.

compromise was struck with Iraq agreeing to the deployment of 500 lightly armed UN personnel.[144] Coalition forces prevented full-scale Iraqi assaults but Baghdad continued to conduct clandestine attacks in regional areas, with the UN guards too lightly armed to ensure Kurdish safety.[145] Operation Provide Comfort was broadly a success and by the time Operation Provide Comfort ended in mid-July 1991, some 500,000 Kurds had returned.[146] The Kurds continued to be subjected to deprivation due to an Iraqi blockade,[147] but the allied intervention meant they enjoyed relative protection and political autonomy.[148]

The Kurds only received such attention as it coincided with the interests of the Coalition and their allies, while little support was given to Shiite rebels who faced sustained assaults in Iraq's south.[149] Such brutality attracted nowhere near the attention that was focused on northern Iraq,[150] but the US eventually sought allied support in enforcing a no-fly zone in southern Iraq to protect Iraqi civilians citing authority under Resolution 688 .[151] Operation Southern Watch created a no-fly zone south of the 32nd parallel patrolled by British, French and American aircraft.[152] This was a welcome development in preventing

144 Annex to UN Security Council. *Letter Dated 91/05/30 from the Secretary-General Addressed to the President of the Security Council.* UN Doc S/22663 (31 May 1991). Paras.1–7. The guards were unable to protect the Kurds while the Coalition's withdrawal prior to any Iraqi political settlement gravely weakened the Kurds' security and breached British promises that Western forces would remain until Iraqi-Kurdish negotiations had concluded (Keen, David. 'Short term interventions and long-term problems: the case of the Kurds in Iraq' in Harriss, John. (Ed.) *The Politics of Humanitarian Intervention* (London, 1995) p.171).

145 Wheeler. *Supra* note 98. p.171.

146 Pope, Hugh. 'Allied Troops Leave North Iraq, Vow to Aid Kurds' *Los Angeles Times.* (16 July 1991).

147 UN Social and Economic Council. *Record on the Human Rights Situation in Iraq.* UN Doc E/CN.4/1992/31 (18 February 1992) Paras.104–105.

148 Human Rights Watch. *Supra* note 84.

149 Pick, Hella. 'Cash strapped UN can do little for Shiite refugees' *Guardian.* (14 June 1991). Hundreds of thousands fled to the inhospitable Mesopotamian Marshes where disease and deprivation were rampant, and any international presence and support was tightly constrained by Iraq (Human Rights Watch. *Supra* note 84).

150 UN Social and Economic Council. *Record on the Human Rights Situation in Iraq.* UN Doc E/CN.4/1992/31 (18 February 1992) Para.120. There were multiple reasons for this, with Coalition forces fearing southern Iraq would secede and re-emerge as a Shiite satellite of Iran. Further issues were an even weaker legal justification for operating in southern Iraq, the difficulties in operating in southern Iraq unless they were permitted to operate from across the Iranian border and a general lack of motivation for Coalition powers to conduct further intervention (Wheeler. *Supra* note 98. p.161).

151 Tyler, Patrick. 'Bush is asking allies to support air action to protect Iraq Shiites' *New York Times.* (17 August 1992).

152 Lancaster, John. 'US moves to toughen Iraq stance' *Washington Post.* (29 August 1992).

atrocities but was far less encompassing than Operation Provide Comfort and failed to prevent ground attacks by Iraqi forces.[153] While the lack of effective intervention in southern Iraq can be seen to detract from Operation Provide Comfort's humanitarian basis, it is important to highlight that selectivity does not preclude an intervention's humanitarianism.[154]

In this way, Operation Provide Comfort was an important development in the evolution of humanitarian intervention given that it involved the use of force within the territory of a sovereign state without its consent. In this respect, it pioneered humanitarian assistance[155] and had some notable successes, particularly in its advancement of civil-military cooperation.[156] Its success relied on the fact that Iraqi forces had already been defeated in the Gulf War and the need to help a NATO ally.[157] Above all, the intervention was possible as the protection of human rights coincided with the interests of those states with the capability to project force effectively. Given Operation Provide Comfort's goal of mitigating the suffering of the Kurds while maintaining Iraq's territorial integrity, it may be seen as a success.[158]

Operation Provide Comfort appears to provide an effective example of humanitarian intervention, where limited force was used to protect an oppressed people, there was little international opposition and it was carried out without jeopardising Iraq's territorial integrity or political independence. Indeed, it likely ensured Kurdistan remained part of Iraq.[159] However, its legal justification is weak, particularly under Resolution 688 . There were attempts to invoke a right of humanitarian intervention under customary international law. A UK Foreign Office legal advisor admitted that Operation Provide Comfort was not 'specifically mandated' by the UNSC but Coalition forces operated under humanitarian intervention's status in customary international law.[160] This was expanded to include the conditions when such interventions

153 Wheeler. *Supra* note 98. p.163.

154 Ibid. p.169.

155 Keen. *Supra* note 144. p.167.

156 Weiss and Collins. *Supra* note 55. p.79.

157 DiPrizio. *Supra* note 85. pp.42–43.

158 DiPrizio. *Supra* note 85. p.27.

159 Freed from Hussein's brutality and protected by an international force, the Kurds flourished, establishing a functioning democracy, and declaring themselves a constituent region of a future Iraqi federation (Fuller. *Supra* note 67. p.113). In many ways, Iraq's Kurds acquired many aspects of statehood, with a democratically elected assembly, their own security forces, and control over foreign and commercial affairs (Akhavan. *Supra* note 82. p.60).

160 Marston. *Supra* note 109. p.827.

could take place. Namely, where there was a 'compelling and urgent' humanitarian catastrophe, the capability of the host state to address the humanitarian concerns, a lack of practical alternatives to intervention and the intervention would need to be 'limited in time and scope'.[161] Gray highlights the importance of this as the first open support of humanitarian intervention by a state since the foundation of the UN.[162] This was not espoused by the US and despite Operation Provide Comfort's humanitarian outcome, it took place in specific circumstances. Iraq's blatant aggression, pariah status and extensive human rights violations ensured that the link between human rights abuses and international security was possible.[163]

Operation Provide Comfort does not create a clear use of precedent for developing humanitarian intervention's status under international law.[164] Although a humanitarian outcome arose from a mission without official sanction, it received no open support and was based on uncertain legal grounds. It is notable that while it took place immediately following the Gulf War to protect Kuwait's national sovereignty, Operation Provide Comfort breached Iraqi sovereignty to protect human rights.[165] Soon after Operation Provide Comfort took place, Harrington speculated that it would not create a precedent but remain a 'historical curio' where intervention was justifiable.[166] This certainly seems to be the case, with the intervention being feasible due to political circumstances. Had Iraq not been militarily weakened in the Gulf War, it is unlikely an intervention would have taken place for humanitarian reasons,[167] especially given that no such intervention took place during the Al-Anfal campaign. Likewise, Operation Provide Comfort was constrained by its reliance on air protection. This restricted it to a limited geographical area and rendered it dependent on airbases in Turkey, whose government was unfavourable to the Kurds.[168] Operation Provide Comfort was motivated by self-interest and while mixed motives do not prevent an intervention having a humanitarian mission

161 Ibid. pp.827–828.

162 Gray, Christine. *International Law and the Use of Force* (Oxford, 2004) p.35.

163 Walling. *Supra* note 24. p.37.

164 Wheeler. *Supra* note 98. p.140, 167–168.

165 This is a point highlighted by Abiew who notes that state-sovereignty was no longer able to shield egregious human rights violations (Abiew, Francis Kofi. *The Evolution of the Doctrine and Practice of Humanitarian Intervention* (The Hague, 1999) p.156). Likewise, Teson claims that Operation Provide Comfort was a 'landmark precedent' on the legality of collective humanitarian intervention (Teson. *Supra* note 33. p.298).

166 Harrington. *Supra* note 90. p.648.

167 DiPrizio. *Supra* note 85. p.42.

168 Keen. *Supra* note 144. p.173.

or outcome, neither can such a unique situation be deemed to strengthen a right of humanitarian intervention under customary international law.

The humanitarian credentials of Operation Provide Comfort are debatable: the international community paid little attention to the use of chemical weapons against the Kurds in the 1980s and only engaged in Operation Provide Comfort when displaced Kurds threatened regional stability. Likewise, the minimal effort taken to protect Iraqi Shiites[169] further demonstrates that the intervention was undertaken in the interests of the US and its allies rather than out of a genuine humanitarian concern. Indeed, DiPrizio notes that humanitarian concern and media pressure were secondary factors in the US launch of Operation Provide Comfort.[170] Rather, concerns over geopolitics and a need to placate its allies were more important, with Washington's need to protect regional stability by ensuring Iraq's territorial integrity while preventing destabilisation of Turkey owing to large numbers of refugees.[171]

## 2 The Rwandan Genocide and Operation Turquoise 1994

Rwanda is a striking example where humanitarian intervention was arguably needed but not forthcoming in a country with a troubled history. Two major ethnic groups, namely the Hutus and the Tutsis, dominated Rwandan society.[172] Ethnic tension was a major problem before and after Rwandan independence.[173] In 1973 General Habyarimana's *coup d'état* established an

169 See *Supra* note 149.

170 DiPrizio. *Supra* note 85. pp.146–147.

171 Ibid.

172 Newbury, David. 'The Clans of Rwanda: A Historical Hypothesis' *Africa: Journal of the International African Institute* (Vol.50 No.4, 1980) p.389. The Hutus were normally farmers while the Tutsis herded cattle. Rwanda's current government denies the existence of ethnic groups, arguing that both Hutus and Tutsis had ancestors with different occupations ('The Jews of Africa: Tutsis' *Economist* (21 August 2004).) Prior to the arrival of colonialism, the differences between Hutu and Tutsi were so vague that it essentially amounted to the number of cattle owned (Pieterse, Jan. 'Sociology of Humanitarian Intervention: Bosnia, Rwanda and Somalia Compared' *International Political Science Review* (Vol. 18(1), January 1997) p.82).

173 Although ethnic divisions existed before the arrival of Europeans, their problems were compounded by European colonisation (Organisation of African Unity *Rwanda: The Preventable Genocide* (2000) Paras.2.3–2.8). Both Hutus and Tutsis shared the same customs, language, and religion but as Rwandan society saw cattle as a sign of wealth, the Tutsis had a privileged position that was reinforced by Germany during the colonisation of German East Africa. During World War I, Belgium took control over the area and turned racialism into an administrative system (Appiah, Anthony and Gates, Henry Louis.

authoritarian, single party regime which discriminated against Tutsis, causing even more Tutsis to flee.[174] Tutsi refugees in Uganda joined with Hutu dissidents to form the Rwandan Patriotic Front (RPF), which sought the repatriation of Tutsis refugees and power sharing.[175] In October 1990, Ugandan Army veterans in the RPF invaded Rwanda, with the ensuing Rwandan Civil War seeing thousands killed, millions left homeless and the collapse of the Rwandan economy.[176] Initially, Rwandan Government Forces (RGF) were able to hold off the RPF with military backing from France, Belgium and Zaire.[177] However, this changed when Paul Kagame took over the RPF and put them on the offensive.[178] RPF military gains combined with international and domestic pressure to force Habyarimana to sign a peace agreement at Arusha, Tanzania in August 1993.[179]

### 2.1 *The UN Assistance Mission in Rwanda* (UNAMIR)

The Arusha Accords ended Habyarimana's single-party-rule and provided for a power-sharing transitional government. Both Habyarimana and the RPF feared a political vacuum that would be filled by paramilitaries and consequently sought a peacekeeping force to help implement the Arusha Accords.[180] The UN Assistance Mission for Rwanda (UNAMIR) was a classic Chapter VI mission[181]

---

*Encyclopaedia of Africa, Volume 1* (Oxford, 2010) p.450). In addition, Tutsi privilege was systematically reinforced while discriminating against the Hutus (Codere, Helen. 'Power in Ruanda' (Sic) *Anthropologica* (Vol.4, No.1, 1962) p.46). Such a system caused resentment among the Hutu majority and amidst the wave of post-World War II decolonisation, the Tutsis tried to maintain their privileges while Hutus pushed for majority rule. In 1959, the Hutus overthrew Rwanda's Tutsi king causing a wave of violence and the exodus of Tutsis to neighbouring countries, with Tutsis being heavily discriminated within Rwanda.

174 Organisation of African Unity. *Supra* note 173. Paras.4.1–4.5.

175 See Ibid. Paras.6.1–6.4.

176 Orr, David. 'Peace of a Sort Heralds End to Years of Misery' *Observer.* (1 August 1993).

177 Khadiagala, Gilbert. *Meddlers or Mediators: African Interveners in Civil Conflicts in East Africa* (Leiden, 2007) p.59.

178 Dallaire, Roméo. *Shake Hands with the Devil: The Failure of Humanity in Rwanda* (London, 2004) p.67.

179 Kuperman, Alan. 'Rwanda in Retrospect' *Foreign Affairs* (Vol.79, No.1, Jan-Feb 2000) p.94.

180 UN Security Council. *Report of the Secretary-General on Rwanda.* UN Doc S/26488 (24 September 1993). Paras.13–14.

181 It was intended for UNAMIR to have a strength of about 2,500 soldiers (UN Security Council. *Report of the Secretary-General on the United Nations Assistance Mission for Rwanda.* UN Doc S/26927 (30 December 1993) Paras. 9–11). UNAMIR was also reliant on the consent of the Rwandan government and with ambiguous Rules of Engagement that were generally seen as prohibiting the use of force except in self-defence (Kuperman. *Supra* note 179. p.104).

under the command of Canadian Major-General Roméo Dallaire and was created by UNSC Resolution 872, with a mandate that included contributing to security in Kigali while monitoring the cease-fire and refugee repatriation.[182]

The UNSC hoped that UNAMIR would be a straightforward mission that would bolster UN credibility after ineffective peace-operations in Somalia and Bosnia.[183] However, France, the US and Russia wanted UNAMIR to have just 500 troops[184] despite the risk of conflict reoccurring that a small Chapter VI force would be unable to contain. Dallaire was aware of the ethnic divisions and the fragility of the peace and proposed Rules of Engagement that would allow UNAMIR to prevent 'crimes against humanity' but he never received a reply from his superiors.[185] Dallaire soon realised how restrictive his mandate was, particularly given that there were extremist Hutu officials plotting to derail the Arusha Accords and exterminate Tutsis,[186] even as the Arusha accords were being negotiated.[187] An informant warned UNAMIR of imminent danger,[188] but little was done.[189] Such information should not have been discounted and it showed UNAMIR was no longer in a traditional Chapter VI situation.

182 UN Doc S/Res/872 (5 October 1993) Para.3.

183 Walling. *Supra* note 24. p.119.

184 Dallaire. *Supra* note 178. p.76.

185 UN Security Council. *Letter Dated 99/12/15 from the Secretary-General Prepared Addressed to the President of the Security Council.* UN Doc S/1999/1257 (16 December 1999) p.9.

186 Gibbs, Nancy. 'Why? The Killing Fields of Rwanda' *Time.* (16 May 1994).

187 Wheeler. *Supra* note 98. p.212.

188 The informant was from the extremist Hutu group *Interahamwe* and warned that Hutu extremists were stockpiling weapons, compiling death-lists of Tutsis and training groups like the *Interahamwe* to exterminate Tutsis (Dallaire. *Supra* note 178. p.142). He offered to reveal the location of the extremists' arms stockpiles, with an agent dispatched by Dallaire verifying their existence and confirming the story was true (Off. *Supra* note 36. p.42).

189 The high-level informant within the Hutu extremist movement proved the violation of the Arusha accords and the threat to UNAMIR's safety (UN Security Council. *Supra* note 185. p.11). Dallaire contacted the UN Department of Peacekeeping Operations (UNDPKO) but was told that UNAMIR's mandate did not permit them to act against the arms caches and that they should inform Habyarimana so RGF could intervene (Dallaire. *Supra* note 178. p.146). However, Habyarimana never followed up and the subject was dropped (Organisation of African Unity. *Supra* note 173. Para.13.34). Kuperman highlights that unreliable informants are common during conflict and that it was prudent to direct the allegations towards Habyarimana (Kuperman. *Supra* note 179. p.113). Dallaire's discovery showed at least one cache existed (Off. *Supra* note 36. p.42). Likewise, large quantities of arms were arriving in Kigali airport, showing the danger. (Lebor, Adam. *Complicity with Evil: The United Nations in the Age of Modern Genocide* (Bury St Edmunds, 2006) p.167).

### 2.2 *The Rwandan Genocide*

On 6 April 1994, unknown perpetrators shot down Habyarimana's plane, with RGF officers disregarding the authority of Prime Minister Uwilingiyimana and taking 'interim control'.[190] Violence soon followed and the killings were initially political rather than ethnic, with prominent moderate Hutus being targeted.[191] Attention swiftly turned towards Tutsis, with the Rwandan government announcing a curfew while Hutu militias and RGF erected roadblocks and extremist Hutu media declared all Tutsis as targets.[192] While the overall death toll is unclear, estimates range between 500,000 to 800,000, accounting for three quarters of Rwanda's Tutsi population alongside thousands of moderate Hutus.[193]

UNAMIR's troop contributing countries were worried about casualties, particularly after recent peacekeeper deaths in Somalia.[194] Hutu extremists were aware of this, particularly UNAMIR's reliance on its Belgian contingent.[195] Consequently, when Prime Minister Uwilingiyimana was murdered, her Belgian peacekeeper guards were killed. Belgium then sought a full withdrawal of UNAMIR to give it the diplomatic cover to withdraw its own troops.[196] Meanwhile, the threat to peacekeepers caused Dallaire to repatriate UNAMIR's ineffective Bangladeshi battalion while other nations followed Belgium in pulling their troops from UNAMIR until Dallaire was left with 450 peacekeepers, predominantly from African countries.[197] This reflected UNSC members focusing on UN troops' safety rather than the safety of the Rwandans and there was a push to withdraw altogether.[198] Although UNAMIR was retained, the UNSC reduced UNAMIR numbers to minimal levels.[199] However, stronger UN action was certainly possible: the rapid evacuation of foreign nationals from Rwanda shows how effective international intervention could have been with

190 UN Security Council. *Supra* note 185. p.15.
191 Gibbs. *Supra* note 186.
192 Power. *Supra* note 77. p.330.
193 Organisation of African Unity. *Supra* note 173. Para.14.80.
194 Doyle, Michael and Sambanis, Nicholas. *Making War and Building Peace* (Princeton, 2006) p.284.
195 Dallaire. *Supra* note 178. p.144.
196 Lebor. *Supra* note 189. p.174.
197 Off. *Supra* note 36. p.64.
198 Wheeler. *Supra* note 98. p.221.
199 UN Security Council. *Security Council Resolution 912 (1994)*. UN Doc S/Res/912 (21 April 1994) Para.8. c.

European soldiers evacuating thousands of Westerners between the 9th and 13th April 1994.[200]

Western public pressure for intervention was minor, given that press coverage of the genocide and support for intervention were both low.[201] It took some time for the international community to call the violence what it was: genocide.[202] On 31 May 1994, the UN Secretary-General announced that there could be little doubt that genocide was taking place.[203] Key policymakers in France, Belgium, the US and the UN were all aware of the massacres taking place but avoided classifying it as genocide, lest it require them to intervene.[204] It was only on 29 April 1994 (three weeks after the genocide began) that the issue of genocide was even discussed by the UNSC.[205] Even while this was going on, the international community failed to challenge the legitimacy of the Rwandan government and never discussed expelling Kigali's representative.[206] This ensured Rwanda was able to take part in and vote on UNSC decisions while the genocide took place.[207] They would also have been aware of the UNSC's reluctance to intervene, allowing the *genocidaires* to be more audacious. This is especially important, as the Rwandan Ambassador would have known that the Arusha Accords required both the Rwandan government and RPF to be committed to the peace process.[208]

---

200 Kuperman. *Supra* note 179. p.103. Even UNAMIR was told to prioritise the extraction of Westerners, with UNDPKO's head, Kofi Annan explicitly telling Dallaire to do so without using force except in self-defence (Power. *Supra* note 77. p.352).

201 Ibid. p.375.

202 On the 25 April, the *New York Times* highlighted that what began as ethnic violence had become 'the methodical killing of Tutsis across the countryside' (Lorch, Donatella. 'Rwandan Refugees Describe Horrors after a Bloody Trek' *New York Times*. (25 April 1994)).

203 UN Security Council. *Report of the Secretary-General on the Situation Rwanda.* UN Doc S/1994/640 (31 May 1994) Para.36.

204 United Nations Human Rights Council. 'Genocide in Rwanda'https://yale.learningu.org/media/uploaded/46340da5-e811-4c72-974c-c1acd896a493 Accessed 10th March 2024. There was nothing clandestine about the genocide, with instructions being explicitly broadcast on Rwandan radio. According to the Czech Ambassador to the UN, the Security Council spent 80% of its time discussing withdrawing UNAMIR and 20% of its time trying to broker a ceasefire (which he compares to wanting Hitler to reach a ceasefire with the Jews) (Melvern, Linda. 'Behind Closed Doors' *The World Today* (Vol.56 No.8–9, August-September 2000) pp.9–11).

205 United Nations Human Rights Council. *Supra* note 204.

206 Ibid.

207 Lebor. *Supra* note 189. p.172.

208 During the Arusha Accords, both Habyarimana and the RPF urged the UN to deploy a monitoring force of 4,260 as soon as possible (UN Security Council. *Supra* note 185. p.7). Such a force was unfeasible due to shortages of both finances and troops, especially given Washington's reluctance to fund such a large force (Power. *Supra* note 77. p.340).

Even after the outbreak of the genocide, the international community focussed on enforcing a ceasefire, which would have allowed the genocide to continue without interference from the RPF.[209] However, the RPF was not content to wait for foreign intervention and the onset of the genocide saw the RPF go on the offensive.[210] Unlike the RGF, the RPF was well trained, well-disciplined and under Kagame's impressive command.[211] RPF forces swiftly advanced and as they made gains, they demanded the withdrawal of foreign troops so they could begin their offensive to take Kigali.[212] Rather than supporting intervention, the RPF saw their victory over the RGF as the best way to stop the genocide and indeed, only their military successes prevented the Rwandan genocide becoming 'a complete holocaust'.[213]

The issue of intervention was problematic for the US. Following the deaths of American troops after a botched operation in Somalia in 1993, Washington feared losing more soldiers and was reluctant to risk its troops.[214] The US was keen to pretend that there was no genocide, lest they be forced to act.[215] Washington maintained both sides were equally culpable of violence, allowing it to avoid intervention but even before the outbreak of the genocide, the US was acutely aware of the risk.[216] While the genocide was ongoing, US President Clinton failed to authorise a single meeting with his foreign policy advisors to discuss US options in Rwanda.[217] Furthermore, the US was constantly

209 Organisation of African Unity. *Supra* note 173. Para.15.13.

210 Kuperman. *Supra* note 179. p.104.

211 Dallaire. *Supra* note 178. p.67.

212 Shaw, Angus. 'Terror, violence control streets of Rwandan city' *Austin American Statesman.* (14 April 1994).

213 Holzgrefe, J.L 'The Humanitarian Intervention Debate' in Holzgrefe, J.L and Keohane, Robert. *Humanitarian Intervention: Ethical, Legal and Political Dilemmas* (Cambridge, 2003) p.17.

214 Lebor. *Supra* note 189. p.50.

215 A Department of Defence memo expressed concern that investigating the Rwandan violence could lead to a finding of genocide that would force the US to act. (Power. *Supra* note 77. p.359).

216 Three months before the genocide began, a CIA report warned that if Rwandan violence reignited, there was a risk of half a million deaths (Des Forges, Alison. 'Shame: Rationalizing Western Apathy on Rwanda' *Foreign Affairs* (Vol.79, May-June 2000) p.141). Similarly, one US government intelligence expert also warned that the resumption of violence risked a worst-case scenario of half a million deaths (Organisation of African Unity. *Supra* note 173. Para.9.13). On the day Habyarimana was killed, US Secretary of State, Warren Christopher received a memo warning that Habyarimana's death created a serious likelihood of widespread violence (Power. *Supra* note 77. p.330). Likewise, US officials were aware of the genocide two days after it began (Des Forges. *Supra* note 216. p.141).

217 Power. *Supra* note 77. p.335.

influencing the UN to prevent UNAMIR from stopping the violence.[218] Given that genocide would force the US to act, Washington avoided using the term and pushed for complete UN disengagement from Rwanda.[219]

International outrage was forcing the UNSC to act. Dallaire suggested expanding UNAMIR, which could secure Kigali then expand outwards to rescue civilians.[220] However, the US opposed Dallaire's plan and pushed for the creation of UN protected safe areas, which ignored the reality that many Tutsis were unable to reach such zones. Although some members of the UNSC supported deploying a UN intervention force to Rwanda, they lacked the capacity to do it themselves and the proposal was rejected by militarily capable states.[221]

Following a recommendation from the Secretary-General, the US acceded to Dallaire's plan and the UNSC voted to bolster UNAMIR to 5,500 soldiers with an expanded mandate to protect civilians.[222] UNAMIR II remained a Chapter VI mission and lacked authority to prevent genocide.[223] Compounding UNAMIR II's difficulties was that despite the efforts of the Special Representative of the Secretary-General, the UN had difficulty in securing troop contributions.[224] As a result, it would take months before UNAMIR II was in a position to fulfil its mandate and by the time the genocide ended, no additional peacekeepers had been deployed.[225]

---

218 Des Forges. *Supra* note 216. p.141. Presidential Decision Directive 25 highlighted that the US 'cannot be the world's policeman' while Congress passed a bill in 1993 requiring 15 days' notice of peacekeeping operations and cutting contributions to UN operations, including peacekeeper funding (Doyle and Sambanis. *Supra* note 194. p.299).

219 Heer, Jeet. 'A Decade after the Horror' *National Post.* (1 April 2004). This was a feature of both the US and UN with a former Pentagon specialist highlighting that both sought to avoid the responsibility of intervening during a genocide (Quoted in Organisation of African Unity. *Supra* note 173. Para.15.17). Overall, it appears that Washington's response to the genocide was built on a cynical belief that Rwanda was of too little strategic use to merit intervention (DiPrizio. *Supra* note 85. p.71).

220 Power. *Supra* note 77. p.378.

221 Wheeler. *Supra* note 98. p.227.

222 UN Security Council. *Security Council Resolution 918 (1994)*. UN Doc/ S/Res/918 (17 May 1994) Paras.3–5.

223 DiPrizio. *Supra* note 85. pp.78–79.

224 UN Security Council. *Supra* note 185. p.25. Western states were reluctant to deploy any troops and while African states offered to bolster UNAMIR, they lacked equipment and logistics (Littlejohn, Michael. 'French Plan Likely to Be Approved in Spite of Opposition' *Irish Times.* (22 June 1994)). Dallaire eventually obtained armoured personnel carriers from the US, but these were little better than 'tons of rusting metal' while the obsolete trucks he received from the British broke down (Dallaire, Romeo. 'The End of Innocence: Rwanda 1994' in Moore, Jonathan (Ed.) *Hard Choices: Moral Dilemmas in Humanitarian Intervention* (1998). p.376).

225 Organisation of African Unity. *Supra* note 173. Para.10.16.

### 2.3 *Operation Turquoise*

Despite knowing about the ongoing genocide, the P5 showed little interest in intervening.[226] The main exception was France, which maintains military and political links with its former colonies and supplied the Habyarimana regime with investment and military aid.[227] French coverage of the genocide and links with Kigali saw a heavy push for intervention among the French public, although Paris insisted it would only intervene with UN authorisation.[228] Even amidst the genocide, other members of the UNSC were reluctant to support French intervention, due to its ties with the Rwandan government.[229] Despite opposition from Dallaire and abstentions by five members of the UNSC, no other state had the will and capability to intervene. On 22 June 1994, the UNSC authorised France to use 'all necessary means' under Chapter VII of the UN Charter.[230] France's Operation Turquoise deployed quickly, showing the pace at which a professional military could have mobilised to halt the genocide.

Initially, France arrived with the assumption that both Hutus and Tutsis were equally guilty of atrocities and President Mitterrand's advisors refused to use their influence in Kigali to stop the genocide.[231] Rather, Paris sought to bolster the Rwandan government, as it had done in 1990.[232] France soon discovered that the Rwandan government was heavily involved with the genocide and Mitterrand declared that the rebels 'are not our enemies, and we are not trying to prevent them from winning the civil war.'[233] French intervention shifted, with the 2,500 French troops being used to establish safe zones for Tutsis.[234] By this point, the RGF was unable to hold the RPF back and by 18 July,

---

226 The US pushed for non-intervention, heavily guided by realpolitik and a desire to avoid another unsuccessful intervention after the failures of US intervention in Somalia in 1993 (DiPrizio. *Supra* note 85. pp.71–75). The UK was similarly reluctant to intervene while Russia and China maintained their prioritisation of sovereignty over human rights (Off. *Supra* note 36. p.70).

227 Dallaire. *Supra* note 178. p.62.

228 Wheeler. *Supra* note 98. pp.231–237.

229 Kraft, Scott. 'France's Big Gamble Pays Off in Rwanda' *Los Angeles Times*. (16 July 1994).

230 UN Security Council. Security Council Resolution 929 (1994). UN Doc S/Res/929 (22 June 1994) Para.3.

231 Organisation of African Unity. *Supra* note 173. Para.15.55.

232 Bonner, Raymond. 'France Backs Away from Battle in Rwanda' *New York Times*. (6 July 1994).

233 Ibid.

234 Randal, Johnathan. 'French Troops Race to Rescue of Tutsis; 1st Effort to Protect Rwandan Civilians' *Washington Post*. (1 July 1994).

the RPF had decisively defeated the RGF, driving 40,000 RGF and militiamen to Zaire (now the Democratic Republic of the Congo) and Tanzania.[235]

Operation Turquoise saved many civilians, with estimates of civilians saved ranging from hundreds[236] to thousands.[237] Dallaire saw Operation Turquoise as a 'humanitarian cloak', allowing France to intervene and bolster RGF against defeat by the RPF.[238] French efforts at impartiality essentially amounted to tacit support for the *genocidaires*, as hate speech continued to be broadcast from the French protected zone and genocide organisers were not seized.[239] The French intervention saved Tutsis but allowed *genocidaires* to flee to Zaire and regroup.[240] Furthermore, Operation Turquoise stoked regional unrest by providing a safe haven to *genocidaires* and allowing them to continue their campaign against the RPF.[241] France arguably did more harm than good, being a key ally of the Rwandan government, failing to use its influence to end the genocide and defending the Rwandan government while the genocide was ongoing.[242] France has since admitted that Operation Turquoise was 'too late and, probably, too little'[243] and the operation can scarcely be called a humanitarian intervention, given it mostly protected the perpetrators rather than the victims of genocide.[244]

235 Orth, Richard. 'Rwanda's Hutu Extremist Insurgency: An Eyewitness Perspective' in Cooke, Susan (Ed.) *Genocide in Cambodia and Rwanda: New Perspectives* (New Brunswick, 2007) p.215. The refugee problem continued to grow with many Hutus fearing reprisal from the advancing RPF and by the 17 July, over one million Rwandans had fled to Zairean refugee camps (UN Security Council. *Supra* note 185. p.29). Furthermore, many refugees were *genocidaires* but French efforts to remain impartial meant *genocidaires* were allowed to flee with their weapons through French safe zones and into refugee camps (Doyle and Sambanis. *Supra* note 194. p.299). These extremists quickly took control of the Hutu refugee camps where they re-armed and catalysed violence in the Democratic Republic of the Congo (United Nations 'Outreach Programme on the Rwanda Genocide and the United Nations' http://www.un.org/en/preventgenocide/rwanda/education/rwandagenocide.shtml Accessed 10th March 2024).

236 Ibid.

237 Quoted in Organisation of African Unity. *Supra* note 173. Para.15.68.

238 Dallaire. *Supra* note 224. p.425.

239 Power. *Supra* note 77. p.380.

240 Orth. *Supra* note 235. p.222.

241 Organisation of African Unity. *Supra* note 173. Para.15.69.

242 Ibid. Para.12.30.

243 BBC News 'Nicolas Sarkozy admits Rwanda genocide 'mistakes''http://news.bbc.co.uk/2/hi/8535803.stm Accessed 10th March 2024.

244 Walling. *Supra* note 24. p.122.

### 2.4 *Humanitarian Intervention, the Rwandan Genocide, and the Failure of* UNAMIR

Although Operation Turquoise had some success, it was authorised and deployed separately from UNAMIR. By placing a Chapter VI and Chapter VII mission in the same operational theatre, the UN's role in Rwanda was complicated further and it is unclear why France could not have used its resources to bolster UNAMIR II.[245] Likewise, Dallaire argues that if France wanted to stop the genocide, they could have simply reinforced UNAMIR.[246] Expanding the size and mandate of UNAMIR seemed the most effective way of responding to the genocide and Nigeria presented a draft resolution to the UNSC proposing this, but dropped it due to Western opposition.[247]

This raises the question as to whether humanitarian intervention would have been unnecessary, had UNAMIR been stronger. Habyarimana claimed peacekeepers were capable of provide security throughout Rwanda but UNAMIR lacked the mandate and force structure to do so.[248] Even in the run up to the genocide, UNAMIR warned of the presence of armed groups, anti-Tutsi broadcasts and the presence of arms caches.[249] Such reports should have been a cause for alarm and when the ceasefire collapsed, UNAMIR found itself peacekeeping in a region that needed peace-enforcement and no steps were taken to adjust the mandate to the 'reality of needs in Rwanda'.[250]

Rules of engagement was another key issue. Dallaire got no response to his suggested rules of engagement, resulting in ambiguity on what measures UNAMIR could take.[251] As the Secretary-General highlighted, 'we have failed in our response to the agony of Rwanda and thus have acquiesced in the continued loss of human lives'.[252] UNAMIR was inadequate and even when it had 2,500 soldiers, it suffered from a variety of deficiencies, particularly in resources, with Dallaire estimating he spent 70% of his time battling UN logistics.[253] Likewise, UNAMIR's personnel were of varying quality[254] and despite

245 UN Security Council. *Supra* note 185. p.49.
246 Dallaire. *Supra* note 224. p.425.
247 Organisation of African Unity. *Supra* note 173. Para.15.11.
248 Wheeler. *Supra* note 98. p.214.
249 UN Security Council. *Report of the Secretary-General on the Situation Rwanda.* UN Doc S/ 1994/640 (31 May 1994) Para.11.
250 UN Security Council. *Supra* note 185. p.33.
251 See *Supra* note 185.
252 UN Security Council. *Report of the Secretary-General on the Situation Rwanda.* UN Doc S/ 1994/640 (31 May 1994) Para.43.
253 Dallaire. *Supra* note 224. p.73.
254 The Belgian contingent were effective combat troops but lacked the tact needed for Chapter VI peacekeeping (Dallaire. *Supra* note 178. pp.112–113) while UNAMIR's largest

Dallaire's efforts at proactivity, he was constrained by his superiors[255] and when he sought to take a proactive role against spoilers, he was prevented from doing so by the Secretariat.[256]

The UN is not a state and is only as strong as its members permit and while there were UN failures, the member states bore much greater responsibility.[257] UNAMIR was heavily criticised in the media and was accused of '[scurrying] for safety, abandoning thousands of refugees who had sought their protection'.[258] However, as UNAMIR was a peacekeeping force and incapable of performing outright intervention, there was little it could have done.[259] UNAMIR still had the capability to perform spoiler prevention despite the ambiguous rules of engagement and restrictive mandate.[260] A stronger UNAMIR could have responded to the genocide when it broke out given the Rwandan government initially included moderate Hutus who were committed to the Arusha Accords.[261] Even when the genocide broke out, confusion over rules of engagement meant UNAMIR troops offered little resistance when threatened by RGF while communication difficulties hindered peacekeeping efforts further.[262]

A stronger response from UNAMIR could have stymied the genocide, with the head of Rwanda's gendarmerie advising Dallaire that *genocidaires* would 'melt away' if they faced an assertive UNAMIR.[263] Despite the worsening situation, UNAMIR's peacekeeping mission remained the same, preventing it from deterring violence and protecting civilians. Had UNAMIR the military capabilities to operate even in Kigali, the genocide could have been mitigated or even

---

contingent was a battalion of poorly trained and ill-equipped Bangladeshis (Power. *Supra* note 77. p.343).

255 Doyle and Sambanis. *Supra* note 194. pp.292–293.

256 UN Security Council. *Supra* note 185. p.14.

257 As the genocide continued, the international community refused to contribute additional troops or strengthen UNAMIR's mandate (United Nations 'Outreach Programme on the Rwanda Genocide and the United Nations' http://www.un.org/en/preventgenocide/rwanda/education/rwandagenocide.shtml Accessed 10th March 2024). Likewise, some TCCs gave orders to their troops that undermined those of Dallaire, weakening UNAMIR's cohesion and effectiveness (Dallaire. *Supra* note 224. p.79). Such weakness was used as an opportunity by the Rwandan government and the RPF to regroup and continue the conflict (Doyle and Sambanis. *Supra* note 194. p.282).

258 'U.S Troops in U.N Peacekeeping' *New York Times* (25 April 1994).

259 UN Security Council. *Supra* note 185. p.9.

260 Ibid. p.24.

261 Kuperman. *Supra* note 179. p.116. Many RGF officers were moderates but felt so isolated, they avoided challenging the extremists, lest they be targeted themselves (Ibid, p.111).

262 Doyle and Sambanis. *Supra* note 194. p.294.

263 Dallaire. *Supra* note 224. p.382.

prevented.[264] The President of Uganda suggested a stronger and more proactive UNAMIR while the Secretary-General proposed a reinforced UNAMIR with a changed mandate, allowing it to 'coerce the opposing forces into a ceasefire, [...] restore law and order and put an end to the killings'.[265] However, turning UNAMIR from peacekeeping to peace-enforcement was never discussed at the UNSC.[266]

UNAMIR had some effectiveness[267] and its personnel protected over 30,000 Rwandans,[268] while Dallaire sought to take action that could have weakened the genocide. On 10 April 1994, Dallaire sought an additional 2,500 troops and a change in the mandate to protect civilians but these never materialised, ensuring UNAMIR's ability to protect civilians was limited, although even small numbers of peacekeepers were able to save thousands of Rwandans.[269] Had UNAMIR retained its original numbers or been strengthened, it could have saved hundreds of thousands of Rwandans.[270]

Dallaire argued that with 5000 properly trained and supported troops and a Chapter VII mandate, he could have stopped most of the genocide.[271] Such a force would have required US support for the necessary logistics and resources.

264 Wheeler. *Supra* note 98. pp.217–218.

265 UN Security Council. *Special Report of the Secretary-General on the United Nations Assistance Mission for Rwanda.* UN Doc S/1994/470 (20 April 1994) Para.13.

266 Wheeler. *Supra* note 98. p218.

267 Despite the inadequacy of his Bangladeshi soldiers, Dallaire cited the effectiveness of his Ghanaian and Tunisian peacekeepers, while UNAMIR scoured Rwanda for survivors with Senegal's Captain Mbaye Diagne having a particular talent for delivering civilians to safety until he was killed by a mortar (Heer, Jeet. 'A Decade after the Horror' *National Post.* (1 April 2004)).

268 Power. *Supra* note 77. p.368.

269 Organisation of African Unity. *Supra* note 173. Para.10.12.

270 Lebor. *Supra* note 189. p.180.

271 This claim supported by a panel of international military leaders who speculated such a force could have saved 500,000 Rwandans (Carnegie Commission on Preventing Deadly Conflict. *Supra* note 24. p.6). Col. Feil agrees, highlighting that 5,000 professional soldiers with the necessary support arms could have significantly stymied the genocide (Feil, Scott. 'Could 5,000 Peacekeepers Have Saved 500,000 Rwandans? Early Intervention Reconsidered' *Institute for the Study of Diplomacy Studies Reports.* (Vol.III, No.2 (April 1997) p.5). Feil's report is driven by the assumption that US forces could have protected Rwandan civilians with little risk to their own troops (Wheeler. *Supra* note 98. p.224). Furthermore, the speed with which European troops were deployed to evacuate foreign nationals shows how quickly troops could have been mobilised (Organisation of African Unity. *Supra* note 173. Para.13.5). Likewise, the OAU's report echoes that a larger and stronger UNAMIR could have 'played a critical role possibly in deterring the conspiracy entirely or at the least [...] in significantly reducing the number of deaths (Organisation of African Unity. *Supra* note 173. Para.10.8).

However, Kuperman disputes this, highlighting that the genocide began so quickly that troops would have taken too long to mobilise to conduct a successful prevention mission.[272] The *genocidaires* were mostly ineffective soldiers[273] and were impotent against the RPF.[274] Intervention did not need not be overwhelming and by avoiding combat areas, limited intervention could still have saved thousands of lives while the *genocidaires* ineffectiveness meant they posed little threat to a professional military.[275]

Prevention is always preferable and the UN never appreciated the necessity of an effective spoiler campaign, showing ignorance or negligence of the threat of genocide and the tensions within Rwandan society. Such warning signs of genocide necessitated the creation of a stronger force with a more robust mandate.[276] While the Rwandan genocide showed a marked failure of humanitarian intervention, it also highlighted that intervention is unnecessary when UN peace-operations are deployed properly. Peace-operations are successful when they have appropriate mandates and sufficient resources to override the problems of a post-conflict society.[277] UNAMIR had neither of these and its key failure was the lack of resources and international support for its efforts. Even without military intervention, a stronger diplomatic response could have saved many lives.[278] The international community avoided taking a strong stance, instead the UN threatened to withdraw UNAMIR, which played

272 Kuperman. *Supra* note 179. p.112.

273 RGF troops 'lived for their two beers a day' while Rwanda's gendarmerie had expanded too quickly and lost discipline, training, and credibility in the process (Dallaire. *Supra* note 178. pp.68–70). Overall, Rwanda's military was a 'minimally capable force' (Feil, Scott. *Preventing Genocide: How the Early Use of Force Might Have Succeeded in Rwanda* (New York, 1998) p.26). Even more ineffective were the armed groups like the *Interahamwe* who were little more than a rabble. Furthermore, the chaos of the genocide saw the RGF's chain-of-command collapsing, greatly diminishing their effectiveness and discipline (Gibbs. *Supra* note 186).

274 Dallaire. *Supra* note 178. p.299.

275 Lebor notes that there is 'no question' that several brigades from a NATO country, if properly armed and equipped (even with light armoured vehicles) would have made short work of the Interahamwe (Lebor. *Supra* note 189. p.180).

276 Kuperman. *Supra* note 179. p.117.

277 Doyle and Sambanis. *Supra* note 194. p.299.

278 Des Forges highlights that on the two occasions when they were criticised by foreign governments, the Rwandan government halted attacks on the Hotel des Milles Collines in Kigali, saving hundreds of lives (Des Forges. *Supra* note 216. p.142). Eventually, the international community criticised the Rwandan government, causing them to soften their tactics. The UN Human Rights Council highlights that if this minor action caused such a result in late April, a strong response by the international community in mid-April could have had a far greater impact (United Nations Human Rights Council. *Supra* note 204).

exactly into the hands of the *genocidaires*. The *genocidaires* were aware that atrocities risked inducing intervention and so sought to conceal the genocide,[279] ensuring the presence of UN peacekeepers or Red Cross workers protected many refugees.[280]

The UNSC's opposition to a stronger UNAMIR meant that the only alternative was humanitarian intervention but such an outright intervention would have been unprecedented.[281] Dallaire suggested military intervention to stop the genocide but only the US had the capabilities to do so effectively.[282] Kuperman notes that there were three potential levels of U.S intervention. Maximum intervention would have required a strong force to halt large scale military conflict and genocide and would have required three brigades plus support units (around 15,000 troops), with a mandate to use force to protect Rwandans.[283] Such a force would have been slow to deploy but the undisciplined *genocidaires* posed little threat to a force as advanced as the US military.[284] Kuperman estimates that while such an intervention might not have completely prevented the genocide, it could have saved an additional 125,000 Tutsis, or 25% of the ultimate toll.[285]

The second option of moderate intervention was an alternative involving the deployment of a single brigade to stop the genocide, while avoiding areas where there was ongoing combat between the RPF and RGF. Such an intervention was politically more feasible and by avoiding ongoing fighting, the US troops would be able to concentrate on rescuing survivors, saving an estimated 100,000 Tutsis.[286]

Finally, there was the option of minimal intervention, relying on the use of air power from bases in neighbouring countries. For example, this could have involved airstrikes against *genocidaire* leaders or strafing RGF threatening civilians.[287] Such airstrikes would have been of limited use but Kuperman

279 Kuperman. *Supra* note 179. p.98.

280 This was not always the case, with Tutsis in the Gikondo Parish Church being slaughtered while Polish missionaries and UNAMIR military observers were forced to watch (Dallaire. *Supra* note 178. pp.279–281). The genocidaires still usually avoided committing atrocities in front of foreign nations to avoid attracting international intervention (Kuperman. *Supra* note 179. p.99).

281 The intervention in Iraq took place amidst an interstate war and the temporary suspension of Iraqi sovereignty (Walling. *Supra* note 24. p.121).

282 Feil. *Supra* note 273. p.9.

283 Kuperman. *Supra* note 179. pp.105–106.

284 Ibid. pp.105.

285 Ibid. pp.107.

286 Ibid. pp.108.

287 Ibid. pp.109–110.

holds that airstrikes could still have saved another 75,000 people for little risk.[288] It is important to note that Kuperman's estimates are conservative and assumed that troops could only be deployed several days after 20 April, the date President Clinton was apparently aware of the genocide. As Des Forges notes, Clinton was aware well before this date[289] and far more civilians could have been saved through a more robust intervention.

Overall, the issue of intervention shows the failures of the UN, with Nigeria's Permanent Representative to the UN noting that there is 'nothing wrong with the UN that is not attributable to its members'.[290] The UNSC was ineffectual, ignoring the high risk of violence and deploying a Chapter VI force. Once the genocide broke out, the UNSC failed to deploy a peace-enforcement mission or even bolster UNAMIR to enable action that was more effective. Instead, UNAMIR's numbers were reduced, further weakening its ability to protect civilians.

Although numerous states condemned the decision to withdraw troops, no state was prepared to mount an intervention.[291] The willingness of African nations to contribute troops to UNAMIR II did show a willingness to take action but UNAMIR II was hindered by operational weaknesses and Western nations' unwillingness to assist.[292] The UNSC was willing to allow French intervention, despite French ties to Rwanda's government. This shows that the members of the UNSC were not opposed to intervention in the region, although as shown by UNAMIR II, they did not want to pick up the cost.[293] Intervention was consequently only possible in Rwanda by a state that had both the willingness and capabilities to intervene. In the end, only France had both, and Operation Turquoise highlights the problems with humanitarian intervention. While many lives were saved, it came too late and indeed, the intervention was conducted in a manner that created further problems in the region by allowing the *genocidaires* to regroup and continue their campaign against the RPF from Zaire.[294] Overall, the Rwandan genocide highlights that even when the UNSC is willing to allow intervention, states will often balk at deploying troops, even if many lives could be saved for low risk.

288 Ibid. p.110.

289 Des Forges. *Supra* note 216. p.142.

290 Quoted in Organisation of African Unity. *Supra* note 173. Para.15.40.

291 Wheeler. *Supra* note 98. p.238.

292 See *Supra* note 224.

293 Ibid.

294 See *Supra* note 235.

## 3 The Kosovo War and Operation Allied Force

By the end of the twentieth century, tensions were arising in Kosovo, an autonomous province within Serbia, a constituent republic of the Federal Republic of Yugoslavia (FRY). Kosovar clamour for independence grew and by 1990, US Senator Bob Dole warned of Serbia's 'brutalization and repression' in Kosovo[295] which was apparent in the run up to the Yugoslav Wars when Serbian President Milosevic conducted a relentless campaign against Kosovo's ethnic-Albanian (Kosovar) majority.[296] Tensions worsened when the Dayton Peace Accords ended the Yugoslav Wars but ignored Kosovars[297] who subsequently sought to exert their constitutional rights within Yugoslavia through passive resistance and the creation of a shadow state.[298] The unofficial Kosovar government achieved little and the mid-1990s saw the emergence of the militant Kosovo Liberation Army (KLA), which began an insurgency campaign for Kosovan independence.[299] By 1998, protests within Kosovo were becoming increasingly violent, while KLA attacks were met with disproportionate Yugoslav military deployments and the targeting of Kosovar civilians.[300]

The conflict in Kosovo alarmed the international community due to fears of reigniting conflict in the Balkans and flows of refugees destabilising neighbouring states.[301] The UNSC convened, with most states highlighting the crisis posed a threat to international peace and condemned both Yugoslav brutality and KLA terrorism. China and Russia agreed Kosovo was a Yugoslavian internal

295 Dole, Robert. 'Human Rights in Yugoslavia' *Congressional Record, 101st Congress.* (27 April 1990) S5201.

296 Gutman, Roy. *A Witness to Genocide* (New York, 1993) p.18.

297 Murphy, Ray. *UN Peacekeeping in Lebanon, Somalia, and Kosovo* (Cambridge, 2007) p.71.

298 Independent International Commission on Kosovo. *Supra* note 31. pp.42–46.

299 UK House of Commons Defence Committee. *Fourteenth Report: Lessons of Kosovo. The Background to Military Intervention* (2000) http://www.publications.parliament.uk/pa/cm199900/cmselect/cmdfence/347/34708.htm Accessed 10th March 2024.

300 Independent International Commission on Kosovo. *Supra* note 31. pp.71–72. So brutal was Belgrade's response that the UN's Secretary-General recalled the atrocities in Bosnia-Herzegovina (UN Doc S/1998/912 (3 October 1998) Para.9) while US Secretary of State Madeleine Albright criticised Serbian actions as 'ethnic cleansing all over again'. (Black, Ian and Stojanovic, Dusan. 'West gets tough with Serbs: Kosovo killings prompt arms ban' *New York Times.* (10 March 1998)).

301 Independent International Commission on Kosovo. *Supra* note 31. pp.229–242. This had been apparent to President H.W Bush who had threatened Belgrade with military force if they ethnically cleansed Kosovo (Shenon, Philip. 'US Says It Might Consider Attacking Serbs' *New York Times.* (13th March 1998)). This was also evident to the UN Secretary-General who highlighted the ongoing atrocities 'the great majority' of which were committed by Yugoslavian forces (UN Doc S/1998/912 (3 October 1998) Para.28).

matter and most members of the UNSC supported an autonomous rather than sovereign Kosovo.[302] The UNSC adopted Resolution 1160, which condemned Serbia's 'excessive force', urged Belgrade-Kosovar negotiations and imposed economic sanctions including an arms embargo.[303]

This did little to restrain Belgrade. Milosevic, now president of Yugoslavia, did not cease his campaign, but exploited Western timidity by continuing his campaign of ethnic cleansing while merely reducing the intensity, resulting in hundreds of civilians being killed and over two hundred thousand displaced.[304] The media coverage of Kosovar refugees and traumatised children gave rise to public support in the US for intervention[305] while UN Resolution 1199 recognised the threat the Kosovo crisis posed to international peace and security and demanded an end to the conflict.[306] Russia and China made it clear they would veto anything authorising military action and Resolution 1199 did not refer to peace-enforcement, which frustrated the US and UK who wanted a stronger mandate.[307] Despite US hegemony, Washington could not act unilaterally on the UNSC, with China and Russia opposing any collective military action on Kosovo.[308] Although an armistice was agreed in October 1998, it swiftly fell apart, with KLA attacks increasing and a resurgent Yugoslav military presence.[309] This resulted in the displacement of hundreds of thousands of Kosovars and the deaths of many others, resulting in Kosovar support increasingly turning from their moderate shadow-government to the more militant KLA.[310]

### 3.1 *Operation Allied Force*

Faced with increasing instability, NATO convened a conference and warned it would use force against any party that failed to attend.[311] The result was the Rambouillet Accords that provided for an autonomous Kosovo within

302 UN Security Council. *53rd Year. 3868th Meeting.* UN Doc S/PV.3868 (31 March 1999).

303 UN Security Council. *Security Council Resolution 1160 (1998).* UN Doc S/RES/1160 (31 March 1998) p.1.

304 UN Security Council. *Report of the Secretary-General Prepared Pursant to the Resolution 1160 (1998) of the Security Council.* UN Doc S/1998/834 (4 September 1998) Para.7.

305 Carey. *Supra* note 63. p.74.

306 UN Security Council. *Security Council Resolution 1199 (1998).* UN Doc S/Res/1199 (23 September 1998).

307 Wheeler. *Supra* note 98. p.261.

308 Franck. *Supra* note 119. p.224.

309 Posen, Barry. 'The War for Kosovo: Serbia's Political-Military Strategy' *International Security* (Vol.24, No.4, Spring 2000) p.43.

310 Independent International Commission on Kosovo. *Supra* note 31. pp.80–83.

311 Hehir, Aidan. *Humanitarian Intervention: An Introduction* (Basingstoke, 2010) p.206.

Yugoslavia and the free movement of NATO personnel. Even as the talks continued, Milosevic amassed troops in Kosovo and initiated Operation Horseshoe, which ethnically cleansed Kosovars at a slow rate to reduce the risk of NATO intervention.[312] Although Kosovar factions accepted the Rambouillet Accords, it was rejected by Milosevic[313] who gambled NATO would refrain from forceful action.[314] Milosevic was proven wrong: on the 24 March 1999, following Belgrade's rejection of the Rambouillet Accords and the continued ethnic cleansing in Kosovo, NATO instituted Operation Allied Force. This authorised air strikes against Yugoslavian forces in Kosovo, resulting in over 38,000 strikes taking place over 78 days, largely by American aircraft.[315] Although there was controversy over the deployment of ground troops,[316] NATO vowed to continue its airstrikes until Milosevic signed the Rambouillet Accords.

As NATO's bombing was at least partially justified as a humanitarian action,[317] the issue of international humanitarian law became especially pressing and NATO claimed it took great efforts to adhere it,[318] particularly in minimising civilian casualties.[319] NATO should have had little trouble defeating Yugoslavia, but in practice,[320] NATO planes were forced to fly at 15,000 feet, drastically

312 DiPrizio. *Supra* note 85. pp.134–139.

313 Milosevic was not entirely opposed to Kosovar autonomy but utterly rejected any NATO military presence (Posen. *Supra* note 309. p.47). He claimed the Rambouillet Accords paved the way for the ethnic cleansing of Kosovo's non-Albanians (Walker, Martin. 'Defiant Milosevic Snubs Ultimatum' *Guardian* (22 March 1999)).

314 Sperling, James and Webber, Mark. 'NATO: From Kosovo to Kabul' *International Affairs* (Vol.85, No.3, May 2009) p.496.

315 UK House of Commons Defence Committee *Supra* note 299.

316 NATO estimated that large numbers of troops would be needed for a successful ground invasion (DiPrizio. *Supra* note 85. p.137). Likewise, the Chairman of NATO's Military Committee, General Naumann, concluded that while NATO would win any ground invasion of Yugoslavian territory, they risked heavy losses (UK House of Commons Defence Committee *Supra* note 299.) While both the UK and France were initially willing to deploy troops in Kosovo, Pentagon intransigence resulted in the US refusing to commit ground troops that greatly weakened the pressure on Belgrade (Carey. *Supra* note 63. p.78). It would not have been feasible for NATO to deploy troops without US support, ensuring the UK's commitment to deploy troops ended. This greatly weakened the threat posed by NATO given the difficulty in securing territory without deploying soldiers. (Murphy. *Supra* note 297. p.74).

317 NATO Press Release 99/12 (30 January 1999).

318 Independent International Commission on Kosovo. *Supra* note 31. p.94.

319 Human Rights Watch. *Civilian Deaths in the NATO Air Campaign* http://www.hrw.org/reports/2000/NATO/Natbm200.htm#P37_987 Accessed 10th March 2024.

320 Yugoslavia struggled with political isolation, an obsolete military and economic stagnation but its military culture was based around forcing invaders into wars of attrition while awareness of NATO's casualty adverseness led Yugoslavia to closely follow NATO's air

reducing their accuracy.[321] Such high-altitude airstrikes also resulted in civilian casualties, which drew international criticism.[322]

Overall, while NATO took precautions to reduce the risk of collateral damage, some five hundred civilians were killed by NATO air strikes.[323] Such an air campaign came under repeated criticism[324] and as the bombings dragged on and Operation Horseshoe continued, NATO realised that air strikes would be insufficient to force Milosevic to the negotiating table. While Clinton had been previously reluctant, he began gathering his Joint Chiefs of Staff to discuss a ground invasion.[325] Soon afterwards, Milosevic surrendered, signing a peace agreement similar to the Rambouillet Accords.[326] Consequently, the UNSC authorised a multinational Kosovo Force (KFOR) under NATO command to establish a secure environment in Kosovo.[327]

When discussing Kosovo and humanitarian intervention, it is first necessary to highlight the extent of the atrocities that led to Operation Allied Force.[328] It can be argued NATO bore responsibility for the increased scale of the ethnic cleansing, given its intervention prompted Belgrade to escalate

---

campaign in the Gulf War and appreciate the importance of air-defence systems (Posen. *Supra* note 309. pp.55)-56.

321 Independent International Commission on Kosovo. *Supra* note 31. p.93.

322 Notably, in May 1999, three people were killed when NATO missiles hit the Chinese embassy in Belgrade while a NATO cluster bomb hit a crowded marketplace, killing fifteen and injuring sixty (Hearst, David. Doughty, Nick and Gittings, John. 'NATO bombers hit Chinese embassy' *Guardian* (8 May 1999)).

323 Human Rights Watch. *Supra* note 319.

324 While air strikes are effective against larger targets such heavy artillery and armour, they could do little to stop civilians being threatened with small arms. General Nauman highlighted that ending atrocities required the deployment of ground troops, while US General Clark (who commanded NATO's bombing campaign) criticised Operation Allied Force's cumbersome decision-making restrictions and the UK's former deputy defence minister lamented how long it took NATO to bring the militarily inferior Yugoslavia to heel (Williams, Carol. 'Conference Highlights Flaws of NATO's Kosovo campaign' *Los Angeles Times* (6 February 2000)).

325 McGeary, Johanna. 'Making a Deal: Why Milosevic Blinked' *Time* (14 June 1999).

326 Ibid. There was a key difference in that peacekeepers deployed would be restricted to Kosovo rather than having free movement throughout Yugoslavia.

327 UN Security Council. *Security Council Resolution 1244 (1999)*. UN Doc S/Res/1244 (10 June 1999) Annex 2, S.4.

328 Figures for the exact numbers of civilians killed are unclear (Independent International Commission on Kosovo. *Supra* note 31. p.83) although estimates go as high as 10,000 (Kifner, John. 'Inquiry Estimates Serb Drive Killed 10,000 in Kosovo' *New York Times* (18 July 1999)). Meanwhile, government forces expelled 90% of Kosovar Albanians from their homes (Human Rights Watch. *Under Orders: War Crimes in Kosovo* http://www.hrw.org/reports/2001/kosovo/undword.htm Accessed 10th March 2024).

this policy. However, this argument relies on the flawed assumption that the ethnic cleansing would have ended without NATO intervention.[329] Despite Belgrade's attempts to blame NATO for the mass displacement, responsibility for this rests with Belgrade and most Kosovars were forced from their homes by Yugoslav soldiers.[330]

The Kosovars were not completely innocent victims, with the KLA carrying out attacks against ethnic Serbs, Roma and Kosovar collaborators with Belgrade.[331] Furthermore, the KLA sought to induce NATO intervention, given this was a key guarantee of Kosovar independence.[332] Although the KLA's actions are not comparable to Belgrade's, such actions weakened international support for intervention and bolstered the idea that both sides were equally culpable.

### 3.2 *Humanitarian Intervention and the Kosovo War*

Operation Allied Force was notable as it was the first time a regional organisation used force against a sovereign country without UN authorisation.[333] NATO states could have argued that they were using force in self-defence, which required action to avert a refugee crisis emanating from the Kosovo conflict.[334]

---

329 Wheeler. *Supra* note 98. p.269.

330 Independent International Commission on Kosovo. *Supra* note 31. pp.88–91.

331 Around 1,000 Serbs and Roma were murdered or missing by the end of the conflict: while some were likely murdered by common criminals or vengeful civilians, many were killed by the KLA either for revenge or to create an ethnically homogenous Kosovar state (Human Rights Watch. *Supra* note 328. After the withdrawal of Yugoslavian forces, there was an exodus of Kosovan Serbs, with KLA troops claiming they no longer needed to carry guns in 'ethnically clean towns' (Kifner, John. 'NATO Tolerates Their Actions … For Now' *New York Times* (15 June 1999) while Human Rights Watch reported over 150,000 minorities had fled Kosovo within six weeks of KFOR's deployment (Human Rights Watch. *Supra* note 328). Even after the conflict and while NATO troops patrolled Kosovo, thousands of Serbs were expelled from their homes and some 1,500 were murdered (Power. *Supra* note 77. p.463). Although rebel Kosovars had committed atrocities, far more were committed by Yugoslavian forces (UN Doc S/1998/912 (3 October 1998) Para.28. Likewise, Human Rights Watch highlighted the far more severe campaign of ethnic cleansing by Belgrade, which included rape and thousands of extrajudicial killings (Human Rights Watch. *Supra* note 328). Overall, nearly the entire Kosovar population was affected, with the expulsion of 1.3 million Kosovars from their homes constituting the single greatest act of ethnic cleansing of the decade (Power. *Supra* note 77. pp.449–450).

332 Independent International Commission on Kosovo. *Supra* note 31. p.132.

333 While NATO had engaged in airstrikes during the Balkan Wars, these were authorised by the Security Council and NATO's 1991 Strategic Concept still highlighted that NATO was 'purely defensive in purpose' (NATO. *The Alliance's New Strategic Concept* http://www.NATO.int/cps/en/NATOlive/official_texts_23847.htm Accessed 10th March 2024).

334 Franck. *Supra* note 119. p.167.

There was a case to be made for this, given Kosovan refugees were threatening regional stability, but this remains a weak argument.

While Western media gave considerable coverage to the Kosovo crisis, it rarely discussed the legality of NATO's intervention.[335] The large numbers being displaced meant the Kosovo crisis posed a risk to regional peace and security, with NATO's strategy being the prevention of a humanitarian catastrophe.[336] Although this had practical grounds (preventing Balkan instability via a refugee crisis), it also had moral justifications.[337] While seemingly humanitarian, NATO claimed to be doing so for the international community, thus relying on implicit authorisation from the UNSC.[338] This is unconvincing, particularly as Russia and China made it clear they would veto any resolution authorising the threat or use of force.[339] Furthermore, even if the UNSC was deadlocked, NATO did not attempt to appeal to the UNGA under the Uniting for Peace Resolution, presumably, as they would not have secured the required majority.[340]

NATO states denied their actions undermined UN authority.[341] The US had not abandoned multilateralism but used flexible interpretations of the UN Charter when it suited American interests despite President H.W Bush seeing the UNSC as fundamental in a 'New World Order'.[342] Although NATO did not offer a single legal justification for its actions, the individual justifications used

335 Carey. *Supra* note 63. p.74.

336 NATO Press Release 99/12 (30 January 1999).

337 Clinton drew parallels with the Holocaust and arguing that military action was 'about our values'. Likewise, US Vice President Gore claimed that the US was 'determined to act to diminish the military power that he has turned ruthlessly toward the Kosovo people.' (CNN 'Clinton: Serbs must be stopped now' http://edition.cnn.com/US/9903/23/u.s.kosovo.04/ Accessed 10th March 2024) NATO's Secretary-General also highlighted that NATO had worked with the UN and OSCE to negotiate a peaceful settlement but that these had failed, leading NATO to conduct military action 'to support the political aims of the international community'. While NATO was not engaging in warfare against Yugoslavia, it did seek to prevent both instability and more violence against civilians in Kosovo alongside NATO's 'moral obligation' to stop Belgrade oppressing the Kosovars NATO Press Release 1999(040) (23 March 1999).

338 Gray. *Supra* note 162. p.39.

339 Independent International Commission on Kosovo. *Supra* note 31. p.142.

340 See Binder, Christine. 'Uniting for Peace Resolution (1950)' Wolfrum, Rudiger (Ed.), *The Max Planck Encyclopaedia of Public International Law* (Online Ed) http://opil.ouplaw.com/view/10.1093/law:epil/9780199231690/law-9780199231690-e568?prd=EPIL Accessed 10th March 2024.

341 This was especially evident with the UK's Foreign Secretary, who claimed it was Milosevic, not NATO, who was challenging UN authority and inaction meant complicity in Belgrade's repression of Kosovo (UK House of Commons Debate (25 March 1999) Col.538).

342 Carey. *Supra* note 63. p.73.

by NATO member states indicate that in the absence of UNSC authorisation, there was some reliance on a right of humanitarian intervention under customary international law.[343] NATO member states also highlighted that they felt authorised to intervene due to previous UNSC resolutions.[344]

Aside from humanitarianism, other justifications were used, particularly relating to national interests. While highlighting the moral cause of intervention, Clinton also argued that American economic interests relied on European stability.[345] Likewise, the UK's Foreign Secretary argued that military action was based on NATO's credibility and the threat to regional peace and security.[346] Wheeler highlights that there was no conflict between humanitarian intervention and self-interest.[347] The UK's Prime Minister Blair claimed that NATO's actions were guided by self-interest and a moral purpose that ultimately merge.[348] This was a key aspect of the British and American approaches, with both Clinton and Blair seeing the intervention as a Just War.[349] Overall, the reasons why each NATO member state engaged in humanitarian intervention are debatable and there was division as to whether NATO should even seek a legal justification at all.[350] Nonetheless, it is clear that it would not have taken place without US leadership.[351]

NATO's air campaign also drew criticism.[352] The main critics were Russia and China who denounced NATO for breaching international law,[353] while

343 Kritsiotis, Dino. 'The Kosovo Crisis and NATO's Application of Armed Force against the Federal Republic of Yugoslavia' *International and Comparative Law Quarterly* (Vol.49, No.2, April 2000) p.340.

344 Krisch, Nico. 'Unilateral Enforcement of the Collective Will: Kosovo, Iraq and the Security Council' *Max Planck Yearbook of UN Law* (Vol.3, 1999) p.82.

345 CNN. *Supra* note 337.

346 UK House of Commons Debate (25 March 1999) Col.538.

347 Wheeler. *Supra* note 98. p.267.

348 Kaiser, Rob and McGuire, Michael. 'Blair Unveils Bold Intervention Doctrine' *Chicago Tribune.* (23 April 1999).

349 Wheeler. *Supra* note 98. p.267.

350 Franck. *Supra* note 119. p.167.

351 DiPrizio. *Supra* note 85. p.136.

352 These included the UN Secretary-General who criticised the US for taking unilateral military action although he also criticised China and Russia for ignoring the atrocities that induced Operation Allied Force (Miller, Judith. 'Annan Takes Critical Stance on U.S. Actions in Kosovo' *New York Times.* (19 May 1999). Likewise, anti-American states such as Libya, Iran and Iraq also condemned the airstrikes, with Iran's Ayatollah Khamenei claiming that NATO sought to use airstrikes to annihilate European Muslims (Washington Institute 'The Arab World, Iran and the Kosovo Crisis' (24 May 1999). http://www.washingtoninstitute.org/policy-analysis/view/the-arab-world-iran-and-the-kosovo-crisis Accessed 10th March 2024).

353 Carey. *Supra* note 63. p.73.

Russia drafted a UNSC resolution condemning NATO's intervention as a violation of the UN Charter.[354] Citing the dangers of precedent, the resolution claimed NATO's actions would cause 'devastating humanitarian consequences' and the intervention constituted aggression,[355] a view supported by few other nations.[356]

Russian and Chinese criticisms of NATO's intervention found little support in the UNSC. The US used humanitarian language to justify intervention, citing the need to prevent a humanitarian catastrophe as well as the threat to international peace and security.[357] Others like Canada highlighted Yugoslavia's breach of previous resolutions while most UNSC members noted the threat that the Kosovo crisis posed to international peace and Belgrade's refusal to come to a peaceful compromise.[358] As the UK put it, NATO's actions were an 'exceptional measure to prevent an overwhelming humanitarian catastrophe'.[359]

Certain states also argued that Russia and China violated the UN Charter by preventing the UNSC from fulfilling its responsibility to maintain international peace and security while other non-UNSC members supported NATO intervention.[360] Likewise, Muslim states saw the UN doing nothing to defend their co-religionists in Kosovo, resulting in NATO's airstrikes being backed by the

354 UN Security Council. *54th Year. 3988th Meeting*. UN Doc S/PV.3988 (24 March 1999) p.2.

355 Ibid. p.3.

356 China saw Kosovo as an internal matter for Yugoslavia (despite Resolution 1199 highlighting that Kosovo posed a threat to regional peace and security) while Namibia argued that NATO's intervention risked creating further conflict. Despite its 1971 intervention in Bangladesh, India claimed that human rights violations did not allow 'unprovoked military aggression', Belarus criticised NATO's 'aggression' while Yugoslavia compared NATO's intervention to Mussolini's invasion of Abyssinia (UN Security Council. *54th Year. 3988th Meeting*. UN Doc S/PV.3988 (24 March 1999) p.3). China's Foreign Minister further condemned NATO's actions in the UNGA, claiming that unauthorised use of force by a regional organisation risked setting a dangerous precedent that weakened the UN's authority in maintaining international peace and security. (Ministry of Foreign Affairs of the People's Republic of China 'Head of the Chinese delegation, Foreign Minister Tang Jiaxuan addressed the 54th UN General Assembly' https://www.mfa.gov.cn/eng/wjb_663304/zzjg_663340/gjs_665170/gjzzyhy_665174/2594_665176/2602_665192/200011/t20001115_598217.html Accessed 10th March 2024).

357 UN Security Council. *54th Year. 3988th Meeting*. UN Doc S/PV.3988 (24 March 1999) p.4.

358 This was a key argument used by the Netherlands, UK, France, Gambia, and Argentina: despite attempts at negotiated settlement, Belgrade's intransigence left NATO with no other option.

359 UN Security Council. *54th Year. 3988th Meeting*. UN Doc S/PV.3988 (24 March 1999) p.12.

360 Namely by Germany (which spoke on behalf of the EU), Bosnia-Herzegovina and Albania (Ibid. p.12).

Organisation of the Islamic Conference that represented 56 Islamic states.[361] In addition, despite India's claims that the Non-Aligned Movement was opposed to peacekeeping outside of the UN, the Movement was divided over Kosovo, to the extent that it was unable to agree on a statement that would reflect a consensus among the members.[362]

The legality of NATO's actions was contested by Yugoslavia, which took a case against ten of NATO's member states to the ICJ, asserting they had violated international law, particularly the prohibitions on the use of force and the violation of state sovereignty.[363] In addition, Yugoslavia sought provisional measures for immediate cessation of each nation's use of force, which was rejected by the ICJ as it lacked jurisdiction.[364] Although the ICJ dismissed the claims against the US and Spain due to a lack of jurisdiction,[365] the ICJ's lack of jurisdiction to institute provisional measures did not preclude it from dealing with the merits of the cases.[366] In the joint hearings on the request for provisional measures, most NATO states refused to comment on the substance

361 Huffington Post 'Intervention Lessons from Kosovo for Syria' http://www.huffingtonpost.com/david-l-phillips/intervention-lessons-from_b_3858228.html Accessed 10th March 2024.

362 While Cuba, Belarus and India wanted the NAM to condemn NATO's airstrikes, they were opposed by Muslim countries like Pakistan, Malaysia and the Gulf States (Inter Press Service 'Third World Nations Split over Kosovo' http://www.ipsnews.net/1999/04/politics-third-world-nations-split-over-kosovo/ Accessed 10th March 2024.). It must be noted that the NAM still maintained its rejection of unilateral humanitarian intervention, even if it was split over the intervention in Kosovo (Movement of the Non-Aligned Countries. 'XIII Ministerial Conference, 8–9 April 2000'. https://web.archive.org/web/20170505034415/http://www.nam.gov.za/xiiiminconf/minconf.txt Accessed 10th March 2024). The NAM also held a ministerial meeting where it rejected any right of humanitarian intervention under international law, deeming it a violation of the UN Charter (UN General Assembly Press Release. *Humanitarian Intervention, Slow Reimbursement rates assailed as Special Committee Reviews Peacekeeping Operations.* UN Press Release GA/SPD/164 (18 October 1999)).

363 International Court of Justice Legality *of Use of Force* (*Yugoslavia v United States*) *ICJ* (*Application instituting proceedings*) (*29 April 1999*). p.3.

364 International Court of Justice *Legality of Use of Force* (*Yugoslavia v United States of America*) (*Provisional Measures, Order of 2 June 1999*). p.2 The ICJ similarly found it lacked jurisdiction against the other respondents. See Bekker, Peter. Legality of Use of Force' *American Journal of International Law* (Vol.93, No.4, October 1999) p.929.

365 International Court of Justice *Supra* note 364. p.1 and International Court of Justice *Legality of Use of Force* (*Yugoslavia v Spain*) (*Provisional Measures*) (*Order of 2 June 1999*). p.1.

366 International Court of Justice *Legality of Use of Force* (*Serbia and Montenegro v Belgium*) (*Request for the Indication of Provisional Measures*) (*Order of 2 June 1999*). Para.46.

of the case but of those that did, many indirectly alluded to humanitarian intervention,[367]while Belgium explicitly argued for such intervention.[368]

Belgium highlighted that the UNSC resolutions provided a basis for Operation Allied Force, it also stated that it acted to end an ongoing humanitarian catastrophe and safeguard human rights, which it argued constituted a *jus cogens* in international law.[369] Furthermore, Belgium argued the 'armed humanitarian intervention' did not violate the UN Charter as it did not threaten Yugoslavia's territorial integrity or political independence and cited the interventions in East Pakistan, Cambodia and Uganda as precedents, particularly as relevant UN organs did not condemn them.[370] Subsequently, the ICJ dismissed the case, given Belgrade was not party to the ICJ when it instituted proceedings.[371] The ICJ proceedings therefore do little to substantiate the legality of Operation Allied Force.

The above shows that while NATO's intervention was seen as a breach of international law by some states, many others supported it. Aside from Russia, China and Namibia, every UNSC member opposed condemning NATO, while Russia's draft resolution was defeated by twelve votes to three. Although it would be inaccurate to see this as supporting NATO's intervention, it highlighted a widespread view that Yugoslavia was responsible for atrocities in Kosovo.[372] Furthermore, the vote was notable as for the first time since the UN's foundation; seven members of the UNSC justified humanitarian intervention without UN authorisation.[373]

Although Secretary-General Annan criticised NATO's unilateral use of force, he did reinforce that NATO's air campaign was necessary.[374] Likewise, the International Independent Commission on Kosovo stated that Operation Allied Force was 'legitimate but not legal' given it breached international law.[375] This is reiterated by Franck who notes that while technically illegal, NATO's intervention was 'mitigated to the point of exoneration' due to the

---

367 Kritsiotis. *Supra* note 343. pp.344–345.

368 Chesterman. *Supra* note 112. p.46.

369 International Court of Justice *Legality of Use of Force (Serbia and Montenegro v Belgium) Provisional Measures, Oral Proceedings* CR *1999/15 (10 May 1999)*. pp.11–12.

370 Ibid. Although Belgium did not invoke Operation Provide Comfort in Iraq. See Gray. *Supra* note 111. p.236.

371 International Court of Justice. *Legality of Use of Force (Serbia and Montenegro v. Belgium) Summary 2004/3 (15 December 2004)*. p.9.

372 Bellamy, Alex. *Global Politics and the Responsibility to Protect* (Abingdon, 2011) p.148.

373 Wheeler. *Supra* note 98. p.281.

374 Miller. *Supra* note 352.

375 Independent International Commission on Kosovo. *Supra* note 31. p.289.

unique circumstances.[376] Despite the widespread opposition to Russia's draft resolution, few UNSC members endorsed humanitarian intervention as a legal doctrine.[377]

The effectiveness of NATO's airstrikes is debatable. They did little damage to Yugoslav ground forces[378] with many analysts holding that it was only the threat of a NATO invasion that induced Yugoslavia's withdrawal[379] and the subsequent role of the UN became divisive following the end of NATO's campaign. As Operation Allied Force went on, NATO stepped up its bombing campaign, which became more effective due to improved weather, the erosion of Yugoslavian air-defences and looser restraints on NATO bombing which ultimately coerced Belgrade to negotiate.[380]

Despite early setbacks, NATO intervention in Kosovo was broadly a success, forcing Serbia to withdraw from Kosovo after three months.[381] This was achieved without a single NATO casualty, while the Kosovar population was broadly protected to the extent that by November 1999, over 94% of Kosovar refugees had returned to Kosovo.[382] Kosovo was governed as an autonomous part of the Federal Republic of Yugoslavia by an interim administration under Resolution 1244.[383] There was controversy as to whether this was a retrospective acceptance of NATO's humanitarian intervention or a de facto recognition of the need to provide for Kosovo's future.[384] Pellet argues that even if Resolution 1244 does not explicitly legitimise NATO's actions, it is inconceivable that the UN would authorise governance of an entity created by aggression.[385] This is debatable as the UNSC is often forced to consider political realities to maintain stability[386] and although China and Russia did not block Resolution 1244, they used the debate to criticise NATO's actions as violating international law.[387]

376 Franck. *Supra* note 119. p.226.
377 Gray. *Supra* note 111. p.234.
378 Posen. *Supra* note 309. p.64.
379 Karon, Tony. 'Milosevic's Famous Cardboard Tank Trick' *Time.* (28 June 1999) This is disputed by Posen who doubts Milosevic saw a ground invasion as forthcoming. (See Posen. *Supra* note 309. p.74).
380 Ibid. p.82.
381 Western, Jon and Goldstein, Joshua. 'Humanitarian Intervention Comes of Age' *Foreign Affairs* (Vol.90 (6), November-December 2011).
382 Independent International Commission on Kosovo. *Supra* note 31. p.206.
383 UN Security Council. *Supra* note 327. Para.5.
384 Gray. *Supra* note 162. p.41.
385 Pellet, Alain. 'State Sovereignty and the Protection of Fundamental Human Rights: An International Law Perspective' *Pugwash Occasional Papers* (February 2000) p.42.
386 White. *Supra* note 22. p.32.
387 UN Security Council. *54th Year. 4011th Meeting.* UN Doc S/PV.4011 (10 June 1999) pp.7–8.

There was neither widespread condemnation nor support for NATO's intervention, showing the complexity of the situation and yet Operation Allied Force comprises the most widely condoned example of humanitarian intervention of modern times.[388] It is important to note the external factors relating to the Kosovo intervention. A key reason for NATO's actions was that senior Washington figures such as Albright and Holbrooke believed that the UN's rigid interpretation of the use of force was the reason behind massacres during the Balkan Wars.[389] After the UN's timidity in Bosnia-Herzegovina, Milosevic was confident he could act unopposed in Kosovo and it is likely that the Kosovo crisis could have been averted, had the international community shown more diligence after the Balkan Wars and avoided the rise of the KLA.[390] NATO had realised how damaging Bosnia-Herzegovina had been to its credibility that provided an impetus for NATO's aerial campaign.[391]

Overall, Kosovo has been described as the 'gold standard' for humanitarian intervention,[392] as well as the 'prime case study' for humanitarian intervention and international law.[393] Despite the opposition of states such as Russia, China and Libya, other states in organisations such as the EU and the OIC[394] refused to condemn NATO's airstrike. This showed considerable support for the use of force outside of the UN Charter. NATO's air strikes without UNSC authorisation were necessitated by the lack of UN action in relation to the Kosovo crisis.

The entire issue of humanitarian intervention and its legality could have been avoided had the UN not been deadlocked. Nonetheless, NATO acted unilaterally and the failure to obtain UN authorisation casts doubt over the legality of NATO's actions. Indeed, it is likely that unilateral action was due to NATO's knowledge that it would not receive the necessary support. Likewise, reliance on 'implicit authorisation' was a dangerous one and risked creating

---

388 Hehir. *Supra* note 311. p.218.

389 Carey. *Supra* note 63. p.79.

390 Independent International Commission on Kosovo. *Supra* note 31. p.56.

391 Sperling and Webber. *Supra* note 314. p.495. This highlights the importance of domestic politics in humanitarian intervention: public support for action contributed to airstrikes in Kosovo, with initial public opinion favouring Operation Allied Force in the key European NATO states of the UK, France, Germany, and the Netherlands (Posen. *Supra* note 309. p.68). NATO fears of casualties precluded deploying soldiers and forced a reliance on high-altitude airstrikes that are far less effective.

392 Huffington Post. *Supra* note 361.

393 Klose, Fabian. 'The Emergence of Humanitarian Intervention' in Klose, Fabian. (Ed.) *The Emergence of Humanitarian Intervention: Ideas and Practice from the Nineteenth Century to the Present* (Cambridge, 2018) p.10.

394 See *Supra* note 360and 361.

an expansionist precedent on the use of force.[395] Ultimately, Kosovo showed the gap between the 'proscribed legality and the perceived legitimacy of intervention'.[396]

## 4 Humanitarian Intervention in the 1990s

The interventions of the 1990s were markedly different from those of the Cold War which took place when the UNSC was less deadlocked. Consequently, there was a growth in interventions with humanitarian justifications.[397] Such interventions were conducted by states that acted multilaterally, with the interventions in Iraq and Kosovo being conducted by coalitions, while Operation Turquoise was undertaken with UN authorisation. Although the end of the Cold War offered the potential to redefine peacekeeping and humanitarian intervention, this was never realised.[398] Peacekeepers were pressured by local parties and NGOs to take a more active role, even while TCCs and the UN secretariat sought to restrict the use of force and prevent a more robust approach.[399] Despite the UN's progress, Chapter VI peacekeeping is not a substitute for humanitarian intervention, which requires far more force than in traditional peacekeeping and with a different approach than regular armed force.[400] By the end of the 1990s, the UN avoided the issues facing peacekeeping by simply removing itself from the dangerous area between peacekeeping and humanitarian intervention.[401] Furthermore, there are issues with

395 Independent International Commission on Kosovo. *Supra* note 31. pp.173–174.

396 Frohlich, Manuel. 'The Responsibility to Protect. Foundation, transformation, and application of an emerging norm' in Klose, Fabian. (Ed.) *The Emergence of Humanitarian Intervention: Ideas and Practice from the Nineteenth Century to the Present* (Cambridge, 2018) p.302.

397 Klose. *Supra* note 393. p.11. See also, *supra* note 20

398 The Security Council underwent a major transformation, authorising far more peace-operations, undergoing a normative change due to greater assumptions on civilian protection and a larger reliance on multilateral peacekeeping tasks (Bellamy. *Supra* note 372. p.171). Despite this, the Security Council was unable to address the conflicts and was too constrained by geopolitics to address mass human rights violations. Above all, the P5 exercised their power for political rather than legal reasons, greatly undermining international law's importance as a restraint on power politics (Chesterman. *Supra* note 112. p.161).

399 Findlay. *Supra* note 26. p.153.

400 International Commission on Intervention and State Sovereignty. *Supra* note 25. Para.7.1.

401 MacQueen, Norrie. 'Cold War peacekeeping versus humanitarian intervention' in Klose, Fabian. (Ed.) *The Emergence of Humanitarian Intervention: Ideas and Practice from the Nineteenth Century to the Present* (Cambridge, 2018) p.251.

relying on states to contribute troops for peace-operations, given states will generally only contribute troops when it is in their own interests.[402] This was especially evident in the difficulties faced by UNAMIR II during the Rwandan genocide.[403] It is unsurprising that in 1994, the UN sought to move to the UNSC authorising 'Coalitions of the Willing' or regional organisations to implement international peace and security.[404]

Nonetheless, the UN remains a major player in the post-Cold War era. Only the UN can give legitimacy to military deployments and even superpowers like the US must seek its authorisation if it is to act within international law.[405] This includes interventions for humanitarian purposes, but the UNSC's actions demonstrate that it only supports humanitarian intervention when authorised by the Council itself.[406] This legitimacy is offset when human rights abuses take place in areas of strategic interest to the P5. The zero-sum game approach of the UNSC means intervention is unlikely to be authorised in such circumstances. Even when atrocities take place in an area of little strategic value and a peace operation is authorised, the P5's self-interest mean they are unwilling to provide the necessary support and they may fear setting a precedent, which could be used against them in the future.[407] Evidently, a key lesson to draw is

402 White. *Supra* note 9. p.128.

403 See *Supra* note 224.

404 Krishnan. *Supra* note 29. p.125.

405 Schlesinger. *Supra* note 7. p.285.

406 Stanulova, Maya. 'Has Humanitarian Intervention Become an Exception to the Prohibition on the Use of Force in Article 2(4) of the UN Charter?' *Atlantic Community* (2010) https://economia.uniroma2.it/ba/globalgovernance/corso/asset/YTo0OntzOjI6ImlkIjtzOjM6IjMyMyI7czozOiJpZGEiO3M6NToiNDE0ODEiO3M6MjoiZW0iO047czoxOiJjIjtzOjU6ImQ2YjgyIjt9 p.9.

407 Although developed countries are the best placed to ensure effective peacekeeping, they usually see no benefit for their involvement (See Carnegie Commission on Preventing Deadly Conflict. *Supra* note 24. p.7). This is critical given that while peace-operations are largely staffed by developing countries, they are primarily funded by developed states (Bosco, David. 'The Price of Peace' *Foreign Policy* (29 May 2013)). This has a major impact on the use of force for humanitarian protection purposes given the P5 comprise five of the world's most powerful militaries (See Koronka, Poppy. 'The 20 Most Powerful Military Forces in the World' *Newsweek* https://www.newsweek.com/most-powerful-military-forces-world-america-china-russia-1621130 Accessed 10th March 2024) and are the best placed to ensure force projection. Even when a peacekeeping mission is authorised and developing countries are willing to supply troops, this means little when developed nations refuse to provide the necessary logistical support, as happened with UNAMIR II in Rwanda.

that prevention is generally better than intervention, given dictators are usually rational, and will back down from a conflict they stand to lose.[408]

Humanitarian intervention might have been redundant had there been stronger and more effective peacekeeping forces, and it is vital for early warning indicators and swift responses to effectively respond. This is a key failing of the UN, with the lack of prevention and contingency plans meaning that when violence occurs, it is usually too late for an effective response.[409] Not only can robust peace-operations help resolve a conflict but also they can also strengthen the UN's hand in future operations. The 1993 peace-operation in Somalia resulted in the West (particularly the US) being especially reluctant to risk casualties or engage in peace-enforcement[410] while Hutu extremists specifically targeted Belgian peacekeepers to ensure their withdrawal from UNAMIR.[411]

Slovenia invoked the UN Charter when they highlighted the UNSC has a primary rather than exclusive responsibility to maintain peace and security.[412] This is particularly relevant given that the UNSC's jurisdiction on such matters is to ensure prompt and effective action.[413] It can therefore be argued that states may take action when the UNSC is unable or unwilling to respond. However, the UNSC's responsibility for peace and security refers to competencies within the UN, ensuring that secondary responsibility is with the UNGA rather than states acting unilaterally or multilaterally.[414] Few nations would argue that states should regularly operate outside of the UN Charter but when

408 Baghdad only initiated the Iran-Iraq war when it saw Tehran's military advantage collapsing (Keegan. *Supra* note 41. p.61) and despite seeing Operation Provide Comfort as a violation of its sovereignty, it knew it was in no position to resist. During the Kosovo crisis, this was especially apparent to Milosevic who rejected the Rambouillet Accords as he felt NATO would not follow through with enforcement (Sperling and Webber. *Supra* note 314. p.496). Both Hussein and Milosevic were ruthless but pragmatic, ensuring they avoided conflicts they would not win and would likely have refrained from commencing atrocities if they faced opposition. Likewise, Rwandan forces were undisciplined and impotent against the RPF, and would likely have stood down from an assertive UNAMIR (Dallaire. *Supra* note 224. p.382).

409 Carnegie Commission on Preventing Deadly Conflict. *Supra* note 24. p.XXI.

410 Wheeler. *Supra* note 98. pp.215–216. See also Weiss, Thomas. *Humanitarian Intervention* (Cambridge, 2018) p.11.

411 Dallaire. *Supra* note 178. p.240.

412 UN Security Council. *54th Year. 3988th Meeting.* UN Doc S/PV.3988 (24 March 1999) p.7. This is codified in the UN Charter. (1 UNTS XVI, 1945) Article 24(1).

413 Ibid.

414 White. *Supra* note 22. p.29.

faced with situations as in Kosovo and Iraq, there was some international support for humanitarian intervention.

Although the UNSC did not authorise the interventions in Iraq and Kosovo, neither did it condemn them. Critically, this was not just due to a veto by the US, the UK or France. Russian attempts to censure Operation Allied Force failed to attract enough support among the non-permanent members of the UNSC, with its proposed resolution being opposed by every member of the UNSC, with the exceptions of Russia, China and Namibia.[415] Although NATO's Operation Provide Comfort in Iraq received no condemnation from the UNSC or UNGA, this is likely as no state wanted to be seen opposing such a humanitarian mission.[416] Despite the interference in Iraq's sovereignty, Baghdad's international isolation ensured no state wanted to be seen defending it.[417] A contrast can be drawn with the Cold War interventions in East Pakistan and Cambodia, which were opposed by most members of both the UNGA and the UNSC, with both interventions escaping UN involvement due to the USSR's veto.[418] Although both the Cold War interventions and those of the 1990s escaped UN censure, those of the 1990s saw greater international acceptance, with the majority of the UNSC refusing to support Russia's resolution condemning NATO actions in Kosovo,[419] and little public opposition to Operation Provide Comfort.[420]

It is debatable whether the status of humanitarian intervention under customary international law was altered by such actions. Although it appeared many states were unwilling to condemn them, this is very different from the explicit endorsement needed to end the uncertainty over humanitarian intervention's legal status. Furthermore, despite the use of humanitarian rhetoric, the above interventions relied on stretching UNSC resolutions rather than any asserted right of humanitarian intervention. The interventions in Iraq and Kosovo all invoked UNSC resolutions as a justification for their interventions even though they used force in a manner far beyond what was originally intended. Given the reluctance of the intervening states to invoke any right of humanitarian intervention under customary international law, it is difficult to argue that such a right exists or has been strengthened.

415 UN Press Office. 'Security Council Rejects Demand for Cessation of Use of Force against Federal Republic of Yugoslavia' www.un.org/press/en/1999/19990326.sc6659.html Accessed 10th March 2024.

416 Wheeler. *Supra* note 98. p.154.

417 See *Supra* note 163.

418 See Chapter 4 *Supra* note 109-note 115 and Chapter 4 *Supra* note 272.

419 See *Supra* note 356.

420 See *Supra* note 118.

Despite its potential for setting a precedent, it would be a mistake to view NATO's intervention in Kosovo as entirely humanitarian. Any humanitarian basis of the operation is far less certain than geopolitical concerns over Balkan stability and a need to protect NATO's credibility.[421] Rather, the intervention merely highlighted existing problems with international law and the use of force to protect human rights.[422] Similarly, the interventions in Rwanda and Iraq were largely motivated by self-interest. Operation Provide Comfort has parallels with India's intervention in East Pakistan in that it had a humanitarian outcome but was only possible due to Iraq's isolation and the fact that it was in NATO's interest to prevent refugees destabilising Turkey.[423] Overall, Weiss notes that the interventions in Iraq and Kosovo operate at 'one end of the spectrum, with the benefits to civilians [...] worth the economic, military and political costs'.[424] At the other end, Weiss places the ineffective response to the conflict in Bosnia, with the response to Rwanda in between the two, but closer to the successful end of the spectrum after July 1994 given the negligible military cost.[425]

Although Operation Turquoise was authorised by the UNSC, its humanitarian credentials are weak, given it took place only when Rwanda's genocidal government was poised to fall. Even then, it mainly protected the perpetrators rather than the victims of the genocide[426] when France could have simply bolstered UNAMIR II or provided logistical support to the African nations willing to contribute troops. It is apparent again that humanitarian intervention will only take place when it coincides with the interests of a state which has both the will and the ability to use military force. This was especially evident in Kosovo where an intervention took place. Although serious human rights abuses were ongoing, these were less egregious than those in Rwanda where demand for intervention was lower.

The key difference being that NATO's credibility and regional stability were of greater concern than humanitarian justifications.[427] Such selectivity seems unjust, especially for people to be left to their fate merely as their suffering does not threaten the interests of stronger states. There are few alternatives: the UN simply cannot override a P5 veto, lest it destroy the foundations upon which

421 DiPrizio. *Supra* note 85. p.145.
422 Independent International Commission on Kosovo. *Supra* note 31. p.297.
423 See *Supra* note 125–138.
424 Weiss. *Supra* note 410. p.117.
425 Ibid.
426 See *Supra* note 244.
427 DiPrizio. *Supra* note 85. p.145.

the UN is built. Neither does the UN have the ability to deploy troops without the support of member states, particularly the P5. This issue helped lead to the Responsibility to Protect doctrine.

## 5 The Responsibility to Protect (R2P)

The end of the Cold War saw newfound optimism for improved collective security, but the UNSC showed itself ineffective at responding to atrocities.[428] The tension between state sovereignty and human rights was becoming even more problematic, developing the concept that sovereignty encompasses responsibility.[429] Given his experience during the Bosnian and Rwandan conflicts, Annan saw a pressing need to balance state sovereignty with the protection of human rights.[430] This led Annan to highlight UN inaction in response to atrocities and remarked on the need for 'two concepts of sovereignty', giving states both rights and responsibilities.[431] Although Annan noted that interventions must conform to international law, neither can the world stand by when atrocities take place, with the intent of the UN Charter's being to protect people rather than shield their abusers.[432] Annan therefore called for an international consensus on an appropriate response to 'massive and systematic human rights violations'.[433]

---

428 International Commission on Intervention and State Sovereignty. *Supra* note 25. Paras.1.1–1.4.

429 This was notably developed in 1993 by the UN's Special Representative on Internally Displaced Persons to protect the growing number of persons displaced by war but who remained within their home state and were thus ineligible for the protections afforded to refugees (Bellamy. *Supra* note 372. pp.10–11).

430 Lebor. *Supra* note 189. p.273.

431 Annan, Kofi. 'Two Concepts of Sovereignty' *Economist* (18 September 1999).

432 Ibid.

433 Ibid. The UK's Foreign Secretary made a speech in 2000 on the need to address crimes against humanity while maintaining international law and state sovereignty. He proposed 'guidelines for intervention in response to massive violations of humanitarian law and crimes against humanity' and when the UNSC was unable to respond, it risked consigning the UNSC to irrelevancy (Cook, Robin. 'Humanitarian Intervention' *British Yearbook of International Law* (Vol.71 No.1 2000) p.646). Consequently, the UK lodged a framework for international intervention with the UN Secretary-General, based on six key points. Namely, the prioritisation of prevention, the use of force as a last resort, the primary responsibility for ending violence remaining with the state where the violence occurs, the responsibility of the international community to intervene where the territorial state was unable or unwilling to respond, the proportionate use of force and the requirement for such intervention to be multilateral.

The Rwandan genocide and the relative effectiveness of the Kosovo intervention led to a push for action,[434] while the concept of sovereignty as involving responsibility gained momentum in 2001, with the International Commission on Intervention and State Sovereignty (ICISS) attempting to forge a consensus on international responses to mass human rights violations.[435] The central theme behind the ICISS was the concept that a state's sovereignty involves a responsibility to protect its citizens but where a state is unable or unwilling to do so, the responsibility must be shared across the international community. Rather than a right to intervene, the ICISS argued for a 'responsibility to protect' with a shift away from a state's rights and towards its responsibilities and human security.[436] R2P can therefore be seen as an attempt to reform and reframe what had previously been known as humanitarian intervention.[437]

Although the ICISS acknowledged that R2P did not exist as a right under customary international law, it did see it as an emerging principle,[438] with even the staunchest advocates of non-intervention accepting some exceptions.[439] However, the ICISS recognised that the issue was controversial and sought to establish a consensus. It therefore felt that 'military intervention for humanitarian protection purposes' should be limited to the criteria of 'right authority, just cause, right intention, last resort, proportional means, and reasonable prospects'.[440]

First is the concept of 'Right authority', with the ICISS highlighting that the UNSC has primary responsibility for maintaining international peace and security.[441] The ICISS also notes the secondary role of the UNGA, particularly

---

This received little support and the framework made no headway (Gray. *Supra* note 111. p.239).

434 Stark, Alex. 'Introduction' in Weiss, Thomas, Thakur, Ramesh, O'Connell, Mary Ellen, Hehir, Aiden, Bellamy, Alex, Chandler, David, Shanahan, Rodger, Gerber, Rachel, Williams, Abiodun and Evans, Gareth. *The Responsibility to Protect: Challenges &Opportunities in Light of the Libyan Intervention* (2011) p.4 http://www.e-ir.info/wp-content/uploads/R2P.pdf Accessed 10th March 2024.

435 Established by the Canadian government, the ICISS was endorsed by Annan who supported the commission remaining outside the UN's auspices to ensure its impartiality and independence (Bellamy. *Supra* note 372. p.16). Notably, the ICISS was comprised of academics from both developed and developing countries (International Commission on Intervention and State Sovereignty. *Supra* note 25. Appendix A).

436 Ibid. Paras.2.22–2.23.

437 Frohlich. *Supra* note 396 p.299.

438 International Commission on Intervention and State Sovereignty. *Supra* note 25. Para.2.24.

439 Ibid. Para.4.13.

440 Ibid. Para.4.16.

441 Ibid. Para.6.7. Although the ICISS acknowledges the Security Council's limitations, they highlight its importance, with violations of the Charter eroding its authority and that no

via the Uniting for Peace Resolution, where military intervention for humanitarian protection purposes could gain legitimacy from the UNGA, even without UNSC authorisation.[442] Ultimately, the ICISS sought to redefine the parameters of intervention, and found broad consensus among states for the concept that their sovereignty involves a responsibility to protect their citizens.[443]

'Just cause' is also critical, given the risks an expansive definition of intervention would involve. The ICISS recommended 'military intervention for humanitarian protection purposes' be strictly limited.[444] It raised the threshold for authorising intervention even higher than existing UNSC practice, despite prior UNSC authorised interventions to restore elected governments or end widespread human rights abuses, which did not involve large-scale deaths.[445] This was to ensure consensus and by taking a conservative stance on intervention, the ICISS hoped to strengthen its support.[446]

'Right intention' is also vital and an intervention to overthrow an authoritarian regime would not qualify, although military intervention for humanitarian protection purposes might require the neutralisation of a regime's capacity to oppress its own citizens.[447] The ICISS recognises that military intervention for humanitarian protection purposes is unlikely to have pure motives and that states will often have to invoke self-interest to their voters to justify the cost and risk involved.[448] As such, the ICISS accepts the reality of mixed motives. The next criteria is 'Last resort'. This states the responsibility to react can only occur once the responsibility to prevent has been exhausted, or at least that alternate measures have no reasonable prospect of success.[449] Military intervention for

other body is better placed to address military intervention for humanitarian protection purposes issues (Ibid. Para.6.9–6.14). Consequently, they sought for a Security Council 'Code of Conduct' agreement whereby the P5 would refrain from using their vetoes in humanitarian emergencies where their vital interests were not involved (Ibid. Para.6.21).

442 Ibid. Para.6.30.

443 Ibid. Para.8.2.

444 Namely to interventions that halted or averted 'large scale loss of life, actual or apprehended, with genocidal intent or not, which is the product either of deliberate state action, or state neglect or inability to act, or a failed state situation; or large scale 'ethnic cleansing,' actual or apprehended, whether carried out by killing, forced expulsion, acts of terror, or rape' (Ibid. Para.4.19). The ICISS ruled out military intervention for humanitarian protection purposes being used for human rights abuses that did not involve ethnic cleansing, such as apartheid, political repression, the restoration of a democratically elected government or the protection of nationals (Ibid. Para.4.25–4.26).

445 Weiss. *Supra* note 410. p.8.

446 Bellamy. *Supra* note 372. pp.19–20.

447 International Commission on Intervention and State Sovereignty. *Supra* note 25. Para.4.33.

448 Ibid. Para.4.35.

449 Ibid. Para.4.37.

humanitarian protection purposes must also use 'Proportional means', involving the minimum use of force to achieve the necessary aim.[450] Finally, it must have 'Reasonable prospects of success', without triggering increased instability and violence.[451]

Overall, the ICISS sought to create a less controversial doctrine than humanitarian intervention, which was too mired in controversy to enjoy widespread support under international law. By avoiding the term 'humanitarian intervention',[452] the ICISS sought to escape humanitarian intervention's contentious past[453] while its parameters would act as a restraint on state misuse of the doctrine.[454] By shifting the debate from a right of intervention and focussing on areas of consensus, R2P is more palatable than humanitarian intervention.[455] To ensure its viability, the ICISS report avoided taking concrete positions and prioritised sovereignty over military force or R2P.[456] The ICISS's impact was therefore limited and it failed to clarify the pressing issues facing R2P.[457]

Momentum for R2P developed further in 2003 with the publication of *A More Secure World* by the Secretary-General's High Level Panel on Threats, Challenges and Change. Essentially, the Panel adopted the substance of the ICISS report with minor alterations.[458] Likewise, R2P saw additional support from the UN member states in 2005 when the UNGA adopted the *World Summit Outcome Document*. It reaffirmed the R2P concept that collective action could

---

450 Ibid. Para.4.39.

451 Ibid. Paras.4.41–4.42.

452 Ibid. Para.1.39.

453 Paris, Roland. 'Responsibility To Protect: The Debate Continues' *International Peacekeeping* (Vol.22, No.2, 2015). p.144.

454 Bellamy, Alex. 'Whither the Responsibility to Protect? Humanitarian Intervention and the 2005 World Summit' *Ethics and International Affairs* (Vol.19, No.2, 2006) p.147.

455 Gray. *Supra* note 111. p.240.

456 Weiss, Thomas. 'Whither R2P' in Weiss et al. *The Responsibility to Protect: Challenges &Opportunities in Light of the Libyan Intervention* (2011) p.7. http://www.e-ir.info/wp-content/uploads/R2P.pdf Accessed 10th March 2024.

457 Hehir, Aidan. The Responsibility to Protect (Basingstoke, 2012) p.49.

458 Bellamy. *Supra* note 372. p.21. The Panel highlighted that the traditional, Westphalian concept of sovereignty included a state's responsibility to safeguard the welfare of its citizens, while collective security also places responsibility on the international community to ensure this (United Nations General Assembly. *Report of the High-Level Panel on Threats, Challenges and Change on a More Secure World: Our Shared Responsibility*. UN Doc A/59/565 (2 December 2004). Para.29). Likewise, it recognised the shift from the 'right to intervene' to the 'responsibility to protect', which was an 'emerging norm' in response to large-scale violence where the relevant state was unable or unwilling to prevent (Ibid. Para.201–203).

be taken under Chapter VII of the UN Charter on an ad-hoc basis after the failure of peaceful methods and in conjunction with regional organisations, where states were failing to protect their citizens from war crimes, genocide, ethnic cleansing and crimes against humanity.[459] In addition, it stressed the international community's responsibility to help states develop the institutions to prevent such occurrences taking place.[460] The *World Summit Outcome Document* was more watered down than the ICISS report to ensure its adoption.[461] Nonetheless, the UNGA endorsement of such a proposal was a major development, although it weakened the case for humanitarian intervention given it only made reference to collective action under the UNSC. Likewise, it is unclear whether the document formulated a new legal norm or a 'framework for political action'.[462] Given the crimes referred to in R2P are already proscribed by international law, R2P is more of a political commitment to enforce existing law rather than establishing new legal norms.[463]

R2P gained impetus and was mentioned by the UNSC in 2006[464] and 2009.[465] It gained further traction in 2009 when the UN's Secretary-General Ban Ki-Moon outlined the three pillars of R2P, namely a state's own responsibility to protect its citizens, the international community's responsibility to provide assistance and the international community's responsibility to respond when the previous two fail.[466] He also highlighted that the R2P endorsed by the UNGA in 2005 was already well established in international law, and must conform to the UN Charter.[467]

459 UN General Assembly. *2005 World Summit Outcome*. UN Doc A/60/L.1 (24 October 2005). Para.139.

460 Ibid.

461 Firstly, the suggestion of intervention outside of the Security Council was dropped, an emphasis was placed on Just Cause and precautionary principles for interventions authorised by the UNSC and the concept of the P5 refraining from using their vetoes was removed (Bellamy. *Supra* note 454. p.155).

462 Gray. *Supra* note 111. p.241.

463 Bellamy, Alex. 'The Responsibility to Protect and the Problem of Regime Change' in Weiss et al. *The Responsibility to Protect: Challenges &Opportunities in Light of the Libyan Intervention* (2011) p.22 http://www.e-ir.info/wp-content/uploads/R2P.pdf Accessed 10th March 2024.

464 UN Security Council. *Security Council Resolution 1674 (2006)*. UN Doc S/Res/1674 (28 April 2006) Para.4.

465 UN Security Council. *Security Council Resolution 1894 (2009)*. UN Doc S/Res/1894 (11th November 2011) Preamble.

466 UN Secretary-General Report. Implementing the Responsibility to Protect. UN Doc A/63/677 (12th January 2009) p.2.

467 Ibid. p.5.

Consequently, R2P restates existing international law rather than creating new obligations but the Secretary-General's report noted humanitarian intervention was a false dichotomy between inaction and full-scale military involvement.[468] Although the Secretary-General's report was welcomed by states, it was more of a blueprint for states rather than the creation of obligations to be implemented.[469] The exact approach states took differed markedly. There was a clear distinction between states (primarily of the Global South) that supported R2P as a norm focussing on prevention, while others saw R2P as a response to the issues concerning humanitarian intervention.[470]

With a permanent seat on the UNSC and both economic and military strength, the UK is an influential advocate for R2P.[471] The US is more reluctant to promote humanitarian intervention as an international norm, and has refrained from using it as a legal justification.[472] France is generally interventionist within the UN framework and for a long time, was the P5's largest

468 Ibid. p.6.

469 Bellamy. *Supra* note 372. pp.39–42.

470 Ibid. p.8.

471 The UK's 2008 National Security Strategy highlighted that collective action and adherence to international law were vital ways of ensuring the UK's national security (UK Cabinet Office. *The National Security Strategy of the United Kingdom 2008* (London, 2008) Para.2.4). While endorsing R2P for situations where states were 'unwilling or unable to protect its citizens from genocide, war crimes, ethnic cleansing or crimes against humanity, or is perpetrating these acts itself' (Ibid.Para.4.75). The UK's 2010 National Security Strategy did not refer to R2P, rather it highlighted that the UK's interests can necessitate humanitarian interventions (UK Cabinet Office. *The National Security Strategy of the United Kingdom 2010* (London, 2010) Para.3.33) although its 2015 NSS noted that the UK would promote UN mechanisms such as R2P 'in line with British values.' (Ibid. Para.5.109). Furthermore, along with France, the UK is one of the few European states with the willingness and ability for force projection (see Hampton, Mary. 'Germany' in Sorenson, David and Wood, Pia Christina (Eds.) *The Politics of Peacekeeping in the Post-Cold War Era* (Abingdon, 2005) p.37).

472 Obama's 2010 National Security Strategy highlighted that military force to protect civilians from a 'grave humanitarian crisis' is sometimes necessary to protect peace and security. Although the NSS states all uses of force must be as a last resort and will seek authorisation through NATO or the Security Council, the US reserves the right to act unilaterally to defend the US and its interests (White House. 'National Security Strategy 2010 (Washington DC, 2010) p.22). Likewise, it notes US endorsement of R2P, with US willingness to intervene multilaterally and bilaterally in response to genocides and mass atrocities, although it makes no endorsement of unilateral US intervention (Ibid. p.48). Obama's 2015 NSS reaffirmed Washington's support for R2P, and the US would continue its commitment to take part in collective responses to mass atrocities (White House. 'National Security Strategy 2015 (Washington DC, 2015) p.22).

contributor of peacekeepers, seeing it as a way to project French power.[473] This can be contrasted with Russia, which has long been suspicious of Western military intervention, with similar fears over R2P.[474] Even as the USSR transformed into Russia, China maintained both its seat on the UNSC and its opposition to intervention into states' domestic matters,[475] although its approach to R2P is more nuanced.[476]

With varying levels of support for R2P among the P5, it is debatable exactly which interventions count as contributing to the development of R2P. Although R2P was arguably involved in the international community response to various twenty-first century crises, these were almost universally inadequate,[477] aside

473 See Coulon, Jocelyn. *Soldiers of Diplomacy: The United Nations, Peacekeeping, and the New World Order* (Toronto, 1994) especially pp.160–165 and p.188. See also, Wood. *Supra* note 35. pp.69–70.

474 Although Russia was willing to support R2P in principle, it had fears that the ICISS would lead to a growth in military interventions outside of those authorised by the Security Council (Bellamy. *Supra* note 463.) While Russia claims to support R2P as evidenced in the 2005 World Summit Outcome, it places a heavy emphasis on states' sovereignty, responsibility, and prevention over armed intervention (Averre, Derek and Davies, Lance. 'Russia, humanitarian intervention and the Responsibility to Protect: the case of Syria' *International Affairs* (Vol.91, No.4, 2015) p.832).

475 Hehir. *Supra* note 457. p.213.

476 China has long maintained that human rights are an internal matter for states, with humanitarian intervention risking 'gun-boat' policy and deteriorating conflicts even further. (Ministry of Foreign Affairs of the People's Republic of China 'Head of the Chinese delegation, Foreign Minister Tang Jiaxuan addressed the 54th UN General Assembly' https://www.mfa.gov.cn/eng/wjb_663304/zzjg_663340/gjs_665170/gjzzyhy_665174/2594_665176/2602_665192/200011/t20001115_598217.html Accessed 10th March 2024). China did not create difficulties in the lead-up to the World Summit where R2P was embraced (Evans, Gareth. 'Responding to Atrocities: The New Geopolitics of Intervention' in *SIPRI Yearbook 2012: Armaments, Disarmament, and International Security* (Oxford, 2012) p.30). China also supported Security Council Resolution 1674 that reaffirmed R2P in protecting civilians from genocide, war crimes, ethnic cleansing, and crimes against humanity (UN Security Council. *Supra* note 464. Para.4). Although a previously staunch advocate of non-intervention, China supports multilateral action and since 1992 began participating in UN peace-operations. At the time of writing, China is the largest contributor of peacekeepers among the P5 (United Nations 'Troop and police contributors' https://peacekeeping.un.org/en/troop-and-police-contributors Accessed 10th March 2024).

477 Evans explicitly rules out the coalition invasion of Iraq in 2003 and Russia's 2008 invasion of Georgia as involving R2P (Evans, Gareth. 'The R2P Balance Sheet after Libya' in Weiss et al. *The Responsibility to Protect: Challenges &Opportunities in Light of the Libyan Intervention* (2011) pp.37–39 http://www.e-ir.info/wp-content/uploads/R2P.pdf Accessed 10th March 2024). Likewise, Russia's invasion of Crimea (ostensibly to protect ethnic Russians) and subsequent annexation received negligible international support and is almost impossible to view as justifiable under R2P. The draft Resolution (UN Security Council. *Draft Resolution* (*On the Situation in Ukraine*). UN Doc S/2014/189 (15 March

from the 2008 Kenya crisis where diplomatic (rather than military) methods were used to maintain Kenyan stability.[478] The most notable example of a military component to R2P took place in response to escalating violence in Libya in 2011. This event has been described as the 'high water mark in the military application of the Responsibility to Protect'.[479]

## 6 The Libyan Civil War and Operation Unified Protector 2011

Located in North Africa, Libya had a tumultuous history before Muammar Gaddaffi came to power.[480] As Gaddaffi made amends for prior terrorist attacks and destroyed unconventional Libyan weapons, the West normalised its relations with Tripoli,[481] which strengthened Gaddaffi's control of Libya. Libya's human rights record remained abysmal and it was not immune from the Arab Spring, which erupted across the Middle East in 2011, with Arabs protesting against the despotism and corruption of their governments.[482]

In February 2011, Libyan protests erupted, catalysed by the mass arrest of government critics, the killing of 1,200 prisoners at the notorious Abu Salim prison and the disproportionately strong response by Libyan forces[483]that

2014)) affirmed Ukraine's territorial integrity and was supported by every member of the Security Council apart from China, which abstained and Russia which vetoed it. See UN Security Council. *69th Year. 7138th Meeting.* UN Doc S/PV.7138 (15 March 2014) p.3. Likewise, a UN General Assembly resolution (UN General Assembly. *Territorial Integrity on Ukraine.* UN Doc A/Res/68/262 (1 April 2014)) deemed the Crimean referendum as illegal. The Resolution was passed with 100 states in favour, 11 against and 58 abstaining. Although non-binding, it highlighted worldwide rejection of Russia's actions.

478 Evans. *Supra* note 477. pp.37–39.

479 Weiss. *Supra* note 410. p. XI.

480 Libya was occupied by numerous empires before achieving independence in 1951 under the pro-Western King Idris I. (BBC News 'Libya profile- timeline' www.bbc.com/news/world-africa-13755445 Accessed 10th March 2024) Idris was overthrown by a military coup in 1969 that brought Col. Muammar Gaddaffi to power, who instituted an authoritarian regime based on pan-Arabism and socialism, similar to that of his idol, Gamal Abdel Nasser of Egypt (Hilsum, Lindsey. *Sandstorm: Libya from Gaddaffi to Revolution* (London, 2012) pp.42–47).

481 Freedom House. 'Freedom in the World 2010: Libya' https://www.refworld.org/reference/annualreport/freehou/2010/en/72133 Accessed 10th March 2024.

482 For further information on the Arab Spring, see Lynch, Marc. *The Arab Uprising* (New York, 2012).

483 Human Rights Watch. *World Report 2012: Libya* (2012) https://www.hrw.org/world-report/2012/country-chapters/libya Accessed 10th March 2024.

saw the country descend into civil war.[484] The disorganised rebels were soon on the defensive[485] and pushed back by loyalist counteroffensives.[486] As the Libyan Civil War continued to escalate, Libya's ambassador to the UN claimed Gaddaffi was committing genocide against Libya's people.[487] Although the ambassador's words were hyperbolic, the civilian casualties were becoming increasingly alarming, with loyalists indiscriminately using artillery and air-strikes on densely populated areas.[488]

The UNSC adopted Resolution 1970, which demanded an immediate end to the violence, referred the Libyan situation to the International Criminal Court (ICC) and imposed an arms embargo along with sanctions on Gaddaffi and his key officials.[489] Gaddaffi failed to comply[490] and by March 2011, the death toll had risen to 1,000 Libyans[491] with Gaddaffi's forces advancing while committing war crimes.[492] Key in this campaign was Gaddaffi's air superiority, with his air force able to operate with impunity.[493] Recognising they would

---

484 The protests soon turned into a civil war, with rebels under the National Transitional Council (NTC) controlling large portions of the country. Although the Libyan military was formidable on paper, decades of sanctions and Gaddaffi's fear of coups meant it was gravely weakened (Apps, Peter and Maclean, William. 'Factbox: Libya's Military: What Does Gaddaffi have left?' Reuters, (1 March 2011) http://www.reuters.com/article/us-libya-military-idUSTRE72027E20110301 Accessed 10th March 2024). Mass desertions by Libyan conscripts ensured Gaddaffi relied on elite units, paramilitaries, and mercenaries notorious for committing atrocities (Vira, Varun and Cordesman, Anthony. 'The Libyan Uprising: An Uncertain Trajectory' *Centre for Strategic and International Studies* (Washington DC, 2011) pp.21–26).

485 Kirkpatrick, David and Fahim, Kareem. 'Allies count on defiant streak in Libya to drive out Qaddafi' *New York Times*. (30 March 2011).

486 Hilsum. *Supra* note 480.p.36.

487 Al Jazeera. 'Libyan Diplomats Defence En Masse' www.aljazeera.com/news/africa/2011/02/201122275739377867.html Accessed 10th March 2024.

488 Vira and Cordesman. *Supra* note 484. p.33. This led to a senior member of the Obama administration warning of an impending 'Srebrenica on steroids' (Rozen, Laura. 'Averting 'Srebrenica on steroids': White House defends Libya operations' *Yahoo News*. http://news.yahoo.com/blogs/envoy/averting-srebrenica-steroids-white-house-defends-libya-operations-20110323-120730-415.html Accessed 10th March 2024).

489 UN Security Council. *Security Council Resolution 1970 (2011)*. UN Doc S/Res/1970 (26 February 2011).

490 Bellamy, Alex and Williams, Paul. 'The new politics of protection? Cote d'Ivoire, Libya, and the responsibility to protect' *International Affairs* (Vol 87, No.4, 2011) p.840.

491 Gazzini, Claudia. 'Was the Libya Intervention Necessary?' *Middle East Report* (No.261, Winter 2011) p.4.

492 Human Rights Watch. *Supra* note 483.

493 Shadid, Anthony and Kareem, Fahim. 'Rebels in Libya Strain to Force a United Front' *New York Times*. (9 March 2011).

be massacred if Gaddaffi's forces continued to have free reign in the skies, the rebels sought an externally imposed no-fly zone.[494]

### 6.1 *UN Security Council Resolution 1973*

The USA was best placed to impose a no-fly zone but was reluctant to do so,[495] given it still had troops deployed in Iraq and Afghanistan.[496] Libya was a far more pressing matter for European nations, given its geographical proximity and importance as a source of oil for several EU states.[497] Without unilateral US involvement, a no-fly zone would require NATO's military capabilities, but NATO refused to act without UNSC authorisation.[498] The rebels' demands for a no-fly zone received support from various sources including the US Senate,[499] the Gulf Cooperation Council and the Arab League.[500]

Although China and Russia favoured a UNSC imposed ceasefire over intervention, the Arab League's support for intervention induced the US to seek measures that were more forceful.[501] The UNSC debated the issue over a draft resolution sponsored by France, the UK and Lebanon (which was acting as the Arab League's representative).[502] Most states supported the use of force for maintaining a no-fly zone and protecting civilians.[503] Consequently,

494 Bronner, Ethan and Sanger, David. 'No Flight Zone in Libya Backed by Arab League' *New York Times*. (13th March 2011).

495 Washington wanted its European allies take the lead on Libya, fearing American involvement would stoke anti-US feeling in the Middle East (Wilson, Scott. 'Obama: U.S. had responsibility to act in Libya' *Washington Post*. (28 March 2011)). Likewise, the Obama administration sought to avoid an interventionist foreign policy, lest military action hinder US economic recovery (Gomis, Benoit. 'NATO: Lessons from Libya' *The World Today* (Vol.67, No.5, May 2011) p.7). This was heightened by the fact the US had no major strategic interests in Libya beyond energy exports and the risks Libya could pose to regional instability (Vira and Cordesman. *Supra* note 484. p.5). Strikingly, the US had little reliance on Libya for oil, which amounted to just 0.5% of US oil imports (International Energy Agency. 'Facts on Libya: Oil and Gas (IEA 21 February 2011) https://web.archive.org/web/20150909200811/https://www.iea.org/media/news/facts_libya.pdf Accessed 10th March 2024).

496 Weiss. *Supra* note 410. p.73.

497 Ibid.

498 MacAskill, Ewen and Borger, Julian. 'No-fly zone plan goes nowhere as US, Russia and NATO urge caution' *Guardian*. (1 March 2011).

499 US Senate. S. RES. 85 112th Congress. (2011) Article.7.

500 Salama, Samir. 'GCC backs no-fly zone to protect civilians in Libya' *Gulf News*. (9 March 2011).

501 Hilsum. *Supra* note 480.p.199.

502 Williams, Paul. 'The Road to Humanitarian War in Libya' *Global Responsibility to Protect* (Vol.3, No.2, June 2011) p.255.

503 It must be noted South Africa and Nigeria highlighted the need to protect Libyan sovereignty and argued for a political solution (UN Security Council. *66th Year. 6498th Meeting.*

Resolution 1973 was adopted with 10 votes in favour and none against, with Germany, India, Brazil, Russia and China abstaining.[504] This authorised the use of force against Libya under Chapter VII of the UN Charter, creating a no-fly zone and authorising 'all necessary measures' to protect civilians, while prohibiting the deployment of occupation forces.[505]

Although Resolution 1973 claimed Libya's actions constituted a threat to international peace and security, it was unclear on how this was the case. It authorised the use of force to protect civilians and civilian areas under imminent attack, resulting in a striking example of an intervention generally considered to be heavily influenced by R2P.[506] A US led operation named Operation Odyssey Dawn was undertaken, joined by several non-NATO nations, including Qatar and the UAE (who were providing significant support to the rebels).[507] Although the inclusion of Arab nations was a useful shield to accusations of imperialism, their contribution to Operation Odyssey Dawn was minor,[508] and the intervention was overwhelmingly conducted by NATO states.[509] Although Operation Odyssey Dawn carried out airstrikes just days after the passing of Resolution 1973 and neutralised Libya's air force,[510] Libyan loyalists continued to advance using tanks and artillery to beat back rebel soldiers.[511] Despite rebel requests for no-fly zones, Operation Odyssey Dawn proved insufficient to alter the war's course in favour of the rebels.

---

UN Doc S/PV.6498 (17 March 2011) p.9). Likewise, military action was questioned by Germany, India, Brazil, Russia, and China. Although Russia endorsed an immediate ceasefire (Ibid. pp.6–10), it abstained rather than vetoing the draft Resolution. Washington maintains it is unclear exactly why, with some feeling Sergei Lavrov (Russia's ambassador to the UN) sought a middle course during Russia's changeover between President Putin and President Medvedev while others feel Lavrov sought to veto Resolution 1973 but was overruled by Moscow (Glasser, Susan. 'Minister No: Sergei Lavrov and the blunt logic of Russian power' *Foreign Affairs* (29 April 2013)).

504 UN Security Council. *Security Council Resolution 1973 (2011)*. UN Doc S/Res/1973 (17 March 2011) Paras.4–6. One of the few states to oppose the intervention was Libya itself that claimed Resolution 1973 was a breach of the Charter, a violation of Libya's sovereignty and a threat to Libyan civilians (Shackle, Samira. 'Libya declares ceasefire' *New Statesman*. (18 March 2011).

505 UN Security Council. *Security Council Resolution 1973 (2011)*. UN Doc S/Res/1973 (17 March 2011) Paras.4–6.

506 Gazzini. *Supra* note 491. p.5.

507 Barry, Ben. 'Libya's Lessons' *Survival* (Vol.53, No.5, October-November 2011) p.5.

508 Vira and Cordesman. *Supra* note 484. p.7.

509 Daalder, Ivo and Stavridis, James. 'NATO's Victory in Libya: The Right Way to Run an Intervention' *Foreign Affairs* (Vol.91, No.2, March/April 2012) p.4.

510 Amnesty International. *Libya: The Forgotten Victims of NATO Airstrikes* (London, 2012) p.5.

511 Kirkpatrick and Fahim. *Supra* note 485.

The US then sought to bring Operation Odyssey Dawn under NATO command and control, which was practical given that the Operation was composed primarily of NATO forces.[512] By the end of March 2011, Operation Odyssey Dawn was turned over to NATO and became Operation Unified Protector, with a mandate to enforce the no-fly zones, protect civilians and arms embargo. By 14 June 2011, it had conducted thousands of sorties,[513] many of which targeted loyalists. Such attacks on regime forces coincided with stronger rebel forces and increased international support, ensuring the rebels greatly improved their capabilities,[514] and eventually took control of Libya.[515]

### 6.2 *Resolution 1973 and the Responsibility to Protect*

Although Operation Unified Protector protected civilians, it avoided unilateral humanitarian intervention, with NATO highlighting that it would not act without UNSC authorisation, while Russia and China warned they would veto any resolution mandating military intervention[516] Resolution 1973 was deliberately vague to ensure viability, with Russia and China subsequently regretting their decision to abstain from voting. This highlights the risk of a UNSC resolution being used to justify force in an unintended manner.

Resolution 1973 was notable as it involved the successful use of force to protect civilians under the auspices of R2P.[517] In this, a key difference can be

512 Daalder and Stavridis. *Supra* note 509. p.3.

513 NATO 'Operational Media Update for 14 June' http://www.NATO.int/NATO_static/assets/pdf/pdf_2011_06/20110615_110615-oup-update.pdf Accessed 10th March 2024.

514 Barry. *Supra* note 507. p.6.

515 A rebel a counteroffensive captured Tripoli (Fahim, Kareem and Kirkpatrick, David. 'Rebels Pour into Central Tripoli Square, Declaring Victory' *New York Times.* (22 August 2011)) forcing Gaddaffi to flee until rebels captured and summarily executed him in October 2011. (Fahim, Kareem, Shadid, Anthony and Gladstone, Rich. 'Qaddafi Seized by Foes' *New York Times.* (21 October 2011)). Although the NTC claimed victory, it faced significant problems, particularly due to its disorganisation and the nature of the Libyan state that was indistinguishable from the regime and relied on Gaddaffi's patronage network rather than an institutionalised bureaucracy (Hilsum. *Supra* note 480.pp.19–20, pp.48–51). The NTC made great efforts to create a new state (Vira and Cordesman. *Supra* note 484. p.64). In addition, it successfully handed over power to a democratically elected government but struggled to assert its authority in a country full of armed militants and was scarcely stronger than the NTC (Hilsum. *Supra* note 480. pp.274–280). At the time of writing, Libya is heavily fragmented and has yet to form a transitional government (*Al Jazeera* 'Libya's parliament to appoint new PM amid rise in tensions' (8th February 2022) https://www.aljazeera.com/news/2022/2/8/libya-parliament-to-appoint-new-pm-amid-rise-in-tensions Accessed 10th March 2024).

516 MacAskill and Borger. *Supra* note 498.

517 Klose, Fabian. 'The Emergence of Humanitarian Intervention' in Klose, Fabian. (Ed.) *The Emergence of Humanitarian Intervention: Ideas and Practice from the Nineteenth Century*

drawn between Operation Allied Force in Kosovo (which was not authorised by the UNSC) Operation Provide Comfort in Iraqi Kurdistan (also unauthorised which involved an interstate conflict) and Operation Unified Protector.[518] Although the UNSC had previously authorised 'all necessary means' for the protection of civilians, this had happened where the sovereign government was either non-existent or consenting. Operation Unified Protector was an 'unprecedented moment' in R2P as it was the first time the UNSC authorised military intervention for humanitarian purposes against the wishes of the relevant sovereign government.[519]

As to whether such force was necessitated, O'Connell argues that Operation Unified Protector failed to establish that military force was used as last resort and had a strong chance of success.[520] Military intervention only came after alternative means failed, namely Gaddaffi's failure to comply with Resolution 1970.[521] It is arguable that the circumstances existed where R2P could be invoked given it can only be invoked to respond to genocide, war crimes, ethnic cleansing or crimes against humanity.[522] Gaddaffi's forces committed extensive war crimes, from targeting civilians to rape.[523] When the case was sent to

*to the Present* (Cambridge, 2018) p.4. This was echoed by the UN Secretary-General who viewed Resolution 1973 as a 'historic decision', whereby the international community fulfilled 'its responsibility to protect civilians from violence perpetrated upon them by their own government' (UN Secretary-General Statement by the Secretary-General on Libya (17 March 2011) www.un.org/sg/STATEMENTs/index.asp?nid=5145 Accessed 10th March 2024).

518 Hehir, Aidan. 'The Permanence of Inconsistency: Libya, the Security Council and the Responsibility to Protect' *International Security* (Vol.38, No.1, Summer 2013) p.141.

519 Bellamy and Williams. *Supra* note 490. p.825. This was a point made by the NTC that addressed the Security Council as Libya's representatives and highlighted that R2P was invoked to save thousands of people while maintaining Libyan sovereignty (UN Security Council. *66th Year. 6620th Meeting.* UN Doc S/PV.6620 (16 September 2011) p.7). Likewise, the head of the European Council highlighted that following the invocation of R2P to protect Libyan civilians, the international community had a 'responsibility to assist' the NTC in its transitional stages (UN General Assembly Press Release. *Sixty-Sixth General Assembly.* UN Press Release GA11151 (22 September 2011)).

520 O'Connell, Mary Ellen. 'How To Lose a Revolution' in Weiss et al. *The Responsibility to Protect: Challenges &Opportunities in Light of the Libyan Intervention* (2011) p. 15 http://www.e-ir.info/wp-content/uploads/R2P.pdf Accessed 10th March 2024.

521 Williams. *Supra* note 502. p.257.

522 Independent International Commission on Kosovo. *Supra* note 31. Para.4.20 and UN General Assembly. *Supra* note 459. Paras.138–139.

523 Human Rights Watch. *Supra* note 483. Grazzini claims war crimes were not being committed given Gaddaffi was suppressing domestic unrest rather than foreign military forces (Gazzini. *Supra* note 491. p.7). This is debatable: there is controversy on whether war crimes can be committed in non-international armed conflicts (Ratner, Stene. 'War

the ICC by the UNSC, the prosecutor made a preliminary determination that there was evidence of crimes against humanity committed by Gaddaffi, his son and his chief of security, resulting in arrest warrants being issued.[524] Gaddaffi did not attempt to conceal his intent, most notably in his Zenga-Zenga speech, which solidified support for intervention.[525]

Given there were grounds to invoke R2P, the question arises as to whether Operation Unified Protector was compatible with R2P or if it exceeded its mandate. For one, it is unclear just how expansive the UNSC's members understood Resolution 1973 to be.[526] It also appears (but remains unconfirmed) that Britain, France, Qatar and the UAE deployed special forces on the ground, potentially breaching Resolution 1973's prohibition on an 'occupation force'[527] while NATO states also breached the arms embargo on Libya.[528]

---

Crimes, Categories of' Gutman, Roy, Rieff, David and Dworkin, Anthony (Eds.) *Crimes of War* (New York, 2007) pp.420–422) but even before the NTC became widely recognised as Libya's representatives, the ICC's prosecutor maintained that Gaddaffi's forces were engaging in war crimes as a matter of policy (Simons, Marlise and MacFarquhar, Neil. 'Hague Court Seeks Warrants for Libyan Officials' *New York Times*. (4 May 2011)).

524 International Criminal Court. *Decision on the 'Prosecutor's Application Pursuant to Article 58 as to Muammar Mohammed Abu Minyar Gaddaffi, Said Al-Islam Gaddaffi and Abdullah Al-Senussi* ICC-01/11-01/11-1 (27 June 2011) p.41.

525 Soon after the rebellion began, Gaddaffi made a speech declaring his forces would 'cleanse Libya, inch by inch, house by house, home by home, alley by alley, and individual by individual' (Qaddafi, Muammar. 'Excerpts from Libyan Leader Muammar al-Qaddafi's Last Televised Address, 22 February 2011' *Foreign Affairs* (4 June 2011)). This Zenga-Zenga speech (from the Arabic for 'alley by alley') demonstrated the lengths to which Gaddaffi would go, with the UK's Minister for North Africa and the Middle East noting that the speech's echoing of Rwanda and Srebrenica forcing NATO to act (Hilsum. *Supra* note 480.p.189–190). Thakur likewise notes that the decisive factor for intervention was Gaddaffi's 'Zenga-Zenga' speech that involved a 'highly credible threat' to the people in Benghazi (Thakur, Ramesh. 'R2P, Libya and International Politics as the Struggle for Competing Normative Architectures' in Weiss et al. *The Responsibility to Protect: Challenges & Opportunities in Light of the Libyan Intervention* (2011) p.13 http://www.e-ir.info/wp-content/uploads/R2P.pdf Accessed 10th March 2024).

526 Lebanon highlighted it could not endorse the use of force against any country but hoped Resolution 1973 would force Gaddaffi's regime to restrain its violence while the UK noted that the use of force to protect civilians was for those under imminent attack (UN Security Council. *66th Year. 6498th Meeting.* UN Doc S/PV.6498 (17 March 2011) p.4). This was echoed by Colombia while Russia expressed its fears that the Resolution would be used to justify large-scale military intervention (Ibid. pp.7–8).

527 Although such troops were far too limited in number to constitute an occupying force, they were nonetheless deployed troops that played a vital role in augmenting Operation Unified Protector -rebel operations (Barry. *Supra* note 507. p.8).

528 Operation Unified Protector members such as the UK, Qatar, the UAE, and France ignored the arms embargo and sent weapons to the rebels with France even deploying soldiers to train rebels in their use (Hilsum. *Supra* note 480.p.207).

This raises questions regarding Operation Unified Protector's role in protecting civilians, given the focus on supporting regime change via rebel groups. Although airstrikes and support to the rebels saved many Libyan's lives with little risk to the intervening powers, it is arguably not a good example of a successful humanitarian intervention.[529] Nonetheless, it is unclear how events would have improved without such intervention and there can be little doubt that Operation Unified Protector succeeded in mitigating atrocities, tipping the balance of the Libyan Civil War and preventing an imminent massacre in Benghazi.[530] Gaddaffi had no interest in compromising with the rebels, had shown a willingness to use force against civilians and would likely have remained in power, leading to a civil war of attrition.[531] This situation would only have deteriorated without outside involvement and although the rebels became more militarily effective, their victory was only possible due to NATO's erosion of Gaddaffi's military capabilities. Without Operation Unified Protector, the rebels would have been defeated, resulting in significant civilian casualties.[532] While Operation Unified Protector had a humanitarian outcome and saved numerous lives, its actions are on dubious legal grounds.

Resolution 1973 authorised 'all necessary measures' for the protection of civilians but Operation Unified Protector exceeded this and it increasingly seemed that its main goal was supporting rebel forces rather than protecting civilians.[533] NATO states initially targeted Gaddaffi loyalists only when they posed a direct threat to civilians but swiftly expanded this, arguing that Gaddaffi's forces posed such a danger to civilians that they could be directly targeted, despite the opposition of states such as South Africa and Russia.[534]

Operation Unified Protector soon went beyond protecting civilians and NATO began actively aiding Libyan rebels,[535] with the 'protection of civilians' mandate being used to justify attacks on loyalists.[536] The key problem was not the use of force to protect civilians but the overthrow of the Gaddaffi regime, given there was no provision for this in Resolution 1973.[537] Although the coalition had a mandate to use all necessary measures in the protection

529 Chollet, Derek. 'The Shame of Srebrenica' *Foreign Affairs* (9 July 2015).

530 Lynch. *Supra* note 482. p.175.

531 Lynch, Marc. 'Obama and the Middle East' *Foreign Affairs* (September/October 2015) p.20.

532 Barry. *Supra* note 507. p.7.

533 Gray. *Supra* note 111. p.249.

534 Barry. *Supra* note 507. pp.5–6.

535 Mangu, André. 'The Arab Spring and the African Union's Reaction to the Crisis' *Africa Insight* (Vol.42, No.1 June 2012) p.8.

536 Hilsum. *Supra* note 480.p.215.

537 Bellamy. *Supra* note 463.

of civilians, it swiftly became a tool of regime change,[538] leading Russia and China to regret their abstention on Resolution 1973.[539] This was highlighted by Russia, which noted the intent of Resolution 1973 was to protect Libyan civilians, but Operation Unified Protector exceeded this,[540] with the head of the Arab League also expressing regret over the intervention.[541]

Operation Unified Protector's engagement in regime change is problematic, as NATO explicitly highlighted its aim was to force Gaddaffi from power[542] and the Operation ended soon after Gaddaffi's assassination. It is arguable that its actions were a necessary part of protecting Libyan civilians: had Operation Unified Protector not targeted loyalists, it would have led to the massacre of civilians as Gaddaffi reasserted control. This is debatable, given NATO was targeting Gaddaffi's military forces and advocating his overthrow. Had NATO sought to protect civilians, Operation Unified Protector could have maintained the no-fly zone and only intervened when civilians were under direct threat.[543] In effect, it operated as the rebels' air support.

NATO's intervention undoubtedly arose from mixed motives, but with a humanitarian aspect.[544] Although NATO did cause civilian casualties,[545] it maintained high standards in preventing such casualties.[546]

---

538 Vira and Cordesman. *Supra* note 484. p.47.

539 Gazzini. *Supra* note 491. p.6.

540 UN Security Council. *66th Year. 6620th Meeting.* UN Doc S/PV.6620 (16 September 2011) p.3.

541 Traynor, Ian. 'Arab League Chief Admits Second Thoughts about Libya Air Strikes' *Guardian.* (21 June 2011).

542 Vira and Cordesman. *Supra* note 484. p.5.

543 Evans. *Supra* note 477. pp.41.

544 Lynch highlights that avoiding an imminent massacre in Benghazi was critical, given the Obama administration could not permit a bloodbath to occur under the eyes of the media (Lynch. *Supra* note 482. p.172). Obama used humanitarian language, arguing that it was in the US' strategic interests to prevent the massacre of civilians and that the US had a responsibility to do so (Wilson. *Supra* note 495). Such humanitarian language was mirrored by conscious NATO efforts to protect civilians. The use of airstrikes was similar to those used by NATO in the 1990s, permitting action without endangering coalition pilots. There was a key difference in the advancement of technology: rapid progress in reconnaissance and precision munitions enabled the use of smart bombs that reduced the risk of civilian casualties (Barry. *Supra* note 507. p.8).

545 Gaddaffi claimed the airstrikes killed 1100 civilians and wounded another 4500, although such figures are certainly exaggerated (Barry. *Supra* note 507. p.7) The *New York Times* estimated that dozens were killed by NATO, with at least 40 confirmed civilian casualties (Chivers, CJ and Schmitt, Eric. 'Libya's Death Toll' *New York Times.* (18 December 2011)).

546 Extensive steps were taken to avoid civilian casualties, with no cluster bombs or dumb bombs being used and most of NATO's 7700 missiles hit their targets without injuring civilians (Ibid.) Amnesty noted that NATO made significant efforts to minimise civilian casualties although scores of civilians were killed, and NATO was reluctant to investigate

## 6.3 *Legitimacy and the Overthrow of Gaddaffi*

Gaddaffi's legitimacy was debatable as he was an unelected dictator, while the National Transitional Council (NTC) claimed popular legitimacy from its inclusion of delegates across Libya.[547] For a government to lose its legitimacy is problematic under international law, even for one as repressive as Gaddaffi's.[548] The rebels enjoyed extensive international recognition and Libyan public support for Operation Unified Protector bolstered its legality.[549] Notably, the use of R2P in Libya was explicitly invoked by the US,[550] Italy,[551] Luxembourg,[552] the Netherlands,[553] Liechtenstein[554] and Norway.[555]

Such support was not universal. South Africa criticised the UNSC's prioritisation of force over diplomacy.[556] Zimbabwe accused NATO of a 'blatant illegal, brutal and callous' intervention in Libya to secure its energy supplies.[557] Namibia referred to the intervention as the greatest threat to the principle of

---

such incidents properly (Amnesty International. *Supra* note 510. pp.5–6). Overall, the precision of NATO's strikes ensured far fewer civilians were killed than the 1999 airstrikes in Kosovo or the 2003 airstrikes in Iraq (Hilsum. *Supra* note 480.p.216) showing the utility of air support in humanitarian protection.

547 Gazzini. *Supra* note 491. p.6.

548 This is a point made by Mangu who argues that NATO's actions were a breach of Resolution 1973, whose provisions made no account for deploying special forces or arming rebels to enact regime change (Mangu. *Supra* note 535. p.8).

549 Thakur. *Supra* note 525. p.13. During the debates surrounding Resolution 1973, several states declared Gaddaffi's' regime had lost its legitimacy by the UK, Lebanon, Germany, Portugal, and Colombia (UN Security Council. *66th Year. 6498th Meeting.* UN Doc S/PV.6498 (17 March 2011) pp.4–8). Likewise, the NTC was widely accepted as Libya's representatives by most members of the General Assembly who supported the Libyan Civil War's outcome (UN General Assembly Press Releases. UN Press Release GA11147-11155 (21–27 September 2011)).

550 UN General Assembly Press Release. *Secretary-General, Opening Annual General Debate, Urges World Leaders to Tackle Global Challenges Decisively for Sake of Future Generations.* UN Press Release GA11147 (21 September 2011).

551 UN General Assembly Press Release. *Examination of Mediation versus Military Intervention to Assist Regions Wracked by Conflict Focus of General Assembly Debate as It Enters Fourth Day.* UN Press Release GA11153 (24 September 2011).

552 Ibid.

553 UN General Assembly Press Release. *General Assembly Debate Considers Global Development at Crossroads, as Least Developed Countries Buckle under Strain of Meeting Most Basic Needs.* UN Press Release GA11154 (26 September 2011).

554 Ibid.

555 UN General Assembly Press Release. *Closing 'Historical and Unforgettable' Annual Debate, General Assembly President Says Time to Shift Gears to Crucial Next Step, 'Turn Talk into Real Impact'.* UN Press Release GA11155 (27 September 2011).

556 UN General Assembly Press Release *Supra* note 550.

557 UN General Assembly Press Release. *Supra Note 519.*

non-intervention in UN history.[558] Mali called for negotiations within Libya and an end of the use of force in the country[559] while Lesotho criticised the African Union's marginalisation during the crisis.[560] Cuba criticised the intervention in a conflict which did not threaten international peace and security, accusing NATO of abusing Resolution 1973 to enact regime change[561] while Nicaragua viewed Operation Unified Protector as 'illegal' and yet another attack on the sovereignty of a UN member state.[562] Venezuela described Operation Unified Protector as an imperialist war, enacted to maintain capitalism and to recolonise Libya.[563]

The above criticisms are notable with African countries seemingly more opposed to the AU's marginalisation during the process, while other criticisms of Operation Unified Protector came from anti-US Latin American countries such as Cuba and Venezuela. Such criticisms seemed motivated by political opportunism rather than legal concerns. By July 2011, the NTC was recognised as Libya's 'legitimate authority' by the Libyan Contact Group, which was composed of over 30 states and organisations including the EU and Arab League.[564] By September 2011, the NTC enjoyed significant international support and both the UN and the AU as Libya's representative, despite lacking control over large parts of Libya, recognised it.[565] This was important given Gaddaffi's role in international affairs.[566]

---

558 UN General Assembly Press Release. *Palestinian Authority President Outlines Application for United Nations Membership as Heads of State, Government Address General Assembly.* UN Press Release GA11152 (23rd September 2011).

559 Ibid.

560 UN General Assembly Press Release. *Supra* note 551.

561 UN General Assembly Press Release. *Supra* note 553.

562 Ibid.

563 UN General Assembly Press Release. *Supra* note 555.

564 Black, Ian. 'Libyan rebels win international recognition as country's leaders' *Guardian.* (15 July 2011). The Libyan Contact Group was established on the 29 March 2011 and advocated for the NTC with representatives from a range of organisation such as the UN, EU, Arab League, and the Organisation of Islamic Conference (UK Foreign and Commonwealth Office. *Libya Contact Group: Chair's Statement* (13th April 2011) https://www.gov.uk/government/news/libya-contact-group-chairs-statement Accessed 10th March 2024). Notably, although an invitee, the African Union was not a member. This is striking given that after Gaddaffi's failed attempts to advance himself within pan-Arabism, he portrayed Libya as a country with an African rather than Arab identity (Ramutsindela, Maano. 'Gaddaffi, Continentalism and Sovereignty in Africa' *South African Geographic Journal* (Vol.91, No.1, 2009) p.3).

565 Fahim, Kareem and Gladstone, Rick. 'Qaddafi Calls New Libya Government a Propped-Up' 'Charade' *New York Times.* (21 September 2011).

566 Libya was heavily involved in international and regional organisations, most notably the African Union, Arab League and United Nations that together formed the nucleus of the

While many African leaders knew Gaddaffi could not remain in power, they feared the destabilisation his departure could bring to the region.[567] The AU expressed its support for the Libyan people's demands for democracy and condemned breaches of International Humanitarian Law by both sides, rejected military intervention in Libya and sought a ceasefire and political solution.[568] Although primarily composed of non-interventionist states, the AU's Constitutive Act highlighted the AU's right to intervene in member states for war crimes, genocide and crimes against humanity, alongside the prohibition on the use of force and non-interference for each state in the internal affairs of others.[569] The AU prohibits unilateral intervention while permitting collective interventions, which is an important evolution in R2P, given the Global South's opposition to intervention and that the Constitutive Act permits intervention without the authorisation of the UNSC.[570] In practice though, the AU has been reluctant to authorise such operations.[571]

A key factor for AU opposition to military intervention arose from Gaddaffi's popularity among the AU's member states,[572] which compromised the AU's impartiality and led the rebels to reject the AU's proposal, as it did not include a call for Gaddaffi's immediate removal.[573] Likewise, the AU called on its members to ignore the ICC's arrest warrant for Gaddaffi.[574] Although South Africa initially voted for Resolution 1973, it soon opposed it, with President Zuma arguing that NATO abused the resolution by shifting from protecting civilians to enacting regime change.[575] Despite its efforts in the Libyan crisis, the AU failed to provide much public diplomacy and swiftly saw itself as an outsider during the conflict. Mangu highlights that African states' outrage was 'crocodile tears', due to their irrelevance when compared to NATO's actions.[576]

---

international response to the Libyan crisis. Gaddaffi was popular for establishing the African Union and generously supporting anti-apartheid movements, including South Africa's African National Congress (Hilsum. *Supra* note 480. pp.140–147).

567 Ibid. p.370.

568 African Union Peace and Security Council. *Communique of the 265 Meeting of the Peace and Security Council of the African Union* PSC/PR/Comm.2 (CCLXV) (10 March 2011) Paras.4–7.

569 Constitutive Act of the African Union (2000). Article 4 (F-H).

570 Bellamy. *Supra* note 454. pp.157–158.

571 Bellamy. *Supra* note 372. pp.14–15.

572 Mangu. *Supra* note 535. p.5.

573 BBC News 'Libya: Benghazi Rebels Reject African Union Truce Plan' (11th April 2011) www.bbc.com/news/world-africa-13035501 Accessed 10th March 2024.

574 'African Union Opposes Warrant for Qaddafi' *New York Times.* (3 July 2011).

575 Roelf, Wendell. 'South Africa says NATO abusing U.N. Resolution on Libya' *Reuters* (14 June 2011) http://www.reuters.com/article/us-libya-safrica-idUSTRE75D2XY20110614 Accessed 10th March 2024.

576 Mangu. *Supra* note 535. p.8.

Also important was the Arab League. Although Gaddaffi was keen to portray himself as heir to Pan Arabism, he alienated other Arab nations with his interference.[577] Across the Arab world, the Libyan protests received immense support due to rebel defiance and the fear Gaddaffi's victory would embolden Arab dictators.[578] Although the Charter of the Arab League requires each member state to treat each other's political systems as internal concerns,[579] it is notable that the Arab League suspended Libya's membership for its crackdown on protestors.[580] Strategic interests culminated in the Arab League requesting a UN imposed no-fly zone,[581] with such an invitation for Western intervention within Arab territory constituting an exceptional occurrence.[582] Furthermore, Arab states such as Jordan and Qatar participated in Operation Unified Protector and made an important symbolic (if not operational) contribution. This was even more interesting given the Arab public had consistently been suspicious of Western intervention,[583] particularly at a time of widespread Arab unrest, with a successful Libyan uprising potentially emboldening Arab uprisings in other states.[584]

The Arab League was motivated more by political interests than any intent to enforce international law. Gaddaffi was a regional pariah and toppling him was popular with both Arab leaders as well as their citizens.[585] This was critical for US involvement, with US Secretary of State, Hillary Clinton and National Security Council Advisor, Samantha Power, arguing that they should push for intervention if they secured Arab backing.[586] Such support gave legitimacy to NATO's actions, while the US refrained from action until support for

577 Hilsum. *Supra* note 480.pp.54–55.

578 Lynch. *Supra* note 482. p.168.

579 Charter of the Arab League (UNTS, 70, 1945) Article VIII.

580 Shenker, Jack. 'Arab League urged to condemn Gaddaffi by angry protesters in Egypt' *Guardian.* (23 February 2011). Support for the no-fly zones was readily apparent in conservative Gulf state such as Saudi Arabia, although it would be a mistake to see this general support for humanitarian intervention, given how repressive most Arab League states are. See Freedom House. *'Freedom in the World 2020'* https://freedomhouse.org/explore-the-map?type=fiw&year=2020 Accessed 12th October 2020.

581 UN Security Council. *Letter Dated 2011/03/14 from the Permanent Observer of the League of Arab States to the United Nations Addressed to the President of the Security Council.* UN Doc S/2011/137 (15 March 2011) Para.1.

582 Bronner and Sanger. *Supra* note 494.

583 Lynch. *Supra* note 482. p.174.

584 Williams. *Supra* note 502. pp.250–251.

585 Hilsum. *Supra* note 480.p.189.

586 Ibid. p.196.

intervention was forthcoming from the UN, NATO and the Arab League,[587] which was also a factor for the UNSC to take into account.[588] Without such support, it is unlikely that the UNSC would authorise such an intervention, with Arab League support being critical in preventing a Russian or Chinese veto.[589]

## 6.4 *Humanitarian Intervention, R2P and Operation Unified Protector*

Resolution 1973 is notable for its swift adoption by the UNSC and for including an expansive mandate, demonstrating that sovereignty is no longer a shield for engaging in massacre.[590] Despite the potential new role for R2P, Operation Unified Protector's impact on R2P's future is debatable. Evans, who co-chaired the ICISS, claimed that Operation Unified Protector was an example of the successful implementation of the R2P doctrine, with the intent of ending 'continuing and imminent mass atrocity crimes'.[591] Operation Unified Protector's success is certainly arguable with its airstrikes saving thousands of civilians in a manner that was cost-effective while avoiding NATO casualties,[592] which are vital factors when the West considers using force for humanitarian purposes. Although Libya remains unstable, Operation Unified Protector avoided mission-creep as happened in the 2003 US invasion of Iraq and prevented the continued commission of atrocities as occurred in Syria.[593] While there was certainly short-term benefits to civilians, the lack of post-intervention assistance led to chaos, and nostalgia for Gaddaffi's rule.[594] Such an intervention was only possible due to a reading of Resolution 1973, which went well beyond what was envisaged by some of the UNSC members that voted for it. Indeed, Russia and China highlighted they would veto any resolution which authorised military intervention.[595]

587 Harwood, John. 'Opportunities and Perils for Obama in Military Action in Libya' *New York Times.* (28 March 2011).

588 The importance of Arab League support was stressed during the Security Council debate on Resolution 1973 from France, the UK, Lebanon, Bosnia, Colombia, China, and the US. (UN Security Council. *66th Year. 6498 Meeting.* UN Doc S/PV.6498 (17 March 2011) pp.2–10).

589 Bellamy, Alex. 'Libya and the Responsibility to Protect: The Exception and the Norm' *Ethics and International Affairs* (Vol.25, No.3, 2011) p.266.

590 Walling, Carrie Booth. *All Necessary Measures: The UN and Humanitarian Intervention* (Philadelphia, 2013) p.214.

591 Evans. *Supra* note 477. p.40.

592 Daalder and Stavridis. *Supra* note 509. p.3.

593 De Waal, Alex. 'African roles in the Libyan conflict of 2011' *International Affairs* (Vol.89, No.2, 2013) p.378.

594 Weiss. *Supra* note 410. p.119.

595 MacAskill and Borger. *Supra* note 498.

These issues raise concerns for R2P, particularly as Resolution 1973 is often cited as an example of R2P in action, but the term was not used in the resolution itself. It is certainly true that Operation Unified Protector involved a sustained military campaign to protect civilians and had a humanitarian outcome in overthrowing Gaddaffi's regime. The stretching of Resolution 1973's mandate means states are likely to be suspicious of further resolutions, which invoke R2P.[596] Nonetheless, Resolution 1973 is historic, given it was the first explicit authorisation of the use of force against a UN member state to compel its government to cease committing atrocities.[597]

Although many states accepted the resulting change of government, there were many unique factors in Operation Unified Protector, which limit its usefulness as a precedent given it took place in a country riven by civil war, without any major threat to intervening forces.[598] In addition, it took place within NATO's spheres of effective operations, in a constrained area and without creating an unmanageable refugee crisis.[599] Likewise, Resolution 1973 sets a precedent that some will seek to avoid, lest a similarly broad UNSC resolution be used to overthrow regimes engaging in atrocities.[600] In addition, the UNSC's key focus was on maintaining international peace and security, while R2P was a secondary factor.[601]

Gaddaffi's international isolation was also a factor. Unlike the Global South's fear of intervention as covert imperialism, Operation Unified Protector came about from the widely recognised NTC's requests for external military support,

596 This is what was elaborated on following the onset of Operation Unified Protector, with Russia expressing its fears that peacekeepers would become dragged into conflicts and the protection of civilians would be used to cloak ulterior motives (UN Security Council. *66th Year. 6531st Meeting*. UN Doc S/PV.6531 (10 May 2011) p.9). Although Brazil supported the use of force for the protection of civilians, it sought clear parameters for its use, lest a vague mandate be used to permit regime change (Ibid. p.11). Meanwhile, South Africa gave Operation Unified Protector as an explicit example where the use of force went beyond a Resolution's mandate to protect civilians to ensure regime change (Ibid. p.18).

597 Walling, Carrie Booth. *All Necessary Measures: The UN and Humanitarian Intervention* (Philadelphia, 2013) p.215.

598 NATO was able to conduct Operation Unified Protector without a major threat posed by Libyan forces, given air strikes swiftly neutralised most of Libya's air defences (Vira and Cordesman. *Supra* note 484. p.18) ensuring Libyan forces posed little danger to coalition forces (Apps and Maclean. *Supra* note 484). Likewise, it involved a dictator clearly stating his intention to commit massacres, with a unified rebel opposition and support from regional groups like the Arab League and the Gulf Cooperation Council (See Frohlich. *Supra* note 396 p.326).

599 Barry. *Supra* note 507. pp.11–12.

600 Ibid.

601 Tsagourias and White. *Supra* note 35. pp.98–99.

with similar demands from regional organisations such as the Arab League, Gulf Cooperation Council (GCC) and Organisation of Islamic Cooperation (OIC).[602] Without such involvement, it is unlikely that Operation Unified Protector would have taken place, highlighting the importance of regional organisations and care must be taken with overemphasising R2P as a norm. Although Russia and China did not oppose Resolution 1973, this was due to the support of the Arab League as a regional actor rather than support for R2P itself.[603] Nonetheless, only a few states have expressed outright opposition to R2P and most of the Global South supported R2P during UNGA dialogues on the subject from 2009–2015.[604]

R2P fails to provide much support for humanitarian intervention under customary international law. Indeed, rather than creating a new international law norm, it seeks to influence the political debate.[605] While Operation Unified Protector would probably not have been authorised without the emergence of R2P,[606] it fails to create a legal precedent based on doctrine. R2P therefore remains as little more than a slogan, with other atrocities in the world remaining unaddressed by the UNSC.[607] This is a key problem with contemporary R2P. Rather than ensuring a response, R2P merely offers a new lens for the P5 to intervene when it is in their interests to do so. R2P makes no changes on the most relevant areas to enabling the use of force for the protection of civilians. It does not reform the UNSC, amend P5 control or create any obligation for the UNSC to act.[608] It perpetuates a system where intervention is only forthcoming if it is the interests of the P5, or at the very least, not against their interests.[609] R2P seeks to create guidelines for governing when interventions can take place, but these are of little use given that the UN is unlikely to support interventions without UNSC approval and even if these occurred, states can merely claim the relevant criteria for intervention are not being fulfilled.[610]

---

602 Hehir. *Supra* note 518. p.138.

603 Hehir. *Supra* note 457. p.13.

604 The few states which are opposed to R2P are Cuba, Venezuela, Sudan, and Nicaragua. (Weiss, Thomas. *What's Wrong the United Nations and How to Fix It* (Cambridge, 2016) p.141).

605 Frohlich. *Supra* note 396 p.309.

606 Williams. *Supra* note 502. p.259.

607 Hehir, Aidan. 'The Illusion of Progress: Libya and the Future of R2P' in Weiss et al. *The Responsibility to Protect: Challenges &Opportunities in Light of the Libyan Intervention* (2011) p.18 http://www.e-ir.info/wp-content/uploads/R2P.pdf Accessed 10th March 2024.

608 Averre and Davies. *Supra* note 474. p.817.

609 Hehir. *Supra* note 518. p.152.

610 Bellamy. *Supra* note 372. pp.167–169.

Such inconsistency is a by-product of the UNSC system. The veto system means the UNSC's response to international crises will remain ad-hoc and subject to self-interest.[611] The key problem with the UNSC's response to crises was lack of will rather than a lack of authority.

Although R2P has potentially replaced humanitarian intervention, it suffers the same shortcomings, being just as selective and primarily used on a political rather than legal basis.[612] As there is no UNSC obligation to act, it does little to alter the problems that existed before the ICISS report.[613] One of the ICISS's chairs noted that R2P was not a norm of customary international law at the time of the panel and neither was it a norm as of 2011.[614] This is still the case and there is little credible evidence that R2P has become a norm at the time of writing. While R2P was widely accepted by the international community, its potential to expand the use of force beyond self-defence and the maintenance of international peace and security remains controversial.[615]

R2P is little better than humanitarian intervention, given it also involves the selective use of force to end atrocities. The key difference is that R2P requires explicit authorisation from the UNSC and this ensures greater legitimacy. This was possible before R2P as the UNSC could already authorise interventions for the protection of civilians. Given that a key reason for R2P was the UNSC's inconsistency towards atrocities in the 1990s, R2P risks failing to resolve the

611 Hehir. *Supra* note 518. *pp.*137–138.

612 The intervention in Libya can be contrasted with NATO's intervention in Syria, where NATO states engaged in an air campaign against the Islamic State despite the vast majority of Syrian civilian casualties being caused by Syrian government forces (Middle East Monitor 'More than 21,000 killed in Syria during 2015' (29 December 2015) https://www.middleeastmonitor.com/20151229-more-than-21000-killed-in-syria-during-2015 / Accessed 10th March 2024) which is also responsible for crimes against humanity (Amnesty International *Between the Prison and the Grave: Enforced Disappearances in Syria* (London, 2015) p.7 and Human Rights Watch *Syria: Criminal Justice for Serious Crimes under International Law* (December 2013) p.1). Even though the war crimes in Libya are scarcely worse than those ongoing in Syria, the international response to atrocities by the Assad regime remains weak, being chiefly limited to condemnations and sanctions. A large part of this is due to Russian support of the Assad regime (Averre and Davies. *Supra* note 474. p.819). Although the failure to react to the Syrian crisis does not render Operation Unified Protector illegitimate, it does highlight the continued selectivity of R2P and shows the intervention in Libya marked an aberration rather than the creation of a new era under international law. (Hehir. *Supra* note 518. p.158). For an analysis on why Libya but not Syria resulted in intervention, see Weiss. *Supra* note 410. pp.75–81.

613 Hehir. *Supra* note 457. p.21.

614 Evans in Weiss et al (2011) p.36.

615 Lu, Catherine. 'Humanitarian Intervention: Moral Ambition and Political Constraints' *International Journal* (Vol.62, Issue 4, Fall 2007) pp.942–943.

issues at hand.[616] R2P does have an advantage as it removes the ambiguity over humanitarian intervention, with the World Summit Outcome Document highlighting that only the UNSC can authorise military force for the protection of civilians.[617] This demonstrates the opposition to humanitarian intervention conducted outside of the UN's auspices, rendering it unlikely that a right of unilateral humanitarian intervention continues to exist under customary international law.[618] In effect, R2P has failed to provide any major progress and existing international law on the matter is essentially the same as in 1990s.[619]

An interesting development arose in 2011 with respect to Russia. During the R2P debate over the Libya crisis, Russia maintained that while intervention to protect civilians was possible under international law, this required the express authorisation of the UNSC and the UN should not become involved as an actor in any civil war.[620] Russia even attempted to invoke R2P for its 2008 invasion of Georgia.[621] Such misuse of the R2P principle seems to highlight the risks associated with its invocation, enabling powerful states to shield military adventurism behind humanitarianism.

Russia's claims received little international support, showing the fears of R2P legitimising imperialism was misplaced.[622] While states can invoke norms such as R2P to try to justify their actions, they will not necessarily be accepted by other states. This can be compared to the norm of self-defence, which is accepted under international law and the most widely cited justification for the use of force.[623] even though it is often misused. Despite its currently ambiguous status, R2P in principle has widespread acceptance[624] and has advanced

616 Hehir. *Supra* note 518. p.159.

617 UN General Assembly. *Supra* note 459. Para.139.

618 See Bellamy. *Supra* note 463.

619 Hehir. *Supra* note 457. p.58.

620 UN Security Council. *66th Year. 6531st Meeting*. UN Doc S/PV.6531 (10 May 2011) p.9. It must be noted that Russia is itself no stranger to military adventurism, notably in its 2014 unilateral intervention of Ukraine (See Treisman, Daniel. 'Why Putin Took Crimea: The Gambler in the Kremlin' *Foreign Affairs* (May/June 2016)) showing its willingness to use force outside of the UN Charter. This will be explored further in Chapter 5.7 The Russia-Ukraine War.

621 Russia claimed the Georgian government was engaging in genocide in the province of South Ossetia (Council for Foreign Relations 'A Conversation with Sergey Lavrov' https://www.cfr.org/event/conversation-sergey-lavrov Accessed 10th March 2024).

622 Bellamy. *Supra* note 372. p.69.

623 Hoffman, Tamás. 'War or peace? – International legal issues concerning the use of force in the Russia–Ukraine conflict' *Hungarian Journal of Legal Studies* (Vol.63, No.3, 2022) p.209.

624 General Assembly debates show there is a consensus on R2P, with few states totally 'remaining outside the R2P fold'. Weiss. *Supra* note 410. p.5.

to its current position at the centre of international law debates, with potential to evolve further.[625] Despite how long it has been since the ICISS convened and the UN endorsed R2P, it continues to be at best, an emerging norm. There is some hope that it will continue in the future: in 2006, Breau noted that UN peace-enforcement was clearly moving in the direction of R2P.[626] Likewise, in 2013, Walling noted the intervention in Libya showed that the norms regarding humanitarian intervention had altered in the twenty-first century.[627] At the time of writing, this remains to be seen, though such debate about humanitarian intervention was given new impetus by the Russia-Ukraine war.

## 7 The Russia-Ukraine War

The dissolution of the USSR in 1991 saw Ukraine gaining independence after centuries of domination by Moscow, via a 'civilised divorce'.[628] The USSR's General Secretary, Mikhail Gorbachev was keen for a successor to the USSR, but such a union would have been impossible without Ukrainian accession.[629] Gorbachev's hopes for a USSR successor were therefore dashed by Ukrainian independence, but Ukraine would remain inextricably linked to Russia for the subsequent decades. Moscow strongly felt the loss of Ukraine, with most contemporary Russians still seeing the two as indivisible (though few Ukrainians agree).[630] Nonetheless, Russia felt its generosity towards Ukrainian independence meant that Kyiv's independence would be largely nominal.[631] Foreign policy was a low priority for the Russian public after the USSR's dissolution and Moscow lacked the will or resources to coerce the newly independent states on its borders,[632] though it retained a stated interest in Russians now located outside Russia's borders.[633] Moscow's ability to enforce this interest in Russians

625 Weiss. *Supra* note 456. p.9.

626 Breau, Susan. 'The Impact of the Responsibility to Protect on Peacekeeping' *Journal of Conflict and Security Law* (Vol.11, No.3, 2006) p.464.

627 Walling, Carrie Booth. *All Necessary Measures: The UN and Humanitarian Intervention* (Philadelphia, 2013) pp.213–214.

628 Plokhy, Serhii. *The Gates of Europe: A History of Ukraine* (New York, 2021). p.325.

629 Plokhy, Serhii. *The Russo-Ukrainian War* (Dublin, 2023). pp.3–4.

630 CNN 'Half of Russians say it would be right to use military force to keep Ukraine out of NATO' https://edition.cnn.com/interactive/2022/02/europe/russia-ukraine-crisis-poll-intl/index.html Accessed 30th November 2023.

631 Trofimov, Yaroslav. *Our Enemies Will Vanish: The Russian Invasion and Ukraine's War of Independence.* (Dublin, 2024) p.13.

632 Reid, Anna. *Borderlands: A Journey Through the History of Ukraine* (London, 2022) p.231.

633 Ivanov, Igor. *The New Russian Diplomacy* (New York, 2002) p.16.

abroad changed under Putin, where the rise of oil prices and Russian nationalism enabled Russia to be far more aggressive, particularly after Russia engaged in extensive military reforms following Russia's military underperformance in the 2008 invasion of Georgia.[634]

Although post-independence Ukraine was peaceful, with generally smooth transitions of power, it struggled with corruption and the economy's control by oligarchs.[635] Such corruption was even more pronounced under President Yanukovych's pro-Russian administration,[636] with the author vividly encountering this when visiting Yanukovych's sprawling Mezhyhirya estate with its petting zoo, luxury car collection and full-scale floating galleon. Tension in Ukraine led to Yanukovych's overthrow,[637] with an EU sponsored power-sharing deal between Yanukovych and opposition leaders being rejected by anti-Yanukovych protesters gathered in Kyiv's Maidan square due to Ukrainian security forces killing protesters and Yanukovych was forced to flee.[638] This was unacceptable to Putin who was in his third decade of controlling Russian politics and was preoccupied with restoring Russia's old sphere of influence.[639]

## 7.1 *Russia's Annexation of Crimea 2014*

Despite Yanukovych's unpopularity in Ukraine, the end of his Moscow-aligned administration was especially problematic for the Ukrainian peninsula of Crimea, where centuries of Russian migration and the mass deportation of its indigenous Tatar population in 1944[640] ensured that the peninsula was strongly pro-Russian in outlook.[641] Crimea also had major symbolic significance to Russia, running from Tsarist Russia through the Soviet era to contemporary Russia.[642] Crimea therefore occupies a key place in Russia's national

634 McNab, Chris. *The Great Bear at War: The Russian and Soviet Army 1917-Present* (Oxford, 2019) pp.328–330.

635 Sixsmith, Martin, with Sixsmith, Daniel. *Putin and the Return of History: How the Kremlin Rekindled the Cold War* (Dublin, 2024) p.123.

636 Kuzio, Taras. *Putin's War Against Ukraine* (Toronto, 2017) p.149.

637 Conradi, Peter. *Who Lost Russia: From the Collapse of the USSR to Putin's War on Ukraine* (London, 2022) pp.247–260.

638 Matthews, Owen. *Overreach: The Inside Story of Putin's War on Ukraine* (London, 2022) pp.87–89.

639 Puri, Samir. *Russia's Road to War with Ukraine: Invasion Amidst the Ashes of Empires* (London, 2022) p.XI.

640 Wilson, Andrew. 'Imagining Crimean Tatar History since 2014: Indigenous Rights, Russian Recolonisation and the New Ukrainian Narrative of Cooperation' *Europe-Asia Studies* (Vol.73, No.5, June 2021) pp. 843–845.

641 Reid. *Supra* note 632. pp.173–181.

642 O'Loughlin, John and Toal, Gerard. 'The Crimea conundrum: legitimacy and public opinion after annexation' *Eurasian Geography and Economics* (Vol.60, No.1, 2019) p.9.

psyche[643] even after it was incorporated to Ukraine by General-Secretary Khrushchev in 1954 out of economic necessity.[644]

Consequently, protests in Crimea influenced by Russia agents were conducted against the new Kyiv government and resulted in the deployment of Russian troops and the imposition of a Crimean puppet government by Russia.[645] This was a major development, marking only the second annexation of a European sovereign state's territory since World War II.[646] Russia claimed that it deployed soldiers at the request of Ukraine's legitimate government[647] and held a referendum offering Crimeans either unification with Russia or the restoration of Crimea's status under Ukraine's 1992 constitution, with no option for the status quo.[648] The official result of the referendum was 97% in favour of unification from a turnout of 83% (which seems unlikely given ethnic Ukrainian and Tatars accounted for nearly 40% of Crimea's population), though a leaked report from Russia's Human Rights Council stated turnout for the referendum was 30%, with half voting for annexation.[649] Likewise, the referendum took place under Russian occupation and amidst misinformation, killings, torture and arbitrary arrests during the referendum's buildup[650] while the referendum was boycotted by Crimea's indigenous Tatars who were strong opponents of the peninsula's annexation.[651] While the referendum was flawed, had the referendum been held fairly, the result would likely still have supported unification with Russia, while the chaos following Yanukovych's overthrow meant little action was taken by Kyiv.[652]

The Crimean invasion brought issues of 'war, occupation and separatism' to the height of European politics in a way not seen since the Yugoslav Wars in the 1990s and followed a Russian tradition of using breakaway regions to threaten

643 Figes, Orlando. *The Story of Russia* (London, 2022) p.288.

644 Sixsmith with Sixsmith. *Supra* note 635. pp.178–179.

645 Galeotti, Mark. *Putin's Wars: From Chechnya to Ukraine* (Oxford, 2022) pp.172–173.

646 The other case being Turkey's invasion and occupation of Northern Cyprus in 1974. See Kershaw, Ian. *The Global Age: Europe 1950–2017* (London, 2018) p.525.

647 United Nations Security Council *7125th Meeting* UN Doc S/PV7125 (3 March 20214) pp.3–4.

648 BBC News. 'Crimea referendum: What does the ballot paper say?' (10 March 2014) https://www.bbc.com/news/world-europe-26514797 Accessed 8th December 2023.

649 Pifer, Steven. 'Crimea: Six years after illegal annexation' *Brookings Institution* (17 March 2020) https://brookings.edu/articles/crimea-six-years-after-illegal-annexation/ Accessed 19th December 2023.

650 Balzer, Harley. 'The Ukraine Invasion and Public Opinion' *Georgetown Journal of International Affairs* (Vol.16, No.1, Winter/Spring 2015) p.81.

651 O'Loughlin and Toal. *Supra* note 642. p.12.

652 Galeotti. *Supra* note 645. pp.174–176.

the states that once governed them, as it did in Georgia and Moldova.[653] Russia's invasion of Crimea is notable as any protective aspect of its invasion in the name of defending Crimeans from Kyiv was done (at most) to pre-empt Kyiv's oppression of Crimea's population rather than due to any such oppression actually taking place.[654] Russia's actions in Crimea were heavily driven by its fear of Ukraine joining NATO, with Putin seeing Ukraine's tilt to the West as an existential threat (though it poses little threat to Russia itself).[655] Although Ukraine sought NATO membership in 2005–2006 under President Yushchenko's pro-Western administration, Yushchenko failed to implement meaningful military reforms and NATO accession was only strongly supported by Ukraine's policy elite rather than society at large, with the Ukrainian public being highly divided on accession.[656]

In 2008, Ukraine (along with Georgia) was promised a future Membership Action Plan for NATO accession, but without any timeframe for when it would take place.[657] Such a decision was a dangerous outcome, given it enraged Russia by treating Ukrainian accession as inevitable but without providing any actual protection to Ukraine.[658] Putin maintains that NATO agreed not to expand 'one inch' further in exchange for Russian acquiescence to German unification in 1990,[659] though there is no written evidence of such a guarantee.[660] Rather, such a claim appears to be based on an unauthorised verbal statement by the then US Secretary of State, with Gorbachev noting that the Warsaw Pact was still in force at the time, meaning it was 'laughable' to foresee Warsaw Pact countries joining NATO.[661] Nonetheless, Ukraine passed a bill

653 Cullen Dunn, Elizabeth and Bobick, Michael S. 'The empire strikes back: War without war and occupation without occupation in the Russian sphere of influence' *American Ethnologist* (Vol.41, No.3, August 2014) pp.405–406.

654 Baranovsky, Vladimir and Mateiko, Anatoly. 'Responsibly to Protect: Russia's Approaches' *Italian Journal of International Affairs* (Vol.51, No.2, 2016) p.62.

655 Balzer. *Supra* note 650. pp.79–80.

656 Puri. *Supra* note 639. pp.77–82.

657 'Russia welcomes NATO offer to repair ties' *The Irish Times* (4 December 2008).

658 Plokhy *Supra* note 629 p.89.

659 Putin, Vladimir. 'Address by the President of the Russian Federation' (21 February 2022) http://en.kremlin.ru/events/president/news/67828 Accessed 8th January 2024.

660 Mirria, Carl. 'Not One Inch, Unless It Is from Lisbon to Vladivostok NATO-Russia Mythmaking and a Reimagined Kyivan Rus' *Journal of Applied History* (Vol.4, 2022) p.132. See also, Sarotte, Mary Elise. 'Not One Inch Eastward? Bush, Baker, Genscher, Gorbachev and the Origin of Russian Resentment toward NATO enlargement in February 1990' *Diplomatic History* (Vol.34, No.1, 2010) pp.139–140.

661 Sixsmith, Martin, with Sixsmith, Daniel. *Putin and the Return of History: How the Kremlin Rekindled the Cold War* (Dublin, 2024) pp.48–49.

rejecting any aspirations of NATO membership in 2010, but retained its goal of EU membership,[662] though EU membership for Ukraine was barely less threatening to Russia than Ukrainian NATO accession.[663] Likewise in 2019, Ukraine passed a constitutional amendment committing Ukraine to join both NATO and the EU.[664] Although Ukraine was not anywhere close to joining NATO in 2022,[665] Russia's perceived threats to its security combined with what Moscow saw as Ukrainian weakness to induce Putin to escalate his attack on Ukraine.

### 7.2 *The Donbas War*

The second stage of Putin's assault on Ukrainian sovereignty was in Ukraine's industrialised eastern region known as the Donbas. In the nineteenth century, the Donbas region had been industrialised and then heavily settled by Russian urban workers, while Ukraine's peasantry rejected such industrial work as alien.[666] Following Ukrainian independence, some in Ukraine (especially from the country's west) sought to distance Ukraine from Moscow but they were opposed by Donbas' politicians, namely former communist party officials and factory bosses.[667] Although opposed to Ukrainian nationalism, the Donbas region lacked Crimea's strongly pro-Russian mindset and there was little support for either Donbas' independence or incorporation into Russia.[668] Nonetheless, following the ease with which Russia took Crimea, Moscow was emboldened to stir up a largely manufactured rebellion in the Donbas region,[669] with the aim of preventing Ukraine joining NATO.[670] Given Donbas' mixed demographics and weaker support for Russia, Moscow's actions in Crimea would not work in the Donbas so Russia's strategy focused on using anti-Maidan protestors (some genuine, some directly sent by Russia) to demand autonomy within Ukraine.[671] Polling by the Kyiv International Institute of Sociology found support for Russian troops in Ukraine as being

662 BBC News. 'Ukraine's parliament votes to abandon NATO ambitions' *BBC News* (3 June 2010).

663 Puri. *Supra* note 639. p.124.

664 'Ukraine president signs amendment on NATO, EU membership' *Associated Press* (19 February 2019).

665 Ramani, Samuel. *Putin's War on Ukraine: Russia's Campaign for Global Counter Revolution* (London, 2023) p.5.

666 Kuzio. *Supra* note 636. pp.172–173.

667 Plokhy. *Supra* note 629 p.47.

668 Sixsmith with Sixsmith. *Supra* note 635 pp.185–192.

669 McNab. *Supra* note 634. pp.351–352.

670 Ramani. *Supra* note 665. p.14.

671 Reid. *Supra* note 632. p.273.

a minority view in South and East Ukraine, even within the Russian claimed Donetsk and Luhansk regions.[672] Simply put, without Russian involvement, there was no chance that the Donbas War would have occurred.[673]

Ukraine responded with what it called an Anti-Terrorist Operation (ATO), a limited military mobilisation to retake the Donbas region. However, Ukraine's regular armed forces were weakened after years of corruption and heavily infiltrated by Russian agents.[674] Consequently, key in the ATO was the use of volunteer battalions who conducted much of the fighting and ranged from oligarch funded private armies to ultranationalists like the Azov Regiment who were effective fighters but bore allegations of war crimes and neo-Nazi ideology.[675]

The presence of far-right personnel in such battalions was swiftly weaponised by Russia to push the myth that Kyiv's government was dominated by fascists.[676] However, there is no evidence of neo-Nazism in Ukraine's current leadership (especially today, given Ukraine's current President Zelensky is Jewish).[677] Eventually, most volunteer battalions were incorporated into Ukraine's armed forces, reducing their politicisation and subjecting them to state control and discipline, with notorious offenders such as the Tornado and Shakhtarsk battalions being disbanded.[678] Integration into Ukraine's military further diluted Azov's far-right ideology until such members formed a small minority.[679] Notably, after integration, Azov's far-right leader was replaced by a professional military officer, with Azov releasing a statement in 2022 condemning both Nazism and Stalinism.[680] Though lightly armed and undertrained, such volunteer battalion proved vital against separatists[681] until the volunteer battalions were integrated into the Ukrainian army.[682]

672 Kyiv International Institute of Sociology. 'The Views and Opinions of South-Eastern Regions Residents of Ukraine: April 2014' *Kyiv International Institute of Sociology* https://www.kiis.com.ua/?lang=eng&cat=reports&id=302&page=7 Accessed 13th December 2023.

673 Puri. *Supra* note 639. p.148.

674 Trofimov. *Supra* note 631. p.16.

675 Galeotti. *Supra* note 645. p.183.

676 Matthews. *Supra* note 638. p.108.

677 Hoffman, Tamás. 'War or peace? – International legal issues concerning the use of force in the Russia–Ukraine conflict' *Hungarian Journal of Legal Studies* (Vol.63, No.3, 2022) p.219.

678 Käihkö, Ilmari. 'A nation-in-the-making, in arms: control of force, strategy and the Ukrainian Volunteer Battalions' *Defence Studies* (Vol.18, No.2, 2018) p.159.

679 Ramani. *Supra* note 665. p.124.

680 Trofimov. *Supra* note 631. p.82.

681 Sanders, Deborah. 'The War We Want; The War That We Get': Ukraine's Military Reform and the Conflict in the East' *The Journal of Slavic Military Studies* (Vol.30, No.1, 2017) p.42.

682 Kuzio. *Supra* note 636. pp.257–259.

Russia initially sought to limit its involvement in the Donbas to funding and permitting Russian volunteers to join the rebels (albeit with Kremlin support)[683] but Ukraine continued to make gains and by August 2014, the separatists were on the brink of collapse, with Ukraine's imminent control of the Donbas border with Russia posing a grave concern to Moscow.[684] As such, on the 24 August 2014, Russia openly sent troops to the Donbas region (a date deliberately chosen to humiliate Ukraine on its independence day).[685] Without such direct Russian intervention, it is likely Kyiv would have recaptured the Donetsk and Luhansk regions.[686]

By September 2014, Russia's defeat of Ukrainian forces in the Donbas led Kyiv to agree to a peace deal brokered in Minsk which involved a ceasefire, the withdrawal of heavy weapons from the front line, the release of all hostages, the decentralisation of power within Ukraine and the return of border control to Ukraine under the Organization for Security and Co-operation in Europe (OSCE).[687] However, the Minsk Agreement had little effect, with both sides continuing to exchange fire[688] while Russia developed its supported forces in the Donbas to a force of thousands of soldiers and an array of heavy weaponry.[689] This took place even as Western states refused to send military equipment to Ukraine to avoid destabilising the peace process.[690]

A second Minsk Agreement was signed in February 2015 but it too proved fundamentally unworkable due to the 'Minsk Conundrum', whereby the Minsk Agreement relied on two irreconcilable differences: upholding Ukrainian sovereignty would require a ceasefire followed by Russian withdrawal and Ukraine holding elections before devolving power to the Donbas regions, while Russia sought the erosion of Ukrainian sovereignty with elections being held before Ukraine establishes dontrol, ensuring the victory of Russia's proxies and the

683 See Puri. *Supra* note 639. p.143.

684 Galeotti. *Supra* note 645. pp.186–187.

685 Kuzio, Taras. 'Euromaidan revolution, Crimea, and Russia–Ukraine war: why it is time for a review of Ukrainian–Russian studies' *Eurasian Geography and Economics* (Vol.59, No.3–4, 2018) pp.533–534.

686 Harding, Luke. *Invasion: Russia's Bloody War and Ukraine's Fight for Survival* (London, 2022) p.209.

687 'Protocol on the results of consultations of the Trilateral Contact Group' (5 September 2014) https://www.peaceagreements.org/view/1363https://www.osce.org/home/123257 Accessed 20th December 2023.

688 Reid. *Supra* note 632. p.286.

689 Kuzio. *Supra* note 685. p.534.

690 Kuzio. *Supra* note 636. p.287.

prevention of Ukraine operating as a sovereign state.[691] Likewise, the Minsk Agreements were impossible to implement given it did not include Russia as a contracting party, but acknowledging Russian involvement in the war would have precluded Russian attendance at Minsk.[692] Indeed, since Russia denied its troops were even in Ukraine, it felt no obligation to withdraw its soldiers from Ukraine, even as its troops conducted major offensives in Ukraine in 2015.[693] Although both sides breached the Minsk Accords,[694] the primary violator of Minsk was Russia, ensuring support for the agreement was further eroded in Ukraine.[695] Furthermore, the Minks Accords have no legitimacy in Ukraine and were seen as an ultimatum signed under duress rather than negotiation.[696]

Russia's invasion of the Donbas saw a marked increase in Ukrainian identity, with Ukrainians uniting across 'ethnic, linguistics, religious and cultural' divides.[697] Furthermore, Ukraine's lacklustre military performance in 2014 spurred intense reforms within the Ukrainian military, utilising Western assistance to build an army of 150,000 by 2022.[698] While Ukraine had aimed to modernise its military to a professional volunteer force between 2006 and 2010, this was incomplete by 2014 when the Donbas war broke out.[699] However, Ukrainians were far more motivated to fight for the Donbas than for Crimea[700] and by 2018, Ukraine had retaken two thirds of the separatist Donbas region and announced that the ATO led by Ukraine's security service (SBU) was to become a Joint Forces Operation led by Ukraine's military.[701] While the Donbas war marked eight years of 'low intensity warfare', it involved rotating thousands of Ukrainian soldiers[702]

691 Allen, Duncan. *The Minsk Conundrum: Western Policy and Russia's War in Eastern Ukraine* (Chatham House, 22 May 2022) p.22.

692 Puri. *Supra* note 639. p.157.

693 Snyder, Timothy. *The Road to Unfreedom: Russia, Europe, America* (London, 2019) pp.191–192.

694 Sixsmith and Sixsmith. *Supra* note 668. p.202.

695 Ramani. *Supra* note 665. pp.76–77.

696 Kuzio. *Supra* note 636. pp.246–247.

697 Plokhy. *Supra* note 629. pp.133–134.

698 Galeotti. *Supra* note 645. p.331.

699 Sanders. *Supra* note 681. pp.33–36.

700 Kuzio. *Supra* note 685. p.539.

701 Sasse, Gwendolyn. 'Ukraine's New Military Engagement in the Donbas' *Carnegie Endowment for International Peace* (3 May 2018) https://carnegieeurope.eu/strategiceurope/76246 Accessed 29th December 2023.

702 Puri. *Supra* note 639. p.137.

which saw 14,200 people killed between 14 April 2014 and 31 December 2021.[703]

With the war in the Donbas ongoing, in April 2019, Vladimir Zelensky was elected as president of Ukraine, defeating the incumbent President Petro Poroshenko with 73% of the vote.[704] A native Russian speaker with Jewish heritage, Zelensky was best known as a comedian and actor but won on a platform based on anticorruption, maintaining Ukraine's orientation towards the West and ending the war with Russia.[705] While advocating peace towards Russia, Zelensky's platform also included pledges for NATO membership and a refusal to relinquish Ukrainian land to Russia.[706] Putin was initially delighted by the election of a Russian-speaking political novice (especially over the Ukrainian nationalist backed Poroshenk), but Zelensky soon proved more resistant to Moscow's demands than it anticipated, likely as Zelensky saw the risks to Ukrainian sovereignty that enacting the Minsk Accords would involve.[707] Zelensky's initially conciliatory strategy towards Russia failed, with Russia accepting Zelensky's concessions but refusing to de-escalate themselves, leading Zelensky to adopt a stronger stance against Moscow.[708] Meanwhile, Zelensky struggled to win over the backing he sought in the White House. US President Donald Trump had offered support in exchange for Zelensky investigating the son of his Democratic opponent, Joe Biden (a quid-pro-quo that Zelensky never acceded to) while when Biden became president, he was insulted by Zelensky's demands for NATO membership and increased military aid.[709] As time went on, Ukrainian disillusionment with Zelensky (particularly due to his failure to tackle corruption) led to his domestic approval ratings dropping to 25–30%.[710] However, Russia soon drastically escalated the war it had been conducting against Ukraine for the previous eight years.[711]

---

703 Office of the United Nations High Commissioner for Human Rights. 'Conflict-related civilian casualties in Ukraine' (27 January 2022) https://ukraine.un.org/sites/default/files/2022-02/Conflict-related%20civilian%20casualties%20as%20of%2031%20December%202021%20%28rev%2027%20January%202022%29%20corr%20EN_0.pdf Accessed 29th December 2023.

704 'Zelenskiy wins Ukraine's presidential election with 73%' *Associated Press* (23 April 2019).

705 'Ukraine elects Volodymyr Zelensky, TV star and political neophyte' *The Economist* (22 April 2019).

706 Trofimov. *Supra* note 631. p.20.

707 Sixsmith with Sixsmith. *Supra* note 635. pp.261–263.

708 Harding. *Supra* note 686. p.47.

709 Foer, Franklin. *The Last Politician Inside Joe Biden's White House and the Struggle for America's Future* (New York, 2023) pp.213–215.

710 Reid. *Supra* note 632. pp.295–296.

711 Azarov Denys, Koval Dmytro, Nuridzhanian, Gaiane and Venher, Volodymyr. 'Understanding Russia's Actions in Ukraine as the Crime of Genocide' *Journal of International Criminal Justice* (Vol.21, No.2, 2023) p.234.

### 7.3 *Russia's Invasion of Ukraine in 2022*

In January 2022, Russia began concentrating large numbers of troops on Ukraine's border, claiming it was conducting military exercises but denying it would invade.[712] While Russia had previously massed troops on Ukraine's borders for conducting exercises, Russia's claims it would also not invade this time were precluded by the sheer size of the deployment, the establishment of field hospitals and the presence of supplies such as large quantities of blood which are too expensive to be used for mere exercises.[713] On Biden's instruction, US intelligence released information on Russia's buildup and imminent attack to the public, with Russia responding with impossible demands such as an end to NATO expansion, the prohibition on Ukraine acceding to NATO and NATO's withdrawal of troops from Eastern Europe, while negotiation attempts by France and the US failed.[714] Despite the threat posed by such a military buildup, many thought Putin was too rational for a full invasion[715] This included Zelensky and his administration, who publicly downplayed the threat of invasion, although the Ukrainian military took the threat seriously enough to begin preparations for invasion.[716]

On the 15 February 2022, Russia's Duma requested Putin to recognise the Donetsk and Luhansk Peoples' Republics as independent states,[717] with Putin doing so via executive order on the 21 February 2022,[718] which was criticised by UN Secretary-General António Guterres as 'a violation of the territorial integrity and sovereignty of Ukraine.'[719] Then on the 24 February 2022, Russia launched a full-scale invasion of Ukraine, marking the first attempt at regime

712 Vindman, Alexander and Cruz Bustillos, Domininc. 'The Day After Russia Attacks What War in Ukraine Would Look Like – and How America Should Respond' *Foreign Affairs* (21 January 2022).

713 See Foer. *Supra* note 709. p.222 and Banco, Erin, Graff, Garrett, Seligman, Lara, Toosi, Nahal and Ward, Alexander. ''Something Was Badly Wrong': When Washington Realized Russia Was Actually Invading Ukraine' *Politico* (24 February 2023).

714 Galeotti. *Supra* note 645. p.343.

715 Allin, Dana. 'Ukraine: The Shock of Recognition' *Survival* (Vol.64, No.2, April-May 2022) pp.202–203.

716 Trofimov. *Supra* note 631. pp.30–31.

717 Roth, Andrew. 'Duma manoeuvre points to Kremlin impatience in Ukraine standoff' *The Guardian* (15 February 2022).

718 Putin, Vladimir. 'Signing of documents recognising Donetsk and Lugansk People's Republics' (21 February 2022) en.kremlin.ru/events/president/news/67829 Accessed 20th January 2024.

719 United Nations Secretary-General. 'Secretary-General's press encounter on Ukraine' *United Nations* https://www.un.org/sg/en/content/sg/press-encounter/2022-02-22/secretary-generals-press-encounter-ukraine Accessed 26th January 2024.

change by Moscow since the USSR's 1968 invasion of Czechoslovakia.[720] Aware of Putin's opinions, Russia's spy agencies fed Putin's bias that there would be little Ukrainian resistance, given most Ukrainians were pro-Russian loyalists who despised their decadent, pro-Western rulers.[721] Likewise, due to Russia's seemingly overwhelming military superiority, Ukrainian resistance was widely expected by Western political and military experts to collapse within seventy two hours.[722] They were soon surprised by the extent of Ukrainian resistance: Ukraine had spent years preparing for such an invasion and were aided by Russia's strategic and tactical errors as well as a severe underestimation of Ukraine's willingness to resist.[723] Russia soon found that the Ukrainian military of 2022 was not like the Ukrainian military of 2014, with years of professionalization and NATO training having an impact, while Ukrainians were highly motivated to defend their homes and rally under Zelensky's leadership.[724] Furthermore, by this point Ukraine had combat experience in conventional modern warfare that exceeded that of Western armies.[725] Ramani summarises that there were four major factors which led to Russia's strategic failure in Ukraine, namely inability to secure air superiority, Russia's overly centralised command structure, the limitations of Russia's irregular combat units such as the mercenary Wagner group and Donbas militias and a failure to secure Ukrainian collaborators.[726] Initially, the West's belief in Ukraine's imminent defeat meant its armament of Ukraine involved limited numbers of weapons suitable for small partisan forces.[727] However, Ukrainian initial military

---

720 Ramani. *Supra* note 665. p.3.

721 Harding. *Supra* note 686. p.37.

722 See Menon, Rajan. 'Ukraine's Best Chance a Successful Offensive Could End the War with Russia' *Foreign Affairs* (12 April 2023) and Grieco, Kelly, Cooper, Evan, Darnal, Aude, Preble, Christoper, Ashford, Emma and Siebens, James. 'Testing Assumptions About the War in Ukraine, One Year Later' *Stimson Centre* (*15 February 2023*) https://www.stimson.org/2023/testing-assumptions-about-the-war-in-ukraine-one-year-later/ Accessed 4th February 2024.

723 Galeotti. *Supra* note 645. pp.345–346.

724 Petraeus, David and Roberts, Andrew. *Conflict: The Evolution of Warfare from 1945 to Ukraine* (London, 2023). p.353.

725 Galeotti. *Supra* note 645. p.192.

726 Ramani. *Supra* note 665. pp.128–133.

727 See Ponomarenko, Illia. 'US delivers 300 more Javelins to Ukraine' *Kyiv Independent* (26 January 2022) Charap, Samuel. 'The West's Weapons Won't Make Any Difference to Ukraine' *Foreign Policy* (21 January 2022) and Scmitt, Eric and Ismay, John. 'U.S. Arms Sent to Ukraine Would Blunt but Not Stop a Russian Invasion' *New York Times* (15 February 2022).

success using its mostly Soviet-era weaponry saw Kyiv begin to receive heavy armament transfers from the West.[728]

Prior to the 2022 invasion, NATO faced numerous challenges and risked going into decline.[729] So severe was this threat, that President Macron of France warned that NATO was experiencing 'brain death'.[730] Likewise, the EU was seen by Putin as divided, and while he previously refrained from invading Ukraine due to the risk of a response from Europe, he now saw Europe as impotent, with its most powerful states distracted by their own domestic issues.[731] Putin expected Western indifference and was surprised by the imposition of sanctions from the West,[732] particularly the extent of sanctions imposed by the EU along with military aid to a non-EU state at war.[733] Rather than compounding European impotence, Putin's invasion saw European solidarity expand, with the EU accelerating Ukraine's attempts for membership while Sweden and Finland sought NATO accession, ensuring Russia was even more isolated.[734] Likewise, NATO 'sprung to life', while the EU bought and delivered lethal aid for the first time in its history.[735] The consequences of Putin's invasion were 'transformative' and in just days, Sweden and Finland abandoned their long-standing neutrality to seek NATO membership, Germany abandoned its policy of military reluctance and post-Brexit UK strongly engaged with continental Europe.[736]

By March 2022, Russia was forced to admit its initial plan was failing and 'repositioned' its goals to secure the Donbas,[737] before announcing its annexation of the Kherson, Zaporizhzhia, Luhansk and Donetsk regions even as parts

728 Trofimov. *Supra* note 631. pp.27–28 and 161–162.

729 Davis, Doug, Steward, Brandon and Slobodchikoff, Michael. 'NATO's Future. The Show Must Go On' in Slobodchikoff, Michael, Davis, Doug and Stewart, Brandon (Eds.) *The Challenge to NATO: Global Security and the Atlantic Alliance* (University of Nebraska Press, 2021) pp.281–288.

730 'Emmanuel Macron warns Europe: NATO is becoming brain-dead' *The Economist* (7th November 2019).

731 Foer. *Supra* note 709. pp.228–229.

732 Reid. *Supra* note 632. p.302.

733 Bosse, Giselle. 'Values, rights, and changing interests: The EU's response to the war against Ukraine and the responsibility to protect Europeans' Contemporary Security Policy (Vol.43, No.3, 2022) pp.531–532.

734 Allin and Jones. *Supra* note 715. p.218.

735 William H McRaven, Peter Orszag and Theodore Bunzel, 'Made in the Alliance How to Shore up the Foundations of Transatlantic Solidarity' *Foreign Affairs* (20 April 2022).

736 Harding. *Supra* note 686. p.7.

737 Reid. *Supra* note 632. p.307.

of them remained under Ukrainian control.[738] However, at the time of writing in March 2024, the war in Ukraine continues, with the war evolving to set battles that favour Russia's advantage in manpower.[739] Russia has been forced to downgrade its goals to focus on the Donbas region and Ukraine has retaken large amounts of territory but its counteroffensive has stalled and as Moscow adapts its tactics and resources, Kyiv risks defeat.[740]

While peace talks were initially held in Belarus at the war's outset, Ukraine showed a willingness to accept neutrality and to abandon its goals of NATO membership (though it refused to accept the loss of land seized by Russia in 2022) while Russia was willing to compromise on 'denazification' and Ukrainian accession to the EU.[741] However, peace negotiations soon broke down, not helped by Russia's decision to send Culture Minister Vladimir Medinsky (a relatively minor official but a noted Russian ultranationalist) as its chief negotiator which seemed like a calculated insult to Ukraine.[742] Further peace talks were held in Istanbul in March 2023, where Ukrainian concessions on neutrality and NATO membership were rejected by Moscow which demanded unconditional surrender.[743] Such concessions by Kyiv were soon withdrawn as Ukrainian battlefield success combined with increased aid from Western states hardened Kyiv's resolve.[744] Likewise, Ukraine drove Russian forces from the Kyiv suburb of Bucha and found severe Russian atrocities, which further increased Zelensky's unwillingness to offer concessions.[745] The discovery of such atrocities ended the Istanbul peace negotiations, with Ukraine feeling its battlefield successes were its best hope for independence from Russia.[746]

### 7.4 *The Impact of the Russia-Ukraine War*

A key factor relating to the invasion is Putin's rejection of Ukraine as a sovereign nation. To Putin, Ukraine was not a real nation and its very existence posed a threat to Russia.[747] This can be seen in his 2021 essay, *On the Historical Unity*

---

738 Sauer, Pjotr and Harding, Luke. 'Putin annexes four regions of Ukraine in major escalation of Russia's war' *The Guardian* (30 September 2022.).

739 Trofimov. *Supra* note 631. p.277.

740 Ryan, Mick. 'Russia's Adaptation Advantage' Foreign *Affairs* (5 February 2024).

741 Ramani. *Supra* note 665. p.147.

742 Matthews. *Supra* note 638. p.276.

743 Trofimov. *Supra* note 631. p.151.

744 Matthews. *Supra* note 638. pp.276–277.

745 Trofimov, Yaroslav. 'Did Ukraine Miss an Early Chance to Negotiate Peace with Russia?' *Wall Street Journal* (5 Jan 2024).

746 Plokhy. *Supra* note 629. p.172.

747 Harding. *Supra* note 686. p.19.

*of Russians and Ukrainians* where he asserts that Russians and Ukrainians are one people, rejecting the idea of Ukrainians as a separate people to Russians as having 'no historical basis – and could not have been any'.[748] Likewise, Putin blamed Ukraine's economic problems on its leaders who were attempting to rewrite history and deny Ukraine's past while colluding with the West to use Ukraine against Russia,[749] while the 'true sovereignty of Ukraine is possible only in partnership with Russia'.[750] In short, Putin's essay was an outright denial of Ukraine's sovereign identity[751] and amounted to a 'historical, political and security predicate for invading [Ukraine]'.[752] Under such an interpretation, Ukraine was not seen as a sovereign nation and therefore outside the protection of international law's strong support for state sovereignty. Rather, Russia's invasion of such a sub-sovereign state would not be an act of aggression but one of national restoration like the unification of East and West Germany.[753]

Russia did not declare its 2022 invasion of Ukraine as a war, but rather as a 'special military operation',[754] to such an extent that Russia bans referring to Russia's actions as a war or invasion.[755] Nonetheless, such semantics have no relevance in international law and Russia's invasion of Ukraine remains an unambiguous case of inter-state of force.[756] The conflict between Russia and Ukraine is a notable one, with the flagrant invasion in 2022 being especially shocking to the world, given the last time one sovereign country had tried to fully conquer another was the Iraqi invasion of Kuwait in 1990.[757] While (for

748 Putin, Vladimir. 'On the Historical Unity of Russians and Ukrainians' (12 July 2021) http://en.kremlin.ru/events/president/news/66181 Accessed 8th December 2023.

749 Ibid.

750 Ibid.

751 Puri. *Supra* note 639. p.2.

752 Rumer, Eugene and Weiss, Andrew. 'Ukraine: Putin's Unfinished Business' *Carnegie Endowment for Peace* (12 November 2021) https://carnegieendowment.org/2021/11/12/ukraine-putin-s-unfinished-business-pub-85771 Accessed 8th December 2023.

753 Harding. *Supra* note 686. p.26.

754 Putin, Vladimir. *Annex to the Letter Dated 24 February 2022 from the Permanent Representative of the Russian Federation to the United Nations Addressed to the Secretary-General: Address by the President of the Russian Federation* UN Doc S/2022/154 (24 February 2022) p.6.

755 See *Human Rights Watch*. 'World Report 2023: Russia' https://www.hrw.org/world-report/2023/country-chapters/russian-federation Accessed 20th January 2024 and *Amnesty International* 'Russia: Kremlin's ruthless crackdown stifles independent journalism and anti-war movement' (10 March 2022) https://www.amnesty.org/en/latest/news/2022/03/russia-kremlins-ruthless-crackdown-stifles-independent-journalism-and-anti-war-movement/ Accessed 20th January 2024.

756 Hoffman. *Supra* note 677. p.208.

757 Fazal, Tanisha. 'The Return of Conquest? Why the Future of Global Order Hinges on Ukraine' *Foreign Affairs* (6 April 2022).

example) the US had engaged in invasions and occupations of sovereign states such as Afghanistan and Iraq, it had not sought to annex them.[758] Russia's actions are especially notable, given that Russia's breach of international law is so blatant. Previously, Russia sought to mask its military force in its 'near abroad' in ways that were 'at least on prima facie acceptable grounds in international law' whereas Russia's 2022 invasion of Ukraine is notable for committing every act defined as aggression in the UN General Assembly resolution 3314.[759]

Immediately following the invasion, a meeting of the UN Security Council saw a draft resolution proposed by dozens of states from across the world that condemned Russia's aggression against Ukraine as a breach of Article 2(4) and demanded an immediate Russian withdrawal.[760] The draft resolution had extensive support on the Security Council and showed Russia's isolation, with Albania condemning Russia as '[staining] the Charter of the United Nations with innocent blood' and 'burying the Charter under the rubble of destruction in Kyiv,'[761] with Mexico invoking its own experiences with colonialism to condemn the invasion.[762] Brazil supported the resolution but interestingly, refused to call Russia's actions an invasion (adopting Russia's term of a 'military operation' instead).[763] The draft resolution was supported by eleven members of the UN Security Council with Global South states like Kenya and Gabon voting alongside Global North members while India and the United Arab Emirates abstained, citing the need for dialogue and de-escalation.[764] Likewise, China abstained, stating its support for territorial integrity but criticising NATO and the need to address Russia's 'legitimate security concerns.'[765] Russia vetoed the resolution, but stood alone in its voting, demonstrating its isolation. The deadlock within the Security Council saw a resolution being passed to send the issue to the United Nations General Assembly[766] (again, with Russia voting against while India, China and the United Arab Emirates abstaining)[767] under the Uniting for Peace resolution[768] with the General Assembly's president invoking

758 Harding. *Supra* note 686. p.152.
759 Hoffman. *Supra* note 677. pp.225–226.
760 UN Security Council. *Draft Resolution* UN Doc S/2022/155 (25 February 2022).
761 UN Security Council. *8979th Meeting*. UN Doc S/PV.8979 (25 February 2022). p.4.
762 Ibid. p.5.
763 Ibid. pp.5–6.
764 Ibid. pp.6–11.
765 Ibid. pp.11–12.
766 UN Security Council. *Resolution 2623* UN Doc S/RES/2623 (27 February 2022).
767 UN Security Council. *8980th Meeting*. UN Doc S/PV.8980 (27 February 2022) p.2.
768 See *Supra* note 118.

the memory of the League of Nation's failure to prevent war that exposed its impotence.[769] The resulting General Assembly debate was illuminating, with Russia's actions being condemned across the globe and even states normally aligned with Russia like China stating their intention to abstain.[770] The resulting resolution saw 141 states voting to condemn Russia's invasions while just five states (Russia, Eritrea, Belarus, Syria and North Korea) opposed the resolution, though thirty five states abstained.[771] A notable number of these abstentions were Global South states, although many other Global South states voted for the resolution. However, it is notable that of those African states which voted for the resolution, few mentioned solidarity with Ukraine and their condemnation was more focused on the war's impact on their own interests, while Russia retains its ability to do business with the Global South.[772] Indeed, it was only the closure of Ukrainian ports by Russia which threatened food security among neutral states in the Global South (especially African states) that led to Russia agreeing to the resumption of Ukrainian food exports from Odessa.[773] However, Russia's actions have been condemned by numerous international, regional and academic organisations as well as states, demonstrating a striking example of widespread condemnation which is 'almost universal' in a way that not even the 2003 invasion of Iraq was.[774]

### 7.5 *Humanitarian Intervention and the Russia-Ukraine War*

The 2022 Ukraine invasion is a highly notable one, marking one of the few wars since World War II where there is a clear aggressor and victim.[775] Nonetheless, Putin still felt the need to justify its actions under international law, advancing several legal justifications for its invasion, though all of these are, at best, dubious.[776] Key in this was that Russia was exercising its right to self-defence under Article 51 of the UN Charter, both individually and collectively with the

769 UN General Assembly. *Eleventh Emergency Special Session* UN Doc. A/ES-11/PV.1 (28 February 2022). p.3.

770 UN General Assembly. *Eleventh Emergency Special Session* UN Doc. A/ES-11/PV.5 (2 March 2022). p.16.

771 UN General Assembly. *Eleventh Emergency Special Session* UN Doc. A/ES-11/PV.5 (2 March 2022). pp.14–15.

772 Ramani. *Supra* note 665. pp.344–366.

773 Trofimov. *Supra* note 631. p.242.

774 Corten, Olivier and Koutroulis, Vaois. 'The 2022 Russia intervention in Ukraine: What is its impact on the interpretation of *jus contra bellum*' *Leiden Journal of International Law* (Vol.36, 2023) pp.998–1000.

775 Plokhy. *Supra* note 629. p.294.

776 See Green, James, Henderson, Christian and Ruys, Tom. 'Russia's Attack on Ukraine and the Jus Ad Bellum' *Journal on the Use of Force and International Law* (Vol.9, No.1, 2022) and

Donetsk and Luhansk People's Republics.[777] Such self-defence claims were initially invoked by Putin in his 24 February 2022 speech, with the speech's transcript being attached to Russia's notification to the UN Secretary-General, with Russia's Permanent Representative to the UN invoking self-defence as the sole justification.[778] Russia also invoked self-defence in its submissions to the ICJ.[779]

However, another justification advanced by Putin and the one most relevant to this book was that Russia was intervening to 'protect people who, for eight years now, have been facing humiliation and genocide perpetuated by the Kiev regime' and end the 'genocide of millions'.[780] This need to protect people within Ukraine's borders from Kyiv had been advanced by Putin to justify the invasion of Crimea,[781] while claims of Kyiv committing genocide in the Donbas were made by Putin when recognizing the Donetsk and Luhansk People's Republics,[782] and were then repeated by Russia's Foreign Minister.[783] Such allegations had echoes with the claims of unilateral humanitarian intervention seen throughout history as researched in this book. Indeed, Moscow has a long tradition of using force to defend those it deems under its protection, from Tsarist Russia through the USSR to contemporary Russia.[784]

---

Moran, Cian. 'The Tribute That Vice Pays to Virtue: An Analysis of Russia's Justifications for the Invasion of Ukraine Under International Law' *Defence Forces Review* (Vol.19, 2022).

777 Putin, Vladimir. *Annex to the Letter Dated 24 February 2022 from the Permanent Representative of the Russian Federation to the United Nations Addressed to the Secretary-General: Address by the President of the Russian Federation* UN Doc S/2022/154 (24 February 2022) p.6.

778 Permanent Representative of the Russian Federation. *Letter dated 24 February 2022 from the Permanent Representative of the Russian Federation to the United Nations addressed to the Secretary-General.* UN Doc S/2022/154 (24 February 2022) p.1.

779 International Court of Justice. *Allegations of Genocide under the Convention on the Prevention and Punishment of the Crime of Genocide (Ukraine v. Russian Federation), (Document (with annexes) from the Russian Federation setting out its position regarding the alleged 'lack of jurisdiction' of the Court in the case)* (7 March 2022) p.4.

780 Putin, Vladimir. *Annex to the Letter Dated 24 February 2022 from the Permanent Representative of the Russian Federation to the United Nations Addressed to the Secretary-General: Address by the President of the Russian Federation* UN Doc S/2022/154 (24 February 2022) pp.5–6.

781 Putin, Vladimir. 'Address by the President of the Russian Federation' (14 March 2014) http://en.kremlin.ru/events/president/news/20603 Accessed 15th February 2024.

782 Putin. *Supra* note 659.

783 'Kiev regime controlled by West, neo-Nazis, Lavrov says' *TASS Russian News Agency.* (5 February 2022).

784 See Moran, Cian. 'Congratulations, you are Being Liberated. Please do not Resist' Russia's Wars and the Protection of Nationals under International Law' *Nordic Journal of International Law* (Vol.92, No.4, 2023) p.558.

This became a particular issue when Russia extended this to 'compatriots abroad' (ethnic Russians living outside Russia),[785] most notably in Georgia and Ukraine. The use of force to protect Russian citizens is dubious under international law, particularly when applied to those who are ethnic Russians rather than Russian citizens or when force is used to protect those who only became Russian citizens through Moscow's policy of passportisation.[786]

In the UNSC, Russia justified its 'special military operation' at the Security Council as not being a war against Ukraine but action taken to protect the residents of the Donbas along with 'denazification and demilitarisation'.[787] This was repeated in the UNGA where Russia reiterated its 'military operation' in support of the Donetsk and Luhansk People's Republics but also 'to protect people who have been subjected to abuse and genocide by the Kyiv regime for eight years'.[788] While Russia claimed its actions were taken to protect people from Kyiv, it must be reiterated that Russia based its justifications around self-defence, insisting its decision was taken under Article 51 of the UN Charter in defending both itself and the Donetsk and Luhansk People's Republics.[789] Likewise, at Russia's Victory Day commemorations on the 9 May 2022, Putin justified Russia's actions in Ukraine as a 'pre-emptive strike' against aggression, with Russia forced to act by NATO's preparation to attack in conjunction with Ukraine.[790] At his 2023 Victory Day speech, Putin cited the need to defend the Donbas' population but focused the justification for the 'special military operation' as a 'real war' being waged against Russia and the West's goal of destroying Russia.[791] A distinction can be drawn between Russia's political rhetoric (where in addition to self-defence, it invokes the need to defend people in Crimea and the Donbas from Kyiv) with its legal justifications when engaging with bodies such as the ICJ and UN, where it solely relies on self-defence.

Rather than formally declaring war, Putin is invoking humanitarian intervention to intimidate and control neighbouring states.[792] Russia has a

785 Milosevich, Mira. *Russia's Westpolitik and the European Union* (Washington DC, 2021) p.4.

786 See Moran. *Supra* note 784.

787 UN Security Council. *Official Records, 26th Year, 8979th Meeting.* UN Doc S/PV.8979 (25 February 2022). p.14.

788 UN General Assembly. *Eleventh Emergency Special Session* UN Doc. A/ES-11/PV.1 (28 February 2022). p.7–8.

789 Ibid.

790 Putin, Vladimir. 'Victory Parade on Red Square' (9 May 2022) en.kremlin.ru/events/president/transcripts/statements/68366 Accessed 20th January 2024.

791 Putin, Vladimir. 'Victory Parade on Red Square' (9 May 2023) http://en.kremlin.ru/events/president/news/71104 Accessed 20th January 2024.

792 Cullen and Bobick. *Supra* note 653. p.409.

longstanding rejection of unilateral humanitarian intervention, citing it as an example of unacceptable force outside of the UN Security Council's jurisdiction.[793] Outright opposition to humanitarian intervention was not mentioned in Russia's 2008 Foreign Policy Concept but Russia reiterated its rejection of military action outside the UN Charter and Security Council, though Russia also claimed a right to act unilaterally to protect its national interests, but 'always on the basis of international law'.[794] In 2013, Russia's Foreign Policy Concept had expanded to reject military operations that undermine international law based on R2P.[795] By 2023, Russia's Foreign Policy Concept maintained opposition to any use of force outside the UN Charter (especially to 'bypass the prerogatives of the UN Security Council') but also highlighted the right to use force in self-defence under Article 51 of the UN Charter.[796] This reflects Russia's actions in Ukraine, given the importance Russia has placed on justifying its actions under self-defence in Article 51 of the UN Charter.

R2P was cited by Russia in 2014 to justify its actions in Crimea and the Donbas, utilising similar justifications used by the West for its operations in Yugoslavia, though Moscow avoids using the term 'humanitarian intervention' or 'R2P' and focuses on Article 51 of the UN Charter involving the right to self-defence.[797] Such claims are dubious, as at no point did Russia show Kyiv's inability to protect the Crimean or Donbas populations, seek UNSC authorisation or Kyiv's consent.[798] Russia traditionally insisted that only the UNSC has the right to authorise force to protect populations (which due to Russia's veto, ensures that such force can only take place with Russian consent) and opposes giving any right to the UN General Assembly to authorise intervention.[799] As

793 President of the Russian Federation. 'The Foreign Policy of the Russian Federation' (28 June 2000) https://nuke.fas.org/guide/russia/doctrine/econcept.htm Accessed 13th January 2024.

794 President of the Russian Federation. 'The Foreign Policy of the Russian Federation' (12 July 2008) https://russiaeu.ru/userfiles/file/foreign_policy_concept_english.pdf Accessed 13th January 2024.

795 President of the Russian Federation. 'Foreign Policy of the Russian Federation' (12 February 2013) https://beijing.mid.ru/en/countries/rossiya/kontseptsiya_vneshney_politiki_rossii/ Accessed 13th January 2024.

796 President of the Russian Federation. 'The Concept of the Foreign Policy of the Russian Federation' (31 March 2023) https://mid.ru/en/foreign_policy/fundamental_documents/1860586/ Accessed 13th January 2024.

797 See Dagi, Dogacan. 'The Russian Stand on the Responsibility to Protect: Does Strategic Culture Matter?' *Journal of Asian Security and International Affairs* (Vol.7, No.3, 2020) pp.381–382.

798 Baranovsky and Mateiko. *Supra* note 654. p.61.

799 Ibid. p.56.

such, while Russia nominally agreed with the idea of R2P against atrocities, it drew strong distinctions between what it sees as the original principles of R2P and the interventionist doctrine of R2P developed by the West.[800] However, Russia's concept of R2P was grounded not in protecting people but in protecting Russians, and even then, R2P was not a main aspect of Russia's stated justifications and Russian R2P focuses on its near abroad rather than any general principle.[801] At any rate, R2P is irrelevant in Ukraine as under R2P, it is Ukraine and not Russia which has the fundamental responsibility in protecting its citizens from atrocities.[802] Nor are such atrocities which might potentially justify humanitarian intervention forthcoming. While Ukrainian forces have committed war crimes, they are far less severe than those committed by Russia[803] The sheer extent of Russian war crimes from torture to rape to the forced transfer of children is notable[804] and despite Russia's claims that it was operating to protect Ukrainian civilians, its invasion has resulted in thousands of civilians being killed due to indiscriminate missile attacks and attacks on civilian infrastructure.[805] As of September 2023, the OCHCR has documented 27,149 civilian casualties, including 9,614 killed and a further 17,535 injured though the OCHCR highlights that the actual number is likely higher, while over six million have

800 Dagi, Dogacan. 'The Russian Stand on the Responsibility to Protect: Does Strategic Culture Matter?' *Journal of Asian Security and International Affairs* (Vol.7, No.3, 2020) p.382.

801 Baranovsky and Mateiko. *Supra* note 654. p.63.

802 Rudolph, James. 'How Putin Distorts R2P in Ukraine' *Open Canada* (7 March 2014) https://opencanada.org/how-putin-distorts-r2p-in-ukraine/ Accessed 13th December 2023.

803 Office of the United Nations High Commissioner for Human Rights. *Report on the Human Rights Situation in Ukraine 1 February-31 July 2023* (4 October 2023) https://ukraine.un.org/sites/default/files/2023-10/23-10-04%20OHCHR%2036th%20periodic%20report.pdf Accessed 12th December 2023 p.44 and Independent International Commission of Inquiry on Ukraine. *Report of the Independent International Commission of Inquiry on Ukraine* UN Doc A/HRC/52/62 (15 March 2023) pp.6–17.

804 See Independent International Commission of Inquiry on Ukraine. *Report of the Independent International Commission of Inquiry on Ukraine* UN Doc A/HRC/52/62 (15 March 2023) p.16, Independent International Commission of Inquiry on Ukraine. *Report of the Independent International Commission of Inquiry on Ukraine* UN Doc A/78/540 (19 October 2023) pp.6–15. Amnesty International. *He's Not Coming Back: War Crimes in Northwest Areas of Kyiv Oblast* (London, 2022) p.5 and Human Rights Watch. 'Ukraine: Apparent War Crimes in Russia-Controlled Areas' *Human Rights Watch* (3 April 2022) https://www.hrw.org/news/2022/04/03/ukraine-apparent-war-crimes-russia-controlled-areas Accessed 12th December 2023.

805 Office of the United Nations High Commissioner for Human Rights. *Report on the Human Rights Situation in Ukraine 1 February-31 July 2023* (4 October 2023) https://ukraine.un.org/sites/default/files/2023-10/23-10-04%20OHCHR%2036th%20periodic%20report.pdf Accessed 4th December 2023 p.34.

fled Ukraine and over five million are internally displaced within Ukraine.[806] If Russia's goal was genuinely to protect people within Ukraine from oppression, then it has failed and instead committed human rights abuses while creating extensive misery for Ukrainians.

Regarding Russia's claims of genocide being committed by Kyiv, there is a lack of evidence. While violence between ethnic Ukrainians and Russians was feared after Ukrainian independence, Russians in Ukraine felt far more secure than other Russians in Russia's 'near abroad' and were an integrated part of the Ukrainian state.[807] Upon independence, Ukraine adopted a purposefully tolerant treatment of its ethnic Russian citizens (the largest outside Russia) who reciprocated by supporting it, ensuring the collapse of the USSR was peaceful while reducing any pressure from the Yeltsin administration to intervene on their behalf.[808] Responding to Russia's allegations to genocide in 2022, Ukraine took a case to the ICJ, arguing that Russia's false accusations of genocide were being used as a justification for Ukraine's invasion[809] and citing several human rights reports for the region which made no mention of Ukraine committing genocide.[810] Ukraine's efforts to invoke the ICJ marked an unprecedented case in ICJ litigation where a state sought ICJ confirmation that it had *not* breached international law.[811] However, Russia's response in the ICJ did not justify its actions under the prevention of genocide but 'based on the United Nations Charter, its Article 51 and customary international law' and emphasised that it justified its actions under Article 51 to the UN Secretary-General and Security Council.[812] Russia insisted it did not invoke genocide under the UN Convention Against Genocide, which is not equivalent to 'a reference' to genocide under customary

806 Independent International Commission of Inquiry on Ukraine. *Report of the Independent International Commission of Inquiry on Ukraine* UN Doc A/78/540 (19 October 2023) p.4.

807 Reid. *Supra* note 632. p.222.

808 Plokhy. *Supra* note 629 pp.32–33.

809 International Court of Justice. *Allegations of Genocide under the Convention on the Prevention and Punishment of the Crime of Genocide (Ukraine v. Russian Federation), Application Instituting Proceedings* (27 February 2022) p.5.

810 International Court of Justice. *Allegations of Genocide under the Convention on the Prevention and Punishment of the Crime of Genocide (Ukraine v. Russian Federation), Application Instituting Proceedings*) (27 February 2022) p.12.

811 Ramsden, Michael. 'Strategic Litigation in Wartime: Judging the Russian Invasion of Ukraine through the Genocide Convention' *Vanderbilt Journal of Transnational Law* (Vol.56, 2023) p.187.

812 International Court of Justice. *Allegations of Genocide under the Convention on the Prevention and Punishment of the Crime of Genocide (Ukraine v. Russian Federation), (Document (with annexes) from the Russian Federation setting out its position regarding the alleged 'lack of jurisdiction' of the Court in the case)* (7 March 2022) p.4.

international or domestic law, that 'provides a general humanitarian environment along with other factors and considerations'.[813] It expanded on this, claiming that the meaning of the term 'genocide' can vary and that there is no singular definition of the term,[814] while reiterating its claims that Russia's actions were justified under Article 51 of the UN Charter and customary international law.[815] Likewise, Russia insisted that 'the Genocide Convention was not referred to as a legal basis for the special military operation' and that genocide was just one factor listed, with Russia's legal justification being based on Article 51 of the UN Charter.[816] Russia's reliance on self-defence as a justification for its actions in Ukraine is notable, but even more important was its reluctance to stand by its initial claims of Kyiv committing genocide. Rather, Russia made such claims parenthetical to its main claims of self-defence, and its agents at the ICJ sought to minimise such statements by drawing a distinction between the use of genocide as 'rhetoric' and using it to invoke the Genocide Convention.[817] As such, Russia sought to use the term genocide as hyperbole to describe the extent of Ukraine's attacks necessitating Russian self-defence.[818] Evidently, Russia sought to utilise the inherent sense of revulsion that the term 'genocide' generates to mitigate criticism of its invasion. However, when confronted with the reality that no such genocide was taking place, Russia was forced to disregard its previous references to genocide and base its legal justification for the invasion on self-defence.

At any rate, in its provisional measures, the ICJ noted that it was doubtful that the Genocide Convention created a right of unilateral humanitarian intervention, even against genocide, as well as that 'Ukraine has a plausible right not to be subjected to military operations by the Russian Federation for the purpose of preventing and punishing an alleged genocide in the territory of

---

813 Ibid. p.6.

814 International Court of Justice. *Allegations of Genocide under the Convention on the Prevention and Punishment of the Crime of Genocide (Ukraine v. Russian Federation), (Preliminary objections of the Russian Federation)* (3 October 2022) p.47.

815 Ibid. pp.27–28 and 49.

816 International Court of Justice. *Allegations of Genocide under the Convention on the Prevention and Punishment of the Crime of Genocide (Ukraine v. Russian Federation), Verbatim Record* CR *2023/17*, pp.34–36.

817 International Court of Justice. *Allegations of Genocide under the Convention on the Prevention and Punishment of the Crime of Genocide (Ukraine v. Russian Federation), Verbatim Record* CR *2023/13*, p.52.

818 Corten, Olivier and Koutroulis, Vaois. 'The 2022 Russia intervention in Ukraine: What is its impact on the interpretation of *jus contra bellum' Leiden Journal of International Law* (Vol.36, 2023) p.1003.

Ukraine'.[819] A joint statement was released by a range of scholars who specialise in genocide and the Holocaust who condemned Russia for weaponising the term genocide, and that such abuse of the term was 'factually wrong, morally repugnant and deeply offensive'.[820] Likewise, a professor of Holocaust Studies rejected the claim that there was any ethnic cleansing (let alone genocide) being conducted against ethnic Russians or Russian citizens in Ukraine.[821] Ukraine's Rada has itself passed a resolution declaring Russia's actions in Ukraine as a genocide, with the same allegation being made by Biden and other Western leaders and parliaments.[822] While such a claim has academic supporters,[823] other experts reject the claim that the actions of either Ukraine or Russia meet the threshold for genocide.[824]

It has been claimed that when Russia invades sovereign states and uses humanitarian intervention as a justification, 'mockery has come full circle'.[825] However, as shown in this book, there have been numerous examples of states abusing humanitarian intervention to justify their own predations. While Russia justifies its actions under self-defence in the UN Charter, its actions are far more reminiscent of Europe's Great Powers in the nineteenth century when the rules governing the use of force were far more expansive.[826] Indeed, Russia's attempts to justify its actions under international law are notable given its arguments have been so widely rejected by states as to confirm the general *opinio juris* against the use of force under international law.[827] Comparisons of Russia's invasion to World War I or World War II, are flawed: Putin is not Hitler and neither is Europe divided into binary alliances, rather Russia is isolated

819 International Court of Justice. *Allegations of Genocide under the Convention on the Prevention and Punishment of the Crime of Genocide (Ukraine v. Russian Federation)*, (Order of 16 March 2022) p.18.

820 Tabarovsky, Izabellea and Finkel, Eugene. 'Statement on the War in Ukraine by Scholars of Genocide, Nazism and World War II' *Jewish Journal* (27 February 2022).

821 Treisman, Rachel. 'Putin's Claim of Fighting against Ukraine 'neo-Nazis' Distorts History, scholars say' *National Public Radio* (1 March 2022).

822 Schabas, William. 'Genocide and Ukraine: Do Words Mean What We Choose them to Mean?' *Journal of International Criminal Justice* (Vol.20, Iss.4, 2022) pp.845–847.

823 See Azarov, Denys, Koval, Dmytro, Nuridshanian, Gaiane and Venher, Volodymyr. 'Understanding Russia's Actions in Ukraine as the Crime of Genocide' *Journal of International Criminal Justice* (Vol.21, Iss.2, 2023) pp.233–264.

824 Schabas, William. 'Genocide and Ukraine: Do Words Mean What We Choose them to Mean?' *Journal of International Criminal Justice* (Vol.20, Iss.4, 2022) pp.856–857.

825 Cullen and Bobick. *Supra* note 653. p.409.

826 Hoffman. *Supra* note 677. p.226.

827 Corten, Olivier and Koutroulis, Vaois. 'The 2022 Russia intervention in Ukraine: What is its impact on the interpretation of *jus contra bellum' Leiden Journal of International Law* (Vol.36, 2023) p.1021.

and its actions are comparable to the Russian Empire's opportunistic actions against the Ottoman Empire in the nineteenth century.[828] This makes the starting point of this book in the nineteenth century even more apt given that the contemporary world is, as in the nineteenth century, one which is 'multipolar and unpredictable'.[829]

828 Oltermann, Philip. 'Don't compare Ukraine invasion to first world war, says 'Sleepwalkers' historian' *The Guardian* (26 June 2022).

829 Ibid.

CHAPTER 6

# Conclusion: The Existence of Humanitarian Intervention under Customary International Law

Based on the research for this book, it is evident that humanitarian intervention has a long pedigree in international law and state practice. Although examples of humanitarian intervention are relatively uncommon,[1] they nonetheless provide a chronological and coherent structure to analyse how it has developed. Furthermore, they demonstrate the conditions under which a humanitarian intervention may be tolerated, even if not explicitly supported. Namely, when the intervention is done in response to systematic and egregious human rights abuses, where the intervention does not threaten regional or global stability, where the intervention is conducted against isolated regimes and especially when the intervention is multilateral in nature.

Nonetheless, the conclusion to draw from the above is that humanitarian intervention no longer exists as a right under international law. Given the invocation of humanitarian intervention in the nineteenth century, there is a strong argument to be made that it had a validity in international law at that time.[2] The fact global hegemons were the main arbiters for authorising force has parallels with today (given the P5's final say on the UNSC's ability to do the same). However, despite the actions of states such as India and Tanzania, modern humanitarian intervention seems most associated with Western values.[3] The founding of the UN nonetheless marked a new era for international law, with sovereign equality among its members altering the validity of previous

1 Heinze argues there are likely just two examples at the time of his writing in 2009: the intervention in East Pakistan and NATO's intervention in Kosovo. (See Heinze, Eric. A. *Waging Humanitarian War: The Ethics, Law, and Politics of Humanitarian Intervention* (New York, 2009) p.77).

2 See Chapter 4. *Supra* note 1. It must be noted that this took place at a time when international law was Euro-centric and focussed on a core of powerful European states rather than on any global consensus. See Oppenheim, Lassa *International Law: A Treatise, Vol. 1-Peace* (London, 1905) pp.48–50. Indeed, Oppenheim claims that while non-Christian nations could be members of the Family of Nations, only the Ottoman Empire and Japan could clearly be deemed members at the time. (Ibid. p.148).

3 Thompson, Andrew. 'Humanitarian interventions, past and present' in Klose, Fabian. (Ed.) *The Emergence of Humanitarian Intervention: Ideas and Practice from the Nineteenth Century to the Present* (Cambridge, 2018) p.337.

 | DOI:10.1163/9789004696396_007

norms relating to intervention.[4] The UN system also emphasised state sovereignty, which restrains intervention, while most states and academics favour a strict interpretation of Article 2(4) of the UN Charter.[5] Furthermore, the inconsistent state practice demonstrates a lack of the requisite practice of states and *opinio juris* for humanitarian intervention to be regarded as a right under customary international law.[6] Even those states that do engage in military operations to protect civilians rarely justify doing so on any basis of humanitarian intervention.[7]

Sovereignty is not a cloak for a state to engage in human rights abuse. While states strive to maintain their sovereignty, contemporary state sovereignty has evolved from that understood prior to 1945, with a dual responsibility to respect other states' sovereignty while protecting the rights of its own citizens.[8] Sovereignty is doubtless a critical aspect of contemporary international law.[9] Although sovereign equality among member states is subordinate to political realities (such as the P5 being the only states with a UNSC veto), sovereignty is widely seen as vital and the need to protect it is frequently invoked against the use of force for humanitarian purposes.[10]

---

4 This was made especially important by decolonization leading to the expansion of the UN to include Afro-Asian states, ensuring a UN culture that was anti-imperialist. (See MacQueen, Norrie. 'Cold War peacekeeping versus humanitarian intervention' in Klose, Fabian. (Ed.) *The Emergence of Humanitarian Intervention: Ideas and Practice from the Nineteenth Century to the Present* (Cambridge, 2018) p.247).

5 Wolf, Daniel. 'Humanitarian Intervention' *Michigan Yearbook of International Studies* (Vol.9, 1988) p.356.

6 International Court of Justice. *Case Concerning the Continental Shelf Judgement* (*Libyan Arab Jamahiriya/Malta*) ICJ Reports 13 (Judgement of 3 June 1985) Para.27.

7 Hoffman, Tamás. 'War or peace? – International legal issues concerning the use of force in the Russia–Ukraine conflict' *Hungarian Journal of Legal Studies* (Vol.63, No.3, 2022) p.217.

8 International Commission on Intervention and State Sovereignty. *The Responsibility to Protect* (Ottawa, 2001) Paras.1.33–1.35.

9 This is evident in Article 2(1) of the UN Charter that highlights the 'sovereign equality' of its members. This was then reaffirmed by the General Assembly's *Friendly Relations Declaration* (UN General Assembly. *Declaration on Principles of International Law Concerning Friendly Relations and Cooperation Among States in Accordance with the Charter of the United Nations.* UN Doc. A/Res/25/2625 (24 October 1970) Annex Preamble).

10 This could be seen in the OAU, whose chairperson notes that its members see sovereignty as a bastion against 'the rules of an unequal world' (UN General Assembly Press Release. *Implications of International Response to Events in Rwanda, Kosovo examined by Secretary-General, in Address to General Assembly.* Press Release GA/9595 (20 September 1999)) while Global South states see it as vital to protect themselves from external coercion (Abiew, Francis Kofi. *The Evolution of the Doctrine and Practice of Humanitarian Intervention* (The Hague, 1999) p.66). See also Thompson, Andrew. 'Humanitarian interventions, past and

This does not mean states are free to commit atrocities against their own citizens[11] and the UNSC adoption of human rights considerations into its decision-making has changed the meaning of sovereignty.[12] Above all, the UNSC has the authority to intervene against member states, but in practice, this is always subject to political interests,[13] particularly among the P5 that comprise the states most capable of force projection.[14] The reality is that a rational response by the P5 means that they will not risk their military personnel in areas where they lack national interests.[15] The role of the UNSC is still important, given few states support humanitarian intervention without UNSC approval.[16] All of the post-UN Charter humanitarian interventions analysed in this book were not condemned by the UNSC, either due to the support of a P5 state (as happened in the cases of Cambodia and East Pakistan) or due to a more widespread acceptance as evident in Iraq and Kosovo. There is arguably a moral difference between unauthorised interventions that have wide international support, and interventions that are widely condemned but avoid censure solely due a P5 veto. Nonetheless, the twentieth century interventions discussed in Chapters 4 and 5 did not receive a UNSC mandate (except for Operation Turquoise, which is an unconvincing example). Such deadlock is a regrettable but foreseeable by-product of the UNSC and its veto system, ensuring humanitarian intervention lacks the necessary support to be accepted under customary international law. Nonetheless, R2P and the intervention in Libya shows that sovereign authority is not a total shield for human rights abuses,[17] while the response to Russia's justifications for its invasion of

present' in Klose, Fabian. (Ed.) *The Emergence of Humanitarian Intervention: Ideas and Practice from the Nineteenth Century to the Present* (Cambridge, 2018) p.331.

11 This is notable with the normally non-interventionist Arab League supporting intervention against Gaddaffi in 2011 or the AU's Constitutive Act permitting its members to intervene against genocide, war-crimes, and crimes against humanity (Hehir, Aidan. *The Responsibility to Protect* (Basingstoke, 2012) pp.200–204).

12 Walling, Carrie Booth. *All Necessary Measures: The UN and Humanitarian Intervention* (Philadelphia, 2013) p.243.

13 Consequently, the international community has repeatedly failed to respond to mass-killings since World War II. See Wolf. *Supra* note 5 p.333.

14 Although strong nations have the greatest means to conduct rescue missions, they are usually disinclined to do so while weaker nations often support peace-support operations but lack the resources to act (Lu, Catherine. 'Humanitarian Intervention: Moral Ambition and Political Constraints' *International Journal* (Vol.62, Issue 4, Fall 2007) p.946).

15 MacQueen, Norrie. *Humanitarian Intervention and the United Nations* (Edinburgh, 2011) pp.122–123.

16 Wheeler, Nicholas. *Saving Strangers: Humanitarian Intervention in International Society* (Oxford, 2010) p.286.

17 Walling. *Supra* note 12. p.268.

Ukraine show that bad faith efforts to instrumentalise international law will be rejected.

Where the UNSC is unable to agree on supporting or opposing a humanitarian intervention, the UNGA would be a useful forum for determining international support.[18] Although its resolutions are not binding, an endorsement by the UNGA would bolster the intervention's legitimacy as a demonstration of support from the international community. Such an action potentially violates the UN Charter, the wording of which permits the use of force only in self-defence or under the auspices of the UNSC.[19] The above examples show humanitarian intervention's status under customary international law is too uncertain to challenge the prohibition on the use of force decisively. As White points out, the UNSC makes such decisions on behalf of the UN and questions regarding which body authorises UN action is an internal matter for the UN rather than detracting from the UN's legitimacy to make such interventions.[20] However, Uniting for Peace could be revived to authorise intervention outside of the UNSC.[21] Since its adoption, Uniting For Peace has been used several times, and it has even been invoked to authorise a peacekeeping force during the 1956 Suez crisis (although with the host state's consent and thus avoided encroaching on the coercive power of the UNSC).[22] Uniting for Peace offers a tool for action when the UNSC is deadlocked, with the UNGA's role as the forum of states giving it the capacity to offer legitimacy for humanitarian interventions, even without UNSC authorisation. Interventions such as Operation Allied Force could have been placed before the UNSC and if vetoed, brought before the UNGA, which would have given NATO's intervention a stronger legal basis.[23] However, Uniting for Peace was enacted during the Cold War's expansion of UNGA power, while the end of the Cold War saw an expansion of the UNSC's

18 The Security Council's role in maintaining international peace and security is primary, not exclusive (International Court of Justice *Certain Expenses Case.* ICJ Report 155. (Advisory Opinion of 20 July 1962). p.163). Furthermore, it is arguable that the General Assembly has a subsidiary role in enforcing international peace and security (White, Nigel. 'The Legality of Bombing in the Name of Humanity' *Journal of Conflict and Security Law* (Vol.5, No.1 2000). p.38).

19 Heinze notes that in addition to a textual reading of the UN Charter prohibiting humanitarian interventions unauthorized by the UNSC, the legality question of Article 2(4) is largely settled in legal circles. Heinze. *Supra* note 1. p.80.

20 White. *Supra* note 18. p.39.

21 Tams, Christian. 'Prospects for Humanitarian Uses of Force.' in Cassese, Antonio (Ed.) *Realizing Utopia: The Future of International Law.* (Oxford, 2012) p.364.

22 Hossain, Kamrul. 'Complementary Role of the United Nations General Assembly in Peace Management' in *USAK Yearbook of International Politics and Law* (Vol.2, 2009) pp.78–83.

23 White. *Supra* note 18. p.42.

competence that renders UNGA action unlikely to be utilised in the post-Cold War era.[24] Ultimately, UNGA resolutions have political significance but are not binding.[25] Consequently, the efficacy of invoking the Uniting for Peace mechanism should not be overstated[26] and its usefulness remains limited as evidenced by its invocation in the Russia-Ukraine War.

## 1 The Role of Public Opinion in Humanitarian Intervention

An important issue when considering the status of humanitarian intervention under customary international law is the role played by public opinion. States have long appreciated the importance of public opinion when considering resorting to force, with democracies and authoritarian regimes alike relying on it.[27]

In the nineteenth century, Britain's increasing democratisation meant it was forced to pay increased attention to public opinion, notably after the Crimean War when press coverage of military blunders forced reform.[28] Likewise, British public pressure influenced Westminster's response in both Greece and Bulgaria and even reactionary Russia was not immune.[29] At the same time, the impact of public opinion should not be overstated and it restricted the relevant governments' options rather than forcing certain actions. A good example was during the Bulgarian Crisis when public opposition to the Ottoman Empire prevented Disraeli from actively backing the Porte,[30] but neither did it force Britain to intervene unilaterally or alongside Russia. Likewise, the creation of an autonomous Greece within the Ottoman Empire satisfied both British

24 Tsagourias and White. *Supra* note 35. p.94.

25 Lebor, Adam. *Complicity with Evil: The United Nations in the Age of Modern Genocide* (Bury St Edmunds, 2006) pp.5–6.

26 Notably, when the General Assembly overwhelmingly voted for a cease-fire during the 1971 India-Pakistan war but was unable to enforce this when India did not comply (Pace, Eric. 'Indians deride U.N move, Pakistanis express doubt' *New York Times*. (9 December 1971)).

27 Western, Jon. 'Prudence or outrage? Public opinion and humanitarian intervention in historical and comparative perspective' in Klose, Fabian. (Ed.) *The Emergence of Humanitarian Intervention: Ideas and Practice from the Nineteenth Century to the Present* (Cambridge, 2018) p.166.

28 France, John. *Perilous Glory: The Rise of Western Military Power* (New Haven 2011) pp.232–233.

29 See Hinde, Wendy. *George Canning* (London, 1973) p.405.

30 Shaw, Stanford and Shaw, Ezel Kural. *History of the Ottoman Empire and Modern Turkey Volume 2* (Cambridge, 1977). p.183.

opposition to Ottoman atrocities while maintaining national strategic interests.[31] Nonetheless, public opinion played a decisive role in the humanitarian interventions of the nineteenth century.[32]

Public opinion was also influential in the interventions of the Cold War, particularly in the case of India, which was a democratic state and more susceptible to public pressure.[33] Public opinion was less important in authoritarian Tanzania and Vietnam, but as Tsarist Russia showed in the nineteenth century,[34] even repressive regimes are not insulated from the demands of their citizens. Western states feared risking their soldiers, especially after the UN mission in Somalia.[35] The impact of mass media on contemporary foreign policy (the 'CNN Effect')[36] is debatable. In none of the case studies in the 1990s was the mass media or public opinion a decisive factor in US policy[37] and extensive media coverage of the Rwandan genocide did not induce a Western response.[38] Western governments are accountable to their electorates and interventions for reasons outside of national security risk domestic political backlash, especially when their own troops are killed for little domestic gain. Despite the seeming hypocrisy whereby states prioritise their own peacekeepers over the lives of civilians (most evident in Belgium seeking UNAMIR's withdrawal after the attack on its peacekeepers),[39] such actions are not necessarily wrong or immoral. States' primary responsibilities are towards its own citizens, ensuring they have a valid reason to resist intervening, especially the large costs associated with intervention in both military and reconstruction terms.[40]

The prioritisation of a nation's peacekeepers is regrettable but understandable. Interventions in the 1990s primarily took place due to security concerns and even then, they were cautious, with air power being especially favoured,[41]

31 See Chapter 3, *Supra* note 75.

32 Heraclides, Alexis and Dialla, Ada. *Humanitarian Intervention in the long Nineteenth Century. Setting the precedent.* (Manchester, 2015) p.228.

33 Schanberg, Sydney. 'Pakistan Divided' *Foreign Affairs* (Vol.50, October 1971).

34 Heraclides and Dialla. *Supra* note 32. p.179.

35 Doyle, Michael and Sambanis, Nicholas. *Making War and Building Peace* (Princeton, 2006) p.284.

36 See Robinson, Piers. 'The CNN effect: can the news media drive foreign policy?' *Review of International Studies* (Vol. 25, No. 2, Apr. 1999), pp. 301–309.

37 DiPrizio, Robert. *Armed Humanitarians: US Interventions from Northern Iraq to Kosovo* (Baltimore, 2002) pp.157–159.

38 Wheeler. *Supra* note 16. p.165.

39 Dallaire, Roméo. *Shake Hands with the Devil: The Failure of Humanity in Rwanda* (London, 2004) p.144.

40 Hehir. *Supra* note 11. pp.140–141.

41 The success of air power in Operation Desert Storm led some in the first Bush administration to see air power as the key to future conflicts, with ground troops merely needed

as in Iraq and Kosovo. Humanitarian concerns may not force interventions but can provide a useful tool for governments to justify their deployment of troops. Nonetheless, neither will it unilaterally cause a state to risk its own troops for little political benefit.[42] While humanitarianism can be a factor, the interventions of the 1990s demonstrate that it will be, at best, a secondary consideration and subordinate to more pressing issues such as security. If we require humanitarian intervention to have a solely humanitarian motive, then humanitarian intervention has not and cannot ever exist.[43] Rather, it arose from a mixture of motives and intentions.[44] Mixed motives do not prevent humanitarian intervention from being valid. In domestic criminal law, few would argue that a person must have no self-interest if protecting another person from violence. The fact that they protected the other person is enough of a justification, and a similar approach could be taken in international law, where the key determinant would be the result and not the motive.[45] Nonetheless, ethical humanitarian motives must at least be 'explicit and prominent', even if they are not the sole or even main motive.[46]

## 2 The Risks Posed by Humanitarian Intervention

It can be argued that the existence of humanitarian intervention risks creating a moral hazard effect, with the prospect of such intervention leading marginalised groups to induce governmental brutality in the hope of securing outside help.[47] However, such claims of moral hazard against persons suffering crimes against humanity risks victim blaming and while the consequences of intervention should be analysed, accusations of moral hazard can be more a tool to defend the status quo.[48]

A more striking criticism of humanitarian intervention is its selectiveness. Although the lack of intervention between 1914 and 1990 has been described as

---

to finish off resistance from enemies who are already devastated by air power. (Hodges, Michael. *AK-47: The Story of the People's Gun* (London, 2007) p.171).

42 Heraclides and Dialla. *Supra* note 32. p.229.

43 Klose, Fabian. 'The Emergence of Humanitarian Intervention' in Klose, Fabian. (Ed.) *The Emergence of Humanitarian Intervention: Ideas and Practice from the Nineteenth Century to the Present* (Cambridge, 2018) p.13.

44 Ibid.

45 Wolf. *Supra* note 5pp.352–353.

46 Weiss, Thomas. *Humanitarian Intervention* (Cambridge, 2018) p.9.

47 Bellamy, Alex. *Global Politics and the Responsibility to Protect* (Abingdon, 2011) p.72.

48 Weiss. *Supra* note 46. p.121.

an 'intermezzo',[49] the lack of intervention to prevent crimes such as genocide undermine the status of humanitarian intervention under customary international law.[50] Even when humanitarianism is a factor, it will not force states to act against their own interests. Despite numerous atrocities across the world in the nineteenth and early twentieth centuries (notably ones conducted by Europe's Great Powers), few humanitarian interventions took place, most notably the lack of response to the Armenian genocide.[51] This continued over the twentieth century, with failure to intervene during the Holocaust making any legal (rather than moral) right of humanitarian intervention debatable.[52] In this way, examples of humanitarian interventions in the twentieth century 'can be count[ed] on our fingers, with digits to spare'.[53]

Although humanitarian interventions are rare and usually coincide with the interests of more powerful nations, they can still have humanitarian outcomes. Cold War interventions saved an admirable amount of people, but they all had a high measure of self-interest involved and rather than humanitarian intervention disciplining realpolitik, the opposite occurred.[54] The fact a state intervenes to stop an atrocity does not require it to intervene against all

49 Segesser, Daniel Marc. 'Humanitarian Intervention and the issue of state sovereignty in the discourse of legal experts between the 1830s and the First World War' in in Klose, Fabian. (Ed.) *The Emergence of Humanitarian Intervention: Ideas and Practice from the Nineteenth Century to the Present* (Cambridge, 2018) p.58.

50 Holzgrefe, J.L 'The Humanitarian Intervention Debate' in Holzgrefe, J.L and Keohane, Robert. *Humanitarian Intervention: Ethical, Legal and Political Dilemmas* (Cambridge, 2003) p.45.

51 During World War I, the Ottoman Empire feared its Armenian community was a potential fifth column and began driving Armenians from Eastern Anatolia (Quatert, Donald. *The Ottoman Empire 1700–1922* (Cambridge, 2000) pp.184–185). Although the official government policy was that this was a wartime evacuation and the Armenians were to be protected, elements within the Ottoman government ensured the evacuations became genocide, with huge numbers being slaughtered (Lewy, Guenter. *The Armenian Massacres in Ottoman Turkey* (Salt Lake City, 2005) p.240). So anaemic was the international response to the Armenian genocide that Hitler disregarded opposition to the Holocaust with the claim '[who] speaks today of the annihilation of the Armenian?' (Bazyler. Michael. 'Re-examining the Doctrine of Humanitarian Intervention in Light of the Atrocities in Kampuchea and Ethiopia' *Stanford Journal of International Law* (Vol.23, 1987) p.593).

52 Franck, Thomas and Rodley, Nigel. 'After Bangladesh: The Law of Humanitarian Intervention by Military Force' *American Journal of International Law* (Vol. 67, 1973) pp.278–279.

53 Donnelly, Jack. 'Human Rights, Humanitarian Crisis and humanitarian intervention' *International Journal* (Vol.48, Autumn 1993) p.622.

54 Lu. *Supra* note Lu. *Supra* note 14. p.946.

atrocities. Political, economic, and military considerations will all influence a state's ability to respond.

In a perfect world, human rights abuses would be met with humanitarian intervention when necessary, ensuring uniformity and consistency. However, such a world does not exist, and this should not discredit situations when an intervention has a primarily humanitarian benefit (if not motive). As Voltaire said, 'the best is the enemy of the good'[55] and an ideal of consistent intervention against atrocities should not detract from when a state ends egregious human rights abuses. The fact such interventions are selective does not render them illegitimate.[56] Even an organisation as globally minded as the UN can be just as selective and when dealing with threats to international peace and security, the UNSC has the discretion rather than the obligation to act. Likewise, the UNSC acts primarily on political calculations rather than legal principles[57] and the major problem in responding to humanitarian crises during the 1990s was not a lack of authority, but of political will. Even if the UNSC was mandated to intervene in cases of genocide and crimes against humanity, faced with having to intervene against their own interests, any member of the P5 could deny the conflict reached the threshold necessary for action.

Perhaps the greatest risk posed by normalising humanitarian intervention is that it will be used as a justification for aggression, which is a major reason for the Global South's opposition to humanitarian intervention.[58] It is also a common realist criticism, which can point to examples such as the Third Reich's invasion of Czechoslovakia for the risks associated with intervention.[59] Likewise, the USSR claimed its interventions in Afghanistan, Hungary and Czechoslovakia were all humanitarian.[60] Even opponents of humanitarian intervention acknowledge that there are situations when intervention might be desirable due to the extent of atrocities.[61] However, the fact a norm can be

55 Voltaire. *La Bégueule*' (Geneva, 1772) p.14.

56 The 2005 *World Summit Outcome Document* notes that collective action will occur on a case-by-case basis and incurs no obligation for states to intervene (UN General Assembly. *2005 World Summit Outcome*. UN Doc A/60/L.1 (24 October 2005). Para.139).

57 Hehir. *Supra* note 11. pp.124–125.

58 See *Supra* note 10. While President, of the Organisation of African Unity, Algeria's President Abdelaziz Bouteflika deemed sovereignty 'our final defence against the rules of an unjust world'. (See UN General Assembly 54th Session, 4th Plenary Meeting. UN Doc A/54/PV.4 (20 September 1999) p.14).

59 See Chapter 3, *Supra* note 30.

60 Bazyler. *Supra* note 51. p.585. Part of the argument was the advance of communism was so vital than any attempt to frustrate it was a denial of human rights (See Franck and Rodley. *Supra* note 52. p.286).

61 Bazyler. *Supra* note 51. p.592.

abused does not extinguish it. The right of self-defence is frequently misused to justify aggression, but this does not detract from its existence.[62] Indeed, when a state attempts to invoke an existing norm of international law to justify its actions, its attempts to rely on such a norm strengthens rather than weakens such a rule.[63] While a legalised norm of humanitarian intervention would offer an additional method for states to justify aggression, it is difficult to argue that in the absence of such intervention, a state would refrain from aggression. States can already justify illegal acts under the UN Charter (as the US and UK did in the 2003 invasion of Iraq) or self-defence. Wheeler therefore argues that humanitarian intervention requires clarification, with intervention being classified in a manner so narrow that the risk of abuse is slim.[64]

## 3 The Importance of Multilateralism

Although it is difficult to argue in favour of the legality of humanitarian intervention under the UN Charter,[65] a customary international law principle does not require constant use to remain in force.[66] Nonetheless, its continued existence would require some level of adherence, particularly given the lack of consensus in favour of humanitarian intervention.[67] As shown in Chapters 4 and 5, states engaging in interventions rely on more traditional justifications,

---

62 This was apparent in 1921 when it was noted that a state seeking war would not avoid declaring it merely due to international law (Anonymous. 'The League of Nations and the Laws of War' *British Yearbook of International Law* (Vol.1, 1920–1921) p.111.) This was re-iterated by Lufty who highlighted that an imperialist power-seeking aggression will do so, irrespective of existing international law. Lufty. *Supra* note 62. p.160.

63 International Court of Justice *Nicaragua v. United States of America* (Judgement of 27 June 1986) ICJ Reports 14. Para 186.

64 Wheeler, Nicholas. 'Legitimating Humanitarian Intervention: Principles and Procedures' *Melbourne Journal of International Law* (Vol.2, Issue 2, 2001) p.555.

65 This is highlighted by Dinstein who argues that only the Security Council has authority under the UN Charter to use force to ensure compliance with human rights. (See Dinstein, Yoram. *War Aggression and Self Defense* (Cambridge, 2017). pp.76).

66 Fonteyne, Jean-Pierre. 'The Customary International Law Doctrine of Humanitarian Intervention: its Current Validity under the UN Charter' *California Western International Law Journal* (Vol.4, 1973–1974) p.234.

67 Humanitarian intervention is opposed by Russia, China, and the Non-Aligned Movement while it has rarely been openly supported by states or invoked (See Gray, Christine. 'The Use of Force for Humanitarian Purposes' in White, Nigel and Henderson, Christine (Eds.) *Research Handbook on International Conflict and Security Law* (Cheltenham, 2013) p.229). This is the case even when stopping genocide or toppling repressive governments (Lu. *Supra* note 14. p.943).

particularly self-defence during the Cold War or the threat posed to international peace and security in the course of the 1990s. The ambiguous support given to such interventions is unlikely to demonstrate that humanitarian intervention's existence under customary international law survived the adoption of the UN Charter and Article 2(4) in particular. This makes it 'difficult if not impossible' to claim that a legal right of unilateral humanitarian intervention continues to exist,[68] while some commentators are far more vociferous in their support of humanitarian intervention than states.[69]

Despite the negative general response to such interventions, there were some situations where criticism was muted, such as in the cases of Uganda and Iraq where despite the illegality of the relevant intervention, international criticism was negligible. The reason for this was that neither threatened the balance of power. Tanzania removed Amin's repressive regime while Operation Provide Comfort stabilised the situation and therefore improved regional stability.[70] While neither intervention received widespread support, they were not subject to any significant degree of criticism. This demonstrates that while a humanitarian intervention may not be explicitly endorsed, it can be tolerated when it provides a humanitarian result that does not threaten the interests of larger powers. While this does not strengthen the status of humanitarian intervention under international law, it can ensure an intervention to save lives may take place on an ad hoc basis.

The fact that so many interventions avoid criticism due to their humanitarian result is important.[71] Nevertheless, it is vital to note that an absence of condemnation is not authorisation.[72] A major challenge with humanitarian intervention is the uncertainty regarding its current status. This was a point made by Annan who highlighted that while unauthorised interventions such as Kosovo might offer a mechanism to end genocide, they risked destabilising the UN's collective security system, which was a flawed but broadly effective mechanism at maintaining international peace and security.[73] Annan highlighted that the emerging norms of intervention to protect civilians should be welcomed though it 'must be based on legitimate and universal principles' and centred on the UNSC.[74]

---

68 Gray. *Supra* note 67. p.253.

69 See Chesterman, Simon. *Just War and Just Peace: Humanitarian Intervention and International Law* (Oxford, 2001) p.47.

70 DiPrizio. *Supra* note 37. pp.146–147.

71 See Ibid. p.86.

72 White. *Supra* note 18. p.33.

73 Annan, Kofi. 'Two Concepts of Sovereignty' *Economist* (18 September 1999).

74 Ibid.

With few contemporary states relying on humanitarian intervention and many explicitly opposing it, there is little justification for unilateral humanitarian intervention, despite its existence at the time of the UN's foundation.[75] This is not to say that the concept of protecting people has ended. The rise of R2P is a critical evolution in the humanitarian intervention debate, which enjoys support that is more widespread, however it is not a new right but a rebranding of existing international law.[76] Nor did the ICISS claim R2P to be part of customary international law.[77] The key problem with R2P lies in the detail and while states generally agree on its existence, it faces many of the same problems of humanitarian intervention in that it risks being used to justify aggression.[78] Although the UNSC's veto system is a check on this, the stretching of Resolution 1973 to include regime change ensures states have reason to be suspicious of R2P's use, while R2P is applied just as selectively as humanitarian intervention and this was most recently evident in the responses to the civil war and humanitarian crisis in Syria.[79]

Although unilateral humanitarian intervention remains illegal under the UN Charter, with any such right being extinguished under customary international law, there appears to be some ways to ensure interventions can avoid condemnation. These are tentative suggestions, given that there are relatively few clear examples of humanitarian intervention to establish a precedent. One way to improve an intervention's viability is through collective action. This was apparent even in the nineteenth century,[80] when multinational interventions reduced the risk of instability and mitigated against a state unilaterally expanding its interests, with unilateral interventions being seen as merely war in the

75 See Chapter 4, *Supra* notes 1 and 33.

76 Gray. *Supra* note 67. p.254.

77 Frohlich, Manuel. 'The Responsibility to Protect. Foundation, transformation, and application of an emerging norm' in Klose, Fabian. (Ed.) *The Emergence of Humanitarian Intervention: Ideas and Practice from the Nineteenth Century to the Present* (Cambridge, 2018) pp.310–311.

78 See *Supra* notes 58–64.

79 Walling summarizes the reasons for lack of intervention in Syria compared to Libya. Namely that there is sharp disagreement among the UNSC about the cause of the violence or the source of sovereign authority within Syria. Meanwhile, the intervention in Libya had both the military capacity and possibility of success to make it viable (Walling. *Supra* note 12. pp.237–239). These arguments are echoed by Frohlich, who also notes the key difference that Syrian intervention was opposed by permanent members of the Security Council (Frohlich. *Supra* note 396 p.329).

80 In 1905, Oppenheim noted that whether humanitarian intervention existed is debatable, but that in time, such interventions might be permissible if done collectively. (See Oppenheim. *Supra* note 2. p.186–187).

traditional sense.[81] This was especially notable in France's 1860 intervention in Syria, where Paris operated with the consent of the other Great Powers.[82] By contrast, Russia's unilateral intervention in Bulgaria posed such a threat to Europe's balance of power that the other Great Powers did not support it, and its gains were reduced at the Congress of Berlin.[83] The importance of collective security is also evident in contemporary international law, with the UN Charter highlighting the ability of regional security organisations to engage in enforcement actions, subject to the UNSC authorisation.[84] Regional organisations have notable advantages, given they are less likely to be perceived as outsiders by local actors, are more familiar with local conditions and have a strong incentive to ensure long-term solutions are achieved.[85] However, they also risk being dominated by regional powers that will pursue their own interests, and regional organisations like the AU often lack the resources to undertake peace-operations on their own.[86] Although a prominent role for regional organisations was envisaged at the UN's founding, these proved ineffectual in subsequent years.[87] Nonetheless, regional organisations saw a marked rise in their use after the Cold War[88] and the *World Summit Outcome* made explicit reference to their role in upholding R2P.[89] This was especially evident in the Libyan conflict where it is unlikely intervention would have taken place without Arab League support.[90]

Collective action is not a panacea for improving an intervention's viability, given that Tanzania's unilateral intervention in Uganda received little condemnation while NATO's collective intervention in Kosovo was met with some criticism. As shown from the nineteenth century onwards, collective interventions are preferable to unilateral actions, given that unilateral interventions

81 Kroll, Stefan. 'The legal justification of international intervention' in Klose, Fabian. (Ed.) *The Emergence of Humanitarian Intervention: Ideas and Practice from the Nineteenth Century to the Present* (Cambridge, 2018) p.78.

82 See Chapter 3, *Supra* note 204.

83 See Chapter, Section 3 (e).

84 UN Charter. (1 UNTS XVI, 1945) Article 53.

85 White, Nigel. 'Towards Integrated Peace Operations: The Evolution of Peacekeeping and Coalitions of the Willing' in Odello, Marco and Piotrowicz, Ryszard (Eds.) *International Military Missions and International Law* (Leiden, 2011) p.22.

86 Ibid.

87 Schlesinger. *Supra* note 7. pp.191–192.

88 Bellamy. *Supra* note 47. p.145.

89 UN General Assembly. *Supra* note 56. Para.139.

90 Bellamy, Alex. 'Libya and the Responsibility to Protect: The Exception and the Norm' *Ethics and International Affairs* (Vol.25, No.3, 2011) p.266.

will be even more subject to selfish national interests.[91] At the same time, collective humanitarian intervention mitigates a state's ability to expand its own interests.[92] A prohibition on unilateral intervention has shortcomings and without it, Cambodians would likely have remained under the Khmer Rouge or Kosovars under Belgrade's control. Normalising unilateral interventions remains risky, with one possible alternative being the expansion of multilateral interventions.[93] Although multilateral intervention does not correlate with legality, it does function as a potential counterweight to humanitarian intervention being abused.[94]

While regional organisations have a vital role to play, their variable intervention capabilities means that a reliance on such organisations to protect areas results in a patchwork of regional security.[95] This is particularly relevant for NATO, which was the only organisation with the willingness and capability of providing military support to the UN.[96] NATO suffered from its own limitations in performing humanitarian interventions, notably its risk averseness to and fear of casualties.[97] A prime example is that although NATO states[98] were willing to use force to protect Iraqi Kurds, this would almost certainly not have happened had the Gulf War not weakened Iraq or if the need to help an ally like Turkey did not exist.[99] This ensured Operation Allied Force was able to maintain a safe zone while minimising danger to its troops.

Likewise, deploying ground troops to Kosovo would have required 100,000 to 200,000 soldiers in order to be successful.[100] Despite RGF's endemic weaknesses, Western states only deployed troops in Rwanda to extract foreign nationals[101] and despite their capabilities, NATO states offered little help

---

91 Donnelly. *Supra* note 53. pp.628–629.

92 Lillich, Richard. 'Intervention to Protect Human Rights' *McGill Journal of International Law* (1969) p.210.

93 Donnelly. *Supra* note 53. p.629.

94 Wolf. *Supra* note 5. p.366.

95 Hehir. *Supra* note 11. p.162.

96 Pauwels, Ann. 'NATO as a peacekeeper, a contradictio in terminis' Paper presented at the 2007 European Society of International Law Biennial Research Forum https://esil-sedi.eu/wp-content/uploads/2018/04/Agora-2-Pauwels.pdf Accessed 10th March 2024.

97 This is not just restricted to NATO: few governments are willing to risk their citizens and resources for humanitarian intervention unless the risks are minimal, or they have other motives. See Heinz. *Supra* note 1. p.143.

98 France left NATO in 1966 but remained a close NATO ally. (Fenby, Jonathan. *France: A Modern History from the Revolution to the War on Terror.* (New York, 2015). p.386). It returned to NATO in 2009. (Ibid. p.445).

99 DiPrizio. *Supra note* 37. p.42–43.

100 DiPrizio. *Supra note* 37. p.137.

101 See Chapter 5, *Supra* note 200.

to African states willing to provide troops for UNAMIR II until Operation Turquoise took place.[102]

To avoid risking casualties, NATO relied heavily on airpower, which is limited as a tool for humanitarian protection. Although airpower is a useful force enabler, it cannot unilaterally win conflicts.[103] While even high-altitude airstrikes can be effective at neutralising large targets and supporting ground troops,[104] this just illustrates airstrikes are useful in support but require ground troops for decisive results. Airstrikes are used extensively not because they were the most effective option but as they are fast, offer a low risk of casualties and reduce the prospect of being dragged into a protracted conflict.[105] Consequently, they are a weak tool but better than nothing, provided they are applied assertively. Overall, airstrikes played an 'important though not decisive' role in securing an end to the Kosovo conflict.[106]

The other key problem with NATO intervention is its association with the interests of the Global North and US hegemony. Although NATO is multinational and includes non-Western countries such as Turkey, the US remains its dominant member and is responsible for the significant majority of NATO's total military expenditure.[107] NATO often lacks the impartiality to make it amenable as a humanitarian intervener to the P5's non-NATO states, particularly Russia, which questioned NATO's continued existence in the post-Cold War era and saw its expansion in Eastern Europe as a threat to Russian security.[108] However, even with its prominent status within NATO, the US cannot unilaterally dictate NATO's action.[109] This is an important restraint on humanitarian intervention

---

102 Chapter 5, *Supra* note 224.

103 O'Connor, Rory. 'To What Degree Can Air Power's Inputs to Battle be Considered Strategic?' *Defence Forces Review* (Vol. 11, 2014) p.121.

104 A recent example being where Syrian Kurds succeeded in recapturing the city of Kobane from the Islamic State but were only able to do so thanks to close air support from NATO and its allies (See Wood, Paul. 'Analysis' in BBC News 'Syrian Kurds 'Drive Islamic State out of Kobane' (26 January 2015) (http://www.bbc.com/news/world-middle-east-30991612 Accessed 8th February 2022).

105 Pape, Robert. 'The True Worth of Air Power' *Foreign Affairs* (Vol.83, 2004) p.116.

106 Wheeler. *Supra* note 16. p.273.

107 This ratio has exponentially increased in recent years. NATO 'Secretary-General's Report 2012' (2012) http://www.NATO.int/cps/en/NATOlive/opinions_94220.htm Accessed 13th October 2020.

108 Gidadhubli, R.G. 'Expansion of NATO: Russia's Dilemma' *Economic and Political Weekly* (Vol.39, No.19, May 2004) p.1885.

109 Pauwels. *Supra* note 96. The prime example is that despite the involvement of major NATO member states such as the US and UK in the 2003 invasion of Iraq, NATO itself had no involvement (NATO 'NATO and the 2003 campaign against Iraq' (1 September 2015) www.NATO.int/cps/en/NATOhq/topics_51977.htm Accessed 13th October 2020). Notably, the

being used to expand the interests of larger states, when even a state as powerful as the US cannot unilaterally impose its will through regional organisations. There is a key role for regional organisations as 'gatekeepers': where intervention is supported by regional organisations, there is a greater likelihood of UNSC authorisation, given this permits timely UN action on humanitarian grounds, in line with regional interests.[110] Indeed, Tams notes that regional intervention is the one type of humanitarian intervention that is likely to be accepted outside of the UN.[111]

Despite the potential role for regional organisations, even those composed of liberal democracies such as NATO cannot claim to operate on behalf of the international community, the only body that can claim this authority is the UN itself.[112] When the UN is unable or unwilling to respond to mass human-rights violations, it gravely undermines the UNSC's credibility and ability to deter such crimes.[113] Maintaining an ad-hoc approach perpetuates the current problems. A successful humanitarian intervention conducted outside of the framework of the UN risks undermining the UN's credibility and legitimacy.[114] Furthermore, as evidenced in the Libyan intervention, even Russia and China (neither of whom supports R2P), can abstain from using their veto on critical UNSC resolutions, given their reluctance to be seen as opponents of international norms.[115]

## 4 The End of Humanitarian Intervention?

If a right of humanitarian intervention exists, 'it is a right that dares not speak its name',[116] and at best, exists in a lacuna. This book has shown that despite extensive academic interest in the area, it is unconvincing to argue

invasion was criticised by key US allies within NATO such as France and Germany. This demonstrates that although the US is influential within NATO, it is not overwhelming.

110 Bellamy, Alex and Williams, Paul. 'The new politics of protection? Cote d'Ivoire, Libya, and the responsibility to protect' *International Affairs* (Vol 87, No.4, 2011). p.848. Problems arise where regional organisations clash. Libya was a prime example that was both an Arab and African nation with the Arab League supporting intervention while the AU opposed it.

111 Tams. *Supra* note 21. p.359.

112 White. *Supra* note 18. pp.36–37.

113 Annan. *Supra* note 73.

114 International Commission on Intervention and State Sovereignty. *Supra* note 8 Para.6.40.

115 Walling, Carrie Booth. *All Necessary Measures: The UN and Humanitarian Intervention* (Philadelphia, 2013) p.225.

116 Holzgrefe. *Supra* note 50. pp.48–49.

that humanitarian intervention continues to exist under customary international law. Humanitarian intervention simply lacks the support among states to demonstrate *opinio juris,* with even the intervention in Kosovo being a 'poor candidate for contributing to customary international law'.[117] A major reason why jurists continued to argue for the existence of humanitarian intervention was the UN's inability to maintain peace and security,[118] which raised questions as to the right of states to utilise force when the UN's institutions fail.[119] R2P has failed to provide much clarity and despite the fanfare over R2P and the intervention in Libya, both failed to provide substantive change in the use of force to protect civilians and merely continued the status quo.[120]

There remains a pressing need to address the use of force to end atrocities. Hehir suggests the creation of a new judicial body to operate alongside the UNSC, charged with recommending responses to 'intra-state humanitarian crises' (including military intervention) where the UNSC is deadlocked.[121] Such judgements could help by catalysing UNSC action or giving legitimacy to states seeking intervention, even if unauthorised by the UNSC.[122] Although such a concept has merit, it is unlikely that the UNSC would permit a new body to erode its power. The most viable option currently available is a continuation of the present system where humanitarian intervention's existence as a right under international law is rejected but that its use can occasionally be overlooked. As highlighted above, this is a qualified and ad-hoc right, which fails to clarify humanitarian intervention's status. Though still a breach of the UN Charter, certain factors seem to improve the chance of avoiding condemnation. While this will still not establish its status under international law, it will allow a response to atrocities when the UNSC is unable or unwilling to act. Above all, the intervention must have a clear humanitarian result without threatening the balance of power or geopolitical stability.

Multilateral interventions are preferable in that they limit one state expanding its interests in a manner that threatens other nations. There are so few examples of humanitarian intervention that drawing concrete conclusions when such interventions may be accepted by the international community is difficult. Furthermore, as Hassan highlights, this has disadvantages in that it permits a state to hide its real motivation in the hope that it is perceived as

117 Heinze. *Supra* note 1. p.78.
118 Bazyler. *Supra* note 51. p.578.
119 Abiew. *Supra* note 10. p.101.
120 See Chapter 5.7.
121 Hehir. *Supra* note 11. pp.232–235.
122 Ibid.

acting on humanitarian grounds. It also leaves discretionary intervention open to abuse, while adding to the lack of clarity surrounding its status.[123] This is an approach commonly used under domestic legal systems. Franck and Rodley give the example of cannibalism, which is widely outlawed, but most people would accept circumstances when cannibalism might be partially justified, such as people adrift on a lifeboat.[124]

Overall, it is far better to have high standards which can be broken in an emergency than to lower standards overall. It is arguable that it is preferable to seek forgiveness than permission and a humanitarian intervention that merely ends atrocities is unlikely to receive sustained criticism from other states.[125] This solidifies humanitarian intervention's ambiguous status under international law, eroding the prohibition on the use of force and the authority of the UN. While humanitarian intervention's continued existence under customary international law is no more, its practice is likely to occasionally surface for some time.

---

123 Hassan, Farooq. 'Realpolitik in International Law: After Tanzanian-Ugandan Conflict Humanitarian Intervention Reexamined' *Willamette Law Review* (Vol.17, Issue.4, Fall 1981) p.889.

124 Franck and Rodley. *Supra* note 52. p.290.

125 Consequently, the best that can be said for humanitarian intervention it is not 'unambiguously illegal' (see Marston, Geoffrey (Ed.) 'United Kingdom Materials on International Law 1986' *British Yearbook of International Law* (Vol.57, 1986) p.619). Likewise, Chesterman notes that humanitarian intervention exists 'in a legal penumbra-sometimes given legitimacy by the Security Council and sometimes merely tolerated by states'. (Chesterman. *Supra* note 69. p.87). Tams notes that international law does not permit humanitarian intervention but there are exceptional circumstances where the international community did not apply the law. See Tams. *Supra* note 21. p.367.

# Bibliography

## Articles


Abu-Manneh, Butrus. 'The Province of Syria and the Mutasarrifiyya of Mount Lebanon (1866–1880)' *Turkish Historical Review* (Vol.4, 2013).

Adelman, Howard. 'Humanitarian Intervention: The Case of the Kurds' *International Journal of Refugee Law* (Vol.4, No.1, 1992).

Akhavan, Payam. 'Lessons from Iraqi Kurdistan: Self Determination and Humanitarian Intervention against Genocide' *Netherlands Quarterly of Human Rights* (Vol.11, No.1, 1993).

Alexandrowicz, C.H. 'Freitas vs Grotius' *British Yearbook of International Law* (Vol.35, 1959).

Allin, Dana. 'Ukraine: The Shock of Recognition' *Survival* (Vol.64, No.2, April–May 2022).

Amer, Ramses. 'The Ethnic Vietnamese in Cambodia: A Minority at Risk?' *Contemporary SouthEast Asia* (Vol. 16, No. 2, September 1994).

Anghie, Antony. 'Francisco de Vitoria and the Colonial Origins of International Law' *Social and Legal Studies* (Vol.5, No.3, 1996).

Anghie, Antony. 'The evolution of international law: Colonial and postcolonial realities' *Third World Quarterly*. (Vol.27 (5), 2006).

Anonymous 'Europe's Poisonous Remedies' *Advocate of Peace through Justice* Vol.84.11, (November 1922).

Anonymous. 'Fall of Idi Amin' *Economic and Political Weekly* (Vol.14, No.21, 26th May 1979).

Anonymous. 'Report on the Present State of the Greek Confederation' *The Eclectic Review* Vol.20 (December 1823).

Anonymous. 'The League of Nations and the Laws of War' *British Yearbook of International Law* (Vol.1, 1920–1921).

Anonymous. 'The Locarno Treaties' *Bulletin of International News* (Vol.1, No.21, 2nd November 1925).

Anonymous. 'The Political State of England and Europe' *The Monthly Magazine of Politics, Literature, and the Belles Lettres* Vol.8 (47), (November 1829).

Averre, Derek and Davies, Lance. 'Russia, humanitarian intervention and the Responsibility to Protect: the case of Syria' *International Affairs* (Vol.91, No.4, 2015).

Azarov Denys, Koval Dmytro, Nuridzhanian, Gaiane and Venher, Volodymyr. 'Understanding Russia's Actions in Ukraine as the Crime of Genocide' *Journal of International Criminal Justice* (Vol.21, No.2, 2023).

Balzer, Harley. 'The Ukraine Invasion and Public Opinion' *Georgetown Journal of International Affairs* (Vol.16, No.1, Winter/Spring 2015).

Baranovsky, Vladimir and Mateiko, Anatoly. 'Responsibly to Protect: Russia's Approaches' *Italian Journal of International Affairs* (Vol.51, No.2, 2016).

Barry, Ben. 'Libya's Lessons' *Survival* (Vol.53, No.5, October-November 2011).

Bazyler. Michael. 'Re-examining the Doctrine of Humanitarian Intervention in Light of the Atrocities in Kampuchea and Ethiopia' *Stanford Journal of International Law* (Vol.23, 1987).

Bekaert, Jacques. 'The Return of the Khmer Rouge' *Southeast Asian Affairs* (1993).

Bekker, Peter. Legality of Use of Force' *American Journal of International Law* (Vol.93, No.4, October 1999).

Bellamy, Alex and Williams, Paul. 'The new politics of protection? Cote d'Ivoire, Libya, and the responsibility to protect' *International Affairs* (Vol 87, No.4, 2011).

Bellamy, Alex. 'Libya and the Responsibility to Protect: The Exception and the Norm' *Ethics and International Affairs* (Vol.25, No.3, 2011).

Bellamy, Alex. 'Whither the Responsibility to Protect? Humanitarian Intervention and the 2005 World Summit' *Ethics and International Affairs* (Vol.19, No.2, 2006).

Bosco, David. 'The Price of Peace' *Foreign Policy* (29 May 2013).

Bosse, Giselle. 'Values, rights, and changing interests: The EU's response to the war against Ukraine and the responsibility to protect Europeans' *Contemporary Security Policy* (Vol.43, No.3, 2022).

Bradshaw, David. 'After the Gulf War: the Kurds' *The World Today* (Vol.47, No.5, May 1991).

Breau, Susan. 'The Impact of the Responsibility to Protect on Peacekeeping' *Journal of Conflict and Security Law* (Vol.11, No.3, 2006).

Briggs, Herbert. 'Power Politics and International Organization' *American Journal of International Law* (Vol.39, No.4, October 1945).

Brown, Phillip. 'The Capitulations' *Foreign Affairs* (Vol.1, No.4, 15th June 1923).

Buchanan, Allen. 'Reforming the international law of humanitarian intervention' in Holzgrefe, J.L and Keohane, Robert. *Humanitarian Intervention: Ethical, Legal and Political Dilemmas* (Cambridge, 2003).

Carey, Henry. 'US Domestic Politics and the Emerging Humanitarian Intervention Policy: Haiti, Bosnia and Kosovo' *World Affairs* Vol.164 (2) (Fall, 2001).

Centre for the Independence of Judges and Lawyers. 'Uganda' *CIJL Bulletin* (Vol.1, No.2, September 1978).

Chiu, Hungdah. 'China's Struggle against the Unequal Treaties, 1927–*1946' Chinese (Taiwan) Yearbook of International Law and Affairs* (Vol.5, 1985).

Chollet, Derek. 'The Shame of Srebrenica' *Foreign Affairs* (9 July 2015).

Codere, Helen. 'Power in Ruanda' (Sic) *Anthropologica* Vol.4, No.1 (1962).

Cook, Robin. 'Humanitarian Intervention' *British Yearbook of International Law* (Vol.71 No.1 2000).

Corten, Olivier and Koutroulis, Vaois. 'The 2022 Russia intervention in Ukraine: What is its impact on the interpretation of *jus contra bellum*' *Leiden Journal of International Law* (Vol.36, 2023).

Cullen Dunn, Elizabeth and Bobick, Michael S. 'The empire strikes back: War without war and occupation without occupation in the Russian sphere of influence' *American Ethnologist* (Vol.41, No.3, August 2014).

Cunningham, Allan. 'The Philhellenes, Canning and Greek Independence' *Middle Eastern Studies* Vol.14, No.2 (May 1978).

Czapliński, Władysław. 'Customary International Law on the Use of Force' *Wroclaw Review of Law, Administration & Economics* (Vol. 8, Iss.2, 2018) p.100.

Daalder, Ivo and Stavridis, James. 'NATO's Victory in Libya: The Right Way to Run an Intervention' *Foreign Affairs* (Vol.91, No.2, March/April 2012).

Dagi, Dogacan. 'The Russian Stand on the Responsibility to Protect: Does Strategic Culture Matter?' *Journal of Asian Security and International Affairs* (Vol.7, No.3, 2020).

De Waal, Alex. 'African roles in the Libyan conflict of 2011' *International Affairs* (Vol.89, No.2, 2013).

Decker, Alice. 'Idi Amin's Dirty War: Subversion, Sabotage, and the Battle to Keep Uganda Clean, 1971–1979' *The International Journal of African Historical Studies* (Vol. 43, No. 3 2010).

Des Forges, Alison. 'Shame: Rationalizing Western Apathy on Rwanda' *Foreign Affairs* 79 (May-June 2000).

Donnelly, Jack. 'Genocide and Humanitarian Intervention' *Journal of Human Rights* (Vol.1, No.1, 2002).

Donnelly, Jack. 'Human Rights, Humanitarian Crisis and humanitarian intervention' *International Journal* (Vol.48, Autumn 1993).

Donnelly, Jack. 'Human Rights, Humanitarian Intervention and American Foreign Policy: Law, Morality and Politics' *Journal of International Affairs* (Vol.37, No.2, 1984).

Drake. 'Will the League of Nations Work' *International Journal of Ethics* (Vol.29 (3) 1919).

Evans, Gareth. 'Responding to Atrocities: The New Geopolitics of Intervention' in *SIPRI Yearbook 2012: Armaments, Disarmament, and International Security* (Oxford, 2012).

'Fall of Idi Amin' *Economic and Political Weekly* (Vol.14, No.21, 26th May 1979).

Fazal, Tanisha. 'The Return of Conquest? Why the Future of Global Order Hinges on Ukraine' *Foreign Affairs* (6 April 2022).

Feil, Scott. 'Could 5,000 Peacekeepers Have Saved 500,000 Rwandans? Early Intervention Reconsidered' *Institute for the Study of Diplomacy Studies Reports* Vol.III, No.2 (April 1997).

Firro, Kais. 'Silk and Agrarian Changes in Lebanon, 1860–1914' *International Journal of Middle East Studies* Vol. 22, No. 2 (May 1990).

Fonteyne, Jean-Pierre. 'The Customary International Law Doctrine of Humanitarian Intervention: its Current Validity under the UN Charter' California *Western International Law Journal* (Vol.4, 1973–1974).

Fox, Gregory, Book Kristen and Jenkins, Isaac. 'The Contributions of United Nations Security Council Resolutions to the Law of Non-International Armed Conflict: New Evidence of Customary International Law' in *The American University Law Review* (Vol. 67, Iss. 3, 2018).

Franck, Thomas and Rodley, Nigel. 'After Bangladesh: The Law of Humanitarian Intervention by Military Force' *American Journal of International Law* (Vol. 67, 1973).

Fuller, Graham. 'The Fate of the Kurds' *Foreign Affairs* (Vol.72, No.2, Spring 1993).

Gazzini, Claudia. 'Was the Libya Intervention Necessary?' *Middle East Report* (No.261, Winter 2011).

Gidadhubli, R.G. 'Expansion of NATO: Russia's Dilemma' *Economic and Political Weekly* (Vol.39, No.19, May 2004).

Glasser, Susan. 'Minister No: Sergei Lavrov and the blunt logic of Russian power' *Foreign Affairs* (29 April 2013).

Gomis, Benoit. 'NATO: Lessons from Libya' *The World Today* (Vol.67, No.5, May 2011).

Green, James, Henderson, Christian and Ruys, Tom. 'Russia's Attack on Ukraine and the Jus Ad Bellum' *Journal on the Use of Force and International Law* (Vol.9, No.1, 2022).

Grigg, Edward. 'The Merits and Defects of the Locarno Treaty as a Guarantee of World Peace' *International Affairs* (Vol. 14, No. 2. Mar- Apr 1935).

Hall, William Edward. *International Law* (Oxford, 1880).

Harrington, Michael E. 'Operation Provide Comfort: A Perspective in International Law' *Connecticut Journal of International Law* (Vol.8, No.2, Spring 1993).

Hasan, K. Sarwar. 'Political Background of the East Pakistan Crisis' *Pakistan Horizon* (Vol.24, No.2, Second Quarter, 1971).

Hassan, Farooq. 'Realpolitik in International Law: After Tanzanian-Ugandan Conflict Humanitarian Intervention Reexamined' *Willamette Law Review* (Vol.17, Issue.4, Fall 1981).

Heffes, Ezequiel. 'Some Reflections on the Theory of Sources of International Law: Re-Examining Customary International Law' *Israel Law Review* (Vol.51, No.3, 2018).

Hehir, Aidan. 'The Permanence of Inconsistency: Libya, the Security Council and the Responsibility to Protect' *International Security* (Vol.38, No.1, Summer 2013).

Hershey, Amos. 'History of International Law since the Peace of Westphalia' *American Journal of International Law* (Vol.6, No.1, Jan 1912).

Hoffman, Tamás. 'War or peace? – International legal issues concerning the use of force in the Russia–Ukraine conflict' *Hungarian Journal of Legal Studies* (Vol.63, No.3, 2022).

Horowitz, Richard. 'International Law and State Transformation in China, Siam, and the Ottoman Empire during the Nineteenth Century' *Journal of World History* (Vol.15, No.4, Dec.2004).

Hossain, Kamrul. 'Complementary Role of the United Nations General Assembly in Peace Management' in *USAK Yearbook of International Politics and Law* (Vol.2, 2009).

Hudson, Manley O. 'Article 24 of the Statute of the International Law Commission' *Yearbook of the International Law Commission* (Vol. II, 1950).

Jahn, Beate. 'Humanitarian intervention – What's in a name?' *International Politics* (Vol 49, Iss.1, 2012).

Käihkö, Ilmari. 'A nation-in-the-making, in arms: control of force, strategy and the Ukrainian Volunteer Battalions' *Defence Studies* (Vol.18, No.2, 2018).

Kloepper, Stephen. 'The Syrian Crisis: 1860–61. A Case Study in Classic Humanitarian Intervention' *Canadian Yearbook of International Law* (Vol.23, 1985).

Krisch, Nico. 'Unilateral Enforcement of the Collective Will: Kosovo, Iraq and the Security Council' *Max Planck Yearbook of UN Law* (Vol.3, 1999).

Krishnan, S. 'UN Peacekeeping, Responsibility to Protect and Humanitarian Intervention' *India Quarterly* (Vol.76, No.1, 2020).

Kritsiotis, Dino. 'The Kosovo Crisis and NATO's Application of Armed Force against the Federal Republic of Yugoslavia' *International and Comparative Law Quarterly* (Vol.49, No.2, April 2000).

Kuperman, Alan. 'Rwanda in Retrospect' *Foreign Affairs* Vol.79, No.1 (Jan-Feb 2000).

Kuzio, Taras. 'Euromaidan revolution, Crimea, and Russia–Ukraine war: why it is time for a review of Ukrainian–Russian studies' *Eurasian Geography and Economics* (Vol.59, No.3–4, 2018).

Langehorne, Richard. 'Reflections on the Significance of the Concert of Vienna' *Review of International Studies* Vol.12, No.4 (October 1986).

Lauterpacht H. 'The Grotian Tradition in International Law' *British Yearbook of International Law* (Vol.23, 1946) p.46.

Lillich, Richard. 'Intervention to Protect Human Rights' *McGill Journal of International Law* (1969).

Lingelbach, William. 'The doctrine and practice of intervention in Europe' *Annals of the American Academy of Political and Social Science* (July 1900).

Lofchie, Michael. 'The Uganda Coup-Class Action by the Military' *The Journal of Modern African Studies* (Vol.10, No.1, May 1972).

Lu, Catherine. 'Humanitarian Intervention: Moral Ambition and Political Constraints' *International Journal* (Vol.62, Issue 4, Fall 2007).

Lufty, James. 'Humanitarian Intervention: The Invasion of Cambodia' *New York Law School Journal of International and Comparative Law* (1980–1981).

Lynch, Marc. 'Obama and the Middle East' *Foreign Affairs* (September/October 2015).

Mangu, André. 'The Arab Spring and the African Union's Reaction to the Crisis' *Africa Insight* (Vol.42, No.1 June 2012).

Marshall, Charles. 'Reflections on a Revolution in Pakistan' *Foreign Affairs* (January 1959).

Marston, Geoffrey (Ed.) 'United Kingdom Materials on International Law 1992' *British Yearbook of International Law* (Vol.63, 1992).

McRaven, William, Orszag, Peter and Bunzel, Theodore. 'Made in the Alliance How to Shore up the Foundations of Transatlantic Solidarity' *Foreign Affairs* (20 April 2022).

Melvern, Linda. 'Behind Closed Doors' *The World Today* (Vol.56 No.8–9, August-September 2000).

Menon, Rajan. 'Ukraine's Best Chance a Successful Offensive Could End the War with Russia' *Foreign Affairs* (12 April 2023).

Mirria, Carl. 'Not One Inch, Unless It Is from Lisbon to Vladivostok NATO-Russia Mythmaking and a Reimagined Kyivan Rus' *Journal of Applied History* (Vol.4, 2022).

Mirsky, Jonathan, 'China's 1979 Invasion of Vietnam: A View from the Infantry' *RUSI* (1 June 1981).

Moran, Cian. 'Congratulations, you are Being Liberated. Please do not Resist' Russia's Wars and the Protection of Nationals under International Law' *Nordic Journal of International Law* (Vol.92, No.4, 2023).

Moran, Cian. 'The Tribute That Vice Pays to Virtue: An Analysis of Russia's Justifications for the Invasion of Ukraine Under International Law' *Defence Forces Review* (Vol.19, 2022).

Murphy, Ray. 'United Nations Military Operations and International Humanitarian law: What Rules Apply to Peacekeepers?' *Criminal Law Forum* (Vol.14, No.2, 2003).

Nanda, Ved. 'A Critique of the United Nations Inaction in the Bangladesh Crisis' *Denver Journal of International Law* (Vol.49, 1972–1973).

Newbury, David. 'The Clans of Rwanda: An Historical Hypothesis' *Africa: Journal of the International African Institute* Vol.50 No.4 (1980).

Nurnberger, Ralph. 'The United States and Idi Amin: Congress to the Rescue' *African Studies Review* (Vol.25, No.1, March 1982).

O'Brien, M.D. 'The Principles of Gladstone's Foreign Policy' *The Westminster Review* (January 1852- January 1914).

O'Connor, Rory. 'To What Degree Can Air Power's Inputs to Battle be Considered Strategic?' *Defence Forces Review* (Vol. 11, 2014).

O'Loughlin, John and Toal, Gerard. 'The Crimea conundrum: legitimacy and public opinion after annexation' *Eurasian Geography and Economics* (Vol.60, No.1, 2019).

Palabiyik, Mustafa Serdar. 'The Emergence of the Idea of 'International Law' in the Ottoman Empire before the Treaty of Paris (1856)' *Middle Eastern Studies* (Vol 50, No.2, 2014).

Paris, Roland. 'Responsibility To Protect: The Debate Continues' *International Peacekeeping* (Vol.22, No.2, 2015).

Pellet, Alain. 'State Sovereignty and the Protection of Fundamental Human Rights: An International Law Perspective' *Pugwash Occasional Papers* (February 2000).

Perry, Harold. 'England and France in the East' *The National Review* (No.6, August 1883).

Pieterse, Jan. 'Sociology of Humanitarian Intervention: Bosnia, Rwanda and Somalia Compared' *International Political Science Review* Vol. 18(1) (January 1997).

Pogany, Istvan. 'Humanitarian Intervention in International Law: the French Intervention in Syria re-examined' *The International and Comparative Law Quarterly* (Vol.34, No.1. January 1986).

Posen, Barry. 'The War for Kosovo: Serbia's Political-Military Strategy' *International Security* (Vol.24, No.4, Spring 2000).

Pruitt-Ham, Bruce. 'Humanitarian Intervention in SouthEast Asia in the Post-Cold War World: Dilemmas in the Definition and Design of International Law' *Pacific Rim Law and Policy Journal* (Vol.3, Issue.2 1994).

Qaddafi, Muammar. 'Excerpts from Libyan Leader Muammar al-Qaddafi's Last Televised Address, 22nd February 2011' *Foreign Affairs* (4 June 2011).

Ramsden, Michael. 'Strategic Litigation in Wartime: Judging the Russian Invasion of Ukraine through the Genocide Convention' *Vanderbilt Journal of Transnational Law* (Vol.56, 2023).

Ramutsindela, Maano. 'Gaddaffi, Continentalism and Sovereignty in Africa' *South African Geographic Journal* (Vol.91, No.1, 2009).

Rendall, Matthew. 'Defensive Realism and the Concert of Europe' *Review of International Studies* Vol.36 No.3 (July 2006).

Robinson, Piers. 'The CNN effect: can the news media drive foreign policy?' *Review of International Studies* (Vol. 25, No. 2, Apr. 1999).

Ryan, Mick. 'Russia's Adaptation Advantage' Foreign *Affairs* (5 February 2024).

Sanaullah, M. 'Second and Third Release from the Second Population Census of Pakistan, 1961' *The Pakistan Development Review* (Vol. 2, No. 1, Spring, 1962).

Sanders, Deborah. 'The War We Want; The War That We Get': Ukraine's Military Reform and the Conflict in the East' *The Journal of Slavic Military Studies* (Vol.30, No.1, 2017).

Sarotte, Mary Elise. 'Not One Inch Eastward? Bush, Baker, Genscher, Gorbachev and the Origin of Russian Resentment toward NATO enlargement in February 1990' *Diplomatic History* (Vol.34, No.1, 2010).

Schabas, William. 'Genocide and Ukraine: Do Words Mean What We Choose them to Mean?' *Journal of International Criminal Justice* (Vol.20, Iss.4, 2022).

Schanberg, Sydney. 'Pakistan Divided' *Foreign Affairs* (Vol.50, October 1971).

Schwartzberg, Steven. 'The Lion and the Phoenix: British Policy towards the Greek Question' *Middle Eastern Studies* Vol.24 (2), (April 1988).

Sharp, Alan. 'Reflections on the Remaking of Europe: 1815, 1919, 1945, Post 1989' *Irish Studies in International Affairs* Vol.8 (1997).
Shepardson, Whitney. 'Nationalism and Free Trade' *Foreign Affairs* (April 1934).
Sperling, James and Webber, Mark. 'NATO: From Kosovo to Kabul' *International Affairs* (Vol.85, No.3, May 2009).
Sterner, Michael. 'The Persian Gulf: The Iran-Iraq War' *Foreign Affairs* (Fall, 1984).
Takeyh, Ray. 'The Iran-Iraq War: A Reassessment' *Middle East Journal* (Vol 64, No.3, Summer 2010).
Temperely, Harold. 'Princess Lieven and the Protocol of 4 April 1826' *The English Historical Review* Vol.39, No.153 (January 1924).
Ullman, Richard. 'Human Rights and Economic Power: The United States versus Idi Amin' *Foreign Affairs* (April 1978).
Van Den Berg, Ruud. 'Promising or Failing? League of Nations and United Nations Organisation' *Tilburg Foreign law Review* (Vol.4, Issue.2, 1994–1995) p.104.
Vindman, Alexander and Cruz Bustillos, Domininc. 'The Day After Russia Attacks What War in Ukraine Would Look Like – and How America Should Respond' *Foreign Affairs* (21 January 2022).
Vira, Varun and Cordesman, Anthony. 'The Libyan Uprising: An Uncertain Trajectory' *Centre for Strategic and International Studies* (Washington DC, 2011).
Wang, Dong. 'The Discourse of Unequal Treaties in Modern China' *Pacific Affairs* (Vol.76, No.3 Fall 2003).
Wenger, Marcha and Anderson, Dick. 'The Gulf War' *Middle East Report* (No.148, Sep-Oct 1987).
Western, Jon and Goldstein, Joshua. 'Humanitarian Intervention Comes of Age' *Foreign Affairs* (Vol.90 (6), November-December 2011).
Wheeler, Nicholas. 'Legitimating Humanitarian Intervention: Principles and Procedures' *Melbourne Journal of International Law* (Vol.2, Issue 2, 2001).
White, Nigel. 'The Legality of Bombing in the Name of Humanity' *Journal of Conflict and Security Law* (Vol.5, No.1 2000).
Williams, Paul. 'The Road to Humanitarian War in Libya' *Global Responsibility to Protect* (Vol.3, No.2, June 2011).
Wilson, Andrew. 'Imagining Crimean Tatar History since 2014: Indigenous Rights, Russian Recolonisation and the New Ukrainian Narrative of Cooperation' *Europe-Asia Studies* (Vol.73, No.5, June 2021).
Wilson, James Lindley and Monten, Jonathan. 'Does Kant Justify Liberal Intervention?' *The Review of Politics* (Vol. 73, No. 4, Fall 2011).
Wolf, Daniel. 'Humanitarian Intervention' *Michigan Yearbook of International Studies* (Vol.9, 1988).
Zhang, Xiaoming. 'China's 1979 War with Vietnam: A Reassessment' *The China Quarterly* (Vol.184, December 2005) Pp. 865–867.

## Books

Abiew, Francis Kofi. *The Evolution of the Doctrine and Practice of Humanitarian Intervention* (The Hague, 1999).

Alexander, Martin. *French History since Napoleon* (London, 1999).

Aminzade, Ronald. *Race, Nation, and Citizenship in Post-Colonial Africa: The Case of Tanzania* (Cambridge, 2013).

Anderson, Jack. *The Anderson Papers* (London, 1973).

Anderson, M.S. *The Eastern Question* (London, 1966).

Anderson, M.S. *The Eastern Question* (London, 1966).

Annan, Kofi. *The Question of Intervention* (1999).

Appiah, Anthony and Gates, Henry Louis. *Encyclopaedia of Africa, Volume 1* (Oxford, 2010).

Aquinas, Thomas. *Summa Theologicae* (1485) https://www.documentacatholicaomnia.eu/03d/1225-1274,_Thomas_Aquinas,_Summa_Theologiae_%5B1%5D,_EN.pdf Accessed 10th March 2024.

Aristotle. *The Art of Rhetoric Book II, Ch.8* (London, 1926).

Arkin, William. Durrant, Damian and Cherni, Marianne. *Greenpeace Study: On Impact: Modern Warfare and the Environment: A Case Study of the Gulf War* (May, 1991) p.49 http://www.greenpeace.org/international/Global/international/planet-2/report/1991/6/on-impact-modern-warfare-and.pdf Accessed 10th March 2024.

Badem, Candan. *The Ottoman Crimean War 1853–1856* (Leiden, 2010).

Bagot, Josceline (Ed.) *George Canning and His Friends, containing hitherto unpublished letters, Jeux d'esprit, etc Volume II* (London, 1909).

Barker, Hannah. *Newspapers, Politics and English Society 1695–1855* (Harlow, 2000).

Bartlett, C.J *Castlereagh* (London, 1966).

Bass, Gary. *Freedom's Battle: The Origins of Humanitarian Intervention.* (New York, 2008).

Bass, Gary. *The Blood Telegram: Nixon, Kissinger, and the Forgotten Genocide* (New York, 2013).

Bassett, Arthur. *Gladstone Speeches: Descriptive Index and Bibliography* (London, 1916).

Bellamy, Alex. 'The Responsibility to Protect and the Problem of Regime Change' in Weiss et al. *The Responsibility to Protect: Challenges &Opportunities In Light of the Libyan Intervention* (2011) p.22 http://www.e-ir.info/wp-content/uploads/R2P.pdf Accessed 10th March 2024.

Bellamy, Alex. *Global Politics and the Responsibility to Protect* (Abingdon, 2011).

Bew, John. 'From an Umpire to a competitor' Castlereagh, Canning, and the issue of international intervention in the wake of the Napoleonic Wars' in Simms, Brendan and Trim, D.J.b (Eds.) *Humanitarian Intervention: A History* (Cambridge, 2011).

Black, Jeremy. *Slavery: A New Global History* (London, 2011).

Blood, Archer. *The Cruel Birth of Bangladesh: Memoirs of an American Diplomat* (Dhaka, 2002).

Boot, Max. *Invisible Armies* (New York, 2013).

Bose, Sugata and Jalal, Ayesha. *Modern South Asia: History, Culture, Political Economy* (Delhi, 1998).

Brewer, David. *The Greek War of Independence* (Woodstock, 2003).

Brown, Norman. *The United States and India, Pakistan, Bangladesh* (Cambridge MA, 1972).

Brownlie, Ian. *International Law and the Use of Force* (Oxford, 2002).

Byron George. Marchand, Leslie (Ed.) *Lord Byron: Selected Letters and Journals* (London, 1982).

Byron, George. Gordon' *Oxford Dictionary of National Biography* (London, 1921).

Byron, George. *Journal in Cephalonia* (1823).

Canning, George. Bagot, Josceline's (Ed.) *George Canning and His Friends, containing hitherto unpublished letters, Jeux d'esprit, etc Volume II* (London, 1909).

Canning, George. *Some Official Correspondences of George Canning Volume 1* (London, 1887).

Canning, George. *Some Official Correspondences of George Canning Volume 2* (London, 1887).

Castlereagh, Robert Stewart. 'Lord Castlereagh's Confidential State Paper of May 5th, 1820' in Ward, Adolphus, William and Gooch, George Peabody (Eds.) *The Cambridge History of British Foreign Policy, 1783–1919* (Cambridge, 2012).

Chandler, David. *A History of Cambodia* (Boulder, 2008).

Chandler, David. *The Tragedy of Cambodian History: Politics, War and Revolution since 1945* (New Haven, 1991).

Chapman, Tim. *The Congress of Vienna: Origins, Processes and Results* (London, 1998).

Charlesworth, Hilary and Chinkin, Christine. *The Boundaries of International Law. A Feminist Analysis* (Manchester, 2000).

Chesterman, Simon. *Just War and Just Peace: Humanitarian Intervention and International Law* (Oxford, 2001).

Childs, John. *Warfare in the Seventeenth Century* (London, 2004).

Chua, Amy. *Political Tribes: Group Instinct and the Fate of Nations* (London, 2019).

Churchill, Charles Henry. *The Druzes and the Maronites under the Turkish Rule from 1840 to 1860* (London, 1862).

Cleveland, William. *A History of the Modern Middle East* (Oxford, 2004).

Cobden, Richard. *The Political Writings of Richard Cobden,* Vol.I, Part II (London, 1835).

Collins, Bruce. *War and Empire: The Expansion of Britain 1790–1830* (Harlow, 2010).

Collins, Ross. 'Traitorous Collaboration: The Press in France 1815–1914' in Collins, Ross and Palmegiano, E.M (Eds.) *The Rise of Western Journalism 1815–1914* (Jefferson, 2007).

Condorelli, Luigi. 'Customary International Law: The Yesterday, Today and Tomorrow of General International Law' in Cassese, Antonio (Ed.) *Realizing Utopia: The Future of International Law*. (Oxford, 2012).

Conradi, Peter. *Who Lost Russia: From the Collapse of the USSR to Putin's War on Ukraine* (London, 2022).

Constant, Benjamin. *Appel aux Nations Chrétiennes en Faveur des Grecs* (Paris, 1825).

Corten, Oliver and Simma, Bruno. *The Law Against War: The Prohibition on the Use of Force in Contemporary International Law* (Oxford, 2010) pp.311–400.

Coulon, Jocelyn. *Soldiers of Diplomacy: The United Nations, Peacekeeping, and the New World Order* (Toronto, 1994).

Craig, Gordon. *Europe since 1815* (New York, 1967).

Crocker, H.W. *Triumph: The Power and Glory of the Catholic Church* (New York, 2001).

Crompton, Louis. *Byron and Greek Love: Homophobia in 19th Century England* (London, 1985).

Dallaire, Romeo. 'The End of Innocence: Rwanda 1994' in Moore, Jonathan (Ed.) *Moral Dilemmas in Humanitarian Intervention* (1998).

Dallaire, Roméo. *Shake Hands with the Devil: The Failure of Humanity in Rwanda* (London, 2004).

Dallaire, Romeo. *They Fight Like Soldiers; They Die Like Children* (London, 2010).

Dallek, Robert. *Partners in Power: Nixon and Kissinger* (New York, 2007).

Dandeker, Christopher. 'War and the Military Establishment' in Freedman, Lawrence (Ed.) *War* (Oxford, 1994).

Davis, Doug, Steward, Brandon and Slobodchikoff, Michael. 'NATO's Future. The Show Must Go On' in Slobodchikoff, Michael, Davis, Doug and Stewart, Brandon (Eds.) *The Challenge to NATO: Global Security and the Atlantic Alliance* (University of Nebraska Press, 2021).

De Vattel, Emer. *The Law of Nations* (1758) http://files.libertyfund.org/files/2246/Vattel_1519_LFeBk.pdf Accessed 10th March 2024.

De Vitoria, Francisco. *De Indis De Jure Belli. Relectiones Theologicae XII. (1583)* http://legalhistorysources.com/Law508/VitoriaDeIndis.htm Accessed 10th March 2024.

De Vogüé, Melchior. *Les Événements de Syrie* (Paris, 1861).

Derry, John. *Castlereagh* (London, 1976).

DiPrizio, Robert. *Armed Humanitarians: US Interventions from Northern Iraq to Kosovo* (Baltimore, 2002).

Disraeli, Benjamin's *The Letters of Disraeli to Lady Chesterfield and Lady Bradford Volume Two* (New York, 1929).

Doyle, Michael and Sambanis, Nicholas. *Making War and Building Peace* (Princeton, 2006).

Doyle, William. *The Old European Order. 1660–1800* (Oxford, 1992).

Droz, Jacques. *Europe between Revolutions 1815–1848* (London, 1967).

Edwards, Richard. *La Syria 1840–1862: histoire, politique, administration, population, religions etmoeurs, événements de1860 d'après des actes officielles et des documents authentiques* (Paris, 1862).

Emerson, E.J. *A History of the Nineteenth Century, Year by Year, Vol.2* (New York, 1901).

Etcheson, Craig. *After the Killing Fields: Lessons from the Cambodian Genocide* (Westport, 2005).

Evans, Gareth. 'The R2P Balance Sheet after Libya' in Weiss et al. *The Responsibility to Protect: Challenges &Opportunities in Light of the Libyan Intervention* (2011) pp.37–39 http://www.e-ir.info/wp-content/uploads/R2P.pdf Accessed 10th March 2024.

Fawaz, Leila Tarazi. *An Occasion for War: Civil Conflict in Lebanon and Damascus in 1860* (Berkeley 1994).

Feil, Scott. *Preventing Genocide: How the Early Use of Force Might Have Succeeded in Rwanda* (New York, 1998).

Fenby, Jonathan. *France: A Modern History from the Revolution to the War on Terror.* (New York, 2015).

Figes, Orlando. *The Story of Russia* (London, 2022).

Findlay, Trevor. *The Use of Force in UN Peace Operations* (Oxford, 2002).

Focarelli, Carlo. *International Law* (Cheltenham, 2019).

Foer, Franklin. *The Last Politician Inside Joe Biden's White House and the Struggle for America's Future* (New York, 2023).

France, John. *Perilous Glory: The Rise of Western Military Power* (New Haven 2011).

Franck, Thomas. 'Interpretation and Change in the Law of Humanitarian Intervention' in Holzgrefe, J.L and Keohane, Robert (Eds.) *Humanitarian Intervention: Ethical, Legal and Political Dilemmas* (Cambridge, 2003).

Franck, Thomas. *Recourse to Force: State Action against Threats and Armed Attacks* (Cambridge, 2002).

Frelick, Bill. 'Operation Provide Comfort: False Promises to the Kurds' in Chaliand, Gerard (Ed.) *A People without a Country. The Kurds and Kurdistan* (London, 1993).

Frohlich, Manuel. 'The Responsibility to Protect. Foundation, transformation, and application of an emerging norm' in Klose, Fabian. (Ed.) *The Emergence of Humanitarian Intervention: Ideas and Practice from the Nineteenth Century to the Present* (Cambridge, 2018).

Fukuyama, Francis. *The End of History and the Last Man* (London, 1992).

Galeotti, Mark. *Putin's Wars: From Chechnya to Ukraine* (Oxford, 2022).

Gathorne-Hardy, Gathorne *Gathorne Hardy, First Earl of Cranbrooke: A Memoir with Extracts from His Diary and Correspondence* (London, 1910).

Gellner, Ernest. 'Nationalism and the New World Order' in Reed, Laura and Kaysen, Carl (Eds.) *Emerging Norms of Justified Intervention* (Cambridge, 1993) pp.152–153.

Gettleman, Marvin and Schaar, Stuart. *The Middle East and Islamic World Reader* (New York, 2003).

Gildea, Paul. *Barricades and Borders: Europe 1800–1914* (Oxford, 1996).

Gladstone, W.E. *The Hellenic Factor in the Eastern Problem with Other Tracts* (Leipzig, 1877).

Gladstone, William Ewart. *Bulgarian Horrors and the Question of the East* (London, 1876).

Gladstone, William Ewart. *Lessons in Massacre* (London, 1877).

Gladstone, William Ewart. *Political Speeches in Scotland: March-April 1880* (Edinburgh, 1880).

Glenny, Misha. *The Balkans 1804–1999* (London, 1999).

Goodwin, Jason. *Lords of the Horizon. A History of the Ottoman Empire* (London, 1998).

Gorce, Pierre. *Histoire du Second Empire, tome troisieme* (Paris, 1906).

Gordon, Thomas. *History of the Greek Revolution, Volume 1* (Edinburgh, 1844).

Gordon, Thomas. *History of the Greek Revolution, Volume 2* (Edinburgh, 1844).

Gray, Christine. 'The Use of Force for Humanitarian Purposes' in White, Nigel and Henderson, Christine (Eds.) *Research Handbook on International Conflict and Security Law* (Cheltenham, 2013).

Gray, Christine. *International Law and the Use of Force* (Oxford, 2004).

Griffiths, Martin, Levine, Iain and Weller, Mark 'Sovereignty and Suffering' in Harris, John. *The Politics of Humanitarian Intervention* (London, 1995).

Grotius, Hugo. *On the Law of War and Peace* (1625). https://socialsciences.mcmaster.ca/econ/ugcm/3ll3/grotius/Law2.pdf Accessed 10th March 2024.

Gutman, Roy. *A Witness to Genocide* (New York, 1993).

Harding, Luke. *Invasion: Russia's Bloody War and Ukraine's Fight for Survival* (London, 2022).

Harris, David. *Britain and the Bulgarian Horrors of 1876* (Chicago, 1939).

Harvey, Dan. *Peacekeepers: Irish Soldiers in Lebanon* (Dublin, 2001).

Hatzopoulos, Marios. 'From resurrection to insurrection: 'sacred' myths, motifs, and symbols in the Greek War of Independence' in Beaton, Roderick and Ricks, David (Eds.) *The Making of Modern Greece: Nationalism, Romanticism, and the uses of the Past (1797–1896)* (Surrey, 2009).

Hearder, Harry. *Europe in the Nineteenth Century 1830–1880* (Harlow, 1966).

Hehir, Aidan. 'The Illusion of Progress: Libya and the Future of R2P' in Weiss et al. *The Responsibility to Protect: Challenges & Opportunities in Light of the Libyan Intervention* (2011) p.18 http://www.e-ir.info/wp-content/uploads/R2P.pdf Accessed 10th March 2024.

Hehir, Aidan. *Humanitarian Intervention: An Introduction* (Basingstoke, 2010).

Hehir, Aidan. *The Responsibility to Protect* (Basingstoke, 2012).

Heinze, Eric. *Waging Humanitarian War: The Ethics, Law, and Politics of Humanitarian Intervention* (New York, 2009).

Henderson, Christine. 'The Centrality of the United Nations Security Council in the legal regime governing the Use of Force' in White, Nigel and Henderson, Christine (Eds.) *Research Handbook on International Conflict and Security Law* (Cheltenham, 2013).

Heraclides, Alexis and Dialla, Ada. *Humanitarian Intervention in the long Nineteenth Century. Setting the precedent.* (Manchester, 2015).

Herslet, Edward. *The Map of Europe by Treaty, Vol. II* (London, 1875).

Hilsum, Lindsey. *Sandstorm: Libya from Gaddaffi to Revolution* (London, 2012).

Hinde, Wendy *George Canning* (London, 1973).

Hitchens, Christopher. *The Trial of Kissinger* (London, 2001).

Holden-Reid, Brian. *The Civil War and the Wars of the Nineteenth Century* (London, 1999).

Holzgrefe, J.L 'The Humanitarian Intervention Debate' in Holzgrefe, J.L and Keohane, Robert. *Humanitarian Intervention: Ethical, Legal and Political Dilemmas* (Cambridge, 2003).

Hupchick, Dennis. *The Balkans from Constantinople to Communism* (New York, 2001).

Ibingira, Grace. 'The Impact of Ethnic Demands on British Decolonisation in Africa: The Example of Uganda' in Gifford, Prosser and Louis, WM. Roger. *The Transfer of Power in Africa: Decolonisation 1940–1960* (New Haven, 1982).

Ivanov, Igor. *The New Russian Diplomacy* (New York, 2002).

Jackson, Robert and Rosberg, Carl. *Personal Rule in Black Africa: Prince, Autocrat, Prophet, Tyrant.* (Berkeley, 1982).

Jelavich, Barbara. *Russia's Balkan Entanglements 1806–1914* (Cambridge, 1991).

Jessup, Philip. *A Modern Law of Nations* (New York, 1948).

Jones, Owen Bennett. *Pakistan: Eye of the Storm* (New Haven, 2002).

Karnow, Stanley. *Vietnam: A History* (London, 1991).

Karns, Margaret and Mingst, Karen. *International Organisations: The Politics and Processes of Global Governance* (Boulder, 2004).

Karoubi, Mohammed Taghi. *Just or Unjust War?* (Aldershot, 2004).

Keegan, John. *The Iraq War* (London, 2004).

Keen, David. 'Short term interventions and long term problems: the case of the Kurds in Iraq' in Harriss, John. (Ed.) *The Politics of Humanitarian Intervention* (London, 1995).

Kershaw, Ian. *The Global Age: Europe 1950–2017* (London, 2018).

Khadiagla, Gilbert. *Meddlers or Mediators: African Interveners in Civil Conflicts in East Africa.* (Leiden, 2007).

Kiernan, Ben. *The Pol Pot Regime: Race, Power, and Genocide in Cambodia under the Khmer Rouge, 1975–1979* (New Haven, 2002).

Kirdar, Nemir. *Saving Iraq: Rebuilding a Broken Nation* (London, 2009).

Kissinger, Henry. *World Order: Reflections on the Character of Nations and the Course of History* (London, 2014).

Klose, Fabian. 'The Emergence of Humanitarian Intervention' in Klose, Fabian. (Ed.) *The Emergence of Humanitarian Intervention: Ideas and Practice from the Nineteenth Century to the Present* (Cambridge, 2018).

Kroll, Stefan. 'The legal justification of international intervention' in Klose, Fabian. (Ed.) *The Emergence of Humanitarian Intervention: Ideas and Practice from the Nineteenth Century to the Present* (Cambridge, 2018).

Kulke, Hermann and Rothermund, Dietmar. *A History of India* (Chatham, 1997) pp.339–340.

Kuzio, Taras. *Putin's War Against Ukraine* (Toronto, 2017).

Laughton, J.K. 'Codrington, Sir Edward.' *Oxford Dictionary of National Biography* (Oxford, 2004).

Lebor, Adam. *Complicity with Evil: The United Nations in the Age of Modern Genocide* (Bury St Edmunds, 2006).

Lepard, Brian. *Rethinking Humanitarian Intervention: A Fresh Legal Approach Based on Fundamental Ethical Principles in International Law and World Religions* (University Park, 2002).

Lewy, Guenter. *The Armenian Massacres in Ottoman Turkey* (Salt Lake City, 2005).

Lynch, Marc. *The Arab Uprising* (New York, 2012).

MacGahan, J.A *Turkish Atrocities in Bulgaria, Letters of the Special Commissioner of the 'Daily News,' J.A. MacGahan, Esq., with An Introduction & Mr. Schuyler's Preliminary Report.* (London, 1876).

Machin, Ian. *The Rise of Democracy in Britain* (Hampshire, 2001).

MacQueen, Norrie. 'Cold War peacekeeping versus humanitarian intervention' in Klose, Fabian. (Ed.) *The Emergence of Humanitarian Intervention: Ideas and Practice from the Nineteenth Century to the Present* (Cambridge, 2018).

MacQueen, Norrie. *Humanitarian Intervention and the United Nations* (Edinburgh, 2011).

Martin, David. *General Amin* (London, 1974).

Martin, Gus. *Understanding Terrorism* (Thousand Oaks, 2006).

Matthews, Ken. *The Gulf Conflict and International Relations* (London, 1993).

Matthews, Owen. *Overreach: The Inside Story of Putin's War on Ukraine* (London, 2022).

McDowall, David. *A Modern History of the Kurds* (London, 2004).

McNab, Chris. *The Great Bear at War: The Russian and Soviet Army 1917-Present* (Oxford, 2019).

Melady, Thomas and Melady, Margaret. *Idi Amin Dada: Hitler in Africa* (Mission, 1977).

Melvern, Linda. *A People Betrayed: The Role of the West in Rwanda's Genocide* (London, 2000).

Mentan, Tatah. *The United Nations Organization: (in)Securing Global Peace and Security* (Bamenda, 2020).

Meredith, Martin. *The State of Africa: A History of Fifty Years of Independence* (London, 2005).

Mingst, Karen and Karns, Margaret. *The United Nations in the Post-Cold War Era* (Oxford, 2000).

Moneypenny, William and Buckle, George (Eds.) *The Life of Benjamin Disraeli, Earl of Beaconsfield, Vol.6* (New York, 1920).

Moses, Dirk. 'The United Nations, Humanitarianism and Human Rights: War Crimes/ Genocide Trials for Pakistani Soldiers in Bangladesh, 1971–1974,' in Hoffman, Stefan-Ludwig (Ed.) *Human Rights in the Twentieth Century* (New York, 2011).

Mowat, R.B. *A History of European Diplomacy 1815–1914* (London, 1922).

Murphy, Derrick and Morriss, Terry. *International Relations: 1879–2004* (London, 2008).

Murphy, John F. *The Evolving Dimensions of International Law: Hard Choices for the World Community.* (Cambridge, 2010).

Murphy, Ray. *UN Peacekeeping in Lebanon, Somalia, and Kosovo* (Cambridge, 2007).

Mysliwiec, Eva. *Punishing the Poor: The International Isolation of Kampuchea* (Oxford, 1988).

Nicholson, Harold. *The Congress of Vienna* (London, 1946).

Nugent, Paul. *Africa since Independence: A Comparative History* (Hampshire, 2004).

O'Connell, Mary Ellen. 'How To Lose a Revolution' in Weiss et al. *The Responsibility to Protect: Challenges &Opportunities in Light of the Libyan Intervention* (2011) p.15 http://www.e-ir.info/wp-content/uploads/R2P.pdf Accessed 10th March 2024.

Oakes, Augustus and Mowat, R.B (Eds.) *The Great European Treaties of the Nineteenth Century* (Oxford, 1918).

Off, Carol. *The Lion, the Fox, and the Eagle: A Story of Generals and Eagles in Rwanda and Yugoslavia* (Toronto, 2000).

Oppenheim, Lassa *International Law: A Treatise, Vol. 1-Peace* (London, 1905).

Orth, Richard. 'Rwanda's Hutu Extremist Insurgency: An Eyewitness Perspective' in Cooke, Susan (Ed.) *Genocide in Cambodia and Rwanda: New Perspectives* (New Brunswick, 2007).

Palmegiano, E.M 'The Fourth Estate: British Journalism in Britain's Century' in Collins, Ross and Palmegiano, E.M (Eds.) *The Rise of Western Journalism 1815–1914* (Jefferson, 2007).

Palmer, Alan. *The Decline and Fall of the Ottoman Empire* (London, 1992).

Pavlowitch, Stevan. *A History of the Balkans 1805–1945* (Harlow, 1999).

Pearce, Malcom and Stewart, Geoffrey. *British Political History: 1867–2001* (London, 2002).

Pears, Edwin. *Forty Years in Constantinople: The Recollections of Sir Edwin Pears 1873–1915* (New York, 1916).

Petraeus, David and Roberts, Andrew. *Conflict: The Evolution of Warfare from 1945 to Ukraine* (London, 2023).

Piric, Fernanda. *The Rule of Laws: A 4,000-Year Quest to Order the World* (London, 2021).

Plessais, Alain. *The Rise and Fall of the Second Empire: 1852–1871* (Cambridge, 1985).

Plokhy, Serhii. *The Russo-Ukrainian War* (Dublin, 2023).

Polunov, Alexander. *Russia in the Nineteenth Century: Autocracy, Reform and Change, 1814–1914* (New York, 2005).
Porch, Douglas. *Wars of Empire* (Kindle Edition, 2012) Chapter 2, Para.6.
Power, Geoffrey. *The Thirty Years War* (Abingdon, 2007).
Power, Samantha. *A Problem from Hell: America and the Age of Genocide* (New York, 2002).
Price, Roger. *Napoleon III and the Second Empire* (London, 1997).
Prunier, Gérard. *The Rwandan Crisis: History of a Genocide* (New York, 1995).
Puri, Samir. *Russia's Road to War with Ukraine: Invasion Amidst the Ashes of Empires* (London, 2022).
Quatert, Donald. *The Ottoman Empire 1700–1922* (Cambridge, 2000).
Ramani, Samuel. *Putin's War on Ukraine: Russia's Campaign for Global Counter Revolution* (London, 2023).
Ratner, Stene. 'War Crimes, Categories of' Gutman, Roy, Dieff, David and Dworkin, Anthony. *Crimes of War* (New York, 2007).
Reid, Anna. *Borderlands: A Journey Through the History of Ukraine* (London, 2022).
Rodogno, Davide. 'The 'principles of humanity' and the European Powers' intervention in Ottoman Lebanon and Syria in 1860–1861' in Simms, Brendan and Trim, D.J.b (Eds.) *Humanitarian Intervention: A History* (Cambridge, 2011).
Rodogno, Davide. *Against Massacre: Humanitarian Interventions in the Ottoman Empire 1815–1914* (Princeton, 2012).
Ronzitti, Natalino. *Rescuing Nationals Abroad Through Military Coercion and Intervention in Grounds of Humanity* (Dordrecht, 1985).
Rowley, Kelvin. 'Second Life, Second Death: The Khmer Rouge After 1978' in Cook, Susan (Ed.) *Genocide in Cambodia and Rwanda: New Perspectives* (New Brunswick, 2007).
Roy-Chaudhury, Rahul. 'The Security Council and the India-Pakistan Wars' in Lowe, Vaughan, Roberts, Adam, Welsh, Jennifer and Zaum, Dominik (Eds.) *The United Nations Security Council and War: The Evolution of Thought and Practice since 1945* (Oxford, 2008).
Russell, Frederick. *The Just War in the Middle Ages* (Cambridge, 1977).
Schanberg, Sydney. 'Cambodia' in Gutman, Roy, Dieff, David and Dworkin, Anthony. *Crimes of War* (New York, 2007).
Schlesinger, Stephen. *Act of Creation: The Founding of the United Nations* (Boulder, 2003).
Schulte, Jan Erik. 'From the Protection of sovereignty to humanitarian intervention? Traditions and developments of United Nations Peacekeeping in the twentieth century' in Klose, Fabian. (Ed.) *The Emergence of Humanitarian Intervention: Ideas and Practice from the Nineteenth Century to the Present* (Cambridge, 2018).
Schulz, Matthias. 'The guarantees of humanity: the Concert of Europe and the origins of the Russo-Ottoman War of 1877' in Simms, Brendan and Trim, D. J.B (Eds.) *Humanitarian Intervention: A History* (Cambridge, 2011).

Segesser, Daniel Marc. 'Humanitarian Intervention and the issue of state sovereignty in the discourse of legal experts between the 1830s and the First World War' in Klose, Fabian. (Ed.) *The Emergence of Humanitarian Intervention: Ideas and Practice from the Nineteenth Century to the Present* (Cambridge, 2018).

Seton-Watson, Hugh. *The Russian Empire 1801–1917* (Oxford, 1967).

Shannon, R.T *Gladstone and the Bulgarian Agitation 1876* (Hassocs, 1963).

Shannon, Richard. *Gladstone: Heroic Minister 1865–1898* (London, 1999).

Shaw, Malcolm. *International Law* (Cambridge, 2017).

Shaw, Stanford and Shaw, Ezel Kural. *History of the Ottoman Empire and Modern Turkey Vol.2* (Salt Lake City, 1977).

Shawcross, William. *Deliver Us from Evil: Warlords and Peacekeepers in a World of Endless Conflict* (London, 2001).

Shirk, Susan. *China: Fragile Superpower* (Oxford, 2007).

Simms, Brendan. *Three Victories and a Defeat: The Rise and Fall of the First British Empire* (New York, 2009).

Sinclair, Andrew. *An Anatomy of Terror: A History of Terrorism* (London, 2003).

Sixsmith, Martin, with Sixsmith, Daniel. *Putin and the Return of History: How the Kremlin Rekindled the Cold War* (Dublin, 2024).

Snyder, Timothy. *The Road to Unfreedom: Russia, Europe, America* (London, 2019).

Sondhaus, Lawrence. *Naval Warfare 1815–1914* (London, 2001).

Spagnolo, John. 'Franco-British rivalry in the Middle East' in Shehadi, Nadim and Mills, Dana Haffer (Eds.) *Lebanon: A history of conflict and consensus* (London, 1988).

Spagnolo, John. *France and Ottoman Lebanon 1861–1914* (London, 1977).

'Stanhope, Leicester Fitzgerald Charles' *Oxford Dictionary of National Biography* (London, 1921).

St Clair, William. *That Greece Might Still Be Free: The Philhellenes in the War of Independence* (Oxford, 1972).

St John, Ian. *Gladstone and the Logic of Victorian Politics* (London, 2010).

Stapleton, Edward (Ed.) *Some Official Correspondences of George Canning Volume 2* (London, 1887).

Stark, Alex. 'Introduction' in Weiss, Thomas, Thakur, Ramesh, O'Connell, Mary Ellen, Hehir, Aiden, Bellamy, Alex, Chandler, David, Shanahan, Rodger, Gerber, Rachel, Williams, Abiodun and Evans, Gareth. *The Responsibility to Protect: Challenges &Opportunities in Light of the Libyan Intervention* (2011) p.4 http://www.e-ir.info/wp-content/uploads/R2P.pdf Accessed 10th March 2024.

Stowell, Ellery. *Intervention in International Law* (Washington DC, 1921).

Stoyanovich, Mihail. *The Great Powers and the Balkans 1875–1878* (London, 1939).

Syse, Henrik. 'Augustine and Just War' in Syse, Henrik and Reichberg, Gregory. *Ethics, Nationalism and Just War: Medieval and Contemporary Perspectives* (Washington D.C, 2007).

Temperely, Harold. *The Foreign Policy of Canning 1822–1827* (London, 1925).

Teson, Fernando. *Humanitarian Intervention: An Inquiry into Law and Morality* (Ardsley, 2005).

Thakur, Ramesh. 'R2P, Libya and International Politics as the Struggle for Competing Normative Architectures' in Weiss et al. *The Responsibility to Protect: Challenges &Opportunities in Light of the Libyan Intervention* (2011) p.13 http://www.e-ir.info/wp-content/uploads/R2P.pdf Accessed 10th March 2024.

Thomas, Caroline. *New States, Sovereignty, and Intervention* (Aldershot, 1985).

Thompson, Andrew. 'Humanitarian interventions, past and present' in Klose, Fabian. (Ed.) *The Emergence of Humanitarian Intervention: Ideas and Practice from the Nineteenth Century to the Present* (Cambridge, 2018).

Thomson, Alex. *An Introduction to African Politics* (London, 2000).

Trachtenberg, Marc. 'Intervention in Historical Perspective' in Reed, Lauren and Kaysen, Carl (Eds.) *Emerging Norms of Justified Intervention* (Cambridge, MA, 1993).

Trim, D.J.B 'Conclusions: Humanitarian intervention in historical perspective' in Simms, Brendan and Trim, D.J.B (Eds.) *Humanitarian Intervention: A History* (Cambridge, 2011).

Trofimov, Yaroslav. *Our Enemies Will Vanish: The Russian Invasion and Ukraine's War of Independence.* (Dublin, 2024).

Tsagourias, Nicholas and White, Nigel. *Collective Security: Theory, Law, and Practice* (Cambridge, 2013).

Vane, Charles (Ed.) *Memoirs and Correspondences of Viscount Castlereagh Volume XII* (London, 1853).

Vanly, Ismet Sheriff. 'Kurdistan in Iraq' in Chaliand, Gerard (Ed.) *A People Without a Country: The Kurds and Kurdistan* (London, 1993).

Vickery, Michael. *Cambodia: 1975–1982* (Boston, 1984).

Volk, Lucia. *Memorials & Martyrs in Modern Lebanon* (Bloomington, 2010).

Voltaire. *La Bégueule*' (Geneva, 1772).

Walker, Martin. *The Cold War: A History* (New York, 1993).

Walling, Carrie Booth. *All Necessary Measures: The UN and Humanitarian Intervention* (Philadelphia, 2013).

Weiss, Thomas and Collins, Cindy. *Humanitarian Challenges and Intervention* (Boulder, 2000).

Weiss, Thomas. 'Whither R2P' in Weiss et al. *The Responsibility to Protect: Challenges &Opportunities in Light of the Libyan Intervention* (2011) p.7 http://www.e-ir.info/wp-content/uploads/R2P.pdf Accessed 10th March 2024.

Weiss, Thomas. *Humanitarian Intervention* (Cambridge, 2018).

Weiss, Thomas. *What's Wrong the United Nations and How to Fix It* (Cambridge, 2016).

Wellington, Arthur. *Despatches, Correspondence, and Memoranda of Field Marshal Arthur, Duke of Wellington Volume V* (London, 1873).

Western, Jon. 'Prudence or outrage? Public opinion and humanitarian intervention in historical and comparative perspective' in Klose, Fabian. (Ed.) *The Emergence of Humanitarian Intervention: Ideas and Practice from the Nineteenth Century to the Present* (Cambridge, 2018).

Westwood, J.N *Endurance and Endeavour: Russian History 1812–1992* (Oxford, 1973).

Wheaton, Henry. *Elements of International Law* (Boston, 1866).

Wheeler, Nicholas. *Saving Strangers: Humanitarian Intervention in International Society* (Oxford, 2010).

White, Nigel. 'Towards Integrated Peace Operations: The Evolution of Peacekeeping and Coalitions of the Willing' in Odello, Marco and Piotrowicz, Ryszard (Eds.) *International Military Missions and International Law* (Leiden, 2011).

White, Nigel. *International Conflict and Security Law* (Cheltenham, 2014).

White, Nigel. *Keeping the Peace: The United Nations and the Maintenance of International Peace and Security* (Manchester, 1997).

Woolsey, Theodore. *America's Foreign Policy* (New York, 1898).

## Governmental and Intergovernmental Sources

African Union Peace and Security Council *Communique of the 265th Meeting of the Peace and Security Council of the African Union* PSC/PR/Comm.2 (CCLXV) (10 March 2011).

*British Parliamentary Papers* LX.1, 139 *'Correspondence with Her Majesty's Embassy at Constantinople Respecting the Affairs of Syria'* (London, 1843).

*British Parliamentary Papers* LXIX.553 *'Papers relating to the disturbances in Syria'* (London, 1860).

*British Parliamentary Papers* LXIX.675 *'Further Papers Relating to the Disturbances in Syria'* (London, 1860).

*British Parliamentary Papers* LXVII.499 *'Papers relating to administrative and financial reforms in Turkey. 1858–61'* (London, 1861).

*British Parliamentary Papers* LXVII.599 *'Reports received from Her Majesty's consuls relating to the condition of Christians in Turkey. 1860'* (London, 1861).

*British Parliamentary Papers* LXVIII.1 *'Convention between Great Britain, Austria, France, Prussia, Russia, and Turkey, respecting measures to be taken for the pacification of Syria.'* (London, 1861).

*British Parliamentary Papers* LXVIII.17 *'Correspondence Relating to the Affairs of Syria 1860–61'* (London, 1861).

British Parliamentary Papers XC.1 *Correspondence respecting the affairs of Turkey* (London, 1877).

British Parliamentary Papers *Correspondence respecting the Conference at Constantinople and the affairs of Turkey XCI.1 (London, 1877).*

Bush George. 'Letter to Congressional Leaders on Iraq's Compliance with United Nations Security Council Resolutions' in *Public Papers of the Presidents of the United States: George Bush 1991 Book 1-January 1 to June 30, 1991* (Washington DC, 1992).

Castlereagh; Richelieu; Wellington. *Cobbett's political register*, (2 December 1815).

Castlereagh *Robert Stewart. Memorandum on the Treaties of 1814 and 1815* (October 1818).

Central Intelligence Agency Information Cable TDCS–315/07612–71 (December 15, 1971) http://2001-2009.state.gov/r/pa/ho/frus/nixon/e7txt/50165.htm Accessed 10th March 2024.

CIA World Factbook 'Cambodia' https://www.cia.gov/the-world-factbook/countries/cambodia/ Accessed 10th March 2024.

CIA World Factbook 'Vietnam https://www.cia.gov/the-world-factbook/countries/vietnam Accessed 10th March 2024.

Conversation between President Nixon and his Assistant for National Security Affairs (Kissinger), Washington (4 June 1971) https://history.state.gov/historicaldocuments/frus1969-76ve07/d136 Accessed 10th March 2024.

Conversation between President Nixon and his Assistant for National Security Affairs (Kissinger) Washington (6 December 1971) https://history.state.gov/historicaldocuments/frus1969-76ve07/d162 Accessed 10th March 2024.

'Correspondence between Great Britain and the United States, respecting the Arrest and Imprisonment of Mr. McLeod, for the Destruction of the Steamboat Caroline' (March, April 1841) *British Foreign and State Papers* (Vol.29. 1840–1841).

Dole, Robert. 'Human Rights in Yugoslavia' Congressional Record, 101st Congress. (27 April 1990).

Federal Research Division of the Library of Congress. *Uganda: A Country Study* (Washington DC, 1990).

*French Documents Diplomatiques 1860* (Paris, 1861).

Hamoodar Rahman Commission Report (1974) http://img.dunyanews.tv/images/docss/hamoodur_rahman_commission_report.pdf Accessed 10th March 2024.

Handwritten Letter from President Nixon to President Yahya (7 August 1971) http://www2.gwu.edu/~nsarchiv/NSAEBB/NSAEBB79/BEBB20.pdf Accessed 10th March 2024.

*Hearing before the Subcommittee on East Asian and Pacific Affairs of the Committee on Foreign Relations, US Senate, 95th Congress, 2nd Session on the Current Situation in Indochina.* (August 1978).

ICISS (International Commission on Intervention and State Sovereignty) *The Responsibility to Protect* (Ottawa, 2001).

IICK (Independent International Commission on Kosovo) *Kosovo Report* (Oxford, 2000).

Independent International Commission of Inquiry on Ukraine. *Report of the Independent International Commission of Inquiry on Ukraine* UN Doc A/78/540.

Intelligence Memorandum, Washington (31 January 1975) https://history.state.gov/historicaldocuments/frus1969-76ve12/d64 Accessed 10th March 2024.

International Energy Agency. 'Facts on Libya: Oil and Gas (IEA 21 February 2011) https://web.archive.org/web/20150909200811/https://www.iea.org/media/news/facts_libya.pdf Accessed 10th March 2024.

Memorandum for the Record (Undated, 1971) https://history.state.gov/historicaldocuments/frus1969-76ve07/d156 Accessed 10th March 2024.

Memorandum from the President's Assistant for National Security Affairs (Kissinger) to President Nixon, Washington (22 February 1971) https://history.state.gov/historicaldocuments/frus1969-76ve07/d118 Accessed 10th March 2024.

'Memorandum from the President's Assistant for National Security Affairs (Scowcroft) to President Ford, Washington' (10 May 1976) https://history.state.gov/historicaldocuments/frus1969-76ve12/d89 Accessed 10th March 2024.

Memorandum from the Staff Secretary of the National Security Council (Davis) to the Deputy Secretary of Defense (Packard) (3 March 1971) https://history.state.gov/historicaldocuments/frus1969-76ve07/d123 Accessed 10th March 2024.

'Memorandum for Secretary Kissinger, Washington' (2 May 1975) https://history.state.gov/historicaldocuments/frus1969-76ve12/d67 Accessed 10th March 2024.

'Memorandum for the President' (10 May 1976) http://www.fordlibrarymuseum.gov/library/exhibits/vietnam/032400045-001.pdf Accessed 10th March 2024.

Memorandum of Conversation, New Delhi, (7 July 1971) https://history.state.gov/historicaldocuments/frus1969-76ve07/d139 Accessed 10th March 2024.

'Minutes of the Secretary of State's Staff Meeting, Washington' (30 April 1975) https://history.state.gov/historicaldocuments/frus1969-76ve12/d65 Accessed 10th March 2024.

National Security Archive Project 'U.S. Consulate (Dacca) Cable, Dissent from U.S. Policy toward East Pakistan, April 6, 1971' http://www2.gwu.edu/~nsarchiv/NSAEBB/NSAEBB79/BEBB8.pdf Accessed 10th March 2024.

NATO 'NATO and the 2003 campaign against Iraq' (1 September 2015) www.nato.int/cps/en/natohq/topics_51977.htm Accessed 10th March 2024.

NATO 'Operational Media Update for 14 June' http://www.nato.int/nato_static/assets/pdf/pdf_2011_06/20110615_110615-oup-update.pdf Accessed 10th March 2024.

NATO 'The Alliance's New Strategic Concept' http://www.nato.int/cps/en/natolive/official_texts_23847.htm Accessed 10th March 2024.

NATO 'Secretary-General's Report 2012' (2012) http://www.nato.int/cps/en/natolive/opinions_94220.htm Accessed 10th March 2024.

Nixon, Richard. 'Third Annual Report to the Congress on United States Foreign Policy.' (9 February 1972).

OAU (Organisation of African Unity) *Rwanda: The Preventable Genocide* (2000).

'Research Study Prepared by the Central Intelligence Agency, Washington' (December 1976) https://history.state.gov/historicaldocuments/frus1969-76ve12/d95 Accessed 10th March 2024.

Telegram 959 from the Consulate General in Dacca to the Department of State (28 March 1971). 2001–2009.state.gov/r/pa/ho/frus/nixon/e7txt/47241.htm Accessed 10th March 2024.

Telegram 540 From the Consulate General in Dacca to the Department of State (28th February 1971) https://history.state.gov/historicaldocuments/frus1969-76ve07/d121 Accessed 10th March 2024.

Telegram 10043 From the Embassy in Pakistan to the Department of State (October 4, 1971) http://2001-2009.state.gov/r/pa/ho/frus/nixon/e7txt/49190.htm Accessed 10th March 2024.

Telegram 11295 from the Embassy in the United Kingdom to the Department of State (December 13, 1971) http://2001-2009.state.gov/r/pa/ho/frus/nixon/e7txt/49207.htm Accessed 10th March 2024.

Telegram 19243 From the Embassy in India to the Department of State (December 15, 1971) http://2001-2009.state.gov/r/pa/ho/frus/nixon/e7txt/49213.htm Accessed 10th March 2024.

Transcript of Telephone Conversation between Secretary of State Rogers and the President's Assistant for National Security Affairs (Kissinger) (3 December 1971).https://history.state.gov/historicaldocuments/frus1969-76ve07/d158 Accessed 10th March 2024.

Transcript of Telephone Conversation between President Nixon and His Assistant for National Security Affairs (Kissinger) (4 December 1971) https://history.state.gov/historicaldocuments/frus1969-76v11/d225 Accessed 10th March 2024.

*Uganda: The Human Rights Situation: Hearings Before the Subcommittee on Foreign Relations (95th Congress, 2nd Session)* (June 1978).

UK Cabinet Office. *The National Security Strategy of the United Kingdom 2008* (London, 2008).

UK Cabinet Office. *The National Security Strategy of the United Kingdom 2010* (London, 2010).

UK Cabinet Office. *The National Security Strategy of the United Kingdom 2015* (London, 2015).

UK Foreign and Commonwealth Office 'Libya Contact Group: Chair's Statement' (13 April 2011) https://www.gov.uk/government/news/libya-contact-group-chairs-statement Accessed 10th March 2024.

UK House of Commons Debate (25 March 1999).

UK House of Commons Defence Committee 'Fourteenth Report: Lessons of Kosovo. The Background to military intervention' (2000) http://www.publications.parliament.uk/pa/cm199900/cmselect/cmdfence/347/34708.htm Accessed 10th March 2024.

US Department of State. *Country Reports on Human Rights Practices for 1987* (Washington, 1988).

US Senate. *Civil War in Iraq: Staff Report to the Committee on Foreign Relations United States Senate* (Washington, 1991).

US Senate. S. RES. 85 112th Congress. (2011).

White House. *National Security Strategy 2010* (Washington DC, 2010).

White House. *National Security Strategy 2015* (Washington DC, 2015).

## Miscellaneous Sources

Binder, Christine. 'Uniting for Peace Resolution (1950)' Wolfrum, Rudiger (Ed.), The Max Planck Encyclopaedia of Public International Law (online Ed) http://opil.ouplaw.com/view/10.1093/law:epil/9780199231690/law-9780199231690-e568?prd=EPIL Accessed 10th March 2024.

Fadel, Mohammed. 'International Law, Regional Developments: Islam' in Wolfrum, Rudiger (Ed.), *The Max Planck Encyclopaedia of Public International Law* (online Ed) opil.ouplaw.com/view/10.1093/law:epil/9780199231690/law-9780199231690-e711?prd=EPIL Accessed 10th March 2024.

Lesaffer, Randall. 'Kellogg-Briand Pact (1928) in Wolfrum, Rudiger (Ed.), The Max Planck Encyclopaedia of Public International Law (Online Ed) http://opil.ouplaw.com/view/10.1093/law:epil/9780199231690/law-9780199231690-e320?rskey=sXnVjt&result=1&prd=EPIL Accessed 10th March 2024.

Ministry of Foreign Affairs of the People's Republic of China 'Head of the Chinese delegation, Foreign Minister Tang Jiaxuan addressed the 54th UN General Assembly' https://www.mfa.gov.cn/eng/wjb_663304/zzjg_663340/gjs_665170/gjzzyhy_665174/2594_665176/2602_665192/200011/t20001115_598217.html Accessed 10th March 2024.

Movement of the Non-Aligned Countries. 'XIII Ministerial Conference, 8–9 April 2000'. https://web.archive.org/web/20170505034415/http://www.nam.gov.za/xiiiminconf/minconf.txt Accessed 10th March 2024.

Pauwels, Ann. 'NATO as a peacekeeper, a contradictio in terminis' Paper presented at the 2007 European Society of International Law Biennial Research Forum https://esil-sedi.eu/wp-content/uploads/2018/04/Agora-2-Pauwels.pdf Accessed 10th March 2024.

Rummel, R.J. 'Statistics of Democide' http://www.hawaii.edu/powerkills/SOD.CHAP8.HTM Accessed 10th March 2024.

Stanulova, Maya. 'Has Humanitarian Intervention Become an Exception to the Prohibition on the Use of Force in Article 2(4) of the UN Charter?' *Atlantic Community* (2010) p.11 https://economia.uniroma2.it/ba/globalgovernance/corso/asset/YTo0OntzOjI6ImlkIjtzOjM6IjMyMyI7czozOiJpZGEiO3M6NToiNDE0ODEiO3M6MjoiZW0iO047czox OiJjIjtzOjU6ImQ2YjgyIjt9 Accessed 10th March 2024.

United Nations Development Programme *UN Human Development Report 1994* (Oxford, 1994) p.47.

United Nations High Commissioner for Refugees 'Statement by Prince Sadruddin Aga Khan, United Nations High Commissioner for Refugees, to the United Nations Economic and Social Council (ECOSOC), Geneva, 16 July 1971' http://unhcr.org/3ae68fd76.html Accessed 10th March 2024.

United Nations 'Outreach Programme on the Rwanda Genocide and the United Nations' http://www.un.org/en/preventgenocide/rwanda/education/rwandagenocide.shtml Accessed 10th March 2024.

United Nations Human Rights Council 'Genocide in Rwanda'. https://yale.learningu.org/media/uploaded/46340da5-e811-4c72-974c-c1acd896a493 Accessed 10th March 2024.

United Nations 'Troop and police contributors' https://peacekeeping.un.org/en/troop-and-police-contributors Accessed 10th March 2024.

Wood, Michael. 'Use of force, prohibition of threat' in Wolfrum, Rudiger (Ed.), The Max Planck Encyclopaedia of Public International Law (Online Ed) http://opil.ouplaw.com/view/10.1093/law:epil/9780199231690/law-9780199231690-e428?rskey=sfhUPW&result=2&prd=EPIL Accessed 10th March 2024.

## NGO Reports

Allen, Duncan. *The Minsk Conundrum: Western Policy and Russia's War in Eastern Ukraine* (Chatham House, 22 May 2022).

Amnesty International. *Amnesty International Report 1977* (London, 1977).

Amnesty International. *Amnesty International Report 1978* (London, 1978).

Amnesty International. *Between the Prison and the Grave: Enforced Disappearances in Syria* (London, 2015).

Amnesty International. *He's Not Coming Back: War Crimes in Northwest Areas of Kyiv Oblast* (London, 2022).

Amnesty International. *Libya: The Forgotten Victims of NATO Airstrikes* (London, 2012).

Amnesty International. 'Russia: Kremlin's ruthless crackdown stifles independent journalism and anti-war movement' (10 March 2022) https://www.amnesty.org/en/latest/news/2022/03/russia-kremlins-ruthless-crackdown-stifles-independent-journalism-and-anti-war-movement/ Accessed 20 January 2024.

Carnegie Commission on Preventing Deadly Conflict *Preventing Deadly Conflict: Final Report* (Washington DC, 1997).

Carus, W. Seth. 'The Genie Unleashed: Iraq's Chemical and Biological Weapons Program' *Washington Institute for Near East Policy Paper No.14* (1989).

Freedom House. *Freedom in the World: The Annual Survey of Political Rights and Civil Liberties 1999–2000.* (New York, 2000).

Freedom House. 'Freedom in the World 2010: Libya' https://www.refworld.org/reference/annualreport/freehou/2010/en/72133 Accessed 10th March 2024.

Freedom House. *'Freedom in the World 2020'* https://freedomhouse.org/explore-the-map?type=fiw&year=2020 Accessed 10th March 2024.

Grieco, Kelly, Cooper, Evan, Darnal, Aude, Preble, Christoper, Ashford, Emma and Siebens, James. 'Testing Assumptions About the War in Ukraine, One Year Later' *Stimson Centre* (15 February 2023) https://www.stimson.org/2023/testing-assumptions-about-the-war-in-ukraine-one-year-later/ Accessed 10th March 2024.

Human Rights Watch. 'Ukraine: Apparent War Crimes in Russia-Controlled Areas' *Human Rights Watch* (3 April 2022) https://www.hrw.org/news/2022/04/03/ukraine-apparent-war-crimes-russia-controlled-areas Accessed 12 December 2023.

Human Rights Watch. 'World Report 2023: Russia' https://www.hrw.org/world-report/2023/country-chapters/russian-federation Accessed 20 January 2024.

International Commission of Jurists. *The events in East Pakistan, 1971* (Geneva, 1972).

International Commission of Jurists. *Violations of Human Rights and the Rule of Law in Uganda* (May 1974).

International Law Association, Committee on the Use of Force (2010–2018), *Final Report on Aggression and the Use of Force, Sydney Conference* (2018).

International Law Commission. 'Draft conclusions on identification of customary international law, with commentaries.' *Yearbook of the International Law Commission* (Vol. II, Part 2, 2018).

Middle East Monitor. 'More than 21,000 killed in Syria during 2015' (29 December 2015) https://www.middleeastmonitor.com/20151229-more-than-21000-killed-in-syria-during-2015/ Accessed 10th March 2024.

Pifer, Steven. 'Crimea: Six years after illegal annexation' *Brookings Institution* (17 March 2020) https://brookings.edu/articles/crimea-six-years-after-illegal-annexation/ Accessed 19 December 2023.

Rumer, Eugene and Weiss, Andrew. 'Ukraine: Putin's Unfinished Business' *Carnegie Endowment for Peace* (12 November 2021) https://carnegieendowment.org/2021/11/12/ukraine-putin-s-unfinished-business-pub-85771 Accessed 8 December 2023.

Sasse, Gwendolyn. 'Ukraine's New Military Engagement in the Donbas' *Carnegie Endowment for International Peace* (3 May 2018) https://carnegieeurope.eu/strategiceurope/76246 Accessed 29 December 2023.

Washington Institute 'The Arab World, Iran and the Kosovo Crisis' (24 May 1999). http://www.washingtoninstitute.org/policy-analysis/view/the-arab-world-iran-and-the-kosovo-crisis Accessed 10th March 2024.

# Index

www.ingramcontent.com/pod-product-compliance
Lightning Source LLC
Chambersburg PA
CBHW071228230926
51849CB00001B/56
*9789004696389*